Lecture Notes in Computer Science 3144

Commenced Publication in 1973
Founding and Former Series Editors:
Gerhard Goos, Juris Hartmanis, and Jan van Leeuwen

Marina Papatriantafilou   Philippe Hunel (Eds.)

Principles of Distributed Systems

7th International Conference, OPODIS 2003
La Martinique, French West Indies, December 10-13, 2003
Revised Selected Papers

 Springer

Volume Editors

Marina Papatriantafilou
Chalmers University of Technology, Department of Computing Science
S-412 96 Gothenburg, Sweden
E-mail: ptrianta@cs.chalmers.se

Philippe Hunel
Université des Antilles et de la Guyane, Campus de Schoelcher
GRIMAAG, Département Scientifique Inter-Facultés
BP 7109, 97275 Schoelcher CEDEX, Martinique, France
E-mail: Philippe.Hunel@martinique.univ-ag.fr

Library of Congress Control Number: 2004109778

CR Subject Classification (1998): C.2.4, D.1.3, D.2.7, D.2.12, D.4.7, C.3

ISSN 0302-9743
ISBN 3-540-22667-2 Springer Berlin Heidelberg New York

Springer is a part of Springer Science+Business Media

springeronline.com

© Springer-Verlag Berlin Heidelberg 2004
Printed in Germany

Typesetting: Camera-ready by author, data conversion by PTP-Berlin, Protago-TeX-Production GmbH
Printed on acid-free paper   SPIN: 11307518   06/3142   5 4 3 2 1 0

Preface

The 7th International Conference on Principles of Distributed Systems (OPODIS 2003) was held during December 10–13, 2003 at La Martinique, French West Indies, and was co-organized by the Université des Antilles et de la Guyane, La Martinique, French West Indies and by Chalmers University of Technology, Sweden. It continued a tradition of successful conferences with friendly and pleasant atmospheres. The earlier organizations of OPODIS were held in Luzarches (1997), Amiens (1998), Hanoi (1999), Paris (2000), Mexico (2001) and Reims (2002).

OPODIS is an open forum for the exchange of state-of-the-art knowledge on distributed computing and systems among researchers from around the world. Following the tradition of the previous organizations, its program is composed of high-quality contributed and invited papers by experts of international caliber in this scientific area. The topics of interest are theory, specifications, design and implementation of distributed systems, including distributed and multiprocessor algorithms; communication and synchronization protocols; coordination and consistency protocols; stabilization, reliability and fault-tolerance of distributed systems; performance analysis of distributed algorithms and systems; specification and verification of distributed systems; security issues in distributed computing and systems; and applications of distributed computing, such as embedded distributed systems, real-time distributed systems, distributed collaborative environments, peer-to-peer systems, cluster and grid computing.

In response to the call for papers for OPODIS 2003, 61 papers in these areas were submitted. The Program Committee, following a peer-review process, selected 19 out of these for presentation at the conference. Each paper, reviewed by at least 4 reviewers, was judged according to scientific and presentation quality, originality and relevance to the conference topics. The distribution of the accepted (respectively, submitted) papers per geographic region was: Asia–Australia, 3 papers accepted (out of 14 submitted); Europe, 11 papers accepted (out of 34 submitted); Central and North America, 5 papers accepted (out of 13 submitted).

Besides the technical contributed papers, the program included invited keynote talks. We were happy that three distinguished experts accepted our invitation to share with us their views of various aspects of the field: Jo Ebergen (Sun Microsystems Laboratories), who gave the luncheon speech on circuits without clocks, Neil Gershenfeld (MIT Center for Bits and Atoms), who talked about physical error correction in building reliable systems out of unreliable components, and Maarten van Steen (Vrije Universiteit Amsterdam), who talked about very large, self-managing distributed systems. Abstracts of the contents of the keynote talks are included in this volume.

Apart from the technical program, OPODIS 2003 also offered a set of satellite events in the form of tutorials, with the themes: Self-stabilization, by

Joffroy Beauquier (Université de Paris 11); Distributed Computing and Information Security, by Roberto Gomez Cárdenas (ITESM-CEM); and Non-blocking Synchronization, by Philippas Tsigas (Chalmers University of Technology).

It is impossible to organize a successful program without the help of many individuals. We would like to express our appreciation to the authors of the submitted papers, and to the program committee members and external referees, who provided useful reviews. Furthermore, we would also like to thank the OPODIS steering committee members, who supervise and support the continuation of the event. We owe special thanks to Yi Zhang for his assistance with the electronic submissions and reviewing system. Finally, one more special thanks to all the other organizing committee members for their precious efforts that contributed to making OPODIS 2003 a successful conference.

Marina Papatriantafilou
Philippe Hunel
OPODIS 2003 Program Co-chairs

Program Committee

Organization

OPODIS 2003 was organized by the Université des Antilles et de la Guyane, La Martinique, French West Indies and by Chalmers University of Technology, Gothenburg, Sweden.

Organizing Institutes

Organizing Committee

Hacene Fouchal	Univ. Reims Champagne-Ardenne, France
Philippe Hunel	Univ. of Antilles-Guyane, La Martinique, French West Indies
Richard Nock	Univ. of Antilles-Guyane, La Martinique, French West Indies
Marina Papatriantafilou	Chalmers Univ. of Technology, Sweden
Jean-Emile Symphor	Univ. of Antilles-Guyane, La Martinique, French West Indies
Yi Zhang	Chalmers Univ. of Technology, Sweden

Steering Committee

During 2003 the Steering Committee of OPODIS consisted of:

Alain Bui	Univ. Reims Champagne-Ardenne, France
Marc Bui	Univ. Paris 8, France
Roberto Gomez-Cardenas	CEM-ITESM, Mexico
Philippas Tsigas	Chalmers Univ. of Technology, Sweden
Vincent Villain	Univ. Picardie Jules Verne, France

Other Supporting and Sponsoring Organizations

The conference was supported and sponsored by the Université des Antilles et de la Guyane, Chalmers University of Technology, Springer-Verlag (publication of this official, postconference proceedings volume), Canon Martinique (preliminary proceedings volume, available during the conference), the Research Ministry of France, the Research Council of Sweden, the French National Centre for Scientific Research (CNRS, GdR Architecture, Réseaux et systèmes, Parallélisme), Microsoft Research, the Department of Tourism in Martinique (Office Départemental du Tourisme de la Martinique, ODTM), the Regional Agency for the Touristic Development of Martinique (Agence Régionale pour le Développement Touristique de la Martinique, ARDTM), the Municipality of Schoelcher, and the ACM French Chapter.

The electronic submission and reviewing system used for OPODIS 2003 was the CyberChair system, authored by Richard van de Stadt.

Referees

Ahmed Ainouche
Johan Andersson
Filipe Araújo
Anish Arora
Hichem Baala
Alina Bejan
Simon Bloch
Olivier Bournez
Jean-Michel Bruel
Franck Butelle
Ken Calvert
Antonio Casimiro
Pranay Chaudhuri
Nawal Cherfi
Bruno Codenotti
Alain Cournier
Ivica Crnkovic
Sivarama Dandamudi
Xavier Defago
Carole Delporte
Stéphane Devismes
Andreas Ermedahl
Hugues Fauconnier
Olivier Festor
German Finez
Lucian Finta
Olivier Flauzac
Pierre Fraigniaud
Johan Fredriksson
Eduardo Garcia
Philippe Gauron
Chryssis Georgiou
Sukumar Ghosh
Anders Gidenstam
Jens Gustedt
Phuong-Hoai Ha
Thomas Herault
Lisa Higham
Taisuke Izumi
Raul Jacinto
Mehmet-Hakan Karaata
Boris Koldehofe
Kishori Konwar
Michael Krajecki

Mikel Larrea-Alava
Victor M. Larios-Rosillo
Patrice Laurencot
Fabrice Le Fessant
Pierre Lemarinier
Erika Mata-Sanchez
Stephan Merz
Hugo Miranda
Lynda Mokdad
Peter Musial
Anders Möller
Yoshihiro Nakaminami
Mikhail Nesterenko
Richard Nock
Mikael Nolin
Florent Nolot
Thomas Nolte
Rui Oliveira
Fukuhito Ooshita
Gabriel Paillard
Catuscia Palamidessi
José-Orlando Pereira
Paul Pettersson
Scott M. Pike
Laurence Pilard
Imran Pirwani
Stefan Pleisch
Vahid Ramezani
Sylvain Rampaceck
Xavier Rebeuf
Antoine Rollet
Launrent Rosaz
Brigitte Rozoy
Sebastien Salva
Kristian Sandström
Pierre Sens
Devan Sohier
Olivier Soyez
Gerard Tel
Henrik Thane
Sébastien Tixeuil
Luis Trejo
Tatsuhiro Tsuchiya
Hasan Ural

Peter Urban
Thierry Val
Edgar Vallejo
Krishnamurthy Vidyasankar
Ramesh Viswanath
Anders Wall

Josef Widden
Mark Wineberg
Wang Yi
Chen Zhang
Hongwei Zhang
Mikael Åkerholm

Table of Contents

Peer-to-Peer Systems, Middleware II

Real-Time and Embedded Systems

Verification, Models, Performance of Distributed Systems

Distributed and Multiprocessor Algorithms II

Author Index

Distributing Bits and Atoms

Neil Gershenfeld

Director
MIT Center for Bits and Atoms
Cambridge, MA 02139, USA

Abstract. The principles used today for developing distributed systems will not scale to the limit of thermodynamically complex engineered systems. The great insight of statistical mechanics is that it is possible to make precise statements about the macroscopic behavior of a system based on knowledge of its microscopic governing equations, without requiring a specification of its internal confirguration. A scalable theory of distributed system design must likewise be able to allocate available local degrees of freedom to accomplish a global goal, without demanding a detailed description of their configuration. Towards that end, I discuss the role of physical error correction in building reliable systems out of unreliable components, and the use of principles from mathematical programming as a language for expressing algorithms in this statistical-mechanical limit.

M. Papatriantafilou and P. Hunel (Eds.): OPODIS 2003, LNCS 3144, p. 1, 2004.

Circuits Without Clocks: What Makes Them Tick?

Jo Ebergen

Asynchronous Design Group
Sun Microsystems Laboratories
Mountain View CA 94043, USA
jo.ebergen@sun.com
http://research.sun.com/projects/async/

Abstract. Most digital circuits have a global clock that dictates when all circuit components execute their basic computation steps. The clock is a convenience for the designer, because the clock synchronizes all basic computations to its ticks. On the other hand, the clock can be a serious inconvenience with respect to speed, power consumption, modularity of design, and reduced electro-magnetic radiation. A clockless circuit is essentially a distributed system in-the-small, where the main challenge is the coordination of all basic computations in a fast and energy-efficient manner. A growing research community is exploring the benefits of circuits without clocks. In this talk I will give a brief overview of clockless circuits, illustrate their potential by means of some 'live' demos, and discuss current challenges.

M. Papatriantafilou and P. Hunel (Eds.): OPODIS 2003, LNCS 3144, p. 2, 2004.

Towards Very Large, Self-Managing Distributed Systems

Extended Abstract

Maarten van Steen

Vrije Universiteit Amsterdam

1 Introduction

As distributed systems tend to grow in the number of components and in their geographical dispersion, deployment and management are increasingly becoming problematic. For long, there has been a tradition of developing architectures for managing networked and distributed systems [2]. These architectures tend to be complex, unwieldy, and indeed, difficult to manage. We need to explore alternative avenues if we want to construct a next generation of distributed systems.

Recently, solutions have been sought to develop self-managing systems. The basic idea here, is that a distributed system can continuously monitor its own behavior and take corrective action when needed. As with many new, or newly introduced, concepts, it is often difficult to separate hype from real content. In the case of self-management (or other forms of *self-∗-ness*), the low signal-to-noise ratio can be partly explained by our poor understanding of what self-management actually means.

2 A Self-Managing User-Centric CDN

In our own research on large-scale distributed systems at the Vrije Universiteit Amsterdam, we have been somewhat avoiding the problem of systems management. However, one of the lessons we learned from building Globe [8], is that supporting easy deployment and management is essential. Partly based on our experience with Globe, we are currently developing a user-centric Content Delivery Network to further explore facilities for self-management. This CDN, called Globule, is designed to handle millions of users, each providing Web content by means of a specially configured Apache Web server.

An important aspect of Globule is that a server can automatically replicate its Web documents to other servers. For each document, a server evaluates several replication strategies, and selects the best one on a per-document basis. This approach allows for near-optimal performance in terms of client-perceived delays as well as total consumed bandwidth [6]. In a recent study, we have also demonstrated that continuous re-evaluation of selected strategies is needed, and that this can be done efficiently [7]. The approach we follow is to regularly perform trace-driven simulations for a specific document, where each simulation entails a single replication strategy. Using a linear cost function defined over performance metrics such as client-perceived latency and consumed bandwidth, we can then compare the effects of applying different strategies. These simulations take in the order of tens of milliseconds in order to select the best strategy for a given document.

M. Papatriantafilou and P. Hunel (Eds.): OPODIS 2003, LNCS 3144, pp. 3–6, 2004.
© Springer-Verlag Berlin Heidelberg 2004

Clearly, Globule should be able to manage itself when it comes to replicating documents, and as far as static content is concerned, such self-management appears to be feasible.

However, much more is needed to develop a CDN such as Globule. For one thing, if we are to replicate documents to where they are needed, it is mandatory that we can locate clients and replica servers in the proximity of those clients. One problem that needs to be solved is letting a Web server determine how close two arbitrary nodes in the system actually are. Fortunately, it turns out that if we consider latency as a distance metric, we can represent the nodes of a widely dispersed distributed system in an N-dimensional Euclidean space [4,5]. In this way, estimating latency is nothing more than a simple computation. In contrast to existing systems, latency estimations in Globule can be obtained in a fully decentralized manner, which, in turn, simplifies overall system management.

By introducing locations and easy-to-compute distances, it becomes feasible to automatically partition the set of nodes comprising a distributed system into manageable parts. For example, by grouping nodes into geographical zones (where the geography is fully determined by the Euclidean space mentioned before), we can assign special nodes to zones in order to manage services, resources, etc. These special nodes, called brokers in Globule, are elected as *super peers* from all available nodes, and together form a separate overlay network using their own routing protocol. Whenever a node in zone A requires services from a zone B (such as, for example, a list of potential replica servers) it simply sends a request to a broker in A which will then forward the request to a broker for B. In Globule, a zone is defined implicitly: it consists of the servers that are closest to a given broker. As a consequence, zones do not overlap. Moreover, adding and removing servers, be they brokers or not, is fully decentralized.

There are many variations on this theme, but it should be clear that grouping nodes into zones and electing brokers for zones are things that can be done in a fully decentralized fashion. There is no need for manual intervention, although there are many unresolved details concerning how this organization can be automatically done.

3   Epidemic-Based Solutions

One could argue that the description of a self-managing system given so far is largely dictated by automating tasks that are currently handled manually. In this sense, self-management is just a next step in the evolution of distributed systems. The question comes to mind if there are radically different alternatives. We are currently exploring epidemic-based systems for management tasks.

In an epidemic-based system, we are generally concerned with reaching eventual consistency: in the absence of any further updates, all nodes should eventually reach the same state. Data are spread by letting each node regularly contact an arbitrary other node, after which the two exchange updates [1]. The problem with this approach for very large systems, is that, in principle, every node should know the entire set of nodes in order to guarantee random selection of a peer. One solution is to maintain, per node, a small list of peers that represents a random sample from all nodes. Maintaining this list is now the key to successfully applying epidemics in very large systems.

In the Newscast system, we take a simple approach. Every node maintains a fixed-size list of length c of *news items*. A news item contains data, the address of its source, and the time when it was published. Once every ΔT time units, each node executes the following steps [3]:

1. Add a fresh (node-specific) news item to the local list.
2. Randomly select a peer from those found in the list.
3. Send all entries to the selected peer, and, in turn, receive all that peer's list entries.
4. Out of the (up to) $2c$ cache entries, keep the c newest ones, and discard the rest.

The selected peer from step 2 executes the last two steps as well, so that after the exchange both nodes have the same list. Note that as soon as any of these two nodes executes the protocol again, their respective lists will most likely be different again.

The lists induce a communication graph with a link from node a to b if b is contained in the list of a. As it turns out, for even a relatively small list size ($c = 20$), we can show that communication graphs are strongly connected for up to hundred thousands of nodes, and by simply increasing c, very large overlay networks of millions of nodes can be accommodated. These networks exhibit properties common to what are known as *small worlds* [9]. We have discovered that these networks are extremely robust: in general, only after the removal of at least 70% of the nodes (and much more for $c > 20$), the network is partitioned into one giant cluster and several (very) small clusters. Most important, however, is that there is no need for centralized control — Newscast networks are completely self-managing.

To illustrate this point, consider how membership is managed in Newscast. First, nodes that want to leave can simply stop communication: they do not initiate a list exchange, nor do they react to exchange requests. This behavior is exactly the same as that of a failing node, and indeed, Newscast treats these two cases identically.

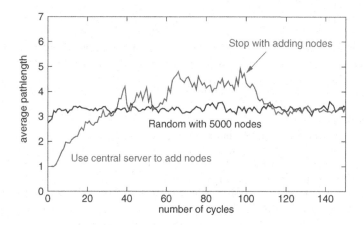

Fig. 1. The effect of continuously adding nodes that contact the same initial node.

Second, when a node wishes to join the network, it need only know the address of one node, with whom it then seeks contact by executing the list exchange protocol (note that its own list is empty). To see to what extent the selection of the initial contact node affects overall behavior, we conducted a series of experiments in which all joining nodes contact *the same* initial node. Clearly, this is a worst-case scenario. Figure 1 shows the effect on the average path length while continuously adding 50 nodes until 5000 nodes have joined. Compared to the "ideal" case, in which each new node contacts another, randomly selected node, we see that soon after nodes are no longer added, the average path length converges to that of the random case. Again, we see self-management at work.

We have used Newscast for various system monitoring tasks, such as estimating the size of the network, load balancing, and broadcasting alarms. In all cases, only a few list exchanges per node are required to reach consistency. As such, it forms a powerful tool for management of large distributed systems, notably because the protocol itself barely requires any management at all.

4   Conclusions

Self-managing systems are in many cases not well understood and as a consequence there is often much ado about nothing. However, it is also clear that we need concepts such as self-management, self-healing, self-organization, and so on, in order to arrive at a next generation of very large distributed systems. Fortunately, self-∗ matters can be made concrete and show to form a promising field that warrants further research.

References

1. A. Demers, D. Greene, C. Hauser, W. Irish, J. Larson, S. Shenker, H. Sturgis, D. Swinehart, and D. Terry. "Epidemic Algorithms for Replicated Database Maintenance." In *Proc. Sixth Symp. on Principles of Distributed Computing*, pp. 1–12. ACM, Aug. 1987.
2. H.-G. Hegering, S. Abeck, and B. Neumair. *Integrated Management of Networked Systems*. Morgan Kaufman, San Mateo, CA, 1999.
3. M. Jelasity and M. van Steen. "Large-Scale Newscast Computing on the Internet." Technical Report IR-503, Vrije Universiteit, Department of Computer Science, Oct. 2002.
4. E. Ng and H. Zhang. "Predicting Internet Network Distance with Coordinates-Based Approaches." In *Proc. 21st INFOCOM Conf.*, June 2002. IEEE Computer Society Press, Los Alamitos, CA.
5. M. Pias, J. Crowcroft, S. Wilbur, T. Harris, and S. Bhatti. "Lighthouses for Scalable Distributed Location." In *Proc. Second Int'l Workshop on Peer-to-Peer Systems*, Feb. 2003. Springer-Verlag, Berlin.
6. G. Pierre, M. van Steen, and A. Tanenbaum. "Dynamically Selecting Optimal Distribution Strategies for Web Documents." *IEEE Trans. Comp.*, 51(6):637–651, June 2002.
7. S. Sivasubramanian, G. Pierre, and M. van Steen. "A Case for Dynamic Selection of Replication and Caching Strategies." In *Proc. Eighth Web Caching Workshop*, Sept. 2003.
8. M. van Steen, P. Homburg, and A. Tanenbaum. "Globe: A Wide-Area Distributed System." *IEEE Concurrency*, 7(1):70–78, Jan. 1999.
9. D. J. Watts. *Small Worlds, The Dynamics of Networks between Order and Randomness*. Princeton University Press, Princeton, NJ, 1999.

Linear Time Byzantine Self-Stabilizing Clock Synchronization

Ariel Daliot[1], Danny Dolev[1]*, and Hanna Parnas[2]

[1] School of Engineering and Computer Science, The Hebrew University of Jerusalem, Israel. {adaliot,dolev}@cs.huji.ac.il

[2] Department of Neurobiology and the Otto Loewi Minerva Center for Cellular and Molecular Neurobiology, Institute of Life Science, The Hebrew University of Jerusalem, Israel. hanna@vms.huji.ac.il

Abstract. Awareness of the need for robustness in distributed systems increases as distributed systems become an integral part of day-to-day systems. Tolerating Byzantine faults and possessing self-stabilizing features are sensible and important requirements of distributed systems in general, and of a fundamental task such as clock synchronization in particular. There are efficient solutions for Byzantine non-stabilizing clock synchronization as well as for non-Byzantine self-stabilizing clock synchronization. In contrast, current Byzantine self-stabilizing clock synchronization algorithms have exponential convergence time and are thus impractical. We present a linear time Byzantine self-stabilizing clock synchronization algorithm, which thus makes this task feasible. Our deterministic clock synchronization algorithm is based on the observation that all clock synchronization algorithms require events for re-synchronizing the clock values. These events usually need to happen synchronously at the different nodes. In these solutions this is fulfilled or aided by having the clocks initially close to each other and thus the actual clock values can be used for synchronizing the events. This implies that clock values cannot differ arbitrarily, which necessarily renders these solutions to be non-stabilizing. Our scheme suggests using a tight pulse synchronization that is uncorrelated to the actual clock values. The synchronized pulses are used as the events for re-synchronizing the clock values.

1 Introduction

Overcoming failures that are not predictable in advance is most suitably addressed by tolerating Byzantine faults. It is the preferred fault model in order to seal off unexpected behavior within limitations on the number of concurrent faults. Most distributed tasks require the number of Byzantine faults, f, to abide by the ratio of $3f < n$, where n is the network size. See [14] for impossibility results on several consensus related problems such as clock synchronization. Additionally, it makes sense to require such systems to resume operation after serious unpredictable events without the need for an outside intervention and/or a restart of the system from scratch. E.g. systems may occasionally experience

---

* This research was supported in part by Intel COMM Grant - Internet Network/Transport Layer & QoS Environment (IXA)

M. Papatriantafilou and P. Hunel (Eds.): OPODIS 2003, LNCS 3144, pp. 7–19, 2004.

short periods in which more than a third of the nodes are faulty or messages sent by all nodes may be lost for some time. Such transient violations of the basic fault assumptions may leave the system in an arbitrary state from which the protocol is required to resume in realizing its task. Typically, Byzantine algorithms do not ensure convergence in such cases, as they sometimes make strong assumptions on the initial state and they focus on preventing Byzantine faults from notably shifting the system state away from the goal. A *self-stabilizing* algorithm bypasses this limitation by being designed to converge within finite time to a desired state from any initial state. Thus, even if the system loses its consistency due to a transient violation of the basic fault assumptions (e.g. more than a third of the nodes being faulty, network disconnected, etc.), then once the system is back within the assumption boundaries the protocol will successfully realize the task, irrespective of the resumed state of the system. For a short survey of self-stabilization see [4], for an extensive study see [11].

The current paper addresses the problem of synchronizing clocks in a distributed system. There are several efficient algorithms for self-stabilizing clock synchronization withstanding crash faults (see [13,18,10] or other variants of the problem [2,15]). There are many efficient classic Byzantine clock synchronization algorithms (for a performance evaluation of clock synchronization algorithms see [1]), however strong assumptions on the initial state of the nodes are typically made, such as assuming all clocks are initially synchronized ([1,9,21]) and thus are not self-stabilizing. On the other hand, self-stabilizing clock synchronization algorithms, which can initiate with arbitrary clock values, typically have a cost in the convergence times or in the severity of the faults contained. Evidently, there are very few self-stabilizing solutions facing Byzantine faults ([12]), all with unpractical convergence times. Note that self-stabilizing clock synchronization has an inherent difficulty in estimating real-time without an external time reference due to the fact that non-faulty nodes may initialize with arbitrary clock values. Thus, self-stabilizing clock synchronization aims at reaching a stable state from which clocks proceed synchronously at the rate of real-time (assuming that nodes have access to physical timers which rate is close to real-time) and not necessarily at estimating real-time. Many applications utilizing the synchronization of clocks do not really require the exact real-time notion (see [16]). In such applications, agreeing on a common clock reading is sufficient as long as the clocks progress within a linear envelope of any real-time interval.

We present a Byzantine self-stabilizing clock synchronization protocol with the following property: should the system initialize or recover from any transient faults with arbitrary clock values then the clocks of the correct nodes proceed synchronously at real-time rate. Should the clocks of the correct nodes hold values that are close to real-time, then the correct clocks proceed synchronously with high real-time accuracy. Thus, the protocol we present significantly improves upon existing Byzantine self-stabilizing clock synchronization algorithms by reducing the time complexity from expected exponential ([12]) to deterministic $O(f)$. Our protocol improves upon existing Byzantine non-stabilizing clock synchronization algorithms by providing self-stabilization while requiring similar complexity measures. The self-stabilization and comparably low complexity is achieved through a deterministic Byzantine self-stabilizing algorithm for pulse synchronization. The synchronized pulse intervals allow for the execution of a

Byzantine Strong Consensus protocol on the clock values in between pulses, thus attaining and maintaining a common clock reading.

Having access to an outside source of real-time is useful. In such case our approach provides a consistent system state when the outside source fails.

A special challenge in self-stabilizing clock synchronization is the clock wrap around. In non-stabilizing algorithms having a large enough integer eliminates the problem for any practical concern. In self-stabilizing schemes a transient failure can cause clocks to hold arbitrary large values, surfacing the issue of clock bounds. Our clock synchronization scheme handles wrap around difficulties.

2 Model and Problem Definition

The environment is a network of processors (nodes) that communicate by exchanging messages. Individual nodes have no access to a central clock and there is no global pulse system. The hardware clocks (referred to as the *physical timers*) of correct nodes have a bounded drift rate, ρ, from real-time. The communication network does not guarantee any order on messages.

The network and/or all the nodes can behave arbitrarily, though eventually the network performs within the assumption boundaries defined below.

Definition 1. *The* **network assumption boundaries** *are:*
1. *Message passing allowing for an authenticated identity of the senders.*
2. *At most f of the nodes are faulty.*
3. *Any message sent by any non-faulty node will eventually reach every non-faulty node within δ time units.*

Definition 2. *A node is* **correct** *at times that it complies with the following:*
1. *Obeys a global constant $0 < \rho << 1$ (typically $\rho \approx 10^{-6}$), such that for every real-time interval $[u, v]$:*

$$(1 - \rho)(v - u) \leq \text{'physical timer'}(v) - \text{'physical timer'}(u) \leq (1 + \rho)(v - u).$$

2. *Operates according to the instructed protocol.*

A node is considered **faulty** if it violates one or more of the above. A faulty node recovers from its faulty behavior if it resumes obeying the conditions of a correct node. For consistency reasons the recovery is not immediate, but rather takes a certain amount of time during which the node is still considered faulty although it behaves correctly[1]. The system performs **within the network assumption boundaries** only following some amount of time of continuous adherence to the network assumption boundaries.

Basic notations:
We use the following notations though nodes do not need to maintain all of them as variables.
- $Clock_i$, the clock of node i, is a real value in the range 0 to $M - 1$. Thus $M - 1$ is the maximal value a clock can hold. Its progression rate is a function of node p_i's physical timer. The clock is incremented every time unit. $Clock_i(t)$ denotes the value of the clock of node p_i at real-time t.

---

[1] For example, a node may recover during the Byzantine Consensus procedure and violate the validity condition if considered correct immediately.

- A *"pulse"* is an internal event for the re-synchronization of the clocks, ideally every $Cycle$ time units. A cycle is the actual (effective) time interval between two successive pulses that a node invokes.
- σ represents the upper bound on the real-time between the invocations of the pulses of different correct nodes (*tightness of pulse synchronization*).
- γ is the target upper bound on the difference of clock readings of any two correct clocks at any real-time. Our protocol achieves $\gamma = 3d + O(\rho)$.
- Let $a, b, g, h \in R^+$ be constants that define the linear envelope bound of the correct clock progression rate during any real-time interval.
- $\Psi_i(t_1, t_2)$ is the amount of clock time elapsed on the clock of node p_i during a real-time interval $[t_1, t_2]$ within which p_i was continuously correct. The value of Ψ is not affected by any wrap around of $clock_i$ during that period.
- $d \equiv \delta + \pi$, where π is the upper bound on message processing time. d is an upper bound on the elapsed real-time from the sending of a message by any non-faulty node until it is received and processed by every non-faulty node.

Using the above notations, a recovered node can be considered correct once it goes through a complete synchronization process, which is guaranteed to happen within *one cycle + consensus_time* of correct behavior, where *consensus_time* represents the time to complete the chosen Byzantine Consensus algorithm.

Basic definitions:

- The **clock_state** of the system at real-time t is given by:

$$clock\_state(t) \equiv (clock_0(t), \ldots, clock_{n-1}(t)).$$

- The systems is in a **synchronized clock_state** at real-time t if $\forall correct\ p_i, p_j$,

$$(|clock_i(t) - clock_j(t)| \leq \gamma) \lor (|clock_i(t) - clock_j(t)| \geq M - \gamma).^2$$

Definition 3. The Self-Stabilizing Clock Synchronization Problem

As long as the system is within the assumption boundaries:

Convergence: *Starting from an arbitrary state, s, the system reaches a synchronized clock_state after a finite time.*

Closure: *If s is a synchronized clock_state of the system at real-time t_0 then $\forall real\ time\ t \geq t_0$,*
   1. clock_state(t) is a synchronized clock_state,
   2. "Linear Envelope": for every correct node, p_i,

$$a \cdot [t - t_0] + b \leq \Psi_i(t_0, t) \leq g \cdot [t - t_0] + h.$$

3   Self-Stabilizing Byzantine Clock Synchronization

A major challenge of self-stabilizing clock synchronization is to ensure clock synchronization even when nodes may initialize with arbitrary clock values. This, as mentioned before, requires handling the wrap around of clock values. The

---

[2] The second condition is a result of dealing with bounded clock variables.

algorithm we present employs as a building block an underlying Byzantine self-stabilizing pulse synchronization procedure. In the pulse synchronization problem nodes invoke pulses regularly, ideally every $Cycle$ time units, and the goal is to do so in tight synchrony. To synchronize their clocks, nodes execute at every pulse Strong Byzantine Consensus on the clock value to be associated with the next pulse event[3]. When pulses are synchronized, then the consensus results in synchronized clocks. The basic algorithm uses strong consensus to ensure that once correct clocks are synchronized at a certain pulse and thus enter the consensus procedure with identical values, then they terminate with the same identical values and keep the progression of clocks continuous and synchronized[4].

3.1 The Basic Algorithm

The basic algorithm is essentially a self-stabilizing version of the Byzantine clock synchronization algorithm in [9]. We call it PBSS-Clock-Synch (for *Pulse-Based Byzantine Self-Stabilizing Clock Synchronization*). The agreed clock time of the next synchronization is denoted by ET (for *Expected Time*, as in [9]). Synchronization of clocks is targeted to happen every $Cycle$ time units, unless the pulse is invoked earlier[5].

PBSS-Clock-Synch
at *"pulse"* event   /* *received the internal pulse event* */
   begin
      $Clock = ET$;
      Abort possible running instance of PBSS-Clock-Synch and Reset all buffers;
      Wait $\sigma(1 + \rho)$ time units;
      $Next_ET = $ Strong-Byz-Consensus$((ET + Cycle) \bmod M)$;
      $Clock = (Clock + Next\_ET - (ET + Cycle)) \bmod M$;   /* *posterior adj.*
      $ET = Next\_ET$;
   end

The internal pulse event is delivered by the pulse synchronization procedure (presented in Section 4). This event aborts any possible on-going invocation of PBSS-Clock-Synch and thus any on-going consensus and resets all buffers. The synchronization of the pulses ensures that the PBSS-Clock-Synch procedure is invoked within σ real-time units[6] of its invocation at all other correct nodes.

The "Wait" intends to make sure that all correct nodes enter the Byzantine Consensus after the pulse has been invoked at all others, without remnants of past invocations. Past remnants may exist only during or immediately following periods in which the system deviates from its assumption boundaries.

---

[3] It is assumed that the time between successive pulses is sufficient for a Byzantine Consensus algorithm to initiate and terminate in between.

[4] The Pulse Synchronization building block does not use the value of the clock to determine its progress, but rather intervals measured on the physical timer.

[5] $Cycle$ has the same function as PER in [9].

[6] The pulse synchronization presented achieves $\sigma = 2d$.

A correct node joins a Byzantine Consensus only concomitant to an internal pulse event, as instructed by the PBSS-Clock-Synch. The Strong-Byzantine-Consensus intends to reach consensus on the next value of ET. One can use a synchronous agreement algorithm with rounds of size $(\sigma + d)(1 + 2\rho)$ or asynchronous style agreement in which a node waits to get $n - f$ messages of the previous round before moving to the next round. We assume the use of a Strong Byzantine Consensus algorithm tolerating f faults when $n \geq 3f + 1$.

The posterior clock adjustment (subsequent to the consensus) adds to the clock value the difference between the agreed time at the next pulse and the node's initial estimate for the time at the next pulse (the value which it entered the consensus with). This is equivalent to adding the elapsed time from the pulse and until the end of the consensus, to the value of ET the node was supposed to hold at the pulse according to the agreed $Next\_ET$. This intends to expedite the time for holding synchronized clocks to the moment following consensus termination rather than to the next pulse event. Take notice that in the case that all correct nodes hold the same ET value at the pulse, then the posterior clock adjustment adds a zero increment to the clock value.

Note that when the system is back within the assumption boundaries following a chaotic state, pulses may arrive to different nodes at arbitrary times, and the ET values and clocks of different nodes may differ arbitrarily. At that time not all correct nodes will join the Byzantine Consensus and no consistent resultant value can be guaranteed. Once the pulses synchronize (guaranteed by the pulse synchronization procedure to happen within a single cycle) all correct nodes will join the same execution of the Byzantine Consensus and will agree on the clock value of the next synchronization. From that time on, as long as the system stays within the assumption boundaries the clocks remain synchronized.

The Strong Byzantine Consensus also ensures that the wrap around of clocks happens at all correct nodes smoothly and at the same cycle.

Note that instead of simply setting the clock value to ET we could use some Clock-Adjust procedure (cf. [9]), which receives a parameter indicating the target value of the clock. The procedure runs in the background, it speeds up or slows down the clock rate to reach the adjusted value within a specified period of time. The procedure handles clock wrap around.

Theorem 1. *PBSS-Clock-Synch solves the Self-Stabilizing Clock Synchronization Problem in the presence of at most f Byzantine nodes, where $n \geq 3f + 1$.*

Proofs of the theorems and more details of the protocols can be found in [6].

3.2   An Additional Self-Stabilizing Clock Synchronization Algorithm

We end the section by suggesting a simple additional Byzantine self-stabilizing clock synchronization algorithm using pulse synchronization as a building block.

Our second algorithm resets the clock at every pulse[7]. This approach has the advantage that the nodes never need to synchronize their clock values. This version is useful for example, when M is relatively small. The algorithm has the disadvantage that for a large value of M, a large *Cycle* value is required. This

---

[7] This approach has been suggested by Shlomi Dolev as well.

enhances the effect of the clock skew, negatively affecting the precision and the accuracy at the end of the cycle.

NOADJUST-CS
at *"pulse"* event   */* received the internal pulse event */*
   begin
      Clock = 0;
   end

4   Self-Stabilizing Byzantine Pulse Synchronization

The nodes execute this procedure in the background. The procedure ensures that different nodes invoke pulses in a close time proximity (σ) of each other. Pulses should be invoked regularly, with a frequency within a linear envelope of any real-time interval and bounds on intervals between two successive pulses.

Basic notations:
In addition to the definitions of Section 2 we use the following notations, though nodes do not need to maintain them as variables.

- $\psi_i(t_1, t_2)$ is the number of pulses a correct node p_i invoked during a real-time interval $[t_1, t_2]$ within which p_i was continuously correct.
- Let $a', b', g', h' \in R^+$ be constants that define the linear envelope bound on the ratio between all real-time intervals and every ψ_i in those intervals.
- $\phi_i(t) \in R^+ \cup \{\infty\}$, $0 \le i \le n$, denotes the elapsed real-time since the last time node p_i invoked a pulse. For a node, p_j, that has not invoked a pulse since the initialization of the system, $\phi_j(t) \equiv \infty$.

Basic definitions:
- The **pulse_state** of the system at real-time t is given by:

$$pulse\_state \equiv (\phi_0(t), \ldots, \phi_{n-1}(t)).$$

- Let G be the set of all possible pulse_states of a system S.
- A set of nodes, N, are called **pulse-synchronized** at real-time t if

$$\forall p_i, p_j \in N, |\phi_i(t) - \phi_j(t)| \le \sigma.$$

- $s \in G$ is a **synchronized pulse_state** of the system at real-time t if the set of correct nodes are pulse-synchronized at some real-time $t_{syn} \in [t, t + \sigma]$.

Definition 4. The Self-Stabilizing Pulse Synchronization Problem

As long as the system is within the assumption boundaries:
Convergence: *Starting from an arbitrary state, s, the system reaches a synchronized pulse_state after a finite time.*
Closure: *If s is a synchronized pulse_state of the system at real-time t_0 then $\forall$real time $t \ge t_0$,*

1. *pulse_state(t) is a synchronized pulse_state,*
2. *"Linear Envelope": for every correct node, p_i,*

$$a' \cdot [t - t_0] + b' \leq \psi_i(t, t_0) \leq g' \cdot [t - t_0] + h'.$$

3. *$\exists cycle_{min} \leq$ effective cycle $\leq cycle_{max}$ such that:*

$$(t - t_0 \leq cycle_{min} \Rightarrow \psi_i(t, t_0) \leq 1) \bigwedge (t - t_0 \geq cycle_{max} \Rightarrow \psi_i(t, t_0) \geq 1).$$

The third condition intends to bound the effective cycle length.

4.1   The Mode of Operation of the Pulse Synchronization Procedure

The Byzantine self-stabilizing pulse synchronization procedure presented is called BSS-Pulse-Synch (for *Byzantine Self-Stabilizing Pulse Synchronization*). A cycle is the time interval between two successive pulses that a node invokes. The input value $Cycle$ is the ideal length of the cycle. The actual real-time length of a cycle may slightly deviate from the value $Cycle$ in consequence of the clock drifts, uncertain message delays and behavior of faulty nodes. In the proof of Theorem 2 (see [6]) the extent of this deviation is explicitly presented, and the bounds on the linear envelope are calculated.

Toward the end of its cycle, every correct node targets at synchronizing its forthcoming pulse invocation with the pulse of the other nodes. It does so by sending an endogenous **Propose-Pulse** message to all nodes. These messages (or just a reference to the sending node) are accumulated at each correct node until it invokes a pulse and deletes these messages (or references). We say that two Propose-Pulse messages are **distinct** if they were sent by different nodes. When a node accumulates at least $f+1$ distinct Propose-Pulse messages it also triggers a Propose-Pulse message. Once a node accumulates $n-f$ distinct Propose-Pulse messages it invokes the pulse. The input to the procedure is $Cycle, n$ and f.

BSS-Pulse-Synch$(Cycle, n, f)$
if $(cycle\_countdown\_is\_0)$ then   */* endogenous message */*
    send "Propose-Pulse" message to all;
    $cycle\_countdown\_is\_0$='False';

if received $f + 1$ distinct "Propose-Pulse" messages then   */* triggered message */*
    send "Propose-Pulse" message to all;

if received $n - f$ distinct "Propose-Pulse" messages then */* pulse invocation */*
    invoke **"pulse"** event;
    $cycle\_countdown = Cycle$;
    flush "Propose-Pulse" message counter;
    ignore "Propose-Pulse" messages for $2d(1 + 2\rho)$ time units;

We assume that a background process continuously reduces $cycle\_countdown$, intended to make the node count approximately $Cycle$ time units on its physical timer. On reaching 0, the background process resets the value back to $Cycle$

and invokes BSS-Pulse-Synch by setting $cycle\_countdown\_is\_0$ to 'True'. A reset is also done if $cycle\_countdown$ holds a value not between 0 and $Cycle$. The value is reset to $Cycle$ in the algorithm, once the "pulse" is invoked, in order to prevent the system from blocking because of initializing with a wrong value in the $cycle\_countdown$ or the program counters. Note that on a premature execution of BSS-Pulse-Synch nodes do not flush the message counter, this can speed up initial synchronization. Observe that nodes typically send more than one messages in a cycle, to prevent cases in which the system may be invoked in a deadlocked state. Note that $Cycle, n$ and f are constants and thus correct nodes do not initialize with arbitrary values of these constants.

Theorem 2. *BSS-Pulse-Synch solves the Self-Stabilizing Pulse Synchronization Problem in the presence of at most f Byzantine nodes, where $n \geq 3f + 1$.*

5   The Self-Stabilizing Byzantine Consensus Algorithm

The Strong Byzantine Consensus module can use many of the classical Byzantine Consensus algorithms. The self-stabilization requirement does not introduce a major obstacle, because the algorithms terminate in a small number of rounds, and $Cycle$ can be set so the termination is before the next pulse and thus before the next invocation of the algorithm. The only delicate point is to make sure that an arbitrary initialization of the algorithm cannot cause the nodes to block or deadlock. Below we specify show how to update the early stopping Byzantine Algorithm of Toueg, Perry and Srikanth [20] to address our needs. The nodes invoke the algorithm with their value of the next ET.

In our environment the nodes advance the phases according to the elapsed time since their pulse. When nodes invoke the procedure they consider also all messages in their buffers that were accepted prior to the invocation.

We use the following notations in the description of the consensus algorithm:

- A *phase* is a duration of $(\sigma + d)(1 + 2\rho)$ clock units on a node's clock.
- A *round* is a duration of two phases.
- A *broadcast* primitive is the primitive defined in [20] (see [6]). Nodes issue an *accept* within the broadcast primitive.

The main differences from the original protocol of [20] are:
- Instead of the General use an imaginary node whose value is the clock values of the individual nodes.
- Agree on whether $n - f$ of the values are identical.
- The fact that the general is not counted as a faulty node requires running the protocol an extra round.

Strong-Byz-Consensus(ET) invoked at node p:
    initialize the **broadcast** primitive;
    $broadcasters := \emptyset;\ v = 0;$
phase $= 1$:
    send($ET, 0$) to all participating nodes;
phase $= 2$:
    if received $n - f$ distinct ($ET', 0$) messages by the end of phase 1 **then**

      send $(echo, I_0, ET', 0)$ to all;
    if received $n - f$ distinct $(echo, I_0, v\prime, 0)$ messages by the end of phase 2
then
      invoke **broadcast**$(p, v\prime, 2)$;
      stop and **return**$(v\prime)$.
round r **for** $r = 2$ **to** $r = f + 2$ **do:**
    if $v \neq 0$ **then**
      invoke **broadcast**(p, v, r);
      stop and **return**(v).
    by the end of round r:
      if in rounds $r\prime \leq r$ **accepted** $(I_0, v, 0)$ and $(q_i, v\prime, i)$ for all i, $2 \leq i \leq r$,
         where all q_i distinct **then** $v := v\prime$;
      if $|broadcasters| < r - 1$ **then stop** and **return**(0);
stop and **return**(v).

Nodes stop participating in the Strong-Byz-Consensus protocol when they are instructed to do so. They stop participating in its broadcast primitive by the end of the round in which they stop the Strong-Byz-Consensus. The only exception is when they stop in the 2nd phase of the algorithm. In this case they stop participation in the broadcast primitive by the end of the 2nd round.

The main feature of the protocol is that when all correct nodes begin with the same value of ET, all stop within 1 round (2 phases). This early stopping feature brings to a fast convergence during normal operation of the system, even when faulty nodes are present. One can employ standard optimization to save in the number of messages, and to save a couple of phases.

Theorem 3. *The Strong-Byz-Consensus satisfies the following properties:*
    Termination: *The protocol terminates in a finite time.*
    If the system is in the assumption boundaries, $n > 3f$, and all correct nodes invoke the protocol within σ of each other, and messages of correct nodes are received and processed by participating correct nodes then:
    Agreement: *The protocol returns the same value at all correct nodes.*
    Validity: *If all correct nodes invoke the protocol with the same value, then the protocol returns that value, and*
    Early-stopping: *in such a case all correct nodes stop within 1 round.*

6   Analysis and Comparison to Other Clock Synchronization Algorithms

Our algorithms require reaching consensus in every cycle. This implies that the cycle should be long enough to allow for the consensus to terminate at all correct nodes. This implies having $Cycle \geq 2\sigma + 3(2f+4)d$, assuming that the consensus algorithm takes $(f + 2)$ rounds of $3d$ each. For simplicity we also assume M to be large enough so that it takes at least a cycle for the clocks to wrap around.

The convergence and closure of PBSS-Clock-Synch follows from the self-stabilization of the pulse synchronization procedure and from the self-stabilization and termination of the Byzantine Consensus algorithm.

Table 1. Comparison of Clock Synchronization Algorithms (ϵ is the uncertainty of the message delay). The convergence time is in pulses for the algorithms utilizing a global pulse system and in network rounds for the other semi-synchronous protocols. PT-SYNC assumes the use of shared memory and thus the "message complexity" is of the "equivalent messages".

Algorithm	Self-Stabilizing /Byzantine	Precision γ	Accuracy	Convergence Time	Messages
PBSS-Clock-Synch	SS+BYZ	$3d + O(\rho)$	$3d + O(\rho)$	$Cycle + 3(2f+5)d$	$O(nf^2)$
NOADJUST-CS	SS+BYZ	$2d + O(\rho)$	$3d + O(\rho)$	$Cycle$	$O(n^2)$
DHSS [9]	BYZ	$d + O(\rho)$	$(f+1)d + O(\rho)$	$2(f+1)d$	$O(n^2)$
LL-APPROX [21]	BYZ	$5\epsilon + O(\rho)$	$\epsilon + O(\rho)$	$d + O(\epsilon)$	$O(n^2)$
DW-SYNCH [12]	SS+BYZ	0 (global pulse)	0 (global pulse)	$M2^{2(n-f)}$	$n^2 M2^{2(n-f)}$
DW-BYZ-SS [12]	SS+BYZ	$4(n-f)\epsilon + O(\rho)$	$(n-f)\epsilon + O(\rho)$	$O(n)^{O(n)}$	$O(n)^{O(n)}$
PT-SYNC [18]	SS	0 (global pulse)	0 (global pulse)	$4n^2$	$O(n^2)$

Note that Ψ_i, defined in Section 2, represents the actual deviation of an individual correct clock (p_i,) from a real-time interval. The accuracy of the clocks is the bound on the deviation of correct clocks from a real-time interval. The clocks are repeatedly adjusted in order to minimize the accuracy. Following a synchronization of the clock values, that is targeted to occur once in a cycle, correct clocks can be adjusted by at most ADJ, where

$$-3d(1 + \rho) - 2\rho\frac{Cycle}{1 - \rho} \le ADJ \le 2d(1 - \rho) + 2\rho\frac{Cycle}{1 + \rho}.$$

Should the initial clock values reflect real-time and their initial states consistent, then this determines the accuracy of the clocks with respect to real-time (and not only in terms of a real-time interval), as long as the system stays within the assumption boundaries and clocks do not wrap around.

The precision, γ, that is guaranteed by Theorem 1 becomes

$$\gamma \ge 3d(1 + \rho) + 2\rho\frac{Cycle}{1 - \rho} + \sigma\rho = 3d + O(\rho).$$

The only Byzantine self-stabilizing clock synchronization algorithms, to the best of our knowledge, are published in [11,12]. Two randomized self-stabilizing Byzantine clock synchronization algorithms are presented, designed for fully connected communication graphs, use message passing which allow faulty nodes to send differing values to different nodes, allow transient and permanent faults during convergence and require at least $3f + 1$ processors. The clocks wrap around, where M is the upper bound on the clock values held by individual processors. The first algorithm assumes a common global pulse system and synchronizes in expected $M \cdot 2^{2(n-f)}$ global pulses. The second algorithm in [12] does not use a global pulse system and is thus partially synchronous similar to our model. The convergence time of the latter algorithm is in expected $O((n-f)n^{6(n-f)})$ time. Both algorithms thus have drastically higher convergence times than ours.

In Table 1 we compare the parameters of our protocols to previous classic Byzantine clock synchronization algorithms, to non-Byzantine self-stabilizing clock synchronization algorithms and to the prior Byzantine self-stabilizing clock synchronization algorithms. It shows that our algorithm achieves precision, accuracy, message complexity and convergence time similar to non-stabilizing algorithms, while being self-stabilizing. The $O(nf^2)$ message complexity as well as the convergence time come from the Byzantine Consensus algorithm used.

Note that the use of global clock ticks does not make the synchronization problem trivial as the nodes will still miss a common point in time where the new clock value is agreed and the clocks adjusted accordingly (see [12]).

Note that if instead of using the pulse synchronization procedure of Section 4, one uses the pulse synchronization of [5] then the precision can improve, but the convergence time would drastically increase.

References

1. E. Anceaume, I. Puaut, *"Performance Evaluation of Clock Synchronization Algorithms"*, Technical report 3526,INRIA, 1998.
2. A. Arora, S. Dolev, and M.G. Gouda, *"Maintaining digital clocks in step"*, Parallel Processing Letters, 1:11-18, 1991.
3. B. Awerbuch, S. Kutten, Y. Mansour, B. Patt-Shamir and G. Varghese, *"Time Optimal Self-Stabilizing Synchronization*, Proceedings of the 25th Symp. on Theory of Computing, 1993.
4. J. Brzeziński, and M. Szychowiak, *"Self-Stabilization in Distributed Systems - a Short Survey*, Foundations of Computing and Decision Sciences, Vol. 25, no. 1, 2000.
5. A. Daliot, D. Dolev and H. Parnas, *"Self-Stabilizing Pulse Synchronization Inspired by Biological Pacemaker Networks"*, Proc. Of the Sixth Symposium on Self-Stabilizing Systems, pp. 32-48, 2003.
6. A. Daliot, D. Dolev and H. Parnas, *"Linear Time Byzantine Self-Stabilizing Clock Synchronization"*, **Technical Report TR2003-89**, Schools of Engineering and Computer Science, The Hebrew University of Jerusalem, Dec. 2003.
7. D. Dolev, J. Halpern, and H. R. Strong, *"On the Possibility and Impossibility of Achieving Clock Synchronization"*, J. of Computer and Systems Science, Vol. 32:2, pp. 230-250, 1986.
8. D. Dolev, H. R. Strong, *"Polynomial Algorithms for Multiple Processor Agreement"*, In Proceedings, the 14th ACM SIGACT Symposium on Theory of Computing, 401-407, May 1982. (STOC-82)
9. D. Dolev, J. Y. Halpern, B. Simons, and R. Strong, *"Dynamic Fault-Tolerant Clock Synchronization"*, J. Assoc. Computing Machinery, Vol. 42, No.1, pp. 143-185, Jan. 1995.
10. S. Dolev, *"Possible and Impossible Self-Stabilizing Digital Clock Synchronization in General Graphs"*, Journal of Real-Time Systems, no. 12(1), pp. 95-107, 1997.
11. S. Dolev, *"Self-Stabilization"*, The MIT Press, 2000.
12. S. Dolev, and J. L. Welch, *"Self-Stabilizing Clock Synchronization in the presence of Byzantine faults"*, Proc. Of the Second Workshop on Self-Stabilizing Systems, pp. 9.1-9.12, 1995.
13. S. Dolev and J. L. Welch, *"Wait-free clock synchronization"*, Algorithmica, 18(4):486-511, 1997.
14. M. J. Fischer, N. A. Lynch and M. Merritt, *"Easy impossibility proofs for distributed consensus problems"*, Distributed Computing, Vol. 1, pp. 26-39, 1986.
15. T. Herman, *"Phase clocks for transient fault repair"*, IEEE Transactions on Parallel and Distributed Systems, 11(10):1048-1057, 2000.

16. B. Liskov, *"Practical Use of Synchronized Clocks in Distributed Systems"*, Proceedings of 10th ACM Symposium on the Principles of Distributed Computing, 1991, pp. 1-9.
17. B. Patt-Shamir, *"A Theory of Clock Synchronization"*, Doctoral thesis, MIT, Oct. 1994.
18. M. Papatriantafilou, P. Tsigas, *"On Self-Stabilizing Wait-Free Clock Synchronization"*, Parallel Processing Letters, 7(3), pages 321-328, 1997.
19. F. Schneider, *"Understanding Protocols for Byzantine Clock Synchronization"*, Technical Report 87-859, Dept. of Computer Science, Cornell University, Aug. 1987.
20. Sam Toueg, Kenneth J. Perry, T. K. Srikanth, *"Fast Distributed Agreement"*, Proceedings, Principles of Distributed Computing, 87-101 (1985).
21. J. L. Welch, and N. Lynch, *"A New Fault-Tolerant Algorithm for Clock Synchronization"*, Information and Computation 77, 1-36, 1988.

Detecting Locally Stable Predicates Without Modifying Application Messages

Ranganath Atreya[1], Neeraj Mittal[1], and Vijay K. Garg[2]*

[1] Department of Computer Science, The University of Texas at Dallas, Richardson, TX 75083, USA
atreya@student.utdallas.edu   neerajm@utdallas.edu
[2] Department of Electrical and Computer Engineering, The University of Texas at Austin, Austin, TX 78712, USA
garg@ece.utexas.edu

Abstract. In this paper, we give an efficient algorithm to determine whether a locally stable predicate has become true in an underlying computation. Examples of locally stable predicates include termination and deadlock. Our algorithm does not require application messages to be modified to carry control information (*e.g.*, vector timestamps), nor does it inhibit events (or actions) of the underlying computation. Once the predicate becomes true, the detection latency (or delay) of our algorithm is proportional to the time-complexity of computing a (possibly inconsistent) snapshot of the system. Moreover, only $O(n)$ control messages are required to detect the predicate once it holds, where n is the number of processes.

1 Introduction

Two important problems in distributed systems are detecting termination of a distributed computation and detecting deadlock in a distributed database system. Termination and deadlock are examples of *stable properties*. A property is stable if it never becomes false once it becomes true. For example, once a subset of processes are involved in a deadlock, they continue to stay in a deadlocked state. An algorithm to detect a general stable property involves collecting the relevant states of processes and channels that are consistent with each other and testing to determine whether the property holds over the collected state. By repeatedly taking such *consistent snapshots* of the computation and evaluating the property over the collected state, it is possible to eventually detect a stable property once it becomes true.

Several algorithms have been proposed in the literature for computing a consistent snapshot of a computation [1,2,3,4,5]. These algorithms can be broadly classified into four categories. They either require sending a control message along every channel in the system [1] or rely on piggybacking control information

---

* Supported in part by the NSF Grants ECS-9907213, CCR-9988225, Texas Education Board Grant ARP-320, an Engineering Foundation Fellowship, and an IBM grant.

M. Papatriantafilou and P. Hunel (Eds.): OPODIS 2003, LNCS 3144, pp. 20–33, 2004.

on application messages [2] or assume that messages are delivered in causal order [4,5] or are inhibitory in nature [3]. As a result, consistent snapshots of a computation are expensive to compute. More efficient algorithms have been developed for termination and deadlock that do not require taking consistent snapshots of the computation (*e.g.*, [6,7,8,9,10,11,12,13,14,15,16]).

Termination and deadlock are examples of stable properties that can be formulated as *locally stable predicates* [17]. A predicate is *locally stable* if no process involved in the predicate can change its state relative to the predicate once the predicate holds. In this paper, we show that it is possible to detect *any* locally stable predicate by repeatedly taking possibly inconsistent snapshots of the computation in a certain manner. Since snapshots are not required to be consistent, it is not necessary to send a control message along every channel of the system. Our algorithm does not inhibit any event of the underlying computation nor does it require channels to be FIFO. Unlike Marzullo and Sabel's algorithm for detecting a locally stable predicate [17], no control information is required to be piggybacked on application messages and therefore application messages do not need to be modified at all. Once the predicate becomes true, the detection latency (or delay) of our algorithm is proportional to the time-complexity of the fastest snapshot protocol. Furthermore, since our approach does not require snapshots to be consistent, it is not necessary to send a control message along every channel of the system when a snapshot is taken.

Our algorithm also unifies several known algorithms for detecting termination and deadlock [6,8,9,10,11]. Some of the examples include Safra's color-based algorithm [9], Mattern's four counter algorithm [8] and Mattern *et al*'s sticky-flag algorithm [10] for termination detection, and Ho and Ramamoorthy's two-phase algorithm [6] for deadlock detection. All of these algorithms can be derived as special cases of the algorithm given in this paper. Note that the two-phase deadlock detection algorithm as described in [6] is actually flawed but can be easily fixed using the ideas given in this paper. Therefore this paper presents a unifying framework for understanding and describing various termination and deadlock detection algorithms.

Although our algorithm does not require application messages to be modified to assist the detection algorithm, it does assume the ability to monitor changes in the values of the relevant variables. This may require modification of the application program. Most of the algorithms for predicate detection make the same assumption and, therefore, may require the application program to be modified to aid in the detection process (*e.g.*, [6,8,10,11,12,16]).

The paper is organized as follows. Section 2 describes the system model and the notation used in this paper. An algorithm for detecting a locally stable predicate is discussed in Section 3. Due to the lack of space, proofs of lemmas and theorems have been omitted. In Section 4, we analyze the performance of the algorithm. We discuss the related work in Section 5. Finally, Section 6 concludes the paper and also outlines directions for future research.

2   Model and Notation

2.1   Distributed Computations

We assume an asynchronous distributed system comprising of multiple processes which communicate with each other by sending messages over a set of channels. There is no global clock or shared memory. Processes are non-faulty and channels are reliable. Channels may be non-FIFO. Message delays are finite but unbounded.

Processes execute *events* and change their states. A *local state* of a process, therefore, is given by the sequence of events it has executed so far starting from the *initial state*. Events are either *internal* or *external*. An external event could be a *send event* or a *receive event* or both. An event causes the local state of a process to be updated. In addition, a send event causes a message or a set of messages to be sent and a receive event causes a message or a set of messages to be received. The event executed immediately before e on the same process (as e) is called the *predecessor event* of e and is denoted by $pred(e)$. The *successor event* of e, denoted by $succ(e)$, can be defined in a similar fashion.

Although it is possible to determine the exact order in which events were executed on a single process, it is, in general, not possible to do so for events executed on different processes. As a result, an execution of a distributed system, referred to as *distributed computation* (or simply a *computation*), is modeled by an (irreflexive) partial order on a set of events. The partial order, denoted by $\rightarrow$, is given by the Lamport's *happened-before relation* (also known as *causality relation*) [18] which is defined as the smallest transitive relation satisfying the following properties:

1. if events e and f occur on the same process, and e occurred before f in real time then e happened-before f, and
2. if events e and f correspond to the send and receive, respectively, of a message then e happened-before f.

Intuitively, the Lamport's happened-before relation captures the maximum amount of information that can be deduced about ordering of events when the system is characterized by unpredictable message delays and unbounded relative processor speeds.

2.2   Cuts, Consistent Cuts, and Frontiers

A state of a distributed system, referred to as *global state*, is the collective state of processes and channels. (A channel state is given by the set of messages in transit.) If every process maintains a log of all the messages it has sent and received so far, then a channel state can be determined by examining the state of the two processes connected by the channel. Therefore, in this paper, we view a global state as a collection of local states. The equivalent notion based on events is called *cut*. A cut is a collection of events closed under predecessor relation. In other words, a cut is a set of events such that if an event is in the set, then its predecessor, if it exists, also belongs to the set. Formally,

$$C \text{ is a cut} \quad \triangleq \quad \langle \forall e, f :: (e = pred(f)) \wedge (f \in C) \Rightarrow e \in C \rangle$$

The *frontier* of a cut consists of those events of the cut whose successors do not belong to the cut. Formally,

$$frontier(C) \quad \triangleq \quad \{ e \in C \mid succ(e) \text{ exists} \Rightarrow succ(e) \notin C \}$$

Not every cut corresponds to a valid state of the system. A cut is said to be *consistent* if it contains an event only if it also contains all events that happened-before it. Formally,

$$C \text{ is a consistent cut} \quad \triangleq \quad \langle \forall e, f :: (e \to f) \wedge (f \in C) \Rightarrow e \in C \rangle$$

Observe that if a cut is not consistent then it contains an event such that one or more events that happened-before it do not belong to the cut. Such a scenario, clearly, cannot occur in a real world. Consequently, if a cut is not consistent then it is not possible for the system to be in a global state given by the cut. In other words, only those cuts which are consistent can possibly occur during an execution.

2.3   Global Predicates

A *global predicate* (or simply a *predicate*) is defined as a boolean-valued function on variables of one or more processes. In other words, a predicate maps every consistent cut of a computation to either true or false. Given a consistent cut, a predicate is evaluated with respect to the values of the relevant variables in the state resulting after executing all events in the cut. If a predicate b evaluates to true for a cut C, we say that C *satisfies* b or, equivalently, $b(C) = $ true. Hereafter, we abbreviate expressions $b(C) = $ true and $b(C) = $ false by $b(C)$ and $\neg b(C)$, respectively. Also, we denote the value of a variable x resulting after executing all events in a cut C by $x(C)$.

In this paper, we focus on a special but important class of predicates called *locally stable predicates* [17]. A predicate is *stable* if once the system reaches a global state where the predicate holds, the predicate holds in all future global states as well.

Definition 1 (stable predicate). *A predicate b is* stable *if it stays true once it becomes true. Formally, b is stable if for all consistent cuts C and D,*

$$b(C) \wedge (C \subseteq D) \Rightarrow b(D)$$

An example of a stable predicate is termination (of a distributed computation) which is expressed as: "all processes are passive" and "all channels are empty". Another important example of a stable predicate is deadlock which occurs when two or more processes are involved in some sort of "circular" wait. (Deadlock is stable under all request models.) A stable predicate is said to be *locally stable* if once the predicate becomes true, no variable involved in the predicate changes its value thereafter. For a predicate b, let $vars(b)$ denote the set of variables on which b depends.

Definition 2 (locally stable predicate [17]). *A stable predicate b is* locally stable *if no process involved in the predicate can change its state relative to b once b holds. Formally, b is locally stable if for all consistent cuts C and D,*

$$b(C) \wedge (C \subseteq D) \quad \Rightarrow \quad \langle \forall\, x \in vars(b) :: x(C) = x(D) \rangle$$

Intuitively, once a locally stable predicate becomes true, not only does the value of the predicate stay the same—which is true, but the values of all variables involved in the predicate stay the same as well. In this paper, we distinguish between property and predicate. A predicate is a *concrete formulation* of a property in terms of program variables and processors states. In general, there is more than one way to formulate a property. For example, the mutual exclusion property, which states that there is at most one process in its critical section at any time, can be expressed in the following ways.

1. $\bigwedge_{1 \leqslant i < j \leqslant n} (\neg cs_i \vee \neg cs_j)$, where cs_i is true if and only if process p_i is in its critical section.

2. $(\sum_{i=1}^{n} cs_i) \leqslant 1$, where cs_i is 1 if and only if process p_i is in its critical section and is 0 otherwise.

Local stability, unlike stability, depends on the particular formulation of a property. It is possible that one formulation of a property is locally stable while the other is not. For instance, consider the property "the global virtual time of the system is at least k", which is abbreviated as $GVT \geqslant k$ [19]. The property "$GVT \geqslant k$" is true if and only if the local virtual time of each processes is at least k and there is no message in transit with timestamp less than k. Let lvt_i denote the local clock of process p_i. Also, let $sent(i, j; k)$ denote the number of messages that process p_i has sent to process p_j so far whose timestamp is at most k. Likewise, let $rcvd(i, j; k)$ denote the number of messages that process p_i has received from process p_j so far whose timestamp is at most k. The property $GVT \geqslant k$ can be expressed as:

$$GVT \geqslant k \;\equiv\; \left(\bigwedge_{1 \leqslant i \leqslant n} lvt_i \geqslant k \right) \wedge \left(\bigwedge_{1 \leqslant i, j \leqslant n} sent(i, j; k) = rcvd(j, i; k) \right)$$

The above formulation of the property $GVT \geqslant k$ is not locally stable because local clock of a process may change even after the predicate has become true. However, we can define an auxiliary variable a_i which is true if and only if $lvt_i \geqslant k$. An alternative formulation of the property $GVT \geqslant k$ is:

$$GVT \geqslant k \;\equiv\; \left(\bigwedge_{1 \leqslant i \leqslant n} a_i \right) \wedge \left(\bigwedge_{1 \leqslant i, j \leqslant n} sent(i, j; k) = rcvd(j, i; k) \right)$$

Unlike the first formulation, the second formulation is actually locally stable. We say that a property is locally stable if there is at least one predicate representing the property that is locally stable. The complexity of determining whether a locally stable formulation for a given stable property exists is an open problem. Termination, deadlock of a subset of processes (under single, AND, OR and k-out-of-n request models) and global virtual time exceeding a given value can all be expressed as locally stable predicates.

3 The Algorithm

In this section, we describe an on-line algorithm to detect a locally stable predicate, that is, to determine whether a locally stable predicate has become true in a computation in progress. A general algorithm for detecting a stable predicate is to repeatedly compute consistent snapshots (or consistent cuts) of the computation and evaluate the predicate for these snapshots until the predicate becomes true. More efficient algorithms have been developed for detecting special cases of stable predicates such as termination and deadlock. Specifically, it has been shown that to detect many stable predicates, including termination and deadlock, it is not necessary for snapshots to be consistent. In this paper, we show that *any* locally stable predicate can be detected by repeatedly taking *possibly inconsistent* snapshots of the underlying computation.

3.1 The Main Idea

The main idea is to take snapshots of the computation in such a manner that there is at least one consistent snapshot lying between any two consecutive snapshots. To that end, we generalize the notion of consistent cut to the notion of *consistent interval*.

Definition 3 (interval). *An interval $[C, D]$ is a pair of possibly inconsistent cuts C and D such that $C \subseteq D$.*

An interval is said to be consistent if it contains at least one consistent cut.

Definition 4 (consistent interval). *An interval $[C, D]$ is said to be consistent if there exists a consistent cut G such that $C \subseteq G \subseteq D$.*

Note that an interval $[C, C]$ is consistent if and only if C is a consistent cut. Next, we give the necessary and sufficient condition for an interval to be consistent.

Theorem 1. *An interval $[C, D]$ is consistent if and only if all events that happened-before some event in C belong to D. Formally, $[C, D]$ is consistent if and only if the following holds:*

$$\langle \forall e, f :: (e \rightarrow f) \wedge (f \in C) \ \Rightarrow \ e \in D \rangle \tag{1}$$

Observe that when $C = D$, the necessary and sufficient condition for an interval to be consistent reduces to the definition of a consistent cut. Now, consider a consistent interval $[C, D]$. Suppose there is no change in the value of any variable in $vars(b)$ between C and D. We say that the interval $[C, D]$ is *quiescent* with respect to b. Clearly, in this case, for every variable $x \in vars(b)$, $x(C) = x(D) = x(G)$. This implies that $b(G) = b(C) = b(D)$. In other words, in order to compute the value of the predicate b for the consistent cut G, we can instead evaluate b for either endpoint of the interval, that is, cut C or cut D. In case b is a stable predicate and $b(D)$ evaluates to true, we can safely conclude that b has indeed become true in the underlying computation. Formally,

Theorem 2. *If an interval $[C, D]$ is consistent as well as quiescent with respect to a predicate b, then*

$$b(D) \;\Rightarrow\; \langle \exists\, G : G \text{ is a consistent cut} : b(G) \rangle$$

Based on the idea described above, an algorithm for detecting a locally stable predicate can be devised as follows. Repeatedly compute possibly inconsistent snapshots of the computation in such a way that every pair of *consecutive* snapshots forms a consistent interval. After each snapshot is recorded, test whether any of the relevant variables—on which the predicate depends—has undergone a change since the last snapshot was taken. In case the answer is "no", evaluate the predicate for the current snapshot. If the predicate evaluates to true, then, using Theorem 2, it can be deduced that the computation has reached a state in which the predicate holds, and the detection algorithm terminates with "yes". Otherwise, repeat the above steps for the next snapshot and so on.

Theorem 2 establishes that the algorithm is *safe*, that is, if the algorithm terminates with answer "yes", then the predicate has indeed become true in the computation. We need to show that the algorithm is also *live*, that is, if the predicate has become true in the computation, then the algorithm terminates eventually with answer "yes". To establish liveness, we use the fact that the predicate is locally stable, which was not required to prove safety. Suppose the predicate b, which is locally stable, has become true in the computation. Therefore there exists a consistent cut G of the computation that satisfies b. Let C and D with $C \subseteq D$ be two snapshots of the computation taken after G. In other words, $G \subseteq C \subseteq D$. Since b is a locally stable predicate and $b(G)$ holds, no variable in $vars(b)$ undergoes a change in its value after G. This implies that the values of all the variables in $vars(b)$ for D is same as that for G and therefore D satisfies b as well. Formally,

Theorem 3. *Given an interval $[C, D]$, a locally stable predicate b and a consistent cut G such that $G \subseteq C$,*

$$b(G) \;\Rightarrow\; ([G, D] \text{ is quiescent with respect to } b) \wedge b(D)$$

Observe that if $[G, D]$ is quiescent with respect to b then so is $[C, D]$. The algorithm, on detecting that no relevant variable has undergone a change in the interval $[C, D]$, evaluates b for D. In this case, $b(D)$ evaluates to true and, as a result, the algorithm terminates with answer "yes".

3.2   Implementation

To implement the detection algorithm described in the previous section, two issues need to be addressed. First, how to ensure that every pair of consecutive snapshots forms a consistent interval. Second, how to detect that no relevant variable has undergone a change in a given interval, that is, all relevant variables have reached a state of quiescence. We next discuss solutions to both the problems.

Ensuring Interval Consistency using Barrier Synchronization: First, we give a condition that is stronger than the condition (1) given in Theorem 1 in the sense that it is sufficient but not necessary for a pair of cuts to form a consistent interval. The advantage of this condition is that it can be easily implemented using only *control messages* without altering messages generated by the underlying computation, hereafter referred to as *application messages*. To that end, we define the notion of *barrier synchronized interval*. Intuitively, an interval $[C, D]$ is barrier synchronized if it is not possible to move beyond D on any process until all events in C have been executed.

Definition 5 (barrier synchronized interval). *An interval $[C, D]$ is* barrier synchronized *if every event contained in C happened-before every event that does not belong to D. Formally,*

$$\langle \forall\, e, f :: (e \in C) \wedge (f \notin D)\ \Rightarrow\ e \to f \rangle \tag{2}$$

Next, we show that a barrier synchronized interval is also consistent.

Lemma 4 (barrier synchronization $\Rightarrow$ consistency). *If an interval is barrier synchronized then it is also consistent.*

It can be verified that when $C = D$, the notion of barrier synchronized interval reduces to the notion of barrier synchronized cut, also known as *inevitable global state* [20]. Now, to implement the algorithm described in the previous section, we use a *monitor* which periodically records snapshots of the underlying computation. One of the processes in the system can be chosen to act as a monitor. In order to ensure that every pair of consecutive snapshots is barrier synchronized, the monitor simply needs to ensure that the protocol for recording the next snapshot is initiated only *after* the protocol for recording the current snapshot has terminated. Recording a snapshot basically requires the monitor to collect local states of all processes. Many approaches can be used depending upon the communication topology and other factors. For instance, the monitor can broadcast a message to all processes requesting them to send their local states. A process, on receiving message from the monitor, sends its (current) local state to the monitor [6]. Alternatively, processes in the system can be arranged to form a logical ring. The monitor uses a token (sometimes call a probe) which circulates through the entire ring gathering local states on its way [9,10,17]. Another approach is to impose a spanning tree on the network with the monitor acting as the root. In the first phase, starting from the root node, control messages move downward all the way to the leaf nodes. In the second phase, starting from leaf nodes, control messages move upward to the root node collecting local states on their way [19]. (The local states are recorded in the second phase and not in the first phase.) Hereafter, we refer to the three approaches discussed above as *broadcast-based*, *ring-based* and *tree-based*, respectively. In all the three approaches, recording of a local state can be done in a lazy manner [10]. In lazy recording, a process postpones recording its local state until its current local state is such that it does not preclude the (global) predicate from becoming true. For instance, in termination detection, a process which is currently *active* can postpone recording its local state until it becomes *passive*.

Let a *session* correspond to taking a single snapshot of the computation. For the kth session, let S_k refer to the snapshot computed in the session, and let $start_k$ and end_k denote the events on the monitor that correspond to the beginning and end of the session. All the above approaches ensure the following:

$$\langle \forall e : e \in frontier(S_k) : e \to end_k \rangle \wedge \langle \forall f : f \in frontier(S_{k+1}) : start_{k+1} \to f \rangle$$

Since sessions do not overlap, $end_k \to start_{k+1}$. This implies that:

$$\langle \forall e, f :: (e \in frontier(S_k)) \wedge (f \in frontier(S_{k+1})) \Rightarrow e \to f \rangle \qquad (3)$$

It can be easily verified that (3) implies (2). Note that non-overlapping of sessions is only a sufficient condition for interval consistency and not necessary. It is possible to ensure interval consistency even when sessions overlap. However, application messages need to be modified to carry control information.

Detecting Interval Quiescence using Dirty Bits: To detect whether one or more variables have undergone a change in their values in a given interval, we use *dirty bits*. Specifically, we associate a dirty bit with each variable whose value the predicate depends on. Sometimes, it may be possible to associate a single dirty bit with a set of variables or even the entire local state. Initially, each dirty bit is in its *clean state*. Whenever there is a change in the value of a variable, the corresponding dirty bit is set to an *unclean state*. When a local snapshot is taken (that is, a local state is recorded), all dirty bits are also recorded along with the values of all the variables. After the recording, all dirty bits are reset to their clean states. Clearly, an interval $[C, D]$ is quiescent if and only if all dirty bits in D are in their clean states.

In case multiple monitors are used to achieve fault-tolerance, a separate set of dirty bits has to be maintained for each monitor. This is to prevent snapshots protocols initiated by different monitors from interfering with each other; otherwise dirty bits may be reset incorrectly.

Combining the Two: To detect a locally stable predicate, the monitor executes the following steps.

1. Compute a snapshot of the computation.
2. Test whether all dirty bits in the snapshot are in their clean states. If not, go to the first step.
3. Evaluate the predicate for the snapshot. If the snapshot does not satisfy the predicate, then go to the first step.

The basic algorithm can be further optimized. In the ring-based approach, the process currently holding the token can discard the token if the local states gathered so far indicate that the global predicate has not become true. For example, this can happen during termination detection when the token reaches a process with one or more dirty bits in their unclean states. The process discarding the token can either inform the monitor or become the new monitor itself and initiate the next session for recording a snapshot. When a session is *aborted early* in this manner, only a subset of processes would have recorded their local states and have their dirty bits reset. In this case, the global snapshot for a session, even if it is aborted early, can be taken to be the collection of *last recorded* local states on all processes.

4   Performance Analysis

We now analyze the performance of the three concrete variants of our detection algorithm, namely broadcast-based, ring-based and tree-based. We evaluate the three approaches with respect to the following criteria:

– **Message Complexity:** It refers to the number of (control) messages generated by the algorithm. These messages are in addition to the application messages generated by the underlying computation.
– **Message Overhead:** It refers to the maximum size of a control message expressed in number of bits.
– **Detection Latency (or Delay):** It refers to the time, measured as the number of message hops, elapsed between when the predicate becomes true to when the detection algorithm terminates.
– **Process Load:** It refers to the number of control messages exchanged—sent or received—by a process.

Let the space-complexity of recording a local state be $O(s)$ bits.

Broadcast-based approach: For this approach, the message complexity per session is $2(n-1)$, where n is the number of processes, and the message overhead for a control message is $O(s)$. Once the predicate becomes true, the algorithm requires at most two more sessions to terminate after the current session has terminated. This is because, after the current session is over, the next session will reset all dirty bits and the session after that will detect the predicate. This translates into $O(1)$ message hops. The monitor is involved in $2(n-1)$ message exchanges per session; it sends $n-1$ messages and receives $n-1$ messages. All other processes are involved in two message exchanges per session; each one of them receives one message and sends one message. Therefore the broadcast-based approach is highly centralized in nature and as such is not suitable for large systems because the monitor may get swamped by messages from other processes.

Ring-based approach: For this approach, the message complexity per session is n and the message overhead for a control message is $O(ns)$. Depending on the property being detected, however, the message overhead may be much lower. For example, for termination detection, it is not necessary to store the local state of each process that has been visited by the token separately. It is sufficient to have one bit to indicate whether all dirty bits seen so far are in their clean states, one bit to indicate whether all processes seen so far are passive, and one integer to store the message deficit—the number of messages sent minus the number of messages received summed over all processes visited so far [9]. The detection latency is two sessions after the current session terminates, which translates into $O(n)$ message hops. This approach is attractive due to its distributed nature because each process is involved in two message exchanges per session; it receives one message and sends one message.

Tree-based approach: This approach lies in between broadcast-based and ring-based approaches. The message complexity per session is $2(n-1)$ and the message overhead for a control message is $O(ns)$. Again, depending on the predicate, the message overhead may be much lower. As in other two approaches, the detection latency is two sessions after the current session terminates. Therefore the detection latency in terms of message hops is $O(h)$, where h is the height of the tree. For a process p, let degree(p) denote the number of neighbors of p in the spanning tree. For example, if p is a leaf node then degree$(p) = 1$. Clearly, process p exchanges $2 * \text{degree}(p)$ messages per session; it sends degree(p) messages and receives degree(p) messages.

5   Discussion

Marzullo and Sabel give an algorithm for detecting a locally stable predicate using the notion of *weak vector clock* [17]. A weak vector clock, unlike the Fidge/Mattern's vector clock [21,22], is updated only when an event that is "relevant" with respect to the predicate is executed. Whenever a process sends a message, it piggybacks the current value of its local (weak) vector clock on the message. Thus Marzullo and Sabel's algorithm requires application messages to be modified to carry a vector timestamp of size n, where n is the number of processes. We are not aware of any other approach specifically developed for detecting a locally stable predicate.

Ho and Ramamoorthy give a two-phase protocol to detect a deadlock in a distributed database system using AND request model [6]. Their two-phase approach is similar to our (broadcast-based) approach in the sense that the snapshots computed in the two phases form a consistent interval. However, their methodology for detecting what part of a process state is quiescent (and what is not) in an interval is flawed. Specifically, their quiescence detection approach works only if status tables maintain information about transactions (and not processes) and transactions follow two-phase locking discipline. Using the results of this paper, their protocol can be easily fixed to work in a more general scenario.

Termination detection algorithms by Safra [9] and Mattern *et al* [10] are similar to our ring-based approach. In Safra's algorithm, a *color* is associated with every machine and the token. A machine turns black when it transitions from active to passive (Rule 3'). When a token visits a black machine, it also turns black (Rule 4). A black machine holding the token turns white after sending the token to its neighbouring machine (Rule 7). Termination is detected when, after one full circulation, all machines were in their passive states, the message deficit is zero, and the token stays white. Mattern *et al* associate a *sticky flag* with every process. A sticky flag normally tracks the state of a process. However, when a process transitions from active to passive, the flag sticks to active until a control message "unsticks" it. Termination is detected when, after one full circulation, all processes along with their sticky flags were in their passive states, and the message deficit is zero. Color and sticky flag play the same role in the two algorithms as dirty bits in ours; both are used to detect if a process went through some activity since last recording its local state. Besides the above two examples, there are several other termination detection algorithms that can be viewed as special cases of our approach for detecting a locally stable predicate such as Mattern's four counter algorithm [8] and Hélary and Raynal's algorithm based on "continuously-passive" flag [11].

Our work is different in the sense that our algorithm is more general and can be used to detect *any* locally stable predicate, and not just termination and deadlock.

6   Conclusion and Future Work

In this paper, we give an efficient algorithm to detect a locally stable predicate based on repeatedly taking (possibly inconsistent) snapshots of the computation in a certain manner. Our algorithm uses only control messages and thus application messages do not need to be modified to carry any control information. It also unifies several known algorithms for detecting two important locally stable predicates, namely termination and deadlock.

At present, we assume that the system is not subject to any failures. In a real world, however, failures do occur and one or more processes may crash. We plan to modify our detection algorithm to work in a faulty environment when one or more processes can fail by crashing. Our algorithm also assumes that it is possible to monitor changes in the values of the relevant variables efficiently. This can be accomplished in two ways. In the first approach, application program is modified such that whenever a relevant variable is assigned a new value, the detection algorithm is informed of the change. In the second approach, which is more desirable, monitoring is done in a transparent manner without modifying the underlying program. While most debuggers such as gdb already have such a capability, their approach is very inefficient. As future work, we plan to investigate efficient ways for monitoring an application program in a transparent manner.

References

1. Chandy, K.M., Lamport, L.: Distributed Snapshots: Determining Global States of Distributed Systems. ACM Transactions on Computer Systems **3** (1985) 63–75
2. Lai, T.H., Yang, T.H.: On Distributed Snapshots. Information Processing Letters (IPL) **25** (1987) 153–158
3. Hélary, J.M., Jard, C., Plouzeau, N., Raynal, M.: Detection of Stable Properties in Distributed Applications. In: Proceedings of the ACM Symposium on Principles of Distributed Computing (PODC). (1987) 125–136
4. Acharya, A., Badrinath, B.R.: Recording Distributed Snapshots Based on Causal Order of Message Delivery. Information Processing Letters (IPL) **44** (1992) 317–321
5. Alagar, S., Venkatesan, S.: An Optimal Algorithm for Recording Snapshots using Casual Message Delivery. Information Processing Letters (IPL) **50** (1994) 311–316
6. Ho, G.S., Ramamoorthy, C.V.: Protocols for Deadlock Detection in Distributed Database Systems. IEEE Transactions on Software Engineering **8** (1982) 554–557
7. Misra, J.: Detecting Termination of Distributed Computations Using Markers. In: Proceedings of the ACM Symposium on Principles of Distributed Computing (PODC). (1983) 290–294
8. Mattern, F.: Algorithms for Distributed Termination Detection. Distributed Computing (DC) **2** (1987) 161–175
9. Dijkstra, E.W.: Shmuel Safra's Version of Termination Detection. EWD Manuscript 998. Available at http://www.cs.utexas.edu/users/EWD (1987)
10. Mattern, F., Mehl, H., Schoone, A., Tel, G.: Global Virtual Time Approximation with Distributed Termination Detection Algorithms. Technical Report RUU-CS-91-32, University of Utrecht, The Netherlands (1991)
11. Hélary, J.M., Raynal, M.: Towards the Construction of Distributed Detection Programs, with an Application to Distributed Termination. Distributed Computing (DC) **7** (1994) 137–147
12. Brzezinski, J., Hélary, J.M., Raynal, M., Singhal, M.: Deadlock Models and a General Algorithm for Distributed Deadlock Detection. Journal of Parallel and Distributed Computing (JPDC) **31** (1995) 112–125
13. Demirbas, M., Arora, A.: An Optimal Termination Detection Algorithm for Rings. Technical Report OSU-CISRC-2/00-TR05, The Ohio State University (2000)
14. Stupp, G.: Stateless Termination Detection. In: Proceedings of the 16th Symposium on Distributed Computing (DISC), Toulouse, France (2002) 163–172
15. Khokhar, A.A., Hambrusch, S.E., Kocalar, E.: Termination Detection in Data-Driven Parallel Computations/Applications. Journal of Parallel and Distributed Computing (JPDC) (2003)
16. Mahapatra, N.R., Dutt, S.: An Efficient Delay-Optimal Distributed Termination Detection Algorithm. Submitted to IEEE Transactions on Parallel and Distributed Systems (2003)
17. Marzullo, K., Sabel, L.: Efficient Detection of a Class of Stable Properties. Distributed Computing (DC) **8** (1994) 81–91

18. Lamport, L.: Time, Clocks, and the Ordering of Events in a Distributed System. Communications of the ACM (CACM) **21** (1978) 558–565
19. Tel, G.: Introduction to Distributed Algorithms. Second edn. Cambridge University Press (US Server) (2000)
20. Fromentin, E., Raynal, M.: Inevitable Global States: A Concept to Detect Unstable Properties of Distributed Computations in an Observer Independent Way. In: Proceedings of the 6th IEEE Symposium on Parallel and Distributed Processing (SPDP). (1994) 242–248
21. Mattern, F.: Virtual Time and Global States of Distributed Systems. In: Parallel and Distributed Algorithms: Proceedings of the Workshop on Distributed Algorithms (WDAG), Elsevier Science Publishers B. V. (North-Holland) (1989) 215–226
22. Fidge, C.: Logical Time in Distributed Computing Systems. IEEE Computer **24** (1991) 28–33

Multiple Agents RendezVous in a Ring in Spite of a Black Hole*

Stefan Dobrev[1], Paola Flocchini[1], Giuseppe Prencipe[2], and Nicola Santoro[3]

[1] University of Ottawa, {sdobrev,flocchin}@site.uottawa.ca
[2] Università di Pisa, prencipe@di.unipi.it
[3] Carleton University, santoro@scs.carleton.ca

Abstract. The *Rendezvous* of anonymous mobile agents in a anonymous network is an intensively studied problem; it calls for k anonymous, mobile agents to gather in the same site. We study this problem when in the network there is a *black hole*: a stationary process located at a node that destroys any incoming agent without leaving any trace. The presence of the black hole makes it clearly impossible for all agents to rendezvous. So, the research concern is to determine how many agents can gather and under what conditions.

In this paper we consider k anonymous, *asynchronous* mobile agents in an anonymous ring of size n with a black hole; the agents are aware of the existence, but not of the location of such a danger. We study the rendezvous problem in this setting and establish a complete characterization of the conditions under which the problem can be solved. In particular, we determine the maximum number of agents that can be guaranteed to gather in the same location depending on whether k or n is unknown (at least one must be known for any non-trivial rendezvous). These results are *tight*: in each case, rendezvous with one more agent is impossible.

All our possibility proofs are constructive: we provide mobile agents protocols that allow the agents to rendezvous or near-gather under the specified conditions. The analysis of the time costs of these protocols show that they are *optimal*.

Our rendezvous protocol for the case when k is unknown is also a solution for the *black hole location* problem. Interestingly, its bounded time complexity is $\Theta(n)$; this is a significant improvement over the $O(n \log n)$ bounded time complexity of the existing protocols for the same case.

Keywords: Mobile Agents, RendezVous, Gathering, Black Hole, Harmful Host, Ring Network, Asynchronous, Anonymous, Distributed Computing.

1 Introduction

In networked systems that support autonomous *mobile agents*, a main concern is how to develop efficient agent-based *system protocols*; that is, to design protocols that will allow a team of rather "simple" agents to cooperatively perform complex system tasks. A main approach to reach this goal is to break a complex task down into more elementary operations. Example of these primitive operations are *wakeup, traversal, gathering,*

---

* Research partially supported by "Progetto ALINWEB: Algoritmica per Internet e per il Web", MIUR Programmi di Ricerca Scientifica di Rilevante Interesse Nazionale.

election. The coordination of the agents necessary to perform these operations is not necessarily simple or easy to achieve. In fact, the computational problems related to these operations are definitely non trivial, and a great deal of theoretical research is devoted to the study of conditions for the solvability of these problems and to the discovery of efficient algorithmic solutions; e.g., see [1,2,3,4].

At an abstract level, these environments, which we shall call *distributed mobile systems*, can be described as a collection $\mathcal{E}$ of autonomous mobile entities located in a graph G. Depending on the context, the entities are sometimes called *robots* or *agents*; in the following, we use the latter. The agents have computing capabilities and bounded storage, execute the same protocol, and can move from node to neighboring node. They are *asynchronous*, in the sense that every action they perform takes a finite but otherwise unpredictable amount of time. Each node of the network, also called *host*, provides a storage area called *whiteboard* for incoming agents to communicate and compute, and its access is held in fair mutual exclusion. The research concern is on determining what tasks can be performed by such entities, under what conditions, and at what cost.

In this paper, we focus on a fundamental task in distributed mobile computing, *rendezvous* in the simplest symmetric topology: the *ring* network. We will consider its solution in presence of a severe security threat: a *black hole*, a network site where a harmful process destroys all incoming agents without leaving a trace.

1.1   Rendezvous

The *rendezvous* problem consists in having all the agents gather at the same node; upon arriving there, each agent terminally sets its variable to *arrived*; there is no a priori restriction on which node will become the rendezvous point.

This problem (sometimes called *gathering*, *point-formation*, or *homing*) is a fundamental one in distributed mobile computing both with agents in graphs and with robots in the plane.

In the case of agents in the graph, the rendezvous problem has been extensively investigated focusing on more limited settings (e.g., without whiteboards) with *two* agents; e.g., see [5,6,7,3,8,9,10]. Almost from the start it became obvious that the possibility (and difficulty) of a solution is related to the possibility (and difficulty) to find or create an *asymmetry* in anonymous and symmetric settings, like the one considered here; to break symmetry in the problem, and thus ensure rendezvous solutions, researchers have used randomization (e.g., [6]), or different deterministic protocols for the two agents (e.g., [10]), or indistinguishable tokens [9]. The case of more than two agents has been investigated in [11,12,13], with only [11] providing a fully deterministic solutions for anonymous ring networks.

Let us stress that *all* these investigations assume *synchronous agents* and this assumption is crucial for the correctness of their solutions.

In contrast, in our setting, both nodes and agents, besides being *anonymous*, are also fully *asynchronous*. The only known results for this setting are about the relationship between *sense of direction* and possibility of *rendezvous* [3]; interestingly, the link between rendezvous and symmetry-breaking is even more clear: rendezvous is in fact equivalent to the *election* problem [3].

1.2   Black Hole Location

Among the severe security threats faced in systems supporting mobile agents, a particularly troublesome one is a *harmful host*; that is, the presence at a network site of harmful stationary processes. The problem posed by the presence of a harmful host has been intensively studied from a programming point of view (e.g., see [14,15,16]), and recently also from an algorithmic prospective [17,18]. Obviously, the first step in any solution to such a problem must be to *identify*, if possible, the harmful host; i.e., to determine and report its location. Depending on the nature of the danger, the task to identify the harmful host might be difficult, if not impossible, to perform.

A particularly harmful host is a *black hole*: a host that *disposes* of visiting agents upon their arrival, leaving *no observable trace* of such a destruction. The task is to develop a mobile agents protocol to determine and report the location of the black hole; the task is completed if, within finite time, at least one agent survives and knows the location of the black hole. The research concern is to determine under what conditions and at what cost mobile agents can successfully accomplish this task, called the *black hole location* problem. Note that this type of highly harmful host is not rare; for example, the undetectable crash failure of a site in a asynchronous network transforms that site into a black hole.

The black hole location problem has been investigated focusing on identifying conditions for its solvability and determining the smallest number of agents needed for its solution [17,18,19]. In particular, a complete characterization has been provided for ring networks [17].

1.3   Our Contributions

In this paper we consider the *rendezvous* problem in a more difficult setting: k asynchronous anonymous agents dispersed in a totally symmetric ring network of n anonymous sites, one of which is a *black hole*.

Clearly it is impossible for all agents to gather since an adversary (i.e., a bad scheduler) can immediately direct some agents towards the black hole. So, the research concern is to determine how many agents can gather. We study this problem and establish a complete characterization of the conditions under which the problem can be solved. The possibility results are summarized in the table shown in Figure 1; these results are *tight*: in each case, rendezvous with one more agent is impossible. It is interesting to observe that at least one of k and n must be known to the agents; however, knowledge of both is not necessary.

Some of these results are unexpected. For example, in an oriented ring all but one agents can indeed rendezvous even if the ring size n is not known, a condition that makes black hole location impossible [17]. In an unoriented ring, at most $k - 2$ agents can rendezvous; surprisingly, if they can not, there is no guarantee that more that $(k-2)/2$ will. It is however always possible to bring all $k - 2$ within distance 1 from each other.

All our possibility proofs are constructive: we provide mobile agents protocols that allow the agents to rendezvous or near-gather under the specified conditions.

Our rendezvous protocol, for the case when k is unknown, is also a solution for the black hole location problem. Interestingly, its bounded time complexity is $O(n)$; this is

	n unknown, k known		n known, k unknown	
ORIENTED	$\forall k$	$RV(k-1)$	$\forall k$	$RV(k-2)$
UNORIENTED	k odd	$RV(k-2)$	k odd or n even	$RV(k-2)$
	k even	$RV(\frac{k-2}{2})$	k even and n odd	$RV(\frac{k-2}{2})$
	$\forall k$	$G(k-2,1)$	$\forall k$	$G(k-2,1)$

Fig. 1. Summary of possibility results.

a significant improvement over the $O(n \log n)$ bounded time complexity of the existing protocols for the same case [17].

Due to space limitation all the proofs are omitted, and can be found at http://sbrinz.di.unipi.it/~peppe/prencipeLNCSopodis03.pdf.

2 Definitions, Basic Properties, and Techniques

2.1 The Framework

The network environment is a ring $\mathcal{R}$ of n *anonymous* (i.e., identical) nodes. Each node has two ports, labelled *left* and *right*; if this labelling is globally consistent, the ring will be said to be *oriented*, *unoriented* otherwise. Each node has a bounded amount of storage, called *whiteboard*.

In this network there is a set $a_1, \ldots, a_k$ of k *anonymous* (i.e., identical) mobile agents. The agents can move from node to neighboring node in $\mathcal{R}$, have computing capabilities and bounded storage, obey the same set of behavioral rules (the "protocol"), and all their actions (e.g., computation, movement, etc) take a finite but otherwise unpredictable amount of time (i.e., they are *asynchronous*). Agents communicate by reading from and writing on the whiteboards; access to a whiteboard is done in mutual exclusion. The agents execute a protocol (the same for all agents) that specifies the computational and navigational steps. Initially, each agent is placed at a distinct node, called its *homebase*, and has a predefined state variable set to *available*. Let us denote by x_i the homebase of agent a_i. Each homebase is initially marked by the corresponding agent.

The agents are aware of the fact that in the network there is a *black hole* (BH); its location is however unknown. In this environment, we are going to consider the *Rendezvous* problem and the *Near-Gathering* problem defined below.

The *Rendezvous* problem $RV(p)$ consists in having at least $p \leq k$ agents gathering in the same site. There is no a priori restriction on which node will become the rendezvous point. Upon recognizing the gathering point, an agent terminally sets its variable to *arrived*. We consider a solution algorithm terminated when at least p agents become *arrived* (explicit termination).

The *Near-Gathering* problem $G(p, d)$ consists in having at least p agents within distance d from each other. As for the Rendezvous problem we consider the algorithm terminated when at least p agents know that they are within distance d from each other and change their state to a terminal state. Clearly, $G(p, 0) = RV(p)$.

The efficiency of a solution protocol is obviously first and foremost measured in the *size* of the solution, i.e. the number of agents that the algorithm will make rendezvous at the same location. A secondary but important cost measure is the amount of *time* elapsed from the beginning to the termination of the algorithm. Since the agents are asynchronous, "real" time cannot be measured. We will use the traditional measure of *bounded time*, where it is assumed that the traversal of a link takes at most one time unit. During the computation some agents will disappear in the black hole, some will survive and eventually gather; for the purposes of bounded time complexity we will consider that the overall computation starts (i.e., we will start to count time) when the first surviving agent starts the algorithm.

2.2   Cautious Walk

In the following we describe a basic tool, first introduced in [17], that we will use in all our protocols to minimize the number of agents that disappear in the back hole.

In our algorithms, the ports (corresponding to the incident links) of a node can be classified as (a) *unexplored* – if no agent has moved across this port, (b) *safe* – if an agent arrived via this port or (c) *active* – if an agent departed via this port, but no agent has arrived via it. Clearly, both *unexplored* and *active* links are dangerous in that they might lead to the black hole; the difference is that *active* links are being traversed, so there is in general no need for another agent to go through that link until the link is declared *safe*.

The technique we use, called *cautious walk*, is defined by the following two rules: **Rule 1.** Whenever an agent moves from node u to node v via an *unexplored* port (turning it into *active*), upon its arrival to v and before proceeding somewhere else, it immediately returns to u (making the port *safe*), and then it goes back to v; **Rule 2.** no agent leaves via an *active* port. In the following, agents will either move only on safe links or move using cautious walk.

2.3   Basic Results

Theorem 1. *In an anonymous ring with a black hole: 1. $RV(k)$ is unsolvable; 2. If the ring is unoriented, then $RV(k-1)$ is unsolvable.*

$RV(p)$ is said to be *non-trivial* if p is a non-constant function of k.

Theorem 2. *If k is unknown, non-trivial rendezvous requires locating the black hole.*

In view of the fact that knowledge of n is necessary for locating a black hole [17], it follows that

Theorem 3. *Either k or n must be known for non-trivial rendezvous.*

3   Characterization and Tight Bounds

3.1   RendezVous When n Is Unknown

An immediate consequence of the fact that n is unknown is that, by Theorem 3, k *must be known* for non-trivial rendezvous to occur. Hence, in the rest of this section we assume that k is known. Let us now examine under what conditions the problem can be solved and how.

Oriented Rings

Theorem 4. $RV(k-1)$ *can be always solved, and this can be achieved in time at most* $3(n-2)$.

To prove this theorem, consider the following protocol **GoRight!**; agents are in two states: *explorer* and *follower*.

PROTOCOL **GoRight!**

1. Initially, everybody is an *explorer*.
2. An *explorer* moves right using cautious walk. If it enters a node visited by another agent, it becomes a *follower*.
3. A *follower* moves right, traversing only safe links.
4. If there are $k-1$ *followers* in one node, the agents there terminate the execution of the protocol.

Lemma 1. *Protocol* **GoRight!** *solves[1] $RV(k-1)$ and terminates in time at most* $3(n-2)$ *since the start of the leftmost agent.*

There are situations in which the $3(n-2)$ time bound is indeed achieved: Consider a scenario where there are agents in the two sites neighboring the black hole. The leftmost (with respect to the BH) agent wakes up first and all other agents join the execution only when an agent arrives to their node. Clearly, the left most agent must wake-up all other agents, and every edge must be traversed using cautious walk.

Unoriented Rings. Since the ring is not oriented, by Theorem 1, $RV(k-1)$ can *not* be solved as two agents can immediately disappear in the black hole. Hence, the best we can hope for is $RV(k-2)$. The result we obtain is rather surprising. In fact, either $k-2$ can gather or no more that $(k-2)/2$ can, with nothing in between.

Theorem 5. *(1) If k is odd, $RV(k-2)$ can always be solved. (2) If k is even, $RV(p)$ can not be solved for $p > (k-2)/2$; however, $RV((k-2)/2)$ can always be solved. (3) $G(k-2,1)$ can always be solved.*

To prove this theorem, we will logically partition the entities in two sets, "clockwise" (or *blue*) and "counterclockwise" (or *red*), where all entities in the same set have a common view of "right". Notice that each agent, although anonymous, can easily detect whether a message on a whiteboard has been written by an agent in the same set or not (e.g, each message contains also an indication of which of the two local ports the writer considers to be "right"). Consider first the case when k is odd (recall k is known).

---

[1] The rendezvous site is not necessarily next to the black hole.

PROTOCOL **GR-Odd**.

1. The agents of each set first of all execute the rendezvous algorithm **GoRight!** for oriented rings, independently of and ignoring the agents of the other set, terminating as soon as $(k-1)/2$ *follower* agents of the same set gather in the same node. (Notice: this will eventually happen, and only to one set, as there is only one set with at least $(k+1)/2$ agents, and eventually only one of those agents will remain *explorer*). Without loss of generality, let this happens to the *red agents*.
2. The node where the $(k-1)/2$ red *followers* have gathered becomes the *collection point*, and one of the *followers* is selected as *left-collector*.
3. Every *follower* or blue *explorer* arriving at the collection point joins the group.
4. The *left-collector* x travels (using cautious walk when necessary) left and tells every *follower* and red *explorer* it encounters to go to the collection point; it does so until it reaches the black hole or the last safe node explored by a blue *explorer*. In the latter case, the *left-collector* leaves a message for the blue *explorer* y informing it of the meeting point, and instructing it to become *left-collector*; it then returns to the collection point. If/when the *explorer* y returns to that node, it finds the message, becomes *left-collector* and acts accordingly.
5. A red *explorer* returning to the collection point during its cautious walk (notice: there is only one) becomes now a *right-collector*.
6. The rules for the *right-collector* are exactly those for the *left-collector*, where "left" is replaced by "right", and viceversa.

Since k is odd, we get

Lemma 2. *There is only one collection point.*

By construction of algorithm **GR-Odd** we have

Lemma 3. *Every edge non-incident to the black hole will be traversed by a collector.*

Because of cautious walk, at most 2 agents will enter the black hole; this fact, combined with Lemma 3, yields the following:

Lemma 4. $k-2$ *agents will gather in the collection point.*

Hence, by Lemmas 2 and 4, Point (1) of Theorem 5 holds. Before proceeding with the proof of the other parts of Theorem 5, let us examine the time costs of Protocol**GR-Odd**.

Theorem 6. *Protocol* **GR-Odd** *terminates in time at most* $5(n-2)$.

Consider now the case when k is even (recall k is known). To prove part (2) of Theorem 5 we first observe that $RV((k-2)/2)$ can always be solved by trivially having each set execute the rendezvous algorithm **GoRight!** for oriented rings, and terminating it when at least $k/2 - 1$ *follower* agents of the same set gather in the same node. To complete the proof, we need to show that, when k is even, rendezvous of a greater number of agents can not be guaranteed.

Lemma 5. *If k is even then* $RV(p)$ *can not be solved for* $p > (k-2)/2$.

We now show that, although we cannot guarantee that more than half of the surviving agents rendezvous, we can however guarantee that *all* the surviving agents gather within distance 1 from each other. To prove this, we use the following protocol **GR-Even**.

First of all, each set executes the rendezvous algorithm **GoRight!** for oriented rings, independently of and ignoring the agents of the other sets, and terminate it when (at least) $k/2 - 1$ *follower* agents of the same set gather in the same node. Notice that it is possible that two (but no more than two) such gathering points will be formed; further notice that they could be both made of agents of the same color!

Let us concentrate on one of them and assume, without loss of generalitazion, that it is formed of *red* agents. By definition, associated with it, there is a red *explorer* that will become a *right-collector* once it realizes the collection point has been formed; among the *followers* gathered there, a *left-collector* has also been selected. Both collectors behave as in **GR-Odd** except that, now, each of them could encounter a collector from the other group (if it exists). Therefore, we need to add the following rules:

1. a *collector* keeps the distance from its collection point. When passing the role of collector to an *explorer*, it passes also the distance information.
2. when a *collector* meets another *collector* (notice: they must be from different groups; further notice, they might actually "jump" over each other):
   a) if they are of the same color, then they agree on a unique site (e.g., the rightmost of the two ones) as the final common collection point;
   b) if they are of different colors, if the distance between the collection points is odd, they agree on the middle node as the final common collection point; otherwise, each chooses the closest site incident on the middle edge as the final collection point of its group.
   c) each goes back to its group and notifies all the agents there of their final collection point.

Lemma 6. *Protocol* **GR-Even** *guarantees that* $(k-2)$ *agents will either rendezvous in the same node or gather within distance* 1.

This completes the proof of Theorem 5. The time efficiency of Protocol **GR-Even** can be easily determined:

Theorem 7. *Protocol* **GR-Even** *terminates in time at most* $5(n-2)$.

3.2   RendezVous When k Is Unknown

An immediate consequence of the fact that k is unknown is that, by Theorem 3, the ring size n must be known for any non-trivial rendezvous to be possible.

Another consequence is that, by Theorem 2, if we want to rendezvous we *must* locate the black hole! Let us examine under what conditions and how the problem can be solved.

Oriented Rings

Theorem 8. *Let* $k \geq 4$. *Then* $RV(k-2)$ *can always be solved.*

To prove this theorem we design a protocol, called *Shadow*, quite different from the ones used when k is known. We associate with each contiguous block of explored nodes a group of agents expanding that block until either (1) the explored block contains $n - 1$ nodes (in which case a final *collection* phase is initiated, collecting the agents into a designated collection point) or (2) the block merges with a neighboring explored block (in which case the corresponding groups of agents are combined into one group expanding the new, bigger block).

The group of agents expanding a block consists of at least one and at most four agents. The agents associated with a block are of two kinds: *explorers* and *shadows* (at most one of each type for each direction). The task of the explorers is to expand the explored block in the opposite directions. The shadows travel between the explorers: their goal is to detect when the block contains $n - 1$ explored nodes. Each node keeps information on which types of agents have visited it so far.

At the beginning, each explored block consists of a single node containing an agent starting as a right explorer. As the blocks grow, they eventually touch and their agents are combined forming one of the following block types.

- A two-agent block (i.e., created by merging two one-agent blocks) has one right- and one left- explorer.
- A three-agent block (i.e., created by merging a two-agents with one-agent block) has two explorers and a right shadow.
- A four-agent block has two explorers and two shadows (one in each direction).

When merging a k-agents block with a j-agents block, if $k + j > 4$, then all additional agents in the block become passive. The activities performed by the agents are quite simple:

explorer: It moves in its assigned direction using cautious walk until either it enters the black hole or it detects a neighbor block (by entering a node already visited by a different explorer).

right (resp., left) shadow: It travels inside the explored block from the rightmost (resp., leftmost) safe node to the leftmost (resp., rightmost) safe node, and count the distance. If the travelled distance is $n - 1$, it becomes a *collector*. If it the distance is less, it returns to the rightmost (resp., leftmost) safe node. If the right (resp., left) boundary of the block has moved in the meanwhile, it repeats the process; otherwise, it waits until a new rightmost (resp., leftmost) node is explored.

collector: A collector agent traverses the explored part and collects all the agents on the way (if an agent meets a collector, it stops its activity and follows the collector). Once the whole explored part has been traversed (i.e., the collector counts $n - 1$ links), all agents have been collected and have gathered at the same place. There is a technical detail: it can happen that both shadows can become collectors. In that case, the gathering point is the node where they meet (or, if they crossed each other on a link, the right endpoint of that link).

passive: It waits to be collected by the collector.

Fig. 2. The Shadow Protocol, where the ring is assumed to be oriented clockwise. The empty circles represent *active* agents; the white squares are the *explorers*, the grey squares the *shadows*, and the black squares the *passive* agents. The fat line evidences the segments delimited by the explorers. The numbers are placed only to clarify how the agents move, and are not used at all during the computation.

The main technical difficulty arises from the fact that the whole process is distributed and the agents are not immediately aware when their block collides with another block. In addition, both ends of a block might collide with neighboring blocks at about the same time, complicating the coordination between the agents of the block. First, let us examine how blocks can collide. There are only few possibilities:

- A right explorer a arrives to a node already visited by a right explorer, but not by a left explorer.
- A right and left explorer of different blocks arrive at the same node v, i.e. they find a mark of an explorer in the opposite direction. (Since cautious walk is used, this need not to occur simultaneously. Instead, the second explorer might arrive to v while the first is busy marking the last link as safe.)
- A right and left explorers of different blocks cross each other over the link separating these blocks.

In the first case, the right explorer a becomes the new left explorer; in the remaining cases, each of the collided explorers becomes a shadow in its original direction. However, this may result in having several left explorers in the block (e.g., in the first case, if the a's block already had a left explorer) or several shadows for a given direction (e.g., if the joining blocks already had shadows). This is resolved in the following way:

- A new left explorer travels to the left through the explored part until it either reaches an unexplored link (i.e., it is the leftmost left explorer of this block) or it reaches a node already visited by a left explorer. In the first case, the explorer starts the algorithm for left explorers, otherwise it becomes a new right shadow.
- A new right shadow travels to the right until it reaches the rightmost safe node or a node already visited by a right shadow. In the first case, it starts the algorithm for right shadows; in the latter case, it becomes a new left shadow.
- A new left shadow travels to the left until it reaches the leftmost safe node or a node already visited by a left shadow. In the first case, it starts the algorithm for left shadows, in second case, it becomes passive.

Lemma 7. *(1) Within finite time there will be only one* right-explorer *and one* left-explorer, *and they will both enter the black hole. (2) Within finite time there will be only* *one* right-shadow *and one* left-shadow. *(3) At least one* shadow *will become* collector, *and a* collector *knows the location of the black hole. (4) Every edge non-incident to the* BH *will be traversed by a collector. (5) There will be a unique collection point. (6)* $k - 2$ *agents will gather in the collection point.*

This completes the proof of Theorem 8. Let us now examine the time costs of this protocol.

Theorem 9. *The protocol* Shadow *terminates in at most* $8(n - 2)$ *time steps since the wake-up of the leftmost agent.*

Let us stress that protocol *Shadows* solves the *black hole location* problem (by Point (3) in Lemma 7). This means that we have obtained a significant improvement over the $O(n \log n)$ time complexity of the existing protocols for the black hole search in oriented rings [17].

Unoriented Rings. Interestingly, we discover for the unoriented case better conditions than those we have found when k was known instead of n.

Theorem 10. *(1) If* k *is odd or* n *even,* $RV(k - 2)$ *can always be solved. (2) If* k *is even and* n *odd,* $RV(p)$ *can not be solved for* $p > \lfloor (k - 2)/2 \rfloor$; *however,* $RV(\lfloor (k - 2)/2 \rfloor)$ *can always be solved. (3)* $G(k - 2, 1)$ *can always be solved.*

We will again logically partition the entities in two sets, "clockwise" or *blue* and "counterclockwise" *red*, where all entities in the same sat have a common view of "right".

To prove Point (1) of Theorem 10 we consider protocol *Blue-Red Shadows*, obtained from protocol *Shadows* applying these modifications:

- Each node now keeps information on which types of agents have visited it for both colors.
- If a left explorer finds a mark of a right explorer of the opposite color, it becomes a right shadow.
- If a left shadow find a mark of a right shadow of the opposite color, it becomes passive.
- A shadow always tries to travel to the furthermost explored node, regardless of the color of the explorer that explored it.
- An agent is collected by a collector, regardless of its color.
- In all other cases, the agents of different color ignore each other.

Note that if all agents are of the same color, the protocol *Red-Blue Shadows* behaves exactly as protocol *Shadow* and its correctness follows. Therefore, in the rest we assume there is at least one agent of each color.

Lemma 8. *(1) Within finite time there will be only one red and one blue right explorer and they will both enter the black hole. There will be no left explorer remaining. (2) Within finite time, there will be only two shadows remaining: Either two right shadows of different color, or a right and left shadow of the same color (if one color has only one agent). (3) Points (3) and (4) in Lemma 7 hold also for protocol* Blue-Red Shadows *in unoriented rings.*

Lemma 9. *(1) If k is odd or n is even, there will be a unique collection point; furthermore, k − 2 agents will gather in the collection point. (2) If k is even and n is odd then $RV(p)$ can not be solved for $p > (k − 2)/2$; however, $RV((k − 2)/2)$ can be achieved.*

We now show that, although we cannot guarantee that more than half of the surviving agents rendezvous, we can however guarantee that *all* the surviving agents gather within distance 1 from each other.

Lemma 10. *Protocol* **Blue-Red Shadows** *guarantees that $(k − 2)$ agents will either rendezvous in the same node or gather within distance 1.*

Theorem 11. *The modified protocol* Shadow *for unoriented rings terminates in at most $8(n − 2)$ time steps.*

4   Concluding Remarks

In this paper we have established tight bounds on the number of anonymous agents that can rendezvous in an anonymous ring in presence of a black hole. Notice that, if there is no black hole in the network, the proposed protocols would not work; i.e., the agents do not rendezvous. This fact is hardly surprising since the rendezvous problem of anonymous agents in anonymous ring without black hole is generally *unsolvable* [3].

References

1. Arkin, E., Bender, M., Fekete, S., Mitchell, J.: The freeze-tag problem: how to wake up a swarm of robots. In: 13th ACM-SIAM Symposium on Discrete Algorithms (SODA '02). (2002) 568–577
2. Barrière, L., Flocchini, P., Fraigniaud, P., , Santoro, N.: Capture of an intruder by mobile agents. In: 14th ACM Symp. on Parallel Algorithms and Architectures (SPAA '02). (2002) 200–209
3. Barrière, L., Flocchini, P., Fraigniaud, P., Santoro, N.: Election and rendezvous in fully anonymous systems with sense of direction. In: 10th Colloquium on Structural Information and Communication complexity (SIROCCO '03). (2003) 17–32
4. Panaite, P., Pelc, A.: Exploring unknown undirected graphs. Journal of Algorithms **33** (1999) 281–295
5. Alpern, S.: The rendezvous search problem. SIAM Journal of Control and Optimization **33** (1995) 673–683
6. Alpern, S., Baston, V., Essegaier, S.: Rendezvous search on a graph. Journal of Applied Probability **36** (1999) 223–231
7. Anderson, E., R.R.Weber: The rendezvous problem on discrete locations. Journal of Applied Probability **28** (1990) 839–851
8. Dessmark, A., Fraigniaud, P., Pelc, A.: Deterministic rendezvous in graphs. In: 11th Annual European Symposium on Algorithms (ESA '03). (2003)
9. Kranakis, E., Krizanc, D., Santoro, N., Sawchuk, C.: Mobile agent rendezvous in a ring. In: 23rd International Conference on Distributed Computing Systems (ICDCS'03). (2003)
10. Yu, X., Yung, M.: Agent rendezvous: A dynamic symmetry-breaking problem. In: ICALP '96. LNCS 1099 (1996) 610–621

11. P.Flocchini, Kranakis, E., Krizanc, D., Santoro, N., Sawchuk, C.: Multiple mobile agent rendezvous in a ring. In: LATIN '04. (2004) accepted for publication.
12. Lim, W., Beck, A., Alpern, S.: Rendezvous search on the line with more than two players. Operations Research **45** (1997) 357–364
13. amd P.B. Hulme, L.T.: Searching for targets who want to be found. Journal of the Operations Research Society **48** (1997) 44–50
14. Hohl, F.: A framework to protect mobile agents by using reference states. In: International Conference on Distributed Computing Systems (ICDCS '00). (2000)
15. Sander, T., Tschudin, C.F.: Protecting mobile agents against malicious hosts. Mobile Agents and Security (LNCS 1419) (1999) 44–60
16. Vitek, J., Castagna, G. In: Mobile Computations and Hostile Hosts. University of Geneva (1999) 241–261
17. Dobrev, S., Flocchini, P., Prencipe, G., Santoro, N.: Mobile agents searching for a black hole in an anonymous ring. In: Proc. of 15th Int. Symposium on Distr. Computing (DISC 2001). (2001) 166–179
18. Dobrev, S., Flocchini, P., Prencipe, G., Santoro, N.: Finding a black hole in an arbitrary network: optimal mobile agents protocols. In: Proc. of 21st ACM Symposium on Principles of Distributed Computing (PODC 2002). (2002) 153–162
19. Dobrev, S., Flocchini, P., c, R.K., Prencipe, G., cka, P.R., Santoro, N.: Searching for a black hole in hypercubes and related networks. In: 6th International Conference on Principles of Distributed Systems (OPODIS '02). (2002) 171–182

Splitters: Objects for Online Partitioning

Jaap-Henk Hoepman

Department of Computer Science, University of Nijmegen
P.O. Box 9010, 6500 GL Nijmegen, the Netherlands
jhh@cs.kun.nl

Abstract. A splitter is a concurrent asynchronous non-blocking object that can partition a collection of contending tokens into smaller groups with certain properties. Splitters are natural objects used to solve a wide range of fundamental distributed computing problems, like renaming and resource allocation. This paper proposes a general definition of splitters, develops their theory, and investigates their implementation in shared memory systems.

Keywords: splitters, shared objects, asynchronous communication, divide & conquer.

1 Introduction

Many fundamental problems in distributed computing can be solved efficiently using a divide and conquer strategy. For asynchronous systems, implementing a suitable divide and conquer strategy sometimes turns out to be a hard problem. To investigate the exact nature of this problem we are motivated to study existing concurrent objects called *splitters*, that have been used to solve this problem in the past, but never received an independent study.

A splitter is a concurrent asynchronous non-blocking object that can partition a collection of contending tokens into smaller groups with certain properties. Conceptually, a splitter has a single input over which it receives incoming tokens, and two or more outputs over which tokens leave the splitter. Each token is assigned to exactly one of the outputs, depending on the contention on the input and the distribution of tokens at the output. The specification of the splitter defines how this assignment takes place. By choosing the right specification, a splitter can be used to partition processors in roughly equal sets, or even to count the number of currently contending processors. In fact, splitters have been used for specific purposes (either implicitly or explicitly) in several distributed algorithms through the years, like mutual exclusion [Lam87], renaming [MA95, AM94,BGHM95], and resource allocation [AHS94].

Because of their occurrence in a wide variety of algorithms, and their fundamental divide-and-conquer nature, we wish to embark on a general study of these splitters in isolation, as a class of objects in their own right. Splitters are a generalisation of counting networks investigated by Aspnes *et al.* [AHS94], and encompass these as well as threshold networks, balancers and smoothing

M. Papatriantafilou and P. Hunel (Eds.): OPODIS 2003, LNCS 3144, pp. 47–57, 2004.

networks. We refer to Sect. 3 for examples of how these (and other) objects can be defined as splitters.

In this paper we report on our initial findings of our study of splitters. Our main contribution is twofold. First of all, we have developed a general model and notation for the description of and reasoning about splitters. This model and notation is described in Sect. 2. Using some natural properties and axioms, we manage to keep this general definition surprisingly simple: almost all splitters can be described by a series of simple inequalities bounding the output contention from above. In Sect. 3 we give some examples of splitter definitions corresponding to splitter like objects used in the literature.

Some of these splitters have been implemented in the read/write memory model; others were implemented using stronger primitives like read-modify-write. In this paper we focus on the implementation of splitters in the read/write shared memory model. As our second contribution, we investigate the implementation of splitters in the read/write shared memory model, showing both impossibility results and splitter constructions. We show for instance that in a read/write memory model, splitters cannot distribute tokens over all their outputs evenly, and that it is unlikely that read/write implementations of non-trivial 2-output splitters exist. These results are presented in Sect. 4.

Finally, we summarise our conclusions and present topics for further research in Sect. 5.

2   Model and Notation

A splitter is a concurrent, asynchronous, non-blocking object shared among n processors[1]. Conceptually, a splitter has a single input x and one or more outputs $y_1, \ldots, y_m$. The total number of outputs is denoted by m. Processors can send one token at a time to the input of a splitter, after which the splitter will assign an output over which the token leaves the splitter (within a bounded number of steps) to join the corresponding output token set. Splitters can either be *one-shot* – in which case tokens stay in the output set forever – or be *long-lived* – in which case tokens may leave the output set travelling back through the splitter to the input.

The interface of a splitter consists of two operations: *Enter* (to enter a splitter and obtain an output) and *Release* (to return back to the input), where the *Release* operation is only defined for long-lived splitters. Tokens using[2] splitters can be in one of four states: *idle, entering, assigned* or *releasing*. Initially, tokens are *idle*. To enter a splitter S (during which it is in the *entering* state), an idle token invokes the operation $y = Enter(S)$, returning the selected output for this token when it finishes. At this point a token becomes *assigned* to output y.

---

[1] Splitters can be realised both in the message passing as well as the shared memory model. In this paper we focus on the shared memory model.

[2] In the remainder of this paper we will assume that tokens are active objects, that maintain state and executes steps by themselves. This makes notation and discussion easier.

For long-lived splitters, an assigned token may invoke the *Release(S)* operation (during which it is in the *releasing* state), after which it becomes idle again. A token is *contending* if it is not idle.

Next we define the state of a splitter.

Definition 2.1. *The state of a splitter is given by the states of all tokens that contend it, and is denote by* σ. *For token t we write* $\sigma(t)$ *for its state in* σ *(where* $\sigma(t) = \perp$ *means t is idle,* $\sigma(t) = \ominus$ *means t is entering,* $\sigma(t) = i$ *means t is assigned to output* y_i, *and* $\sigma(t) = \ominus\!\!\rightarrow$ *means t is releasing). Similarly, we write* $\sigma(t) : v$ *to denote the state equal to* σ *except that t has state v. A state is called a* steady state *if all contending tokens are assigned to an output.*

The state of a splitter can alternatively be expressed using the *contention* at the input and the outputs of the splitter. Let z denote an input or an output of a splitter S. For $z = x$ 'a token at z' means a token is contending S, while for $z = y_i$ 'a token at z' means a token assigned to output y_i. We distinguish the following four different contention measures.

point contention $\eth^t z$ of S at time t: the number of tokens at z at time t.

maximal point contention $\delta^t z$ of S at time t: the maximal number of tokens at z at any time t' within the busy prefix of S at t.

interval contention $\Delta^t z$ of S at time t: the total number of *different* tokens (i.e., not counting doubles) at z in the busy prefix of S at t (this measure is also called interval contention in [AAF$^+$99]).

total contention $\nabla^t z$ of S at time t: the total number of tokens (counting doubles) at z in the busy prefix of S at t.

Here, the busy prefix of S at t is defined as the time interval between t and the last $t' \leq t$ where all tokens are idle on S. Note that if the same token contends more than once during a busy prefix, it contributes only once to the interval contention.

We usually omit the superscript t. Note that δy_i, Δy_i and ∇y_i are measured over the busy prefix of S, and not over the busy prefix of y_i itself. This means that if during the busy prefix of S only one token enters and leaves y_i several times (say three), then $\nabla y_i = 3$. See also Fig. 1, which shows a particular run over a 2-output splitter being accessed by 4 different tokens a, b, c and d. Note that $\eth \leq \delta \leq \Delta \leq \nabla$, and equality always holds for one-shot splitters.

The implementation of a splitter should be *adaptive*, meaning that the number steps needed to enter or release a splitter depends solely on the number of contending tokens. Note that adaptive splitters are *wait-free* by default.

The behaviour of a splitter S is defined by its invariant $\mathsf{Inv}(S)$. $\mathsf{Inv}(S)$ is a predicate over the states σ of S. We write $\sigma \models P$ if predicate P holds in state σ. An implementation of a splitter S must ensure that for each state σ that can occur during an execution over S, $\sigma \models \mathsf{Inv}(S)$ holds. Because we are interested in splitters as objects that can partition a collection of contending tokens into smaller groups, we restrict the invariant of a splitter to be a predicate over the input and output contentions of the splitter only. In other words, for splitter

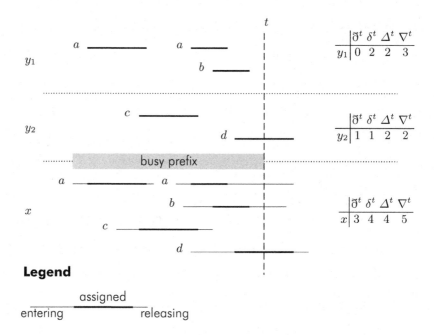

Fig. 1. A run over a long-lived splitter and the resulting contentions.

S with m outputs, $\mathsf{Inv}(S)$ is a predicate over input contention dx and output contentions dy_i, where the symbol d ranges over $\eth$, δ, Δ or ∇.

Tokens are only allowed to enter the splitter if that does not invalidate the invariant. A typical example is an invariant that restricts the maximal number of contending tokens to a constant. We only consider *smooth* long-lived splitters, where no such restriction is placed on the release operation: a token should always be able to release itself (see below).

2.1 Properties and Axioms

Splitters satisfy the following properties, and are further defined by the following axioms.

Clearly, the contention is always greater or equal to 0.

Property 2.2. For any state σ and input or output z of a splitter S, we have $\eth z \geq 0$, $\delta z \geq 0$, $\Delta z \geq 0$ and $\nabla z \geq 0$.

As already stated earlier, the four contention measures form an increasing series.

Property 2.3. For any state σ and input or output z of a splitter S, we have $\eth z \leq \delta z \leq \Delta z \leq \nabla z$. Equality always holds if S is one-shot.

Proof. Follows from the fact that if a token contends at time t it also contends at the busy prefix of t, and the fact a token never contends with itself. Equality holds for one-shot splitters, because tokens never leave.   □

Point contention on the outputs cannot exceed contention on the input. Similarly for total contention.

Property 2.4. For any state σ of splitter S with m outputs, $\sum_{i=1}^{m} \eth y_i \leq \eth x$ and $\sum_{i=1}^{m} \nabla y_i \leq \nabla x$, with equality holding in the steady state.

Proof. If a token is assigned to output y_i at time t it is contending at time t. For point contention we also need the fact that, no token is assigned to two outputs simultaneously. For total contention, we use the fact that all duplicates are counted. Equality in the steady state follows from the fact that no tokens are unassigned in the steady state.   □

Note that this property does not hold for the interval contention (or the maximal point contention) on the outputs. Suppose for an m output splitter, the first m tokens are spread evenly over all outputs and stay there. Then the $m + 1$-th token enters and leaves m times, which is assigned to a different output each time. Then during this interval $\Delta x = m + 1$ and $\Delta y_i = 2$ so $\sum_{i=1}^{m} = 2m$.

For a definition of a splitter to be meaningful, it must satisfy the following axioms. First, the initial state with no tokens contending must be a legal state.

Axiom 2.5 *Let σ be the state of splitter S with all tokens idle. Then $\sigma \models \mathsf{Inv}(S)$.*

Second, if a token has entered, it must be able to legally obtain some output.

Axiom 2.6 *For all states σ of a splitter S, if $\sigma \models \mathsf{Inv}(S)$ and for some token t we have $\sigma(t) = \oplus$, then there is an i with $1 \leq i \leq m$ such that $\sigma(t) : i \models \mathsf{Inv}(S)$.*

For long-lived splitters, similar axioms govern the behaviour of the splitter when tokens are released.

A token must always be able to release itself.

Axiom 2.7 *For all states σ of a splitter S, if $\sigma \models \mathsf{Inv}(S)$ and for some token t we have $\sigma(t) = i$ with $1 \leq i \leq m$, then $\sigma(t) : \oplus \models \mathsf{Inv}(S)$.*

Moreover, a releasing token must be able to leave the splitter and return to the idle state.

Axiom 2.8 *For all states σ of a splitter S, if $\sigma \models \mathsf{Inv}(S)$ and for some token t we have $\sigma(t) = \oplus$ then $\sigma(t) : \bot \models \mathsf{Inv}(S)$.*

We restrict our attention to *smooth* splitters that we define next.

Definition 2.9. *A splitter S with m outputs is called* smooth *if its invariant $\mathsf{Inv}(S)$ can be specified by a collection of $m + 1$ inequalities of the form*

$$d_0 x \leq f_0(\sigma)$$
$$d_i y_i \leq f_i(\sigma) \text{ for all } i, \ 1 \leq i \leq m \ ,$$

where for each i with $0 \leq i \leq m$, d_i is any of the four contention measures $\eth$, δ, Δ or ∇, and each f_i is a function mapping splitter states to integers.

We note that it does not make much sense to consider non-smooth splitters, because any implementation of a splitter must be smooth anyway: if the implementation assigns any number of tokens to a particular output, then each of these tokens can be delayed indefinitely until all other tokens appear on their outputs, after which the delayed tokens are released one by one.

Note that circularity in the definition is not a problem, because the functions together specify a predicate that is either true or false in any specific state, depending on whether all inequalities are true or not in that state.

A few more observations about the form of the invariant can be made.

Because there is no difference in contention measures for one-shot splitters, we always use the total contention ∇ in the description of the invariant for one-shot splitters.

Observe that by feeding a splitter with a lot of tokens, and subsequently releasing all tokens except those at output y_i, we get $\eth y_i = \eth x$. This means we cannot even impose a condition like $\eth y_i \leq \eth x - 1$. Hence, $\eth x$ is not commonly used in the definition of $\mathsf{Inv}(S)$.

Finally, note that for any constant c, if for all t we have $\eth \leq c$ then also $\delta \leq c$. But this only holds for constants. Clearly $\eth y_i \leq \eth x$ does not imply $\delta y_i \leq \eth x$ (although $\eth y_i \leq \delta x$ for all t does imply $\delta y_i \leq \delta x$). We conclude that also $\eth y_i$ is not commonly used in the definition of $\mathsf{Inv}(S)$, because its role can be taken by δy_i.

3   Examples

To give a feel for the class of smooth splitters, we present several splitters that have appeared in the literature (albeit under different names) using the notation we developed. We first consider one-shot splitters, and then present some long-lived splitters.

3.1   One-Shot Splitters

Aspnes *et al.* [AHS94] have defined several splitter-like objects in their treatment of counting networks, like a *balancer*,

$$\nabla y_1 \leq \left\lceil \frac{\nabla x}{2} \right\rceil \wedge \nabla y_2 \leq \left\lfloor \frac{\nabla x}{2} \right\rfloor,$$

a *counting network*

$$\text{For all } i, 1 \leq i \leq m: \nabla y_i \leq \left\lceil \frac{\nabla x - i + 1}{m} \right\rceil,$$

and a *k-smoothing network*

$$\text{For all } i, 1 \leq i \leq m: \nabla y_i \leq \min \{\nabla y_j \mid j \neq i\} + k .$$

Note that equality in the first two invariants above is guaranteed to hold in the steady state due to Prop. 2.4. Our definition of the k smoothing network is atypical: the original definition states that in the steady state $|\nabla y_i - \nabla y_j| \leq k$ for all i, j.

Analogous to the threshold networks defined by Aspnes et al. [AHS94], we can define a *threshold network* for threshold w with the invariant

$$\nabla y_1 \leq \left\lfloor \frac{\nabla x}{w} \right\rfloor \wedge \nabla y_2 \leq \nabla x - \left\lfloor \frac{\nabla x}{w} \right\rfloor .$$

In the context of renaming, splitters have also been used extensively, like the one shot "fast-path" renaming building block [MA95,Lam87] (where y_1 corresponds to *stop*, y_2 corresponds to *right*, and y_3 corresponds to *down* as in [MA95]):

$$\nabla y_1 \leq 1 \wedge \nabla y_2 \leq \nabla x - 1 \wedge \nabla y_3 \leq \nabla x - 1$$

3.2   Long-Lived Splitters

Long-lived splitters are necessary to implement long-lived renaming. Buhrman *et al.* [BGHM95] used a long lived splitter in their initial phase of a fast long-lived renaming protocol that had the following invariant

$$\text{For all } i, 1 \leq i \leq 3: \delta y_i \leq \max(1, \delta x - 1) .$$

Other splitters are for example the long lived "fast-path" renaming building block of Afek *et al.* [AAF$^+$99]

$$\delta y_1 \leq 1 \wedge \nabla y_2 \leq \nabla x - 1 \wedge \nabla y_3 \leq \nabla x - 1 ,$$

and the long lived "fast-path" renaming building block of Moir *et al.* [MA95]

$$\delta y_1 \leq 1 \wedge \delta y_2 \leq \delta x - 1 \wedge \delta y_3 \leq \delta x - 1 .$$

Note that the Moir *et al.* splitter is more permissive than the Afek *et al.* splitter, and that in fact the implementation of the Moir *et al.* splitter given in [MA95] can reach the state $\Delta y_2 = \delta x$ in the following scenario. Token 1 enters and stops, i.e., is assigned to y_1. Then token 2 enters and goes right (i.e., is assigned to y_2), and subsequently leaves. The same happens to token 3. Then $\delta x = 2$, $\Delta y_2 = 2$ but $\delta y_2 = 1$.

We see that the difference between the Moir *et al.* splitter and the Afek *et al.* splitter (as discussed in [AAF$^+$99]) is that the former is defined using the maximal point contention on the input, whereas the latter is defined using the total contention.

4   Constructions and Impossibility Results

In this section we investigate the wait-free implementation of splitters in the shared memory model. We start with a few impossibility results.

Splitters cannot distribute tokens over their outputs tightly (and evenly) if they are only implemented using read/write atomicity. This is formalised in the following theorem.

Theorem 4.1. *Let S be a splitter with $m > 1$ outputs. Suppose for some constant $c > 1$ we can select constants $c_1, \ldots, c_m$ such that for all states σ of S with $dx = c$ we have*

$$f_i^S(\sigma) \leq c_i$$

and

$$\sum_{i=1}^{m} c_i < c + \frac{m-1}{2} \ .$$

Then a read/write implementation of S does not exists

Proof. Consider the following construction for renaming $c > 1$ tokens, where splitter S is used in a one-shot fashion. W.l.o.g. then $dx = \nabla x$ and $dy_i = \nabla y_i$ (see Prop. 2.3).

Let the c tokens enter S. The conditions of the theorem guarantee that no more than c_i tokens leave the splitter over output y_i. Run at each output y_i a renaming algorithm (e.g., [AF00]) that renames the at most c_i incoming tokens to at most $2c_i - 1$ names. We must use distinct name-sets for each different output of the splitter. This is possible because $f_i^S(\sigma)$ is bounded a priori by c_i.

Then the total number of names assigned to the c incoming tokens is no larger than

$$\sum_{i=1}^{m} (2c_i - 1) = 2 \sum_{i=1}^{m} c_i - m$$

Herlihy and Shavit [HS93] showed that wait-free renaming of c processes to less than $2c - 1$ names cannot be implemented using read/write atomicity. So this is the case if $2 \sum_{i=1}^{m} c_i - m < 2c - 1$.   □

Moreover, a splitter implemented using only reads and writes cannot partition a set of tokens into two non-empty sets.

Theorem 4.2. *Define $M = \{1, \ldots, m\}$. Let S be a splitter with $m > 1$ outputs. Suppose there exists an index set $I \subset M$ such that for all states σ of S with $dx > 0$ we have*

$$\sum_{i \in I} f_i(\sigma) < \max(2, dx) \quad and \quad \sum_{i \in M-I} f_i(\sigma) < dx \ .$$

Then a read/write implementation of S does not exist.

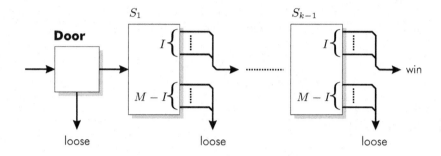

Fig. 2. Construction used in the proof of Th. 4.2.

Proof. We show that if both properties hold, we can build a test-and-set object of which we know no read/write implementations exist [LAA87,Her91]. The construction is sketched in Fig. 2. Again, splitter S is used in a one-shot fashion. W.l.o.g. then $dx = \nabla x$ and $dy_i = \nabla y_i$ (see Prop. 2.3).

Let there be $k > 1$ processors for which we wish to implement a test-and-set object. The processors first have to pass through a "door" implemented using a single multi-writer shared variable DOOR, initially *open*. To pass through the door, processors execute the following protocol.

> **if** DOOR $=$ *closed*
> **then return** *leave*
> **else** DOOR $\leftarrow$ *closed*
>   **return** *pass*

Only processors that pass enter the following setup of splitters, each with their own token. Note that at most k tokens enter, and that at least one processor finds the door open and enters with a token.

Let some index set I satisfy the conditions of the theorem. Connect $k - 1$ copies of the splitter S as follows. Tokens leaving splitter S_i on an output y_i with $i \in I$ enter splitter S_{i+1}. Tokens leaving splitter S_i on another output (with $i \notin I$) loose the test-and-set immediately. Tokens leaving splitter S_{k-1} on output y_i with $i \in I$ win the test-and-set.

By the properties of the splitter, simple induction shows that at least one token and at most $k - i$ tokens leave splitter S_i on an output y_i with $i \in I$ (and hence enter splitter S_{i+1}). Hence at splitter S_{k-1} there is exactly one token leaving splitter S_k on output y_i with $i \in I$ and winning the test-and-set.

This only leaves us to show that any processor loosing does not strictly precede the eventual winner [Hoe99,AGTV92]. This is guaranteed by the door placed before the first splitter: it is easy to see that no processor strictly precedes (in accessing the door) any processor that passes the door. □

Given this theorem, it is unlikely that read/write implementations for non-trivial splitters with 2 outputs exist.

Next, we investigate read/write implementations of splitters with 3 outputs. Given Th. 4.2, the best we can hope for is a splitter like

$$\nabla y_1 \leq f_1(\sigma)$$
$$\wedge \ \nabla y_2 \leq \nabla x - f_1(\sigma)$$
$$\wedge \ \nabla y_3 \leq \nabla x - f_1(\sigma)$$

where $f_1(\sigma) \leq \frac{1}{2}\nabla x$.

Theorem 4.3. *Splitter S defined by*

$$\delta y_i \leq \frac{2}{3}\delta x, \quad for \ 1 \leq i \leq 3.$$

has a read/write implementation.

Proof. Use any optimal long-lived renaming algorithm (like [AF00]) to rename the δx incoming tokens to $2\delta x - 1$ names. Map a token with name i to output $y_{(i \bmod 3)+1}$. Then $\delta y_i \leq \frac{2}{3}\delta x$.

In a read-modify-write setting, any reasonable splitter can be implemented.

Theorem 4.4. *Let S be a splitter satisfying the axioms in Sect. 2.1 shared with n processors. This splitter can be implemented using a single n processor read-modify-write register.*

Proof. Observe that the state of a splitter as given in Def. 2.1, is a set of token states. We let the read-modify-write register store this set of states (in the most general case the size of the register must be unbounded).

Initially, we let the register denote the empty set. Observe, that by Ax. 2.5, this initialisation of the register is proper.

An entering token reads the register and selects any output y_i of his choice that satisfies $\mathsf{Inv}(S)$ (such an output always exist by the Ax. 2.6). A leaving token reads the register and changes its own state to idle and writes it back. This is also a correct action, due to Ax. 2.7 and Ax. 2.8.   □

5   Conclusions and Further Research

We have presented a general definition of splitters as a concurrent asynchronous non-blocking object that can partition a collection of contending tokens into smaller groups. This general definition turns out to be surprisingly simple: almost all splitters can be described by a series of simple inequalities bounding the output contention from above.

Any splitter can be constructed using read-modify-write registers. For the case where only read/write registers can be used, we have presented some constructions and some impossibility results. These results can be extended. In particular, there are still gaps between our upper and lower bounds. Moreover, it is an interesting question to give characterisations of splitters in terms of their place in Herlihy's hierarchy [Her91].

Also, we would like to investigate the construction of larger splitters from smaller ones, similar to the way balancers are used to construct counting networks [AHS94].

References

[AAF+99]   AFEK, Y., ATTIYA, H., FOUREN, A., STUPP, G., AND TOUITOU, D. Long-lived renaming made adaptive. In *18th PODC* (Atlanta, GA, USA, 1999), ACM Press, pp. 91–103.

[AGTV92]   AFEK, Y., GAFNI, E., TROMP, J., AND VITÁNYI, P. M. B. Wait-free test-and-set. In *6th WDAG* (Haifa, Israel, 1992), A. Segall and S. Zaks (Eds.), LNCS 647, Springer-Verlag, pp. 85–94.

[AM94]   ANDERSON, J. H., AND MOIR, M. Using k-exclusion to implement resilient, scalable shared objects. In *13th PODC* (Los Angeles, CA, USA, 1994), ACM Press, pp. 141–150.

[AHS94]   ASPNES, J., HERLIHY, M., AND SHAVIT, N. Counting networks. *J. ACM* **41**, 5 (1994), 1020–1048.

[AF00]   ATTIYA, H., AND FOUREN, A. Polynomial and adaptive long-lived $(2k-1)$-renaming. In *14th DISC* (Toledo, Spain, 2000), M. Herlihy (Ed.), LNCS 1914, Springer, pp. 149–163.

[BGHM95]   BUHRMAN, H., GARAY, J. A., HOEPMAN, J.-H., AND MOIR, M. Long-lived renaming made fast. In *14th PODC* (Ottawa, Ont., Canada, 1995), ACM Press, pp. 194–203.

[Her91]   HERLIHY, M. P. Wait-free synchronization. *ACM Trans. Prog. Lang. & Syst.* **13**, 1 (1991), 124–149.

[HS93]   HERLIHY, M. P., AND SHAVIT, N. The asynchronous computability theorem for t-resilient tasks. In *25th STOC* (San Diego, CA, USA, 1993), ACM Press, pp. 111–120.

[Hoe99]   HOEPMAN, J.-H. Long-lived test-and-set using bounded space. Tech. rep., University of Twente, 1999. www.cs.kun.nl/~jhh/publications/test-and-set.ps.

[Lam87]   LAMPORT, L. A fast mutual exclusion algorithm. *ACM Trans. Comput. Syst.* **5**, 1 (1987), 1–11.

[LAA87]   LOUI, M. C., AND ABU-AMARA, H. H. Memory requirements for agreement among unreliable asynchronous processes. In *Advances in Computing Research*, F. P. Preparata (Ed.), vol. 4. JAI Press, Greenwich, CT, 1987, pp. 163–183.

[MA95]   MOIR, M., AND ANDERSON, J. H. Wait-free algorithms for fast, long-lived renaming. *Science of Computer Programming* **25**, 1 (1995), 1–39.

Partial Replication: Achieving Scalability in Redundant Arrays of Inexpensive Databases

Emmanuel Cecchet[1], Julie Marguerite[2], and Willy Zwaenepoel[3]

[1] INRIA, Projet Sardes, 655, Avenue de l'Europe, 38330 Montbonnot St Martin, France
Emmanuel.Cecchet@inrialpes.fr
[2] ObjectWeb consortium, 655, Avenue de l'Europe, 38330 Montbonnot St Martin, France
Julie.Marguerite@inrialpes.fr
[3] Ecole Polytechnique Fédérale de Lausanne, 1015 Lausanne, Switzerland
willy.zwaenepoel@epfl.ch

Abstract. Clusters of workstations become more and more popular to power data server applications such as large scale Web sites or e-Commerce applications. There has been much research on scaling the front tiers (web servers and application servers) using clusters, but databases usually remain on large dedicated SMP machines. In this paper, we focus on the database tier using clusters of commodity hardware. Our approach consists of studying different replication strategies to achieve various degree of performance and fault tolerance.

Redundant Array of Inexpensive Databases (RAIDb) is to databases what RAID is to disks. In this paper, we focus on RAIDb-1 that offers full replication and RAIDb-2 that introduces partial replication, in which the user can define the degree of replication of each database table.

We present a Java implementation of RAIDb called Clustered JDBC or C-JDBC. C-JDBC achieves both database performance scalability and high availability at the middleware level without changing existing applications. We show, using the TPC-W benchmark, that partial replication (RAIDb-2) can offer better performance scalability (up to 25%) than full replication by allowing fine-grain control on replication. Distributing and restricting the replication of frequently written tables to a small set of backends reduces I/O usage and improves CPU utilization of each cluster node.

1 Introduction

Clusters of workstations are already an alternative to large parallel machines in scientific computing because of their unbeatable price/performance ratio. Clusters can also be used to provide both scalability and high availability in data server environments such as eCommerce application servers. When the database tier is running on commodity hardware, application performance becomes database bound [7].

Database replication has been used as a solution to improve availability and performance of distributed databases [2, 11]. Even if many protocols have been designed to provide data consistency and fault tolerance [4], few of them have been used in commercial databases [17]. Gray et al. [9] have pointed out the danger of replication and the scalability limit of this approach. However, database replication is

M. Papatriantafilou and P. Hunel (Eds.): OPODIS 2003, LNCS 3144, pp. 58–70, 2004.

a viable approach if an appropriate replication algorithm is used [1, 12, 20]. Most of these recent works only focus on full replication. In this paper, we propose a partial replication solution that offers fine-grain control over replication and compare it to full replication.

Redundant Array of Inexpensive Databases (RAIDb) is an analogy to the existing RAID (Redundant Array of Inexpensive Disks) concept, that achieves scalability and high availability of disk subsystems at a low cost. RAIDb is the counterpart of RAID for databases. RAIDb aims at providing better performance and fault tolerance than a single database, at a low cost, by combining multiple database instances into an array of databases. RAIDb levels provide various performance/fault tolerance tradeoff [8]. In this paper, we will only focus on RAIDb-1 (full mirroring) and RAIDb-2 (partial replication).

We propose C-JDBC, a Java middleware that implements the RAIDb concept. We evaluate the different replication techniques using the TPC-W benchmark [18]. C-JDBC proves that it is possible to achieve performance scalability and fault tolerance at the middleware level using partial replication. We show that partial replication offers a significant improvement (up to 25%) compared to full replication by reducing both the communication and the I/O on the backend nodes.

The outline of the rest of this paper is as follows. Section 2 gives an overview of the RAIDb architecture. Section 3 presents C-JDBC, a Java implementation of RAIDb and section 4 details the various RAIDb levels implementations. Section 5 describes the experimental platform and an analysis of the benchmark workloads. Experimental results are presented in section 6. Section 7 discusses related work and we conclude in section 8.

2   Redundant Array of Inexpensive Databases

One of the goals of RAIDb is to hide the distribution complexity and provide the database clients with the view of a single database like in a centralized architecture. As for RAID, a controller sits in front of the underlying resources. The clients send their requests directly to the RAIDb controller that distributes them among the set of RDBMS (Relational DataBase Management System) backends. The RAIDb controller gives the illusion of a single RDBMS to the clients.

In general, RAIDb does not require any modification of the client application or the RDBMS. However, some precautions have to be taken care of, such as the fact that all requests to the databases must be sent through the RAIDb controller. It is not allowed to directly issue requests to a database backend as this might compromise the data synchronization between the backends.

RAIDb defines levels providing various degree of replication that offer different performance/fault tolerance tradeoffs [8]. Note that RAIDb is just a conceptual analogy to RAID. Data distribution in RAIDb uses a logical unit which is a database table, whereas RAID uses a physical unit defined by a disk block.

2.1   RAIDb-1: Full Replication

RAIDb level 1 is similar to disk mirroring in RAID-1. Databases are fully replicated. RAIDb-1 requires each backend node to have enough storage capacity to hold all database data. RAIDb-1 needs at least 2 database backends, but there is (theoretically) no limit to the number of RDBMS backends.

The performance scalability is limited by the capacity of the RAIDb controller to efficiently broadcast the updates to all backends.

RAIDb-1 provides speedup for read queries because they can be balanced over the backends. Write queries are performed in parallel by all nodes, therefore they execute at the same speed as the one of a single node. However, RAIDb-1 provides good fault tolerance, since it can continue to operate with a single backend node.

2.2   RAIDb-2: Partial Replication

RAIDb level 2 features partial replication. Unlike RAIDb-1, RAIDb-2 does not require any single node to host a full copy of the database. This is essential when the full database is too large to be hosted on a node's disks. Each database table must be replicated at least once to survive a single node failure. RAIDb-2 uses at least 3 database backends (2 nodes would be a RAIDb-1 solution).

As RAID-5, RAIDb-2 is a good tradeoff between cost, performance and data protection.

3   C-JDBC: A RAIDb Software Implementation

JDBC™, often referenced as Java Database Connectivity, is a Java API for accessing virtually any kind of tabular data [19]. We have implemented C-JDBC (Clustered JDBC), a Java middleware based on JDBC. C-JDBC works with any existing RDBMS that provides a JDBC driver. The client application does not need to be modified and transparently accesses a database cluster as if it were a centralized database. The RDBMS does not need any modification either, nor does it need to provide distributed database functionalities.

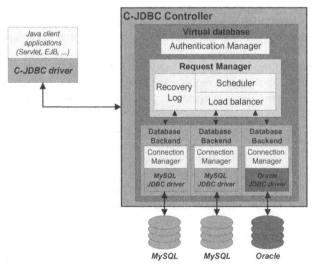

Fig. 1. C-JDBC overview

3.1 C-JDBC Overview

Fig. 1 gives an overview of the different C-JDBC components. The client application uses the generic C-JDBC driver that replaces the database specific JDBC driver. The C-JDBC controller implements a RAIDb controller logic and exposes a single database view, called virtual database, to the driver. A controller can host multiple virtual databases. The drivers and the controller use sockets to communicate.

The authentication manager establishes the mapping between the login/password provided by the client application and the login/password to be used on each database backend. All security checks can be performed by the authentication manager. It provides a uniform and centralized resource access control.

Each virtual database has its own request manager that defines the request scheduling, caching and load balancing policies. The "real" databases are defined as database backends and are accessed through their native JDBC driver. If the native driver is not capable of connection pooling, a connection manager can be added to perform such a task.

The C-JDBC controller also provides additional services such as monitoring and logging. The controller can be dynamically configured and administered using an administration console that uses XML files describing the controller configuration.

3.2 C-JDBC Request Manager

The request manager is a major component of the C-JDBC controller that implements the RAIDb logic. It is composed of a scheduler, a load balancer and a recovery log. Each of these components can be superseded by a user-specified implementation.

When a request comes from a C-JDBC driver, it is routed to the request manager associated to the virtual database. The *scheduler* is responsible for ordering the requests according to the desired isolation level. Moreover, consecutive write queries may be aggregated in a batch update so that they perform better. According to the application consistency, some write queries can also be delayed to improve the cache hit rate. Once the request scheduler processing is done, the requests are sequentially ordered and sent to the *load balancer*.

RAIDb-2 load balancers need to know the database schema of each backend. The schema information is dynamically gathered. When the backend is enabled, the appropriate methods are called on the JDBC DatabaseMetaData information of the backend native driver. Database schemas can also be statically specified by the way of the configuration file. This schema is updated dynamically on each *create* or *drop* SQL statement to reflect each backend schema. Among the backends that can treat the request (all of them in RAIDb-1), one is selected according to the implemented algorithm. Currently implemented algorithms are round robin, weighted round robin and least pending requests first (the request is sent to the node that has the least pending queries).

Once a backend has been selected, the request is sent to its native driver through a connection manager that can perform connection pooling. The ResultSet returned by the native driver is transformed into a serializable ResultSet that is returned to the client by means of the C-JDBC driver.

3.3   C-JDBC Fault Tolerance

C-JDBC implements a recovery log that records all write statements between checkpoints. The log can be used to recover from a failure by rolling forward requests from a previous checkpoint. It can also be used to add dynamically a node (when the system is online) by replaying all write requests since a known checkpoint that has been restored on the node.

Horizontal scalability is what is needed to prevent the C-JDBC controller from being a single point of failure. We use the JGroups [3] group communication library to synchronize the schedulers of the virtual databases that are distributed in several controllers. Only write requests are multicasted using a total order to manage concurrency control and update caches at each controller site.

4   RAIDb Level Implementations

C-JDBC assumes that the underlying RDBMS provides ACID properties for transactions and that there is always at least one node that has the needed tables to execute a query. For instance, in dynamic content servers, one of the target environments for RAIDb clusters, we know a priori what queries are going to be issued. Therefore, it is always possible to distribute the tables in such a way that all queries can be satisfied (essentially by making sure that for each query there is at least one replica where we have all the tables for that query).

4.1   RAIDb-1

RAIDb-1 usually does not require parsing the requests, since all backends have a full copy of the database and can therefore execute any query. When a client issues a CREATE TABLE statement, the table is created on every node.

We have implemented optimistic and pessimistic transaction-level schedulers with deadlock detection. To detect the deadlocks, we need to know the database schema and parse the requests to check which tables are accessed by each query. A simple query level scheduler that let the backends resolve the deadlocks is also provided.

One thread is dedicated to each backend to send write requests sequentially. The load balancer ensures 1-copy serializability [4] and post write queries in the same order in each thread queue. The user can define if he wants to send the result as soon as one, a majority or all backends complete the request. If one backend fails, but others succeed to execute the write request, then the failing backend is disabled, because it is no more coherent. Then the recovery log can be used to recover from this failure.

Connections are started lazily when a backend is involved in a query. After a write query inside a transaction, one connection per backend has been allocated for the transaction. Transaction commit or rollback use the same principle as write queries. The user can define if he wants only one, a majority or all nodes to commit before returning. If one node fails to commit, but others succeed, the failing node is automatically disabled.

Finally, read requests are executed on a backend according to a user defined algorithm. We have implemented round-robin (RR), weighted round-robin (WRR) and least pending requests first (LPRF) which selects the node with the fewest pending queries (which should be approximately the less loaded node in an homogeneous environment).

4.2   RAIDb-2

RAIDb-2 has to maintain a representation of each backend database schema. The query has to be parsed to be routed to the right set of backends. We have implemented the same set of schedulers as RAIDb-1. Read and write queries are implemented almost the same way as in RAIDb-1 except that the requests can only be executed by the nodes hosting the needed tables. The set of nodes is computed for each request to take care of failed or disabled nodes.

Unlike RAIDb-1, when a node fails to perform a write query or to commit/rollback a transaction, it is not disabled. In fact, only the tables that are no longer coherent are disabled (that is to say, removed from the backend schema). If a commit/rollback fails on one node, all tables written on this node during the transaction are disabled. This way, RAIDb-2 allows continued service by a backend, after a partial failure which leaves most of its tables up-to-date.

Completion policy is also user definable and can be completely synchronous (wait for all nodes to complete) or more relaxed by waiting only for a majority or just the first node to complete.

New database table creation policy can be defined to achieve any degree of replication for a table. The user can define a set of nodes where the table can possibly be created and a policy determining how to choose nodes in this set. The policy can range from all nodes to a fixed number of nodes (at least 2 nodes to ensure fault tolerance) chosen according to a selectable algorithm (currently random and round-robin). Those policies prove to be useful to distribute and limit the replication of created tables in the cluster.

5   Experimental Environment

5.1   TPC-W Benchmark

The TPC-W specification [18] defines a transactional Web benchmark for evaluating e-Commerce systems. TPC-W simulates an online bookstore. We use the Java servlets implementation from University of Wisconsin [5] with the patches for MySQL databases. As MySQL does not support sub-selects, each such query is decomposed as follows: the result of the inner select is stored in a temporary table; then, the outer select performs its selection on the temporary table and drops it after completion.

Of the 14 interactions specified in the TPC-W benchmark specification, six are read-only and eight have update queries that change the database state. TPC-W specifies three different workload mixes, differing in the ratio of read-only to read-write interactions. The browsing mix contains 95% read-only interactions, the shopping mix 80%, and the ordering mix 50%. The shopping mix is considered the most representative mix for this benchmark. The database scaling parameters are 10,000 items and 288,000 customers. This corresponds to a database size of 350MB.

5.2   Configurations

In this section, we describe the 3 main configurations evaluated in our experiments.

5.2.1   SingleDB

In this configuration, MySQL is directly accessed using the MySQL native JDBC driver on a single database backend without using C-JDBC. This reference measurement is referred to as SingleDB in the experimental reports.

5.2.2   RAIDb-1

There is no choice about data placement with RAIDb-1 since the whole database is replicated on each node. We present results using two different load balancing algorithms for read queries: RAIDb-1 RR uses a simple round-robin distribution whereas RAIDb-1 LPRF uses the least pending request first distribution defined in 4.1. For the write queries, we choose a completion policy that returns the result as soon as one backend has completed the execution of the query.

5.2.3   RAIDb-2

Table 1 summarizes the table replication in the different RAIDb-2 configurations ranging from 3 to 6 nodes. Note that the temporary table that is used to implement sub-selects can only be created on the nodes having a copy of the needed tables. The *customers, address, items, authors* and *countries* tables are replicated on all nodes.

Table 1. Database table replication for RAIDb-2 configurations.

TPC-W database tables	3 nodes			4 nodes				5 nodes					6 nodes					
	1	*2*	*3*	*1*	*2*	*3*	*4*	*1*	*2*	*3*	*4*	*5*	*1*	*2*	*3*	*4*	*5*	*6*
customers	■	■	■	■	■	■	■	■	■	■	■	■	■	■	■	■	■	■
address	■	■	■	■	■	■	■	■	■	■	■	■	■	■	■	■	■	■
orders	▨	■	■	▨	■	▨	■	▨	■	■	▨	■	▨	■	▨	■	■	■
order_line	▨	■	■	▨	■	▨	■	▨	■	■	▨	■	▨	■	▨	■	■	■
credit_info	▨	■	■	▨	■	▨	■	▨	■	■	▨	■	▨	■	▨	■	■	■
items	■	■	■	■	■	■	■	■	■	■	■	■	■	■	■	■	■	■
authors	■	■	■	■	■	■	■	■	■	■	■	■	■	■	■	■	■	■
countries	■	■	■	■	■	■	■	■	■	■	■	■	■	■	■	■	■	■
shopping_cart	■	□	■	■	□	■	■	■	□	■	■	■	■	□	■	■	■	□
shopping_cart_line	■	□	■	■	□	■	■	■	□	■	■	■	■	□	■	■	■	□
temporary table	▨	■	■	▨	■	▨	■	▨	■	■	▨	■	▨	■	▨	■	■	■

Legend:
- ■ Replicated on this node in all mixes
- ▨ Replicated in the browsing mix only
- □ Not replicated on this node

The heaviest query in term of CPU usage is the best seller query that performs a join between 5 tables (*orders, order_line, items, authors* and the temporary table). This query can only be executed on the nodes having a copy of these tables. The best seller query occurs 4566, 2049 and 261 times for the browsing, shopping and ordering mixes, respectively. Restricting the orders table replication for the browsing mix induces a performance penalty and results in load imbalance. We have measured a performance drop of 42% when only half of the nodes can perform the best seller query. Therefore we choose to replicate all tables needed for the best seller query in the browsing mix only.

Like for RAIDb-1, we present results using two different load balancing algorithms for read queries: RAIDb-2 RR uses a simple round-robin distribution whereas RAIDb-2 LPRF uses the least pending request first distribution defined in 4.1. Table creation policy uses 2 nodes chosen using a round-robin algorithm among the nodes having a copy of the *orders* table.

5.3 Methodology

For each workload, we use the appropriate load generator and record all SQL requests sent by the application server to the database. The resulting trace file contains all transactions received by the database during one hour.

We have written a multithreaded trace player that replays the trace as if requests were generated by the application server. This way, we can test every configuration with the exact same set of queries.

We always use a separate machine to generate the workload. The trace player emulates 150 concurrent client sessions. We first measure the throughput of a single database without C-JDBC. Then, we evaluate the various C-JDBC configurations using a dedicated machine to run the C-JDBC controller.

5.4 Software Environment

The TPC-W benchmark trace is generated using Apache v.1.3.22 as the Web server and Jakarta Tomcat v3.2.4 [10] as the servlet server.

The Java Virtual Machine used for all experiments is IBM JDK 1.3.1 for Linux. We always use a pessimistic transaction level scheduler in C-JDBC controllers. We experiment two different load balancing algorithms: round-robin (RR) and least pending requests first (LPRF). All experiments are performed without query caching in the controller.

We use MySQL v.4.0.8gamma [13] as our database server with the InnoDB transactional tables and the MM-MySQL v2.0.14 type 4 JDBC driver.

All machines run the 2.4.16 Linux kernel.

5.5 Hardware Platform

We use up to six database backends. Each machine has two PII-450 MHz CPU with 512MB RAM, and a 9GB SCSI disk drive. In our evaluation, we are not interested by the absolute performance values but rather by the relative performance of each configuration. Having slower machines allows us to reach the bottlenecks without requiring a large number of client machines to generate the necessary load.

A number of 1.8GHz AMD Athlon machines run the trace player and the C-JDBC controllers. We make sure that the trace player does not become a bottleneck in any experiment. All machines are connected through a switched 100Mbps Ethernet LAN.

6 Experimental Results

We measure the number of SQL requests performed per minute by each configuration. We only report the best result of three runs at the peak point for each configuration. In all experiments, the average CPU usage on the controller node was below 8% with very little variations between configurations.

6.1 Browsing Mix

Fig. 2 shows the throughput in requests per minute as a function of the number of nodes for each configuration using the browsing mix. The single database configuration saturates at 129 requests per minute.

RAIDb-1 RR starts with a linear speedup with a throughput of 261 requests per minute with 2 nodes. The 6 nodes configuration reaches 542 requests per minute, representing a speedup of 4.2. RAIDb-1 LPRF achieves 628 requests per minute due to a better load balancing. However, the speedup remains below 5 with 6 nodes. This is due to the implementation of the best seller query. The temporary table needs to be created and dropped by all nodes whereas only one will perform the select on this table. This is a good example of the danger of replication.

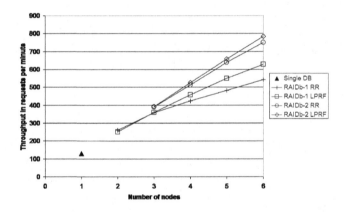

Fig. 2. Maximum throughput in SQL requests per minute as a function of database backends using TPC-W browsing mix.

RAIDb-2 configurations limit the temporary table creation to 2 nodes. The results show a better scalability with RAIDb-2 RR achieving 750 requests per minute with 6 nodes (speedup of 5.8). RAIDb-2 LPRF improves RAIDb-1 LPRF performance by 25% and achieves a small superlinear speedup of 6.1 at 784 requests per minute. We attribute this good performance to the better temporary table distribution and the limitation of the replication of the shopping cart related table.

6.2 Shopping Mix

Fig. 3 reports the throughput in requests per minute as a function of the number of nodes for the shopping mix, which is often considered as the most representative workload. The single database without C-JDBC achieves 235 requests per minute at the peak point.

RAIDb-1 RR scalability is similar to the one observed for the browsing mix with a peak at 996 requests per minute with 6 nodes. RAIDb-1 LPRF performs better mainly due to the reduction of the best seller queries compared to the browsing mix. RAIDb-1 LPRF achieves 1188 requests per minute with 6 nodes.

RAIDb-2 RR gives the least scalable performance. We will explain the problem using the table replication distribution presented in table 1 with the 6 nodes configuration. When the load balancer wants to execute a query on the *orders*, *order_line* and *credit_info* tables and its current index is positioned on node 1, 2 or 3, the index is moved to the next available node having these tables, namely node 4. The same phenomenon appears with any of the shopping cart tables that will be executed by node 1 if the index is currently on node 4, 5 or 6. We notice a ping-pong effect of the index between nodes 1 and 4.

We can reduce this effect by alternating the table replication order. Instead of replicating shopping cart related tables on nodes 1, 2 and 3 we can replicate them on nodes 1, 3 and 5. Therefore, order related table replicas will be moved from nodes 4, 5 and 6 to nodes 2, 4 and 6. With this new configuration, we obtain a throughput of 887 requests per minute which is better than the previous RAIDb-2 RR configuration saturating at 820 requests per minute. But still, RAIDb-2 with a round robin load balancing algorithm remains the least scalable configuration (among the configurations using replication) due to its uneven load distribution.

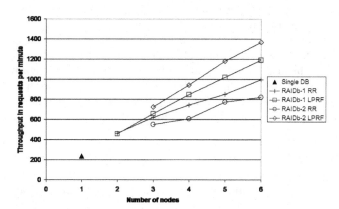

Fig. 3. Maximum throughput in SQL requests per minute as a function of database backends using TPC-W shopping mix.

RAIDb-2 LPRF shows the benefits of fine grain partial replication over full replication with 1367 requests per minute at the peak point with 6 nodes. With this dynamic load balancing algorithm, partial replication provides a linear speedup up to 5 nodes. The 6 nodes setup achieves a speedup close to 5.9.

6.3   Ordering Mix

Fig. 4 shows the results for the ordering mix for each configuration.

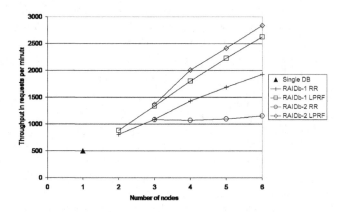

Fig. 4. Maximum throughput in SQL requests per minute as a function of database backends using TPC-W ordering mix.

We observe that round robin load balancing gives poor performance for RAIDb-1 and becomes a real bottleneck for RAIDb-2. Even when trying to reduce the ping-pong effect using the alternate distribution used for the shopping mix, we obtain a throughput of 1561 requests per minute with 6 nodes compared to 1152 requests per minute for the original RAIDb-2 RR configuration.

The load imbalance of the round robin algorithm is accentuated when the workload becomes more write intensive. Simple algorithms such as Least Pending Request First alleviate this problem and give significantly better results. The improvement from RAIDb-1 RR to RAIDb-1 LPRF is 700 requests per minute, from 1923 to 2623 requests per minute. RAIDb-2 LPRF achieves 2839 req/min with 6 nodes offering the best throughput of all tested configurations for this mix.

7   Related Work

Since the dangers of replication have been pointed out by Gray et al. [9], several works have investigated lazy replication techniques [15]. The limitations of these approaches are described in [11]. Ongoing efforts on eager replication have also been going on with the recent release of Postgres-R [12]. Several groups are focusing on group communications for asynchronous replication [20] or partial replication [16]. These works are performed at the database level whereas our approach is to implement replication techniques at the middleware level independently of the database engine.

Commercial solutions such as Oracle Real Application Clusters [14] or IBM DB2 Integrated Cluster Environment [6] are based on a shared storage system to achieve both performance scalability and fault tolerance. RAIDb targets shared nothing architectures build with commodity hardware.

Existing works in clusters of databases mainly use full replication. RAIDb also supports partitioning and partial replication. Postgres-R implements basic mechanisms for partial replication [11]. Updates are broadcasted to all nodes that decide whether they have to perform the update or not. RAIDb maintains a knowledge of each backend database schema and broadcast the updates only to the concerned nodes. To the best of our knowledge, our work is the first to evaluate partial replication tradeoffs and to compare its performance with other replication techniques.

8 Conclusion

We have presented C-JDBC, a RAIDb (Redundant Array of Inexpensive Databases) software implementation in Java. We have evaluated the performance of RAIDb-1 (full replication) and RAIDb-2 (partial replication) using the TPC-W benchmark on a 6 nodes cluster.

RAIDb-1 performs well on read-mostly workloads where load can be easily balanced, however write performance limits scalability when increasing the number of replicas. RAIDb-2 allows us to tune and control the degree of replication of each table. By limiting the write broadcasts to smaller sets of backends, RAIDb-2 shows always better scalability (up to 25%) over full replication when using a dynamic load balancing algorithm such as Least Pending Request First.

Round-robin load balancing provides poor performance scalability even using a cluster composed of homogeneous nodes. When tables are replicated on a small number of nodes, partial replication becomes very sensitive to load balancing. That is why round-robin is not well suited for partial replication and it becomes a bottleneck for workloads with a high write ratio.

C-JDBC is an open-source project hosted by the ObjectWeb consortium. Source code and documentation are available for download from http://c-jdbc.objectweb.org.

References

1. Christiana Amza, Alan L. Cox, Willy Zwaenepoel – Conflict-Aware Scheduling for Dynamic Content Applications – *Proceedings of USITS 2003*, March 2003.
2. Christiana Amza, Alan L. Cox, Willy Zwaenepoel – Scaling and availability for dynamic content web sites – *Rice University Technical Report TR02-395*, 2002.
3. Bela Ban – Design and Implementation of a Reliable Group Communication Toolkit for Java – Cornell University, September 1998.
4. P.A. Bernstein, V. Hadzilacos and N. Goodman – *Concurrency Control and Recovery in Database Systems* – Addison-Wesley, 1987.
5. Todd Bezenek, Trey Cain, Ross Dickson, Timothy Heil, Milo Martin, Collin McCurdy, Ravi Rajwar, Eric Weglarz, Craig Zilles, and Mikko Lipasti – Characterizing a Java Implementation of TPC-W – *3rd Workshop On Computer Architecture Evaluation Using Commercial Workloads* (CAECW), January 2000.
6. Boris Bialek and Rav Ahuja – IBM DB2 Integrated Cluster Environment (ICE) for Linux – IBM Blueprint, May 2003.
7. Emmanuel Cecchet, Julie Marguerite and Willy Zwaenepoel – Performance and scalability of EJB applications – Proceedings of OOPSLA'02, November 2002.

8.   Emmanuel Cecchet, Julie Marguerite and Willy Zwaenepoel – Reduandant Array of Inexpensive Databases – INRIA Research Report n°4921, September 2003.
9.   Jim Gray, Pat Helland, Patrick O'Neil and Dennis Shasha – The Dangers of Replication and a Solution – *Proceedings of the 1996 ACM SIGMOD International Conference on Management of Data*, June 1996.
10. Jakarta Tomcat Servlet Engine – http://jakarta.apache.org/tomcat/.
11. Bettina Kemme– Database Replication for Clusters of Workstations – *Ph. D. thesis nr. 13864*, Swiss Federal Institute of Technology Zurich, 2000.
12. Bettina Kemme and Gustavo Alonso – Don't be lazy, be consistent: Postgres-R, a new way to implement Database Replication –*Proceedings of the 26th International Conference on Very Large Databases*, September 2000.
13. MySQL Reference Manual – MySQL AB, 2003.
14. Oracle – Oracle9*i* Real Application Clusters – Oracle white paper, February 2002.
15. E. Pacitti, P. Minet and E. Simon – Fast algorithms for maintaining replica consistency in lazy master replicated databases – *Proceedings of VLDB*, 1999.
16. A. Sousa, F. Pedone, R. Oliveira, and F. Moura – Partial replication in the Database State Machine – *Proceeding of the IEEE International Symposium on Networking Computing and Applications* (NCA'01), 2001.
17. D. Stacey – Replication: DB2, Oracle or Sybase – *Database Programming & Design 7*, 12.
18. Transaction Processing Performance Council – http://www.tpc.org/.
19. S. White, M. Fisher, R. Cattel, G. Hamilton and M. Hapner – *JDBC API Tutorial and Reference, Second Edition* – Addison-Wesley, ISBN 0-201-43328-1, november 2001.
20. M. Wiesmann, F. Pedone, A. Schiper, B. Kemme and G. Alonso – Database replication techniques: a three parameter classification – *Proceedings of the 19th IEEE Symposium on Reliable Distributed Systems (SRDS2000)*, October 2000.

A Peer-to-Peer Approach to Enhance Middleware Connectivity

Erik Klintskog[1], Valentin Mesaros[2], Zacharias El Banna[1,3], Per Brand[1], and Seif Haridi[3]

[1] Distributed Systems Lab., Swedish Institute of Computer Science, Kista, Sweden,
{erik, zeb, perbrand}@sics.se

[2] Computer Science Dpt., Univ. catholique de Louvain, Louvain-la-Neuve, Belgium,
valentin@info.ucl.ac.be

[3] IMIT - Royal Institute of Technology, Kista, Sweden
seif@it.kth.se

Abstract. One of the problems of middleware for shared state is that they are designed, explicitly or implicitly, for symmetric networks. However, since the Internet is not symmetric, end-to-end process connectivity cannot be guaranteed. Our solution to this is to provide the middleware with a network abstraction layer that masks the asymmetry of the network and provides the illusion of a symmetric network. We describe the communication service of our middleware, the Distribution Subsystem (DSS), which carefully separates connections to remote processes from the protocols that communicate over them. This separation is used to plug-in a peer-to-peer module to provide symmetric and persistent connectivity. The P2P module can provide both up-to-date addresses for mobile processes as well as route discovery to overcome asymmetric links.

1 Introduction

Development of distributed applications is greatly simplified by using programming systems that offer abstractions for shared state, e.g., distributed objects as in JavaRMI or CORBA. Considerable research and work has been done on protocols for shared state [1,2], mechanisms [3], and systems [4,5] to make them more transparent without sacrificing efficiency. The existing shared-state protocols have usually been, implicitly or explicitly, designed for connectivity-symmetric networks, e.g., LANs and clusters. By *symmetric connectivity* between two machines we understand the fact that they both can connect to each other via the physical network. On the other hand, we speak about *asymmetric connectivity* between two machines when only one of them is able to connect to the other one.

However, symmetry is not guaranteed on the Internet, in particular due to firewalls and Network Address Translators. Consequently, when the state-sharing protocols make use of messaging based on static IP addresses and assume symmetric connectivity over the Internet, they fail to work properly. In the light of

M. Papatriantafilou and P. Hunel (Eds.): OPODIS 2003, LNCS 3144, pp. 71–82, 2004.

this unfortunate fact, many take the view that shared-state abstractions are just not possible for asymmetric networks [6], or that new and completely different kinds of shared-state protocols are necessary. We do not share this opinion. Instead, existing shared state protocols can be directly used on top of a network abstraction layer that masks the asymmetry of the physical network.

The problem of asymmetric connectivity has been targeted at the networking layer using proxy-based architectures. Communication is routed through fixed way-points [7,8], thus a way-point, or proxy, guarantees connectivity. This solution is static in its configuration, and requires an infrastructure for hosting the proxy. A more promising solution is to explicitly separate the name of a process from its identity [9,10]. Name-to-address resolution can then be performed at application/middleware level, allowing for customizable strategies. This approach coincides with results from the peer-to-peer field. Organizing processes in peer-to-peer (P2P) infrastructures [11,12], or overlay networks, has in [13] been shown to efficiently solve process mobility. However, their solution requires potentially inefficient indirection of messages and does not provide a solution for asymmetric connectivity.

The remainder of the paper is organized as follows. We continue by stating the contribution of this paper. Then, in Section 2 we introduce our middleware library. In Sections 3 and 4 we describe the design and the implementation of our abstract notion of remote processes. In Section 5 we present a P2P extension to increase connectivity for our middleware. The basic messaging performance of our middleware is evaluated in Section 6. We discuss related work in Section 7, and then conclude.

1.1 Contribution

This paper presents the design and implementation of an efficient, simple-to-use process abstraction, called a DSite. The abstraction separates the notion of a process name from its address and hides details of the underlying network by offering an end-to-end asynchronous and reliable messaging service.

The implementation of the DSite allows for simple customization of strategies for failure detection and connection establishment. This is indicated by the second contribution of this paper: the usage of P2P techniques to overcome asymmetry when establishing connections. By organizing processes in a P2P network, DSites have access to a service that provides decentralized name-to-address resolution and name-to-valid-route discovery.

2   The Distribution Subsystem

The Distribution Subsystem (DSS) is a middleware library, designed to provide distribution support for a programming systems [14]. A programming system connected to the DSS results in a distributed programming system[1]. Distribution

---

[1] The system is implemented in C++ as a library and it is available for download at http://dss.sics.se

support is on the level of language entities/data structures, over an interface of abstract entities. Associated with an abstract entity type is a consistency model, e.g., sequential consistency for shared objects. The DSS provides one or more consistency protocols for each supported abstract entity type.

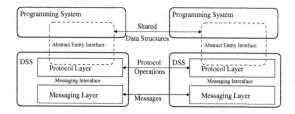

Fig. 1. The structure of the DSS middleware library. The figure depicts two processes sharing data structures using the DSS. The distribution model for the two programming systems is on the level of shared data structures. Within the DSS, the protocol layer exchanges protocol operations with other protocol instances. The bottom layer of the DSS, the messaging layer, is responsible for passing the protocol operations to the correct process.

Central in the DSS is the consistency protocol framework. This framework enables simplified development of protocols, indicated by the large suite of efficient protocols provided by the DSS [14]. The key component in this framework is an efficient and expressive inter-process service. As shown in Figure 1, the DSS is internally divided into two layers: a protocol layer that implements the consistency protocols and a messaging layer that implements all tasks related to inter process interaction, e.g., messaging. The focus of this paper is on the messaging layer. Hereinafter, we refer to a process that executes the DSS as a *DSS-node*.

At any point in time a DSS-node may know other DSS-nodes, these nodes are refereed as the *known set*. During the course of computation, references to DSS-nodes are passed among DSS-nodes, thus the *known set* changes. At any one time a DSS-node needs to communicate with a subset of the *known set*, this subset is constantly changing. Furthermore, it is perfectly possible that a DSS-node will never communicate with a given node in the *known set*. Each DSS-node is assigned a globally unique identity. In addition, a DSS-node's identity is separated from its address; this is an important requirement [10] for supporting mobile processes.

3   DSite, Representing a Process

The DSS represents known DSS-nodes as first-class data structures, called DSites. A known DSS-node is referenced from the consistency protocol module of the DSS. The task of the DSite is to provide two services: a seamless connection and communication service, and an asynchronous failure detection service. DSites can be passed within messages using the communication service of other DSites, possibly causing the introduction of a DSite in the other DSS-node. Within a DSS-node there exists at most one copy of a particular DSite.

The provided messaging service is asynchronous and guarantees reliable, in-order, message delivery (modulo failure of the receiving process). Failures are reported from the messaging layer to the protocol layer. A DSite continuously monitors the DSS-node it represents and classifies accessibility into one of the three following states:

No-problem. The DSS-node can be reached.

Communication-problem. The DSS-node is currently not accessible. This perception is local to this DSite instance. Other DSite instances, represent-ing the same DSS-node, located at other DSS-nodes can have different per-ceptions. This state is not permanent, the state of the DSite can change later to No-problem or Crash-failure.

Crash-failure. The DSS-node has crashed and will never be reachable again from any DSS-node in the network. This is a global perception; all DSite instances representing the DSS-node will either be in the state Communication-problem or already in the state Crash-failure.

3.1   Channel Establishment

Within the DSS, two types of channels can be established to the node represented by a DSite. A direct channel, e.g., a TCP connection, or an internal indirect channel, called *virtual circuit*. A virtual circuit is constructed using a route of intermediary nodes (we will enter in more details in Section 5). Messages sent over a virtual circuit are passed over existing direct connections from one node to another, along the path of the route. Whether a DSite is connected directly or routed is transparent to the consistency-protocol module.

3.2   DSite API

In this section we briefly describe the interface provided to the protocol layer by a DSite and vice versa. For the reason of clarity, the interface is slightly simplified. Messages are passed as lists of appropriate data structures, e.g., integers, strings, DSites and application data structures.

send(site, msg) causes the messaging layer to transport the given message to the node identified by the given site. The protocol layer exports the following interface to the messaging layer:

receive(msg, site) called by the messaging layer when a message is received. The site argument identifies the sender of the message.

siteChangedState(site, fault) called by the messaging layer when **site** has changed its fault state[2].

---

[2] When specialized failure detectors are used, there are provisions for turning detection on and off.

4   Dividing the Labor

Realizing reliable messaging for middleware requires consideration of a multitude of requirements. These requirements include in-order messages delivery, reliable transportation, opening and closing of connections, interfacing to OS-specific services, and channel establishment. In order to efficiently fulfill them and provide a portable and extendable system, we have divided the functionality of the DSite into three separate tasks:

Session specific tasks. Fundamental tasks for correctness of the service a DSite provides, i.e., end-to-end message delivery. This includes ensuring reliable, in-order message delivery, (de)serialization of messages, deciding when to open connections and when to close connections.

Environment specific tasks. Connection establishment and detecting DSS-node faults tasks. These tasks are generally subject to customization, depending on the needs of the application and what the environment offers and can simply be defined as external services.

Operating system specific tasks. Link/channel tasks, that are closely related to the specifics of the operating system a DSS-node executes on, e.g., implementing socket handling.

4.1   DSite Subcomponents

The three tasks defined in the previous section are reflected in the division of the DSS into three subcomponents (see Figure 2). Session specific tasks are located within the protocol layer in the Asynchronous Protocol Machine (APM). Application specific tasks of DSite handling is located in the Communication Service Component (CSC). Operating system specifics regarding communication are located in the IO-factory. The APM is implemented as a C++ library that requires connecting to an instance of the CSC and the IO-factory. The other subcomponents are represented as abstract C++ classes in order to simplify custom implementations.

The division of the DSS into three separate subcomponents makes the middleware easier to maintain and extend. All three subcomponents interact over small, well specified, interfaces, enabling application developers to implement specialized CSC and IO-factory subcomponents independently. Furthermore, the design is in the line of separating names from addresses: the APM is responsible for the identity (the name), while the CSC is responsible for addressing, i.e., for actually establishing connections.

4.2   A Layered Approach

A DSite is realized as an extendable structure of five sub-objects, located in APM, CSC, and IO-factory (see Figure 2). Each object within the structure represents a certain task related to remote process interaction.

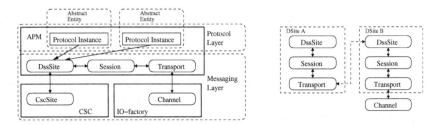

Fig. 2. To the left, the layout of the DSS and its three separate software subcomponents. The protocol layer and parts of the messaging layer are located in the same software subcomponent, the APM. The figure also depicts the location of the subobjects that represent the DSite structure. The APM does abstract messaging and the CSC/IO-factory does the actual messaging. The figure to the right, depicts how a DSite A uses DSite B to construct a virtual circuit.

There are three objects located within the APM. First, the **DssSite** that provides the protocol layer interface and acts as the internal DSite reference. Second, the **Session Object** that maintains communication sessions and ensure reliable, in-order delivery even in the case of volatile connections. Third, the **Transport Object** is responsible for serializing messages[3], according to the channel type, and put serialized representations onto the channel.

Establishing connections to, and monitoring the status of, a DSS-node is assigned to the **CscSite**, located in the CSC. Establishing connections is done upon request from the **DssSite**. When a connection is established, it is passed to the **DssSite**. The actual connection has the form of a *channel* in the case of a direct connection, whereas in the case of an indirect connection it has the form of a route, or virtual circuit, i.e., a sequence of **DssSites** describing the path to the target process. The **CscSite** is also responsible for monitoring the status of the target process; a continuous task. Detected errors are reported to the **DssSite**.

A direct connection to another process (in the form of a TCP socket, or another transport medium) is represented by a **Channel** object, located in the IO-factory. It is allocated and linked to a Transport object when a connection is established and removed when the channel is lost or closed.

4.3   Maintaining a Dynamic DSite Structure

A DSite is always represented by at least a **DssSite** connected to a **CscSite**. The other objects exist on a by-need basis, allocated when needed and deallocated when no longer needed. The Session object is allocated when the DSite is needed for actual communication, and lazily removed when there is no further

---

[3] in cooperation with the application, running on top of the DSS

communication needed[4]. A Transport object is allocated by the session object when a direct or an indirect connection to a DSS-node exists.

This design allows for a compact representation of a DSite. A DSite used only for identification is represented by a simple **DssSite** object. A disconnected DSite object with unsent messages is represented by a **DssSite** object together with a Session object.

The DSS creates DSites from descriptions commonly received along with consistency-protocol messages. DSites are automatically created when received, and automatically removed when no longer needed. Detecting obsolete DSites is done during periodic checks by a mark-and-sweep algorithm. Consequently, a DSS-node closes non-used connections automatically.

4.4   API Between Subcomponents

The interfaces that a DSite object's subcomponent interact through represent both synchronous and asynchronous functions. For simplicity basic functionality regarding identity/address serialization or connection of two objects is not described. The APM exports the following interface to the CSC, through the **DssSite**:

directConnectionEstablished(Channel), called when a direct connection has been established for the **DssSite**.

routeFound(DssSites[]) is used to inform a DSite that it should set up a virtual circuit through the sites in **DssSites[]**.

stateChange(newState), the CSC has deduced that the fault state has change and that affected protocols should be informed.

The following interface is provided to the APM by the CSC (CscSite):

establishConnection(), is called when a **DssSite** needs to communicate. Later on, the CSC will call either **directConnectionEstablished** or **routeFound**.

closeConnection(Channel), is called by the **DssSite** when no communication is needed.

disposeCssSite(), tells the CSC that the **DssSite** has been reclaimed within the APM and so should the CscSite.

A detailed description of the IO-factory interface toward the CSC and the APM is intentionally left out due to space limitations. In short, the interface can be described as a high-level socket abstraction.

5   A Peer-to-Peer Approach

P2P overlay networks implicitly offer name-based communication and routing [11,12,15]. The organization of the overlay network is fully decentralized. To structure the network, each participating process is required to connect to a certain number of so-called neighbor processes. As long as each participant

---

[4] Removal is partly controlled by the amount of communication needs of other DSites, i.e., resource management.

maintains the connections it is assigned, the algorithm guarantees connectivity within the group. A P2P lookup algorithm (here we are looking for nodes rather than data) can be used to find routes between participants of the overlay network.

In this section we give a description of how the CSC is extended in our Oz-DSS[5] implementation with a P2P module to enhance connectivity, followed by a discussion.

5.1   Adding a P2P Module to CSC

The "P2P module" acts as a service for the **CscSite**, providing name-to-address resolution and name-to-valid-route discovery functionality. The module is responsible with the node management in the P2P system, and with the organization of the corresponding overlay structure for the chosen P2P protocol. The P2P module is to be used when direct connections cannot be established due to connection asymmetry in the network, or outdated addresses, e.g., in the case of mobile hosts. The resulting system provides an illusion of a symmetric and quasi-static network over a highly asymmetric and dynamic network. The P2P module has access to all the channels opened for the APM and is allowed to open channels on its own.

5.2   A Flooding-Based P2P Module

In order to verify our approach, we implemented a simple P2P-based connection establishment schema based on flooding, similar to Gnutella (gnutella.wego.com). More efficient P2P algorithms, based on DHTs, could also be used. However, the point here is to validate the interface between the APM and the CSC.

When a **DssSite** asks its **CscSite** to establish a connection, the **CscSite** first tries to open a direct connection using the last known address. Only if that fails will the P2P module be asked for a route-and-address discovery.

The P2P module, in this flooding approach, then broadcasts a request to the neighbor set. Subsequently, they forward it to all their neighbor processes. The request forwarding ends when either the message time-to-live (TTL) expires or the target process is found. When reached, if that is the case, the target process sends its current address together with a path list along the reverse path. Upon successful return, the **CscSite** compares the received address with the one locally cached. If the address has changed (this could be the case for a mobile host), the **CscSite** tries to connect directly to the new address. If that fails, or if the address has not changed, it sets up a virtual circuit using the returned path. Thus, connectivity can be improved both in case of mobility and in case of asymmetric connectivity, e.g., hosts behind firewalls, NATs or physical network limitations in ad-hoc networks. The CSC can also try to shorten the route before handing it to the APM.

---

[5] Oz-DSS is a prototype that extends the programming language Oz with distribution support, using our DSS middleware. It is available for download at http://dss.sics.se

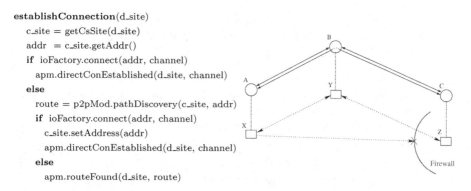

```
establishConnection(d_site)
   c_site = getCsSite(d_site)
   addr  = c_site.getAddr()
   if ioFactory.connect(addr, channel)
      apm.directConEstablished(d_site, channel)
   else
      route = p2pMod.pathDiscovery(c_site, addr)
      if ioFactory.connect(addr, channel)
         c_site.setAddress(addr)
         apm.directConEstablished(d_site, channel)
      else
         apm.routeFound(d_site, route)
```

Fig. 3. Overcome asymmetric connectivity by using the name-to-valid-route discovery service. Since node A cannot connect directly to node C, it looks for a path through node B. On the left hand side we show pseudo-code representing the steps at node A.

In Figure 3 we show a simple example of three nodes, where the name-to-valid-route discovery service is used. The DSS-nodes are denoted by circles, whereas the machines they run on to are denoted by rectangles. In this example, node A receives, through the action of some consistency protocol, a reference to the target node C and tries to connect to it. As node A can not connect directly to node C, it makes use of the name-to-valid-route service provided by the P2P module, and thus it obtains a route to node C through node B which will be used to create a virtual circuit between A to C through B. We also show the pseudo-code representing the steps at node A.

5.3   Routing for Scalability

We have seen how the use of name based routing can extend the DSS function-ality to cater for firewalls, NATs and mobility. In addition the P2P module can also extend the DSS with respect to scalability.

There is an appreciable cost with each direct connection in terms of memory and system resources. Thus large *known sets* are not, within reason, a problem, rather keeping a large number of direct connections might be. A DSS-node may be at the limits of its available resources and unable to accept additional incom-ing connections without serious performance degradation. With the P2P routing available as backup, the loaded node can now deliberately refuse additional con-nections requests, thus indirectly forcing the communication to take place over the already existing connections.

6   Evaluation of the DSS

The functionality provided by the DSite structure simplifies interprocess com-munication for the protocol layer of the DSS. However, this functionality does not come for free; it imposes a certain overhead compared to raw socket use. In this section we show that the overhead is relatively small, especially when considering Internet communication.

Table 1. The time it takes to send sequences of 1000 request-reply messages for three different applications on two different network configurations. The times normalized to the time of the socket application are shown in parentheses.

Process-Configuration	Socket	DSS – channel	DSS – virtual circuit
100Mbit LAN (ping 0.096ms)	92ms (1.0)	116ms (1.26)	287ms (2.51)
Internet (ping 51.504ms)	51073ms (1.0)	51137ms (1.0)	53404ms (1.04)

We compared a small socket application against the DSS in two settings. First, using a TCP channel for interprocess communication. Second, using a virtual circuit (over established TCP channels). All applications send a request from one process, the source, to another process, the target. Upon receiving the request, the target process sends a reply message back to the source. The reception of the reply message finishes a request-reply call. This sequence is repeated 1000 times. The tests were conducted over two network configurations: a fast LAN (0.096 ms) at SICS, and Internet (51.5 ms) setting with computers located in Sweden and Belgium. For the virtual circuit test we used one intermediary node, also in Sweden, 80km (ping 4ms) away from the source node.

The results are shown in Table 1. The socket application can be seen as the practical maximum communication speed that could be obtained (the IO-factory used by the DSS uses TCP). The overhead imposed by the DSite structure is surprisingly small, only 26%. When considering WAN settings with higher latency, the overhead is negligible. Maintenance of the virtual circuit introduces an extra 50% overhead added to the extra network hop in the LAN setting, resulting in a 250% overhead compared to raw socket communication. However, the difference is only 4% when communicating over the Internet.

7   Related Work

The JXTA specifications (www.jxta.org) define a set of basic protocols for a number of P2P services such as discovery, communication, and peer monitoring. JXTA only provides unreliable communication using the notion of pipes. Contrary to JXTA, the DSS implements reliable communication. Furthermore, the DSS is much more than a data-storage system; it is a generic middleware library supporting a wide variety of abstract entity types.

The Intentional Naming System – *INS* [16] provides resource discovery and service location for dynamic and mobile networks. The so-called resolvers in *INS* form an overlay network used to discover new services and perform late binding, i.e., a mechanism that integrates name resolution and message routing. The idea of using the lookup procedure of the P2P algorithms for routing messages in our system is very close to the late binding mechanism. However, the overlay network in *INS* is organized into a spanning tree and is intended for relatively small systems. *INS* is focused on service location, rather than process location, as is our approach. In our approach, we take advantage of the P2P lookup algorithms to extend, improve and scale up our middleware to be able to deal with asymmetric networks, mobility, firewalls, and NATs.

The research in [13] (Internet Indirection Infrastructure – *i3*) is focused on the idea of employing a P2P based overlay network to support host mobility and to provide a rendezvous-based communication abstraction. In our approach we also organize the system into a P2P overlay network. However, whereas in *i3* the rendezvous points are used for indirection, and thus, storing extra routing state, in our proposal we use the P2P lookup algorithms for process location, directly, and message routing, indirectly. Moreover, whereas *i3* is an independent infrastructure that has to be deployed explicitly, in our solution we propose that the very nodes of a given distributed system dynamically organize themselves to maintain communication in asymmetric networks.

8   Future·Work

Currently, the DSS design is built on the assumption of a non-hostile environment. We are currently working on making the DSS a secure platform, by adding encrypted channels based on public key negotiated session keys, and unforgeable DSS-node/DSite identifiers and adresses. Furthermore, we plan to investigate and experiment more with DHT-based algorithms in our prototype P2P component. The properties of the structured P2P algorithms, the scalability robustness, full decentralization and self-organizing make them prime candidates for our middleware system.

9   Conclusion

We described a messaging model based on a first class notion of a remote process, a DSite. The DSite abstraction hides details of the underlying network, and provides a simple to use asynchronous messaging interface. The DSS, the middleware library that implements the DSites, is designed to be both efficient and extendable. The efficiency of the design is shown in our evaluations.

The DSS matched with a suitable P2P module extends the usefulness of the DSS to asymmetric networks. The P2P algorithms work as a connection fallback when direct connections are either impossible or resource inefficient. Direct connection establishment is not possible when dealing with mobility (mobile processes), firewalls, and NATs.

Previously our middleware (as well as other shared state systems), incorporating many state-of-the-art consistency protocols, required symmetric networks to work. In this paper we show how this limitation can be overcome by incorporating suitable P2P algorithms, greatly extending the application domain.

Acknowledgments. We wish to express thanks to Anna Neiderud and Emil Gustavsson; Anna for the work on a prototypical messaging layer and Emil for discussions about using P2P to overcome asymmetric connectivity.

This work was partially supported by the Information Society Technologies programme of the European Commission, Future and Emerging Technologies under IST-2001-33234 PEPITO, and by grants from the Swedish Agency for Innovation Systems (Vinnova) and the Swedish Research Council.

References

[1] Herlihy, M., Warres, M.: A tale of two directories: implementing distributed shared objects in Java. Concurrency: Practice and Experience **12** (2000) 555–572

[2] Tilevich, E., Smaragdakis, Y.: NRMI: Natural and efficient middleware. In: 23rd International Conference on Distributed Computing Systems. (2003) 252–

[3] Maassen, J., Kielmann, T., Bal, H.: Efficient replicated method invocation in Java. In: ACM 2000 Java Grande Conference. (2000) 88–96

[4] Aridor, Y., Factor, M., Teperman, A.: cJVM: A single system image of a JVM on a cluster. In: International Conference on Parallel Processing. (1999) 4–11

[5] Holder, O., Ben-Shaul, I., Gazit, H.: Dynamic layout of distributed applications in FarGo. In: International Conference on Software Engineering. (1999) 163–173

[6] Waldo, J., Wyant, G., Wollrath, A., Kendall, S.: A note on distributed computing. In: Mobile Object Systems – Towards the Programmable Internet. Volume 1222. (1996) 49–64

[7] Maltz, D.A., Bhagwat, P.: MSOCKS: An architecture for transport layer mobility. In: 7th Conference on Computer Communications. (1998) 1037–1045

[8] Perkins, C.: IP mobility support, RFC 2002 (1996)

[9] O'Toole, J., Gifford, D.: Names should mean what, not where. In: 5th ACM European Workshop on Distributed Systems. (1992)

[10] Snoeren, A., Balakrishnan, H., Kaashoek, M.: Reconsidering internet mobility. In: 8th Workshop on Hot Topics in Operating Systems. (2001)

[11] Stoica, I., Morris, R., Krager, D., Kaashoek, M., Balakrishnan, H.: Chord: A scalable peer-to-peer lookup service for internet applications. In: ACM SIGCOMM. (2001) 149–160

[12] Ratnasamy, S., Handley, M., Karp, R., Shenker, S.: Application-level multicast using content-addressable network. In: 3rd COST264 International Workshop on Networked Group Communication. Volume 2233. (2001) 14–29

[13] Stoica, I., Adkins, D., Zhuang, S., Shenker, S., Surana, S.: Internet Indirection Infrastructure. In: ACM SIGCOMM. (2002) 73–88

[14] Klintskog, E., Banna, Z.E., Brand, P., Haridi, S.: The design and evaluation of a middleware library for distribution of language entities. In: 8th Asian Computing Conference. (2003) 243–259

[15] L. Onana, S. El-Ansary, P.B., Haridi, S.: Dks (n, k, f): A family of low communication, scalable and fault-tolerant infrastructures for p2p applications. In: 3rd IEEE International Symposium on Cluster Computing and the Grid. (2003) 344–350

[16] Adjie-Winoto, W., Schwartz, E., Balakrishnan, H., Lilley, J.: The design and implementation of an intentional naming system. In: 17th ACM Symposium on Operating System Principles. (1999) 186–201

Multicast in $\mathcal{DKS}(N, k, f)$ Overlay Networks[*]

Luc Onana Alima[1], Ali Ghodsi[1], Per Brand[2], and Seif Haridi[1]

[1] IMIT-Royal Institute of Technology (KTH)
{onana,aligh,seif}@imit.kth.se,
[2] Swedish Institute of Computer Science (SICS)
perbrand@sics.se

Abstract. Recent developments in the area of peer-to-peer computing show that structured overlay networks implementing distributed hash tables scale well and can serve as infrastructures for Internet scale applications.

We are developing a family of infrastructures, $\mathcal{DKS}(N, k, f)$, for the construction of peer-to-peer applications. An instance of $\mathcal{DKS}(N, k, f)$ is an overlay network that implements a distributed hash table and which has a number of desirable properties: low cost of communication, scalability, logarithmic lookup length, fault-tolerance and strong guarantees of locating any data item that was inserted in the system.

In this paper, we show how multicast is achieved in $\mathcal{DKS}(N, k, f)$ overlay networks. The design presented here is attractive in three main respects. First, members of a multicast group self-organize in an instance of $\mathcal{DKS}(N, k, f)$ in a way that allows co-existence of groups of different sizes, degree of fault-tolerance, and maintenance cost, thereby, providing flexibility. Second, each member of a group can multicast, rather than having single source multicast. Third, within a group, dissemination of a multicast message is optimal under normal system operation in the sense that there are no redundant messages despite the presence of outdated routing information.

Keywords: Peer-to-Peer Computing, Distributed Algorithms, Multicast, Distributed Hash Tables.

1   Introduction

The need for making effective use of the huge amount of computing resources attached to large scale networks such as the Internet is driving research in peer-to-peer (P2P) computing. Recent developments in this area show that structured overlay networks implementing distributed hash tables scale well and can serve as infrastructures for P2P applications. [1,9,8,2].

In an effort to contribute to this new trend, we are designing and developing a family of infrastructures termed $\mathcal{DKS}(N, k, f)$[1], for constructing P2P

---

[*] This work was funded by the European project IST-2001-32234, PEPITO and Vinnova PPC project in Sweden.

M. Papatriantafilou and P. Hunel (Eds.): OPODIS 2003, LNCS 3144, pp. 83–95, 2004.

applications. Each instance of $\mathcal{DKS}(N, k, f)$ is an overlay network that implements a distributed hash table and which has a number of desirable properties including low cost of communication due to a novel technique for maintaining routing information, scalability, logarithmic lookup length, fault-tolerance and high guarantees of locating any data item that was inserted in the system.

1.1 Motivations and Contributions

Multicast is an important primitive for many distributed applications, such as content distribution and video conferencing. Traditional approaches for multicast work well in small scale systems. For large scale systems with extreme dynamism, such as P2P systems, the multicast problem must be addressed in a different fashion that enables creation of scalable, fault-tolerant groups in which multicast messages are delivered to all group members without any redundant messages. How to achieve this in the $\mathcal{DKS}(N, k, f)$ family is the main contribution of this paper.

Multicast in large scale and highly dynamic environments such as peer-to-peer environments has been addressed according to two main approaches. In the first approach exemplified by [3], the idea is to construct a multicast dissemination tree. However, this approach has at least two drawbacks. First, non-member nodes of a multicast group maintain information about the multicast dissemination tree. Furthermore, the number of messages sent for a given multicast is, in the worst case, in the order of the actual size of the underlying overlay network (i.e., Pastry). In the second approach exemplified by [6] a new CAN is created for the multicast group. But the dissemination of multicast messages does not ensure zero redundancy, because of the possibility of imperfect partitioning of the coordinate space.

The design presented in this paper follows the second approach as in [6], although it differs in some respects significantly. The main contributions of our design are: (i) Members of a multicast group self-organize in an instance of $\mathcal{DKS}(N, k, f)$ in a way that allows co-existence of groups of different sizes, degree of fault-tolerance, and maintenance cost, thereby, providing flexibility. (ii) As in [6], each member of a group can multicast, rather than having single source multicast like in [3]. (iii) In contrast to [6], within a group, dissemination of a multicast message is optimal under normal system operation in the sense that there are no redundant messages despite the presence of outdated routing information. This is achieved thanks to a "correcting broadcast" algorithm inspired by our previous work [4].

1.2 Roadmap

The rest of the paper is structured as follows. In Section 2, we give an overview of the preliminary design of the $\mathcal{DKS}(N, k, f)$ family. In section 3, we discuss how multicast groups are created, how nodes join a multicast group and present the algorithm used to transmit a multicast message to all members of a group without any redundancy. Thereafter we validate and evaluate our multicast scheme in section 4. Finally, Section 5 summarizes the paper.

2   Overview of $\mathcal{DKS}(N,k,f)$ Design

In this section, we recall the key ideas behind the preliminary design of the $\mathcal{DKS}(N,k,f)$ family [1].

2.1   Underlying Assumptions

For the design of the $\mathcal{DKS}(N,k,f)$, we model a distributed system as a set of *processes* linked together through a *communication network*. Processes communicate by message passing. The communication network is assumed to be *connected, asynchronous, reliable*, and *FIFO*. By reliable, we mean that every message injected into the communication network eventually is delivered to its destination, provided that the latter remains connected to the communication network.

To set up a $\mathcal{DKS}(N,k,f)$ system, it is assumed that: k is an integer greater or equal 2. The maximum number of nodes that can be in the system is $N = k^L$ where L is assumed to be large enough to achieve very large distributed systems. f is the fault-tolerance parameter. Each peer knows the parameters N, k and f, thus can compute L.

2.2   The Identifier Space and Notations

In designing $\mathcal{DKS}(N,k,f)$ systems, we assume, like in most P2P infrastructures [9,8], that nodes of a $\mathcal{DKS}(N,k,f)$ and objects managed by these nodes are uniquely identified by identifiers taken from the same logical space.

In this paper, we assume that the identifier space, denoted $\mathcal{I} = \{0, 1, \cdots, N-1\}$ is organized as a ring. We use for $a, b \in \mathcal{I}$, $a \oplus b$ for $(a + b)$ modulo N.

Next in the paper, we shall need to determine whether a given identifier belongs, going in the clockwise direction, to a part (or interval) of the identifier space. For this reason, we use an appropriate boolean function $\hat{\in}$, which will serve that purpose. For simplicity of notation, we shall use infix notation for the function $\hat{\in}$.

2.3   Key/Value Pairs Management

A $\mathcal{DKS}(N,k,f)$ overlay network implements a distributed hash table that serves for efficient storage and retrieval of key/value pairs. Let (t, v) be a key/value pair, where t is a key and v is the value associated with t. When inserted in a $\mathcal{DKS}(N,k,f)$ network, this pair is stored at the first node met moving on the identifier space starting from the hashed identifier of t, in the clockwise direction.

2.4   Levels and Views

Any $\mathcal{DKS}(N, k, f)$ network is built in a manner that allows each lookup to be resolved by following a path of a virtual k-ary spanning tree of height $\log_k(N)$ ensuring logarithmic lookup path length. To achieve this, each node in a $\mathcal{DKS}(N, k, f)$ network has $\log_k(N)$ *levels* numbered from 1 to L, where $L = \log_k(N)$. From now on, we shall use $\mathcal{L}$ for $\{1, 2, \cdots, L\}$.

When at level $l \in \mathcal{L}$, a node n has a *view* V^l of the identifier space. The view V^l consists of k equal parts, denoted I_i^l, $0 \leq i \leq k - 1$, and defined below level by level. Next, we use $\mathcal{K}$ for $\{0, 1, \cdots, k - 1\}$.

At level 1: $V^1 = I_0^1 \cup I_1^1 \cup I_2^1 \cup \cdots \cup I_{k-1}^1$, where $I_0^1 = [x_0^1, x_1^1[$, $I_1^1 = [x_1^1, x_2^1[$, $\cdots$, $I_{k-1}^1 = [x_{k-1}^1, x_0^1[$, $x_i^1 = n \oplus i\frac{N}{k}$, for $0 \leq i \leq k - 1$.

At level $2 \leq l \leq L$: $V^l = I_0^l \cup I_1^l \cup I_2^l \cup \cdots \cup I_{k-1}^l$, where $I_0^l = [x_0^l, x_1^l[$, $I_1^l = [x_1^l, x_2^l[$, $\cdots$, $I_{k-1}^l = [x_{k-1}^l, x_1^{l-1}[$, $x_i^l = n \oplus i\frac{N}{k^l}$, for $0 \leq i \leq k - 1$.

2.5   Responsibilities

Let n be an arbitrary $\mathcal{DKS}(N, k, f)$ node. Let l, $1 \leq l \leq L$, and let $V^l = \cup_{0 \leq j \leq k-1} I_j^l$ be the view that node n has at level l. With respect to node n, for each I_j^l, $0 \leq j \leq k - 1$, there is a node $R(I_j^l)$ that node n considers *responsible* for I_j^l. Intuitively, the responsible for I_j^l represents the node that n will contact, for example, when trying to resolve a key identifier that belongs to I_j^l.

We denote by $S(x)$, for an identifier x, the successor[1] of x.

For an arbitrary node n and an arbitrary level $l \in \mathcal{L}$, the responsible for I_i^l, $i \in \mathcal{K}$ is $S(x_i^l)$. Each node is itself responsible for I_0^l for any $1 \leq l \leq \log_k(N)$.

2.6   Routing Information

To ensure logarithmic ($\log_k(N)$) lookup length, each node n of a $\mathcal{DKS}(N, k, f)$ system maintains a routing table RT, which is of type $RT:\mathcal{L} \to (\mathcal{K} \to \mathcal{I})$ Hence, $(RT(l))(i)$ denotes the responsible for the interval I_i^l. Sometimes, for the sake of clarity, we write RT_n, to emphasize that the routing table under consideration is that of node n.

In addition to the above routing table, each node n maintains a pointer denoted p, to its predecessor on the ring. The predecessor of a node n is the first node met when moving in the counterclockwise direction starting from n. So, in total, each node needs only $(k - 1)\log_k(N) + 1$ for the purpose of the lookup.

2.7 $\mathcal{DKS}(N, k, f)$ Networks Construction and Maintenance

A $\mathcal{DKS}(N, k, f)$ is built as described in [1]. The core idea is that the join and leave operations are handled by local atomic actions that ensure a consistent

---

[1] The successor of an identifier t is the first node encountered, moving in the clockwise direction, starting at t.

interleaving of concurrent joins, leaves and other operations, such as multicast and broadcast. Typically, these local atomic operations involve very few nodes.

Given that concurrent joins at different parts of the circle can take place by the same time, and that when a node joins it obtains an approximate routing table, it is possible that routing entries can be out of date.

Handling such out of date information is the distinguishing property of the $\mathcal{DKS}(N, k, f)$ infrastructures. Indeed, rather than using separate stabilization mechanism to be run periodically, the $\mathcal{DKS}(N, k, f)$ design adopts another approach in which erroneous or out-of-date routing entries are detected and corrected on-the-fly. We intuitively present the technique used in the next subsection.

We refer the reader to [1] for the handling of failures.

2.8   Correction-on-Use

The correction-on-use technique builds on two simple observations.

Observation 1: By piggybacking the level and the interval information in lookup or insert messages, a remote node n' can determine upon receipt of a message from n, whether the routing entry used by n to send the received message was correct.

Observation 2: Upon receipt of a message from a remote node n', a node n becomes aware of the existence of n', and can therefore determine whether it should consider n' as responsible some of its routing entries.

To exploit the first observation, each node n maintains a *back list*[2], which consists of at most the first f nodes encountered in the counter-clockwise direction, starting at node n. We recall by the definition of responsibilities, that at a node n, for any l $(1 \leq l \leq \log_k(N))$, and any $i \in \mathcal{K}$, $(RT_n(l))(i) = S(n \oplus i\frac{N}{k^l})$. This invariant will hold in any configuration of the system where each node has correct routing information. Therefore, if a node n sends the level (i.e., l) and the interval information (i.e., i) while sending message to a node n', then node n' upon receipt of the message can determine whether the entry used by n was correct. With respect to node n', the entry used by n to send a message carrying l and i, is correct *only if* node n' is the successor of $(n \oplus i\frac{N}{k^l})$. So, node n', using its back list, can determine whether a node in its back list is a better approximate successor for $n \oplus i\frac{N}{k^l}$.

When a node n' detects that there is a better approximate successor for $n \oplus i\frac{N}{k^l}$, node n' sends a BADPOINTER message to node n. This message serves to inform node n that the entry it used to contact n' is outdated. In addition, the BADPOINTER message carries the address of a node C, that node n' believes is the best candidate for correcting the routing entry used by n. The best candidate C is selected from the *back list* of n'.

---

[2] The *back list* component is one of the enhancements we have made on the preliminary design.

When node n receives such a BadPointer message, it updates its routing table and repeats the operation (e.g., lookup request, key/value pair insertion request, broadcast) that led it to contact n', but now the message is sent to C.

The exploitation of the second observation is immediate. Indeed, when a node n receives a message from a remote node n', node n checks its routing table to determine whether it should have n' in its routing table. If this is the case, node n updates its routing table accordingly.

2.9   Lookup in a $\mathcal{DKS}(N, k, f)$

The protocol for resolving keys in a $\mathcal{DKS}(N, k, l)$ overlay network is an interval routing protocol that serves not only for resolving keys, but also for correcting outdated routing entries. As we have already sketched the idea of detection and correction of outdated routing entries, in this section, we only present briefly how keys are resolved.

When a node n receives a lookup request for key identifier t, from its user, node n checks if t is between its predecessor, p, and itself. If this is the case, node n does a local lookup to find the value associated to t. The result is returned to the user. Otherwise, node n triggers a forwarding process that goes level by level, and that consists in routing lookup messages toward the successor of t. Each lookup message carries necessary information (level and interval) for detection and correction of outdated routing entries. When the node n', successor of t is reached, node n' performs a local lookup to retrieve the value associated to t. The result is forwarded backward on the reverse path to the origin of the lookup.

Inserting key/value pairs in the system is similar to the lookup. In addition, messages induced by key/value pairs insertion are also used for detection and correction of routing entries.

3   Multicast in $\mathcal{DKS}(N, k, f)$

In this section, we show how groups are created and managed in $\mathcal{DKS}(N, k, f)$ overlay networks. We first give the underlying principle in Subsection 3.1. Then in Subsection 3.2 we explain the creation of groups. Subsection 3.3 gives an explanation of how nodes join a given group. Finally in Subsection 3.5, we present a "correcting broadcast" that serves to forward multicast messages in an optimal way within a group.

3.1   The Principle

The multicast in $\mathcal{DKS}(N, k, f)$ is inspired from [7]. However, our design differs from the one given in [7] in many aspects. First, in [7], the identifier space is a d-dimensional space while in $\mathcal{DKS}(N, k, f)$, the identifier space is a ring. Second, CAN relies on active correction for maintaining routing information while $\mathcal{DKS}(N, k, f)$ uses correction-on-use. Third, the broadcast algorithm used for multicast message forwarding in CAN is not optimal, as it does not eliminate redundant messages under normal system operation.

Our design borrows from [7], the idea of creating new instances of $\mathcal{DKS}(N, k, f)$ overlay networks for multicast groups. The idea is as follows. Let O be an instance of $\mathcal{DKS}(N, k, f)$. A node in O can decide to create a multicast group identified by g. Members of g self-organize in an instance G_g of $\mathcal{DKS}(N, k, f)$. The instance G_g is created and maintained as the underlying overlay network O. Information about group membership is distributed over the members of the group, as each group is represented by a specific instance of a $\mathcal{DKS}$.

To multicast a message within a group g from a member node n, the multicast message is handed out to n. Then node n simply starts a "correcting broadcast" process that serves to forward the message only to members of g. The challenging part is to design the "correcting broadcast" for forwarding multicast messages while ensuring that under normal system operation, there are no redundant messages. The broadcast must be "correcting", because in a $\mathcal{DKS}(N, k, f)$ overlay network representing a group, members can have erroneous routing information due to the way nodes are inserted in the group, and also because of leave or failure of group members.

3.2   Group Creation

Let O be an instance of $\mathcal{DKS}(N, k, f)$. We write N_O, k_O and f_O the values of the parameters N, k and f for the creation of the overlay network O. Let n be a node of O and assume that node n wants to create a new group identified by g. Then, node n first determines the characteristics of the group g. These include:

- k_g: the arity parameter within the group. This parameter serves for the construction of the topology of the overlay representing the group g.
- N_g: a power of k_g that denotes the maximum number of members that the group g can have. This number serves to determine the ring onto which group members are mapped.
- f_g: the fault-tolerance parameter within the group. This parameter serves also to determine the size of the back list.
- H_g: the hash function used to map nodes in O onto the ring of maximum size N_g.

Then, once these parameters are set up, node n inserts itself as the first node of the group. The characteristics of the group, g, and the address of node n are made available such that other nodes of O interested in g can join the group g. The joining of a group deserves some explanations that we give in the next subsection.

3.3   Joining a Group

A node n_j that wants to join the group g must know the characteristics of g and at least one node that belongs to g.

Assume node n_j knows the characteristics of a group g and some node n, member of g. Then, using H_g, node n_j computes its potential position, a number in $\{0, .., N_g - 1\}$, in the overlay network associated to group g. Then node, n_j starts a join process similar to the one used to insert nodes in O, except that now, because N_g can be small compared to N_O, we must resolve collisions during insertion. In the current design, we adopt the "first come first in" policy. As a consequence, it is possible for some nodes to continuously be rejected due to collisions when they want to join a group g. Addressing this issue is the subject of a future work.

Once a node n_j is inserted in a group g, node n_j makes available the characteristics of g and the addresses of some nodes it knows are in g. This way, the group information diffuses.

3.4   Illustration

The principle of the multicast group in $\mathcal{DKS}(N, k, f)$ overlay networks is illustrated in Figure 1. In this figure, panel $a)$ shows a $\mathcal{DKS}(N = 32, k = 2, f = 3)$ instance in which only nodes with identifiers 4, 11, 15, 19, 25 and 28 are present. Let us call this instance O. Panel $b)$ shows a $\mathcal{DKS}(N = 16, k = 4, f = 2)$ representing a multicast group with identifier $g = 4$, in which nodes 28, 25, 19 and 15 of O are members. Note that because of the hashing function for the multicast group $g = 4$, denoted H_4, each of the nodes 28, 25, 19 and 15 receives a new identifier relatively to this multicast group. For example, node 28 receives 1 as its identifier in the multicast group $g = 4$. Panel $c)$ shows a $\mathcal{DKS}(N = 8, k = 2, f = 1)$ representing a multicast group with identifier $g = 2$ in which nodes 4, 11 and 15 of O are members. Note that each node of O that is member of the multicast group $g = 2$ receives a new identifier relatively to this group.

3.5   Correcting Broadcast

The main difficult part of multicasting to groups in $\mathcal{DKS}(N, k, f)$ is to achieve optimal forwarding of messages. To overcome this difficulty, we build on our previous work on broadcasts [4], which we adapt to fit our need for multicast. The proposed algorithm allows multicast messages to be delivered to all members of a group without any redundant messages. In addition, it allows members of a group to correct their routing information on-the-fly, leading to efficient use of the bandwidth. From this on-the-fly correction of erroneous routing information comes the name "correcting broadcast".

We shall proceed in two steps. First, we give the principle of the correcting broadcast in Subsection 3.5. Next, we present a formal description of the algorithm in Subsection 3.

The principle. Each node n maintains a mapping GT_n that takes a group identifier, g, then returns N_g, k_g, f_g and the routing table, RT_g, of n for the

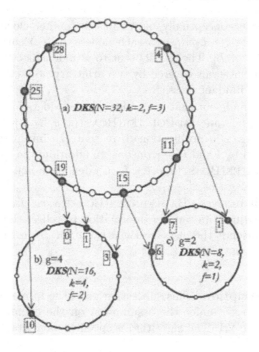

Fig. 1. Two groups based on a $\mathcal{DKS}(32, 2, 3)$.

overlay network associated to g. For practical reasons, we assume that each node can be in at most *MaxGroup* groups.

Let u be the application layer at a node n, member of a group g. When u wants to multicast an information x, u sends a BCASTREQUEST(x, g) message to n.

Upon receipt of BCASTREQUEST(x, g), node n starts a broadcast process using the routing table associated to group g. In this broadcast process, node n conceptually moves in the counter clockwise direction to deliver a BCAST$(x, g, l, i, Limit)$ to each node node n' considers responsible by n. The parameters of the BCAST message are: x, the information to be multicast. l and i serve for the correction-on-use. Actually, l and i represent the interval for which node n considers n' responsible for. The *Limit* parameter, serves the receiving node n' for determining which part of the ring associated to g, node n' should cover during the broadcast process.

When a node n receives a BCAST(x, g, l, i, L) from a node n', node n first adjusts (if necessary) its routing table for the group g to reflect the presence of n' in the overlay network associated to g^3. Second, node n checks whether it is actually the node that n' should consider responsible for the interval represented by l and i. If this is the case, node n delivers the information x to its application

---

[3] This action is performed for correction-on-use.

layer. Then, node n conceptually moves in the counter clockwise direction to deliver a BCAST$(x, g, l, i, Limit_x)$ to each node x that n considers responsible within the interval $]n, L[$. The $Limit_x$ sent to a node x is computed such as to guarantee that the intervals covered by two arbitrary nodes are disjoint. This is the key to avoid redundant messages.

If node node n finds out that it shouldn't be considered responsible by node n', then node n sends an BADPOINTER(BCAST$(x, g, l, i, L), C$) message to n'. This message serves as a notification to n' that the information it has about interval represented by l and i is erroneous. In addition, the parameter C in the message BADPOINTER(BCAST$(x, g, l, i, L), C$) denotes a node that n knows and believes is the successor of $n' \oplus i \frac{N}{k^l}$.

When a node n' receives a BADPOINTER(BCAST$(x, g, l, i, L), C$) from another node n, node n' adjusts its routing information to reflect the presence of node C, thereafter it re-sends the message BCAST(x, g, l, i, L) to the new responsible for its interval i at the level l.

The formal description. This subsection gives the formal description of the "correcting broadcast" under the assumption on the communication network made in Subsection 2.1. The algorithm is specified as a set of rules of the form

$$\frac{Event}{\text{ACTION}}$$

where EVENT is the reception of a message and ACTION is a sequence of statements that is executed atomically upon receipt of EVENT. For a node n to send a message MSG(*param*) to another node n', node n executes the statement **send**$(n : n' : \text{MSG}(param))$.

We assume that each node n has a mapping GT that takes a group identifier g and returns a 4-tuple (RT_g, N_g, k_g, f_g) where RT_g is the routing table of n for the multicast group g, N_g is the maximum size of this group, k_g is the search arity within this group and f_g is the fault-tolerance degree in this group. We call GT the group table of the node. Note that in addition to GT, each node has the routing table for the underlying $\mathcal{DKS}(N, k, f)$ instance.

4   Simulation Results

To validate our multicasting scheme we have simulated the algorithm in our stochastic discrete event simulator developed by our team using the Mozart[5] programming system. We focused on the following metrics:

Redundancy, the percentage of redundant messages. *Coverage*, the percentage of those nodes that received each multicast message. *Average Lookup Length*, the average number of hops a multicast message takes from the source to each destination. *Badpointer Traffic*, the number of BADPOINTER messages induced by the correction-on-use.

Algorithm 3.1 Correcting Broadcast

Message types:
    $\textsc{BcastRequest}(x, g)$
    $\textsc{Bcast}(x, g, l, i, L)$
    $\textsc{BadPointer}(\textsc{Bcast}(x, g, l, i, L), C)$

Variables:
    GT

Rules:

$R_1 ::$ **receive**$(u : n : \textsc{BcastRequest}(x, g))$

    $(RT_g, N_g, k_g, f_g) := GT(g)$
    $Limit := n$
    for $l = 1$ **to** $\log_{k_g}(N_g)$ **do**
        for $i = k_g - 1$ **downto** 1 **do**
            if $(RT_g(l))(i) \; \hat{\in} \;]n, \; Limit[$ **then**
                send$(n : (RT_g(l))(i) : \textsc{Bcast}(x, g, l, i, Limit))$
                $Limit := n \oplus i \frac{N_g}{(k_g)^l}$
            fi
        od
    od

$[]$

$R_2 ::$ **receive**$(n' : n : \textsc{Bcast}(x, g, l, i, L))$

    $(RT_g, N_g, k_g, f_g) := GT(g)$
    Adjust RT_g with n'
    if $n \oplus i \frac{N_g}{(k_g)^l} \hat{\in}]p, n]$ **then**
        deliver x to application layer
        $Limit := L$
        for $\tau = 1$ **to** $\log_{k_g}(N_g)$ **do**
            for $j = k_g - 1$ **downto** 1 **do**
                if $(RT_g(\tau))(j) \; \hat{\in} \;]n, \; Limit[$ **then**
                    send$(n : (RT_g(\tau))(j) : \textsc{Bcast}(x, g, \tau, j, Limit))$
                    $Limit := n \oplus j \frac{N_g}{(k_g)^\tau}$
                fi
            od
        od
    else
        $C :=$ best approximate successor from back list
        send$(n : n' : \textsc{BadPointer}(\textsc{Bcast}(x, g, l, i, L)), C)$
    fi

$[]$

$R_3 ::$ **receive**$(n : n' : \textsc{BadPointer}(\textsc{Bcast}(x, g, l, i, L)), C)$

    Let RT_g be the routing table of n for g
    Adjust RT_g with C
    send$(n : C : \textsc{Bcast}(x, g, l, i, L))$

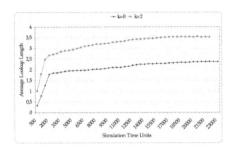

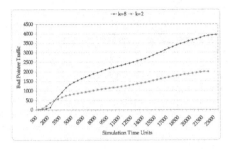

Fig. 2. Average Lookup Length

Fig. 3. Number of BADPOINTER messages

The results from all the experiments showed that the multicast messages were received by every node in the group. Furthermore, no redundant messages were sent in any of these experiments.

Figures 2 and 3 compare two multicast groups, $\mathcal{DKS}(N = 8^3, k = 8, f = 5)$ and $\mathcal{DKS}(N = 2^9, k = 2, f = 5)$. Each group is initiated with 100 joining members, and thereafter 900 broadcasts are interleaved with 100 additional joins over time.

Figure 2 shows that the $\mathcal{DKS}(N, k, f)$ system can be instantiated with a larger value for k to obtain a lower average lookup length. However, as Figure 3 shows, this will come at the cost of higher number of BADPOINTER messages.

5   Concluding Remarks and Future Work

We shown how multicast is achieved in $\mathcal{DKS}(N, k, f)$ overlay networks. The main idea lies on the fact that for each new group, a specific instance of $\mathcal{DKS}(N, k, f)$ is created and maintained exactly as for the underlying overlay network. Very large groups can be created at the cost of large amount of data for multicast group. Interestingly, each group is created with specific characteristics, such that smaller and bigger groups can co-exist. For example, powerful nodes can be in many or larger groups while less powerful node restrict themselves to smaller groups.

With a given group, each multicast message is transmitted in an optimal way under normal operation, i.e. there is no redundant message. Because of the dynamism (join, leave and failure), members of a group can have outdated routing information relatively to groups, the proposed "correcting broadcast" fixes outdated routing information on-the-fly, thus avoiding unnecessary bandwidth consumption. The proposed multicast scheme has been validated by simulations. We performed preliminary experiments that confirmed our expectations: no redundant messages are sent, and any multicast message sent to a group is received by every member. The simulations showed that the correcting broadcast effectively updates incorrect routing information. Moreover, each group can be tuned to adjust the trade-off between the efficiency and the cost of multicasting.

Acknowledgments. We would like to thank Mr. Thomas Sjöland for correcting some typos in the preliminary version of this paper.

References

1. Luc Onana Alima, Sameh El-Ansary, Per Brand, and Seif Haridi. DKS(N, k, f): A Family of Low Communication, Scalable and Fault-Tolerant Infrastructures for P2P Applications. In *3rd International Symposium on Cluster Computing and the Grid - CCGRID2003*, Tokyo, Japan, May 2003.
2. S. Banerjee, B. Bhattacharjee, and C. Kommareddy. Scalable application layer multicast. Technical Report UMIACS-TR 2002-53 and CS-TR 4373, 2002.
3. M. Castro, P. Druschel, A-M. Kermarrec, and A. Rowstron. SCRIBE: A large-scale and decentralised application-level multicast infrastructure. *IEEE Journal on Selected Areas in Communications (JSAC) (Special issue on Network Support for Multicast Communications*, 2002.
4. A. Ghodsi, L. O. Alima, S. El-Ansary, P. Brand, and S. Haridi. Self-Correcting Broadcast in Distributed Hash Tables. In *15th IASTED International Conference, Parallel and Distributed Computing and Systems*, Marina del Rey, CA, USA, November 2003.
5. Mozart Consortium. http://www.mozart-oz.org, 2003.
6. Sylvia Ratnasamy, Paul Francis, Mark Handley, Richard Karp, and Scott Shenker. A Scalable Content Addressable Network. Technical Report TR-00-010, Berkeley, CA, 2000.
7. Sylvia Ratnasamy, Mark Handley, Richard Karp, and Scott Shenker. Application-level Multicast using Content-Addressable Networks. In *Third International Workshop on Networked Group Communication (NGC '01)*, 2001.
8. Antony Rowstron and Peter Druschel. Pastry: Scalable, Decentralized Object Location, and Routing for Large-Scale Peer-to-Peer Systems. *Lecture Notes in Computer Science*, 2218, 2001. citeseer.nj.nec.com/rowstron01pastry.html.
9. I. Stoica, R. Morris, D. Karger, M. Kaashoek, and H. Balakrishnan. Chord: A Scalable Peer-to-Peer Lookup Service for Internet Applications. In *ACM SIGCOMM 2001*, pages 149–160, San Deigo, CA, August 2001.

Real-Time Framework for Distributed Embedded Systems

Khaled Chaaban, Paul Crubillé, and Mohamed Shawky

HEUDIASYC laboratory, UMR CNRS 6599
University of Technology of Compiegne
BP 20529, 60205 Compiegne Cedex, France
{chaaban, crubille, shawky}@hds.utc.fr

Abstract. This paper presents a software framework called SCOOT-R[1] that was developed in our laboratory to design and implement real-time distributed applications. This architecture allows the exchange of objects between processes running on interconnected computers. It is based on client/server model with real-time extensions. The paper describes the possibilities of our approach to allow the integration of independently designed modules in a coherent real-time system. Finally, we present a typical automotive application involving our system: real-time accurate vehicle positioning on a digital map.

1 Introduction

Real-time systems differ from other software systems by a stricter criterion of correctness of their applications. The correctness of a real-time application not only depends on the delivered result but also on the time when it is produced [1]. Examples include highly complex systems such as flight controllers, automotive applications and industrial automation systems, etc.

The increased complexity of embedded real-time systems leads to increasing demands with respect to engineering requirements: high-level design, early error detection, reusability, integration, verification and maintenance. The embedded computing hardware resources in real-time systems must usually meet stringent specifications for safety, reliability, limited hardware capacity, etc.

The context of our research works depicted in this paper is the automotive field. In fact, the embedded applications in a vehicle are complex. Components are supplied by various industrial sub-contractors. Some applications are critical for the security of people. Furthermore, a vehicle can contain several tens of processors and a complex interconnection structure[2].

---

[1] SCOOT-R stands for Server Client Object Oriented for the Real-Time. This Work was supported in part by the European Project ROADSENSE (ROad Awareness for Driving via a Strategy that Evaluates Numerous Systems; http://www.eu-projects.com/roadsense/).

[2] Recent Renault Laguna: 20 processors, BMW Series 7: up to 60 processors.

M. Papatriantafilou and P. Hunel (Eds.): OPODIS 2003, LNCS 3144, pp. 96–107, 2004.

The objective of this paper is to present our software framework SCOOT-R, its main features and services to design and implement distributed real-time applications. SCOOT-R is the acronym for "Server and Client Object Oriented for the Real-Time".

The rest of this paper is organized as follows: Section 2 describes the requirements that led to the development of this system. Section 3 describes the features of SCOOT-R that make it a good framework for prototyping multi-sensor automotive applications. Section 4 presents the main services provided by the system. A typical application involving our solution is given in Section 5: real-time accurate vehicle positioning on a digital map.

2   SCOOT-R Architecture

Our solution presents a framework for software development; resting on a set of basic services built as a middleware layer above a real-time kernel. SCOOT-R offers a framework for distributing tasks on multi-processing unit architecture, along with communication and synchronization services.

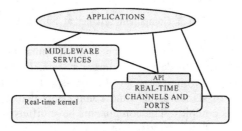

Fig. 1. Overview of SCOOT-R environment

The architecture includes also additional support to verify real-time constraints and to implement fault-tolerant strategies.

The whole system is conceived so that it is possible to prove, before launching, that all deadlines of applications will be respected including in the worst case of load and of tolerated faults. All these features have been implemented in our prototype.

2.1   Component Oriented Architecture

It is now recognized that object-oriented techniques are well suited to the design and implementation of distributed real-time applications [8]. Objects may be used to encapsulate a great variety of hardware devices used in such applications and to make abstraction of the low-level interfaces details.

The modular architecture concept has been widely used in SCOOT-R: nearly each element of the system, including the core, is a module (or a set of modules). At the programming level, it means that nearly all the classes inherit from the same common class.

The integration of intelligent sensors in a distributed system encourages the request-based model. Moreover, the use of a client/server model facilitates the object modeling of the system. Each client and server of the system is modeled by an object. One can easily make his own custom modules in C/C++, and SCOOT-R provides the interface to the other modules (sensors, display systems, etc).

A real-time system will be constituted by interconnected hardware components (Fig. 2). Each of these hardware components supporting one or several software components, each one corresponds to an application implemented by a set of servers, of clients and possibly of other tasks.

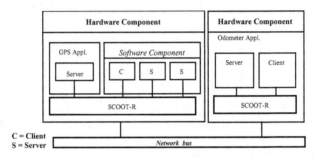

Fig. 2. Component oriented architecture

In classic engineering fields, a component is a self-contained subsystem that can be used as a building block in the design of a larger system. The component provides the specified service to its environment across the well-specified component interfaces.

The development of standard real-time components that can be run on different hardware platforms is complex. The components have different timing characteristics on different platforms. Thus a component must be adapted and re-verified for each HW-platform to which it is ported, especially in safety-critical systems. Hence, we need to perform a timing analysis for each platform to which the system is ported.

The basic requirements when designing real-time components for efficient reuse are to create components that are memory efficient, fulfill the requirement on the worst case execution time, and are easy to use and reuse.

In SCOOT-R, servers and clients are implemented as descendants of generic classes of the SCOOT-R API while writing a minimum of code and while expressing the temporal terms to which clients and servers subscribe. A component in our system can contain several clients and/or servers SCOOT-R that cooperate between them to provide the results expected by the component interfaces. Using SCOOT-R API, the clients and servers stubs are written as very classical and human readable C++ classes.

2.2 Client/Server Model

The integration of intelligent sensors in our applications has led us to consider the communications between components on a transactional basis. The sensor delivers its data not only when it is solicited but also when it's processing is achieved. So, the communication is best implemented on a request based client/server model. This approach allows sensor dependent and independent code to be implemented by independent programmers teams.

SCOOT-R communication layers cover from network to presentation layers and lies on the physical layer of the used network (IEEE-1394). The presentation layer encapsulates the full set of communication features in an object oriented API.

2.3 Distributed and Real-Time Approaches

SCOOT-R clients and servers exchange data while respecting a real-time contract, which is specified as a set of standardized constraints. Table 1 illustrates these temporal contracts and the results in case of non-respect of the rules.

Table 1. Real-time contracts

Constraint attribute	Client side comments	Server side comments
Response time in worst case.	This time includes the response time and the communication time in the worst case. If it expires, the transaction fails with "timeout" error. The server is considered defective and may be replaced by a redundant server.	Response time of the server in worst case. The non-respect of this time indicates a software misconception rather than hardware or network error.
Recovery time on simple error	This clause is an engagement of the server and a request of the client.	Maximum time of registering of the server in the case of deactivation of the server or some incidents such as a reset on the FireWire bus.
Min_Period	Maximum rate of request to be respected by the client. It must be compatible with the server constraint.	Maximum rate of requests for each client. This value multiplied with *Max_clients* limits the processor resources needed by the server.
Max_clients	N/A	Maximum number of clients supported by the server.

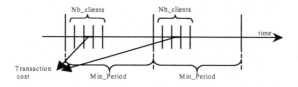

Fig. 3. Transactions chronogramme.

As each transaction consumes some CPU time, the total server activity is calculated using "Min_Period" and "Max_clients". The load distribution on the processing units is thus validated (Fig. 3).

The SCOOT-R extension for the client/server model consist of these temporal clauses. This extension is decisive to achieve the SCOOT-R goals.

2.4 Dynamic Reconfiguration and Redundancy Management

Fault-tolerance may be implemented by different ways [3]. We decided to use partial replication of the critical system modules. We consider either software or hardware replication or both.

In fact, we focused on the server redundancy. In Fig. 4, a replication of a GPS server is illustrated. A specific algorithm will permit the activation of the better server registered in the services database replicated in each node of the network (§ 3.2).

For the application to be fault tolerant, the restoration time of the service should be compatible with the temporal constraints announced by the application.

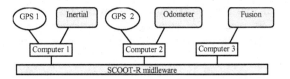

Fig. 4. Redundancy approach.

Another aspect of redundancy is the selection of the best component providing a given information. Let's consider an accurate positioning system of a vehicle functioning by fusion of inertial and GPS data. Another server yields position using GPS and Odometer data. A quality indicator is associated with each server.

This quality may depend on the vehicle physical environment (adherence, speed...). Each fusion module evaluates its quality. When the positioning data is needed, SCOOT-R provides the value having the best quality indicator. Let's assume that "GPS-inertial fusion" module will be providing the best value. In case of "Inertial" module failure, the quality indicator of the "GPS-inertial fusion" module decreases significantly. Hence, SCOOT-R selects dynamically the "GPS-odometer fusion" module.

3   SCOOT-R Services Operation

SCOOT-R needs a communication media providing a deterministic access time and transmission delay in order to provide the real-time services presented hereafter.

3.1   Network Time Stamping

The provision of a system-wide global time base with sufficient accuracy is a fundamental prerequisite for the design of a distributed real-time system [7]. To get round the problem of broadcasting the global time, we used double time-reference techniques based on network and local time stamping. The IEEE-1394 bus offers a service of high rate synchronization (8 KHz) that permits to obtain a global time between two bus reconfigurations (node added or removed).

The application should manage the transition between these independent global times (before and after reconfiguration) using the local time of the local node.

3.2   Servers Registration and Access to Services by Clients

In SCOOT-R API, upon setting up a server, a server object is created. As soon as the server quality indicator becomes non-zero, the server launches a procedure to introduce itself to all the nodes on the bus (registration procedure). If the service role (same service name) is already taken by another server, it will wait until the quality of the current server becomes less than its own quality to win the arbitration. So, the server that has the best quality will provide the service.

This registration procedure needs a safe broadcast protocol and a decision algorithm to elect the winner among the registration submissions for a given service.

This broadcast protocol should guaranty that all nodes will receive all the emitted messages through a custom acknowledge mechanism. The decision algorithm selects the most recent request based on the common network time stamping.

In case of adding a new node on the bus, it should be informed of all the previously registered services of the other nodes. For FireWire bus [4] or for MOST bus [5], a global reconfiguration is made whose over-cost is lumped and may be bounded. The same procedure is used for the node suppression or other major network incidents.

At the client side, a transaction is performed by sending a request message and getting back a reply message within the specified time. If this specified delay has expired, the server will be overwhelmed. Its quality is lowered for a period of purgatory during which it will lose all arbitrations. So the nuisance capacity of a failed server is limited.

In order to explain the philosophy of our client/server model, the Fig. 5 illustrates two statecharts of a normal behavior of our system.

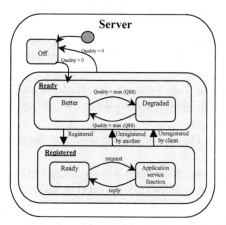
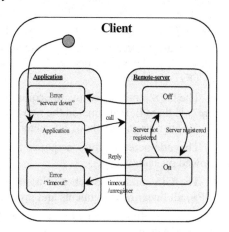

QSS = set of qualities of all servers in the whole network.

Fig. 5. Statechart of a SCOOT-R server and client

At the server side, one server leaves state "off" and can be registered as soon as its quality becomes greater than zero. It will be registered if it has the highest quality of all others servers of the network for the same service.

The "remote_server" object (client side network interface) has two steady states: the state "on" and the state "off". The application starts the transaction by invoking of the *call()* method of the "remote_server" object.

Every node maintains a table of services containing their description, including the node address, the port associated to the server, the size of data, names of data types and parameters of the temporal contract. All the services are identified by their names. This table is updated by the servers registration algorithm and is reset at each global reconfiguration.

In order to provide a distributed real-time communication service, SCOOT-R communication stack integrate both the synchronization and client/server communication management services.

4 Automotive Application Using SCOOT-R

Our lab is involved in the European project ROADSENSE whose goal is to provide a framework for establishing robust Human Machine Interface requirements that will drive technology change.

Part of our contribution is the design of a distributed real-time architecture (Driver Behavior Interface Test Equipment). For this purpose, we use SCOOT-R as a development framework for distribution and communication techniques.

4.1 Application Context

This modular application (Fig. 6a) is a small sub-set of the ROADSENSE application. It permits the accurate positioning in real-time of a car on a digital cartography GIS (Geographical Information System) [10].

In our application, GPS, Odometer sensors are necessary for the vehicle localization. These sensors and other tasks like the fusion and GIS are encapsulated in SCOOT-R modules.

The GPS module permits to acquire GPS data frames through the serial bus and to provide them in real-time on the network as a SCOOT-R server. We use a differential GPS with a precision about 4-5 meters at 1 Hz.

The odometer module acquires through a PC-card the speed and the distance flowed by each wheel.

The GIS module searches in a circle of radius R and center C (measured by the GPS) all linear road segments and provides them in SCOOT-R format (Fig. 6b).

The first fusion module combines GPS and Odometer data. So the accurate position is kept between the GPS 1 Hz messages and during the GPS masking that can still for several seconds. In order to improve the precision, the vehicle position is projected on the GIS map by the second fusion module. Furthermore, using the accurate position, the GIS module sends pertinent information to the display module.

The commutation from fusion1 to fusion2 module is done in a bounded time without disturbing the clients invocations on fusion1 module. So, when the fusion2 module is ready to operate, the client access it and continue its transactions.

On the other hand, when the fusion1 server doesn't respond at time to the client requests, it will be considered as defective and the client transaction will fail. The server will be replaced by the server of fusion2 module. The client should wait until this replacement process has been completed before initiating another transaction.

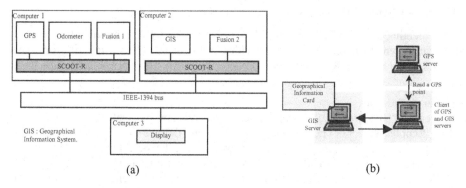

Fig. 6. (a) General architecture of the accurate positioning, (b) Communications client/server, GPS – GIS

4.2 Real-Time Application Constraints

In this sub-section, we explain the real-time requirements of the application that led to use SCOOT-R. The precision of the positioning resides on the data quality, on the dating precision and on the communications and processing delays.

Furthermore, we need that the global imprecision degradation to be less than one meter (GPS imprecision + 1 meter). Let's consider a vehicle with a nominal speed of 30 m/s; note that one-meter corresponds to 3/100 seconds at this speed. This precision should be preserved between the GPS messages and during GPS masking.

Using the SCOOT-R time-stamping mechanism for a distributed environment, the degradation does not exceed 10 μs.

The access by the fusion modules to the odometer data and for the "fusion2" module to the data produced by the "fusion1" module should be done in a strictly bounded delay for the application to operate properly. More critical even is the access to the «display» server, as unexpected delay can't be taken into account by a predictive algorithm. If each of these data communication is less than 1/100 second, our application delivers correct results (if the other aspects of it's design are correct).

In Fig. 7, a uniform speed is represented by the oblique dashed line (45°). GPS data are acquired at 1 Hz while the odometer data are acquired at 100 Hz. We present at the Y-axis the imprecision intervals. Between the GPS acquisition time (t_{gps}) and the odometer acquisition time (t_{tod}), we have the real value of the vehicle position. After t_{od}, we do not have a real measure of the position, and the vehicle model changes dynamically (region between upward and downward curved dashed lines).

The dynamic model of the vehicle uses odometer data to compute its position at instant t_{od} . We add the imprecision of the GPS data acquisition time to the imprecision of the GPS module (≈ 5 meters). Imprecision of odometer data and of data acquisition time degrade the results quality. These computations are achieved and displayed slightly later; so predictive model is used to provide results at the display time rather than at the acquisition time.

4.3 GPS Client and Server Using SCOOT-R

Implementing a SCOOT-R client/server service is done by defining new C++ classes for exchanged data, server and client sides stubs. These classes inherit from base classes of the SCOOT-R library.

Server definition
To create a "GPS" server, a descendant class "server_gps" is created from the generic class "scooter_server". The method *get_buffer_in()* defines the object type received from the client and *get_buffer_out()* defines the object type returned by the server. The "accept" method is called at every transaction initiated by any client of the "GPS" service. In this example it consists in providing to the client, the information on the actual position and speed of the vehicle.

The server definition also includes needed functions to supply the constraints listed in table 1. For the "gps_server" implementation, "worst_case" will be set to 20 ms, "max_at_once_clients" to 10, "min_period" to 100 ms and "max_recover" to 200 m

Server invocation
At the application level, an instance of the previously defined server class is created, then one has to manage properly the quality of the server using the *set_quality()* method.
In order to use the server defined previously, a new class is defined by inheritance from the basic client class.

For the "gps_client" side, "worst_case" will be set to 50 ms, "min_period"" to 100 ms and "max_recover" to 200 ms.

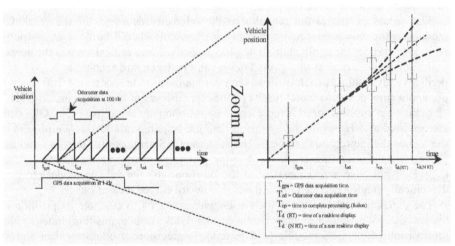

Fig. 7. Position imprecision and computation delays

Client application accessing the server
Once a local object is created as an instance of the previous "remote_server_gps" class, the "fusion" or "GIS" applications use the *call()* method from this object to get

back the GPS data from the "gps" server. In the case of GPS masking, the quality of the "gps" server becomes zero and the "SERVER_DOWN" error will occurred.

4.4   Worst Case Time Analysis for the Distributed Application

For each computer, a local RMA (Rate Monotonic Analysis) [11] is performed to determine the worst-case behavior for each activity. We take into consideration the maximum number of clients for each server. So, each computer is validated as a hardware component. In table 2, we present only the results for computer 1.

Table 2. RMA for computer 1

	Worst delay	*CPU time per activity*
ISR (Interrupt Service Routine) for timer, IEEE-1394, serial line and high priority task	0	500 µs at 100 Hz
Odometer server	500 µs	100 µs+50 µs(per transaction) * 8 clients = 500 µs
Fusion 1 computation & server	1 ms	1ms + 50 µs* (8 clients) = 1,4 ms
SCOOT-R overhead	2,4 ms	200 µs
GPS server	2.6 ms	60 µs * 8 clients < 500 µs

Knowing the list of clients and servers and the size of messages sent on the network, we can compute the worst time for each node to send a message.

Table 3. Clients and servers per computer

Computer name	Clients	Servers
Computer 1	GIS, Display	GPS, Odometer, Fusion 1
Computer 2	GPS, Odometer, Display,Fusion1	GIS, Fusion 2
Computer 3 (display)	No clients	Display

In order to simplify the computation, we estimate that:

$$MAT \leq nb\_nodes*MET \qquad (1)$$

Where MAT = Media Access Time, and MET = Maximum Emission Time.
In our example, we have four calculators in the network. So, from the previous:

$$MAT \leq 4*MET \qquad (2)$$

Where, $MET = 10µs+Max\_Length/speed$
− Max_Length = Maximum size of messages in bytes.
− $Speed$ = Transmission speed on the IEEE-1394 bus in Mb/s.
In case of messages with maximum size of 8000 bytes and a bus speed of 400 Mb/s, we obtain:
$MET = 30$ µs, $MAT = 120$ µs.
Let's note that the 10µs in the last formula corresponds to the arbitration period on the IEEE-1394 bus.

Table 4. Computation and network delays

	Number of Modules	Clients	Data size per message	Server response time (load)	Transaction time
Computer 1	*6*	*GIS*	1 Kbytes	2 seconds	(6 + 7) *MAT
		Display			(6 + 3) *MAT
Computer 2	*7*	*GPS*	2000 bytes	30 ms	(7 + 6) *MAT
		Odometer			(7 + 6) *MAT
		Display			(7 + 3) *MAT
Computer 3	3	*Display*			

Moreover, the arbitration mechanism on the IEEE-1394 bus is guaranteed by a fairness interval for asynchronous transactions. The fairness interval ensures that each node wishing to initiate a transaction gets fair access to the bus [4]. Table 4 recapitulates these metrics.

5 Conclusion

This paper has given a presentation of the architecture and current status of the SCOOT-R project, aiming at building a distributed run-time support for applications with hard real-time and fault-tolerance constraints. Our solution rests on a set of basic services built as a middleware layer above a real-time kernel. Essential protocols for the fault-tolerance, like synchronization of clocks, replication and reliable diffusion are implemented. Special attention was given to the communication subsystem since it is a common resource to middleware services developed.

Our existing vehicle positioning application benefit from the SCOOT-R middleware. The application requires bounded end-to-end communication delays guaranteed by our communication subsystem, as well as fault-tolerant replication.

The temporal specifications of components consist of specify some deadlines values. Static and dynamic verifications permit to assure the deadlock and the respect of the temporal constraints of the system.

The redundancy management in the system doesn't require specific efforts of design and development to dynamically replace a server or to activate a redundant function. This enables an evolution of the services without interruption.

References

[1]   A. Burns, S. Poledna and P. Barrett. "Replica determinism and flexible scheduling in hard real-time dependable systems". IEEE transactions on Computers, No. 2, Vol. 49, 2000.

[2]   M. Stûmpfle, F. Hermes, V. Friesen, F. Muller, X. Chen, S. Bachhofer, D. Jiang, K. Ly, C. Gauger, and P. Stiess. "COSIMA- A Component System Information and Management Architecture". IEEE Intelligent Vehicles symposium 2000, USA Oct 3-5, 2000.

[3] P. Chevochot, I. Puaut. "Scheduling Fault-Tolerant Distributed Hard Real-Time Tasks Independently of the Replication Strategies". Proc. of the 6th International Conference on Real-Time Computing Systems and Applications, Hong-Kong, China, December 1999.

[4] D. Anderson. FireWire System Architecture IEEE-1394, MinDShare, Inc, 1998.

[5] Most Group. "Digitization opens the way for new standard". Automobilentwicklung. March 2000 (http://www.mostcooperation.com).

[6] T. Abdelzaher, M. Bjorklund, S. Awson, W.-C. Feng, F. Jahanian, S. Johnson, P. Arron, A. Mehra, T. Mitton, A. Shaikh, K. Shin, Z. Wang, H. Zou. "ARMADA Middleware and Communication Services". IEEE Workshop on Middleware for Distributed Real-Time Systems and Services, San Francisco, California, December 1997.

[7] H. Kopetz & al. "A synchronization Strategy for a Time-Triggered Multicluster Real-Time System". Proc. of the 14th IEEE Symposium on Reliable Distributed Systems, Bad Neuenahr, Germany, 13-15 September 1995.

[8] H. Koptez. "Components-Based Design of large Distributed Real-Time Systems". The 14th IFAC Workshop on Distributed Computer Control Systems, pages 171--177, Seoul, 1997

[9] Douglas C. Schmidt, Aniruddha Gokhale, Timothy H. Harrison, and Guru Parulkar. "A High-performance Endsystem architecture for Real-time CORBA". IEEE Communications Magazine, Vol-14 No. 2, Feb 1997.

[10] M. EL Najjar, P. Bonnifait, "A Road Reduction Method using Multi-Criteria Fusion", IEEE Intelligent Vehicles Symposium, Versailles, France, June 17-20 2002.

[11] L. Sha & al. "Generalized Rate-Monotonic Scheduling Theory: A framework for Developing Real-Time systems". Proceedings of the IEEE, Vol. 82, No. 1, pp 68-82, 1990.

[12] K. Yaghmour. "The Real-Time Application Interface", Proceedings of the Linux Symposium, July 2001.

[13] Real-time CORBA, Object Management Group. Joint revised submission OMG document orbos/99-02-12 Ed, March 1999.

[14] F. Nashashibi. "RTm@ps: a framework for prototyping automatic multi-sensor applications". IEEE Intelligent Vehicles Symposium, Oct 3-5, 2000.

[15] B. Steux, PhD thesis: RTMAPS, un environnement logiciel dédié à la conception d'applications embarquées temps-réel. Utilisation pour la détection automatique de véhicules par fusion radar/Vision. Ecole des mines de Paris, France, December 2001.

[16] M. Shawky, S. Favard, P. Crubillé, "A computing Platform and its tools for feature extraction from on-vehicle image sequences", 3rd IEEE Annual conference on Intelligent Transportation Systems, 1-3 Octobre 2000, Dearborn, Michigan, USA.

[17] M. Shawky, P. Crubille and P. Bonnifait , "Archiving and Indexing of Large Volume Sensor Data of an Equipped Vehicle", DRIIVE'99, July 1999, Helsinki, Finlande.

[18] K. Chaaban, P. Crubille and M. Shawky, "SCOOT-R: A framework for distributed real-time applications", Work In Progress for the 24h IEEE Real-Time Systems Symposium, December 2003, Cancun, Mexico.

Self-Organization Approach of Communities for P2P Networks

Kazuhiro Kojima

AIST, 1-2-1 Namiki, Tsukuba, Ibaraki, Japan
k.kojima@aist.go.jp

Abstract. Locating contents is an essential function, but it presents a
very difficult and challenging problem for large-scale Peer-to-Peer (P2P)
systems. Many P2P systems, protocols, architectures, and search strategies are proposed for this problem. In this paper, we focus on the self-
organization of a community structure based on user preferences for P2P
systems. We propose these methods to improve P2P search performance:
1) Extended Pong, 2) Pong Proxy, 3) QRP with Firework 4) Backward
Learning, and 5) Community Self-Organization Algorithm. We evaluate
the performance of the self-organized community network through simulations. These results show that the self-organized community network
maintains a high query hit rate without overflow.

1 Introduction

Peer-to-Peer (P2P) protocols and applications such as Gnutella[1] and Freenet[2]
extend the power of Internet users. The current major P2P application is sharing
of multimedia content. In the future, P2P systems will be applied to distributed
search engines, knowledge management, and myriad Internet applications. However, P2P systems present many problems, one of which is Locating Contents

In Gnutella protocol v0.4, a flooding algorithm is used to locate contents as
shown in Fig. 1(a). Peer A sends a Query tagged with a maximum Time-To-
Live (TTL) to its all neighbors on the overlay network. Each peer forwards the
Query to its neighbors. When the Query string partially or exactly matches a file
name stored locally, the peer replies with the QueryHit. Though this algorithm
is very simple and robust even when peers are joining or leaving the system,
it lacks scalability. A system comprising a large number of peers is inundated
with Queries even if peers do not forward Queries that they have forwarded
previously.

This paper proposes an approach to locating contents, a self-organization of
communities based on the user's preferences. It is very natural to introduce a
structure of community into P2P systems. Communities in the real world and
cyberspace are formed by people who have similar preferences. For example, they
form mailing lists, chat rooms, and Bulletin Board Systems (BBSs). Information
required by members is propagated efficiently into the community, so that it is
expected that the query hit performance improves without overflow. In Fig. 1,

M. Papatriantafilou and P. Hunel (Eds.): OPODIS 2003, LNCS 3144, pp. 108–119, 2004.

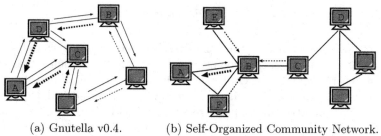

(a) Gnutella v0.4.   (b) Self-Organized Community Network.

Fig. 1. Network topologies of Gnutella and the Self-Organized Community Network. In these figures, Peers A and B, and Peers C and D have identical preferences. Solid arrows represent message $X \in \{Ping, Query\}$ and broken arrows represent reply message $Y \in \{Pong, QueryHit\}$. The thickness of the broken arrows represents the number of reply Pong messages for a Ping.

(a) Gnutella Header.

Descriptor ID	Payload Descriptor	TTL	Hop	Payload Length
0 15	16 17	18	19	22

(b) Pong.

port	IP Address	Number of Files Shared	Number of Kilobytes Shared
0 1	2 5	6 10	11 13

(c) Extended Pong.

port	IP Address	PeerDigest
0 1	2 5	6 32005

Fig. 2. Structure of message: (a), (b), and (c) are the Gnutella header, Pong, and proposed extended Pong, respectively. (a) In Ping, the Payload Length is 0. That is, Ping comprises only a header. (c) The proposed extended Pong includes a PeerDigest.

an example of the Gnutella network and the self-organized community P2P systems are shown, respectively. It is assumed that Peers A and B have the same preferences; similarly, Peers C and D do also. In the Gnutella network, if Peer A sends a Query to the Gnutella network, Peers C and D must receive and forward the Query as shown in Fig. 1(a). Hence, Peers C and D are troubled with that trivial Query message. In self-organized community P2P systems, Peer A sends a Query to Peer B directly because it has the same preferences, as shown in Fig. 1(b), thereby decreasing the load on Peers C and D.

The remainder of this paper proceeds as follows: Section 2 presents a Community Self-Organization Algorithm based on users' preferences; Section 3 shows through simulations that a self-organized community network maintains a high query hit rate without overflow; Section 4 addresses related work; and Section 5 concludes the discussion and proposes future work.

2   Improvement of P2P Protocols

There are evident communities in some conventional client-server web applications such as mailing lists, chat rooms, and BBSs. These communities are maintained by centralized servers. On the other hand, decentralized and distributed P2P systems have no such servers. In a social network, a so-called acquaintance network[3], communities are frequently self-organized by local interactions. This study implements local interactions to a decentralized P2P system using 1) Ping-Pong and 2) Bloom filters.[4] Next, we briefly explain these key technologies.

2.1   Key Technologies

Ping-Pong. In Gnutella protocol v0.4, a peer uses Ping to probe the network actively for other peers. Gnutella protocol messages comprise a header and payload. A Ping has only a header portion, as shown in Fig. 2(a). A peer receiving a Ping forwards it to its neighbors and responds with a Pong, which contains its own IP address and the Port number and the amount of data it is sharing on the Gnutella network. The payload part of a Pong message is shown in Fig. 2(b). The number of Pings increases exponentially through replication and forwarding, thereby flooding the network with Ping-Pongs.

Bloom Filter and QRP. A Bloom filter[4] is a quick and space-efficient data structure for representing a set of N elements to support membership queries. An array of M bits and K independent hash functions is used for a Bloom filter. A Bloom filter may generate false positives. According to the analysis in [5], the false positive rate is given as

$$f = \left(1 - e^{-\frac{K}{r}}\right)^{K},\tag{1}$$

where r represents the number of bits per element, M/N. Some exemplary values of false positive rates are

$$M/N = 6 \quad K = 4 \; f = 0.0561 \qquad M/N = 8 \quad K = 6 \quad f = 0.0215$$
$$M/N = 12 \; K = 8 \; f = 0.00314 \quad M/N = 16 \; K = 11 \; f = 0.000458$$

We can choose a reasonable value of M/N and K by considering the expected false positive rate.

Rohrs proposed a Query Routing Protocol (QRP)[6] for Gnutella networks. In QRP, keywords are hashed and embedded in a Bloom filter. The Bloom filter of each peer is sent and forwarded to its neighbors so that the Bloom filter is propagated throughout the network. Queries are routed according to the QRP without a flooding algorithm.

2.2   Improvements

The above subsection briefly explained Ping-Pong, Bloom filters, and QRP. We extend these important elements to improve the P2P system performance.

Extended Pong. We extend a Pong message so that we can use Bloom filters to self-organize communities. The Extended Pong (ExPong) includes a Bloom filter as shown in Fig. 2(c). In web cache systems[7], a Bloom filter is called a Summary Cache[8] or Cache Digest[9]. In this paper, a Bloom filter of the ExPong is called a PeerDigest. The PeerDigest of Peer i is represented as $digest_i$.

We restrict the shared contents within such document files having extensions as .html, .ps, and .pdf. Shared .pdf or .ps files are transformed into text files by pdftotext or ps2text. Keywords are extracted from these text files using text mining techniques.[10] Moreover, users can choose additional keywords independently. It is considered that $digest_i$ shows the preference of the Peer i because these keywords are embedded into the PeerDigest.

PeerDigest Cache and Pong Proxy. In Gnutella protocol v0.6[1], a hierarchical structure is defined as Ultra Peer and Leaf Peer. The Gnutella backbone is dominated by connections of Ultra Peers because Leaf Peer connects only to Ultra Peers. Ultra Peer serves as a proxy or server like Clip2 Reflector or Napster, thereby reducing redundant Pings and Queries.

In this paper, we propose a Pong Proxy instead of a hierarchical structure to reduce Ping-Pongs. Each peer has two PeerDigest Caches $cache_l (l = 1, 2)$. Pairs $(address_j, digest_j)$ are cached into the $cache_l$, where $address_j$ is $ip_j{:}port_j$ of Peer j. The first and second neighbors of Peer i are represented as $nbr_{i,l}(l = 1, 2)$. The index l of $cache_l$ and $nbr_{i,l}$ indicates the degree of neighbors. If Peer j receives a Ping from Peer i, Peer j responds with an ExPong including $digest_j$. Moreover, Peer j responds with ExPongs including $digest_k (k \in nbr_{j,1})$. Peer i caches $digest_j$ and $digest_k$s into $cache_{i,1}$ and $cache_{i,2}$, respectively. In this manner, Peer j plays the role of Pong Proxy.

If each peer sends Pings to all first neighbor peers, as in Gnutella v0.4, the network load will increase as a result of the ExPongs because the ExPong size is usually very large. We also improve the Ping-ExPong protocol in the following respect. Each peer sends Pings to $MaxCon$ peers that are selected randomly from $cache_1$. The peer responds with $MaxCon$ ExPongs that are selected randomly from $cache_1$. Hence, the upper bound for the total size of ExPongs that a peer will receive is given as

$$upper\ bound = MaxCon \times (1 + MaxCon)$$
$$\times Size_{\text{ExPong}}. \tag{2}$$

It is fair to add that the Gnutella peer also sends and forwards Pings to $MaxCon$ peers in simulations of Section 3.

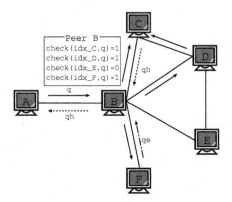

Fig. 3. QRP with Firework and Backward Learning. Peer A sends the Query to Peer B. Query routing is decided by $check(digest_j, q)(j \in nbr_{B,1})$ at Peer B. q, qh, and qe show the Query, QueryHit, and QueryError, respectively.

QRP with Firework. According to the Pong Proxy, each peer has information about the contents shared by its neighbors. We use the PeerDigests for query routing.

In Fig. 3, Peer A sends a Query: q, including search keywords, to Peer B. If Peer B has no content for the Query, Peer B must forward the Query. Routing of the Query is implemented as follows: Peer B checks whether keywords of q are in $digest_j(j \in nbr_{B,1})$ or not. It is given as

$$check(digest_j, q) = \{true, false\}. \tag{3}$$

If keywords exist in $digest_j(j \in nbr_{B,1})$, Peer B forwards the Query to Peer j. In Fig. 3, Peer B forwards the Query to Peers C, D, and F. If $check(digest_j, q)$ is false for all first neighbors, the Query is forwarded to Peer $j(\in nbr_1)$, which is selected randomly. This process is equivalent to a Random Walk Search.

Backward Learning. In Fig. 3, Peer B forwards the Query to Peers C, D, and F. If Peer F has no content for the Query and is in Dead Lock, Peer F returns QueryError: qe to Peer B. According to the QueryError, Peer B modifies $digest_F$ as

$$digest_F^{(m)} = 0, \ m = h_k(q) \ (k = 1, \cdots, K),$$

where $digest^{(m)}$ is the m-th bit of $digest$ and h is a hash function. On the other hand, if Peer C has content sought by the Query, Peer C replies to Peer B with QueryHit: qh. The QueryHit: qh is backwarded to the Peer A by way of Peer B. According to the QueryHit, each mediate peer and originator routed by random walk strategy modifies $digest$ as

$$digest_j^{(m)} = 1, \ m = h_k(q) \ (k = 1, \cdots, K),$$

where $j(\in nbr_{i,1})$ shows the next or last mediate peer.

procedure _Self-Organization (Peer i)

    calculate sim_{ij} for all Peers $j \in nbr_{i,2}$
    $nbr_{i,2} = sort \; nbr_{i,2}$ according to sim_{ij}
    Peer j =top of $nbr_{i,2}$
    connect to Peer j
    add Peer j to $nbr_{i,1}$ and $cache_{i,1}$
    remove Peer j from $nbr_{i,2}$ and $cache_{i,2}$

    if($Con_i > MaxCon_i$)
        Peer k = *select* from $nbr_{i,1}$ at random
        disconnect Peer k
        remove Peer k from $nbr_{i,1}$ and $cache_{i,1}$

Fig. 4. Pseudo code of the proposed Community Self-Organization Algorithm. In the following simulations of Section 3, $MaxCon = 4$.

2.3   Community Self-Organization Algorithm

This subsection presents the Community Self-Organization Algorithm (CSOA). The above section mentioned that the PeerDigest shows the respective preferences of peers. Therefore, we can use PeerDigest to self-organize communities based on respective users' preferences.

We must define the similarity of the preference between Peer i and Peer j, sim_{ij}. That similarity is defined as

$$sim_{ij} \equiv count(digest_i \wedge digest_j), \tag{4}$$

where $\wedge$ is an AND operator and $count(\cdot)$ is a function that counts bits with 1.

Self-organization is implemented as follows. Firstly, Peer i calculates the similarity $sim_{i,j}$ between itself and the second neighboring Peers $j (\in nbr_{i,2})$. Secondly, Peer i selects the Peer j that has the largest value of $sim_{i,j}$. Thirdly, if the number of current connections Con_i is greater than the maximum connections $MaxCon_i$, then Peer i randomly selects Peer $k (\in nbr_{i,1})$ to disconnect. Finally, Peer i disconnects Peer k and connects to Peer j. The pseudo-code of this self-organization algorithm is shown in Fig. 4. This algorithm is very simple and requires only local information, that is, the PeerDigests of the first and second neighbor peers. Moreover, this local information is obtained by local interactions: Ping-ExPong and Pong Proxy.

3   Simulations

Simulator of complex systems such as Gnutella is not an easy task. We provided a simple setup for the following simulations.

- Initial Topology
  The initial topology of a network is given as a random network, as shown
  in Fig. 10(a). The network comprises 500 peers. Each peer has four random
  outgoing links; therefore $MaxCon_i = 4$. The number of peers is constant in
  the following simulations. We also simulated cases wherein the network is
  growing, but identical results to these were obtained.
- Community
  All peers are classified into five communities. Each peer is assigned randomly
  to one of these communities. There are no explicit community structures in
  the initial network topology as shown in Fig. 10(a).
- Contents and Keywords
  Each keyword is an integer value for simplicity.[2] The number of keywords,
  N, is 500. The keywords are divided to five classes: $KC_i(i = 0, \cdots, 4)$. Class
  KC_i comprises the inherent 100 keywords and 20 keywords which belong to
  the class $KC_{i+1}(KC_5 = KC_0)$. The content associated with each keyword
  is an integer equal to the keyword.
- PeerDigest
  The hash functions are built by first calculating the MD5 signature of the
  keyword string, which yields 128 bits, then dividing the 128 bits into four
  32-bit unsigned integer values, then finally taking the modulus of each 32-bit
  unsigned integer value by the PeerDigest size M[8]. MD5 is a cryptographic
  message digest algorithm that hashes arbitrary length strings to 128 bits. The
  bits per element M/N is set to four in the following simulations; therefore,
  the theoretical false positive rate is 0.160.
- LocalStorage
  In real P2P systems, most users have no shared local storage; they are called
  Free Riders[11]. However, in simulations, peers have the same local storage
  capacity for simplicity. We define the local storage capacity factor as

$$\alpha \equiv \frac{LSC}{NC}, \tag{5}$$

where LSC and NC are the local storage capacity and the number of contents assigned to a community, respectively. If $\alpha \geq 1$, each peer can store all
contents shared by its own community on the local storage. If $\alpha < 1$, LRU
cache replacement is used for stored content.
- Uploader and Downloader
  All local storage locations are initially empty. Contents are provided by specific peers called Upload-Only Members (UOMs). The remaining peers are
  Download-Only Members (DOMs). We assumed that the number of UOMs
  is 10% of all peers. In Fig. 10(a), UOM and DOM peers are shown as big
  and small circles, respectively.
- Message Size and Buffer
  The TTL of Ping and Query are set to $five$. We define the size of each message as shown in Table 1. According to the above assumption, $MaxCon_i = 4$,
  the upper bound eq.(2) is 0.64 M-byte. The message buffer, that is, the number of messages that Peer i can process in a single time step, is represented

Table 1. Message size.

Message Type	Message Size [byte]
Ping	22
Pong	35
ExPong	32027
Query	50
QueryHit	100
QueryError	50

as mb_i. Each peer has the same size mb. If the number of messages received is greater than the size of mb, the overflowed messages are dropped.

– Time Step

Each peer generates a Query and Ping every 10 and 1000 time steps. CSOA is applied every 1000 time steps.

3.1   Performance

We compared the performance of the proposed method with Gnutella protocol v0.4. Respective performances were evaluated by the success rate of search, network load, average HOP of the successful Query, and the average number of QueryHit. We implemented several simulations under various parameter values, that is, the local storage capacity factor α and the message buffer mb. This paper describes results of simulations under $\alpha = 1.0$ or 0.25 and $mb = 100$ or 20.

Results represent an average of 10 simulations; they are shown in Figs. 5-8. In those figures, results of Gnutella v0.4 and the proposed method are shown by the broken line with open squares and the solid line with filled squares, respectively.

The success rates converge to 1.0 for Gnutella v0.4 and the proposed method with $\alpha = 1.0$, $mb = 100$, as shown in Fig. 5(a). Moreover, the average HOP converges to 0, as shown in Fig. 7(a) because each peer has local storage of sufficient capacity to store the contents and a message buffer that is sufficient to receive the messages. However, Gnutella v0.4 induces a flood of Ping-Pongs and Queries in an early time step as shown in Fig. 6(a). The network load of Gnutella v0.4 converges to the lower value after the peak. When the size of the local storage is limited, the network load of Gnutella v0.4 converges to the higher value, as shown in Fig. 6(b). When the size of the message buffer is also limited, as many Queries are dropped out; the average number of QueryHit decreases and the success rate converges to the lower value of 0.68, as shown in Fig. 8(c) and Fig. 5(c).

The proposed method does not engender a rapid increase of the network load. Network loads of the proposed method converge to the lower value, as shown in Fig. 6. In Fig. 5, even though the size of local storage and message buffer are limited, the success rate of the proposed method converges to 1.0.

We also simulated the proposed method without the CSOA to clarify the reason why the self-organized community network retains the high success rate value: the network retains the initial topology, as shown in Fig. 10(a) and the

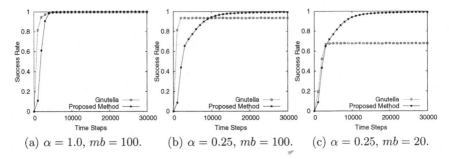

(a) $\alpha = 1.0$, $mb = 100$.   (b) $\alpha = 0.25$, $mb = 100$.   (c) $\alpha = 0.25$, $mb = 20$.

Fig. 5. Performance: success rate.

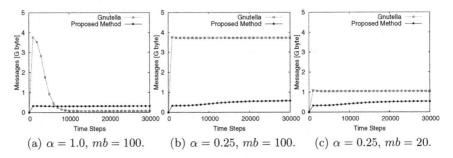

(a) $\alpha = 1.0$, $mb = 100$.   (b) $\alpha = 0.25$, $mb = 100$.   (c) $\alpha = 0.25$, $mb = 20$.

Fig. 6. Performance: network load.

routing of Queries is implemented by QRP with Firework. Results of the success rate, network load and average number of QueryHit are shown in Fig. 9. These three values of the proposed method without the CSOA are lower than the values of the original proposed method.

According to these results, we inferred the following answer to the question above. In the proposed method without the CSOA, the probability that the first neighbors have the same preference is a low value; thereby, the routing strategy is equivalent to a Random Walk Search. If $\alpha \geq 1$, the search strategy is improved gradually to QRP with Firework by backward learning based on QueryError and QueryHit. However, if $\alpha < 1$, as the contents on the local storage are replaced by the LRU replacement policy, the PeerDigest will be inconsistent with the current contents shared by the distant peers. Many Queries are dropped out according to the TTL limitation.

On the other hand, in the self-organized community network shown in Fig. 10(b), each peer has several first neighbors that have identical preferences. As QRP with Firework replicates and forwards a Query based on eq.(3), the probability that the Query is replicated is higher than in the random network. Hence, the probability of locating contents will be a high value. This effect that is induced by the community structure and replication of Query is called the Community Effect

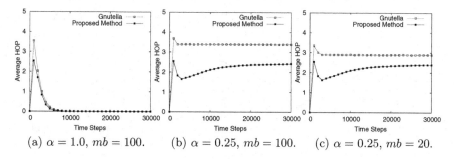

(a) $\alpha = 1.0$, $mb = 100$.   (b) $\alpha = 0.25$, $mb = 100$.   (c) $\alpha = 0.25$, $mb = 20$.

Fig. 7. Performance: average value of HOP.

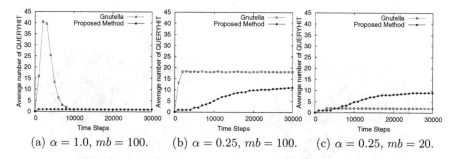

(a) $\alpha = 1.0$, $mb = 100$.   (b) $\alpha = 0.25$, $mb = 100$.   (c) $\alpha = 0.25$, $mb = 20$.

Fig. 8. Performance: average number of QueryHit.

4   Related Work

Freenet[2] uses a slightly more sophisticated method than Gnutella. All contents are labeled with a Global Unique IDentifier (GUID) obtained by a hash function. Each peer maintains a routing table comprising (GUID, Peer's IP Address) pairs; queries are forwarded according to this table. This method is equivalent to a steepest ascent hill climbing algorithm (with backtracking) in one-dimensional GUID space.

A more elegant approach is a protocol based on the Distributed Hash Table (DHT) [13]-[16]. In DHT systems, peers are organized into a well-defined structure based on content GUID and peer GUID.

In both systems, network topology is self-organized based on GUID such that the local storage of each peer is expended by its own unneeded contents.

5   Conclusion

This paper introduced the self-organization approach of community structure into P2P systems and proposed methods. Simulation results show that the self-organized community network maintains a high query hit rate without overflow. However, we did not consider that peers often go offline in the above simulations. Therefore, future work will address simulations under such dynamic conditions.

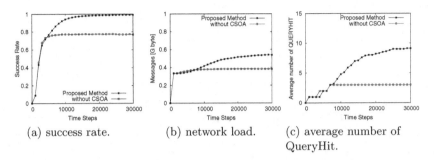

(a) success rate.   (b) network load.   (c) average number of
                                          QueryHit.

Fig. 9. The effect of community structure: CSOA is the Community Self-Organization
Algorithm.

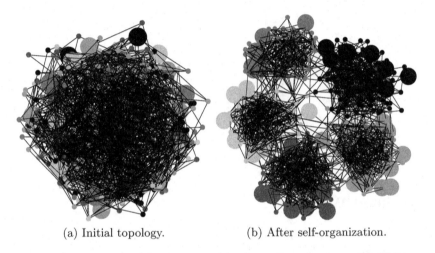

(a) Initial topology.   (b) After self-organization.

Fig. 10. Network topology (a) Initial and (b) after self-organization (30 CSOAs were
applied). Network topology is illustrated using the spring embedded model[12]. All
peers are classified into five communities. The gray scale of each circle represents each
community. Big and small circles represent UOMs and DOMs, respectively. In this
figure, the number of UOMs is 50 peers and the number of DOMs is 450 peers.

We are developing software that uses methods proposed in this paper: the
peer servant is TellaGate and the browser is TellaScope

The proposed Community Self-Organization Algorithm is based on local interactions. Recently, Davidsen and co-workers proposed a model of acquaintance networks.[19] In their model, the network is self-organized from an initial
random network to a SmallWorld network[17][18] characterized as having: 1)
short path length, 2) high clustering[17], and 3) scale-free or exponential link
distributions[18]. The proposed CSOA in this paper and Davidsen's algorithm
are based on similar local interactions; indeed, the Self-Organized Community
Network has short path length ($L \simeq 3.0$) and a high clustering ($C \simeq 0.14$) property. However, in Davidsen's model, not every node has an internal state such

as PeerDigest. How do Small World properties influence the self-organization processes? Future works will address this question.

References

1. RFC-Gnutella. http://rfc-gnutella.sourceforge.net/
2. I.Clarke, O.Sandberg, B.Wiley, and T.W.Hong: Freenet: A distributed anonymous information storage and retrieval system. Proc. the OCSI Workshop on Design Issues in Anonymity and Unobservability (2000).
3. Stanley Milgram: The Small-World Problem. Psychology Today **1** (1967) 60–67.
4. B.Bloom: Space/time trade-offs in hash coding with allowable errors. Communications of the ACM **13**(7) (1970) 422–426.
5. M.Mitzenmacher: Compressed Bloom Filters. Proc. of the 20th ACM Symposium on Principles of Distributed Computing (2001).
6. Christopher Rohrs: Query Routing for the Gnutella Network. http://rfc-gnutella. source-forge.net .
7. D.Wessels: Squid. http://squid-cache.org .
8. L.Fan, P.Cao, J.Almeida, and A.Broder: Summary cache: A scalable wide-area Web cache sharing protocol. IEEE/ACM Transactions on Networking **8**(3) (2000) 281–293.
9. A.Rousskov and D.Wessels: Cache digests. Computer Networks and ISDN Systems **30**(22-23) (1998) 2155–2168.
10. Y.Matsuo and M.Ishizuka: Keyword Extraction from a Document using Word Co-occurrence Statistical Information (in Japanese). Trans. of the Japanese Society for Artificial Intelligence, **17**(3) (2002) 217–223.
11. E.Adar and B.A.Huberman: Free Riding on Gnutella. First Monday **5**(10) (2000).
12. Graphviz. http://www.research.att.com/sw/tools/graphviz .
13. B.Zhao, J.Kubuatowicz and A.Joseph: Tapestry: An Infrastructure for Wide-area fault-tolerant Location and Routing. University of California, Berkeley Computer Science Division, Technical Report, UCB/CSD-01-1141 (2001).
14. A.Rowstron and P.Druschel: Pastry: Scalable, decentralized object location and routing for a large-scale peer-to-peer system. Proc. of the 18th IFIP/ACM International Conference on Distributed System Platforms (2001).
15. I.Stoica, R.Morris, D.Karger, M.F.Kaashoek, and H.Balakrishnan: Chord: A Scalable Peer-to-peer Look-up Service for Internet Application. Proc. of the ACM SIGCOMM Conference (2001).
16. S.Ratnasamy, P.Francis, M.Handley, and R.Karp: A Scalable Content-Addressable Network. Proc. of the ACM SIGCOMM Conference (2001).
17. D.J.Watts: Small-Worlds. Princeton Univ. Press (1999).
18. R.Albert, H.Jeong, and A.-L.Barabási: Error and attack tolerance of complex networks. Nature **406** (2000) 378–381.
19. Jörn Davidsen, Holger Ebel, and Stefan Bornholdt: Emergence of a Small World form Local Interactions: Modeling Acquaintance Networks. Physical Review Letters **88**(12), 128701 (2002).

The Role of Software Architecture in Configuring Middleware: The ScalAgent Experience

Vivien Quéma and Emmanuel Cecchet

Sardes project, LSR-IMAG laboratory
INRIA Rhône-Alpes 655, Avenue de l'Europe
F-38334 Saint-Ismier Cedex, France
`Vivien.Quema@inria.fr`

Abstract. Middleware has emerged as an important architectural component in modern distributed systems. It provides many solutions allowing to hide the management of the distribution of services and computations to the developers. However, its configuration becomes more and more complex, since it must fit application requirements, while adapting to the underlying system capacities. In this paper we propose a customization tool to automate the configuration of the ScalAgent message-oriented middleware. The tool uses the application description (into an Architecture Description Language) to determine and configure the set of middleware modules required to ensure non-functional properties required by the application. It is controlled by an algorithm that tries to minimize some non-functional property management costs. Our performance measurements clearly show the customization advantages.

Keywords: Middleware, architecture description languages, configuration, components.

1 Introduction

The use of the Internet and the increasing number of equipments embedding increasing intelligence leads to the development of new services. Developing these services raises numerous problems both from the development and run-time points of view: flexibility since already deployed applications must cooperate; scalability since thousands of devices may be involved, thus raising the problem of controlling the exchange of large volumes of information; extensibility since new devices join and leave the services dynamically; configurability since the application should support simultaneously a wide spectrum of devices with different requirements.

The ScalAgent platform has been designed to support the construction, deployment and operation of such services. It is composed of: (1) an asynchronous component model, (2) a message-oriented middleware (MOM) that provides components with an execution infrastructure and an asynchronous messaging service, and (3) a set of tools for the various users involved in the application

M. Papatriantafilou and P. Hunel (Eds.): OPODIS 2003, LNCS 3144, pp. 120–131, 2004.

life-cycle (designers, programmers, integrators, administrators). These tools are centered around an architecture description language (ADL) that allows the description of the application as an assembly of interacting components.

In its current form, the ScalAgent infrastructure allows component-based applications to be constructed, deployed and operated on large-scale distributed systems. Available ADL-based tools allow a high level of customization and configurability at the application level. However, a difficult task that remains to be done is the MOM configuration. Indeed, the MOM is made of several modules that provide various non-functional properties: component and/or message persistency, execution atomicity, causal ordering of messages, etc. Required modules and their attributes are described in configuration files (one per site).

Providing these configuration files may be a challenge, especially for large-scale distributed applications involving a large number of components with different non-functional requirements. This often results in a similar configuration of the different nodes hosting the application: each non-functional property is enforced on each node. For performance reasons, it is not desirable (sometimes even not possible) that the MOM systematically provides support for all the non-functional properties.

Many techniques have been proposed to build (dynamically) configurable middleware: reflection [1,2], components [3,4], aspects [5,6], etc. Nevertheless, they do not provide tools to systematically configure the middleware. This paper presents the work we have done to fill this gap. It describes a middleware configuration tool that has been implemented within the ScalAgent platform. The originality of this tool is that it uses the ADL description of the application to determine the required middleware configuration. For that purpose, the ADL has been extended in order to enable application developers to specify non-functional properties required by the application. The main contribution of this paper is to show that with very simple extensions to an existing ADL and by implementing appropriate algorithms, middleware configuration can be both simplified and optimized. As a proof of concept, we present the configuration algorithm used to configure the causal ordering property and we show that the performance gain brought by the configuration is significant.

The paper is organized as follows: related work is surveyed in section 2. The ScalAgent platform is described in section 3. Section 4 describes the configuration tool. It presents the extensions brought to the ADL and the customization algorithm. Section 5 details the algorithm used to configure the causal ordering property and section 6 concludes the paper.

2 Related Work

Over the past decade, system customization has become an increasing area of interest. This is mainly due to the growing weight of non-functional properties in the overall system behavior. Many research projects have thus addressed this issue. The Aster project [7] proposes a formal method for reasoning about matching of a customized software bus with some application requirements. The problem raised by this approach is that formal specification of software components and application requirements is a complex task, especially for large-scale distributed applications. The Lasagne project [5] proposes to compose aspects [8] at run-time to enable dynamic customization of systems. Composition is achieved by a run-time weaving mechanism that uses reflective techniques to perform a context-sensitive selection of aspects. According to Lasagne designers, the main drawback of this method is the run-time performance overhead. QuO [9] aims at providing a quality of service (QoS) support for CORBA applications. It defines a QoS description language, a runtime kernel and libraries of system condition objects for measuring and controlling QoS. This approach is interesting but only targets client-server interactions.

The software architecture community also addressed some configuration issues for component-based applications. For that purpose, ADLs have been developped. ADLs have in common the objective of providing the structural view of a software system. They are based on the commonly accepted concepts of an architecture: components that define computational units, connectors that define types of interactions between components, and the configuration that defines an application structure in terms of the interconnection of components through connectors. Existing ADLs differ on the exploitation of the application description: UniCon [10], Olan [11], C2 [12] provide assistance for the construction of the designed system. Other ADLs, like Rapide [13] or Wright [14], provide assistance for the analysis of the system: they use a formal description of the application to generate a model on which model checking techniques are applied. To our knowledge, few ADLs of the first category allow the specification of non-functional properties associated with both the components and the connectors.

3   The ScalAgent Platform

The ScalAgent platform provides an asynchronous component model, an execution infrastructure (a message-oriented middleware or MOM), and a set of tools easing the description, the configuration and the administration of applications made of components interacting via the MOM.

3.1   The Component Model

The ScalAgent component-based programming model has been inspired by the actor paradigm [15]. Components execute concurrently and communicate through an "event → reaction" pattern. Similarly to other component models, a component is made of a functional and a control part, defined by their interfaces. Moreover, the component model allows hierarchical compositions: an assembly of components may be manipulated as a component, called composite which, can itself be encapsulated within another composite.

3.2   The MOM

The MOM[1] [16] serves as an execution infrastructure for the above presented component model. It is represented by a set of servers organized in a bus architecture (see Fig. 1).

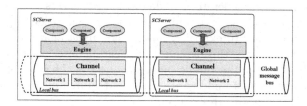

Fig. 1. Two interconnected servers details.

Each server is made up of three types of components implemented in the Java language: an engine — responsible for the creation and execution of components —, a channel— in charge of routing messages coming from the engine to the networks —, and several networks that implement the basic message-based communication layers: HTTP, TCP/IP, SOAP.

These components can be extended with software modules responsible for non-functional properties. We distinguish properties related to components (e.g. persistency, atomicity, monitoring) and properties related to communication links (e.g. security, causal ordering). To execute correctly, each module owns attributes that must be configured. For example, the "persistency" module has two attributes for each component it persists: the first attribute gives information about the persistency technique (e.g. hard disk, database, etc.) while the second one specifies the location where the data has to be stored.

3.3   The ADL-Based Tools

The ScalAgent platform provides several tools centered around the Olan ADL [11]. A description tool is used to specify the application architecture as an assembly of interacting components. A deployment tool is used to install the actual components into their target environment and to set up the links between them. An administration tool is used to monitor and reconfigure the application.

4   Middleware Configuration

The ADL-based tools described in the previous section allow fine-grained configuration of applications. Nevertheless, they do not provide any assistance for

---

[1] The ScalAgent MOM is developed by the ScalAgent Distributed Technologies company and is freely available on the Web. http://www.objectweb.org/joram/

the middleware configuration. This latter task is very difficult since applications may involve a large number of components, with various non functional requirements. This often results in either a bad configuration or no configuration at all. This causes the middleware to be homogeneous: nodes enforce non functional properties for application components that do not necessarily require them. This is a major drawback for applications involving devices with limited resources.

Our proposal is to generate a middleware that meets application requirements. This is achieved by extending the ADL specification capacity so as to enable the programmer to explicitly specify non-functional properties required by the application. Given this extended application description, a configuration algorithm is in charge of the middleware configuration. The goal of the algorithm is to determine the set of middleware modules required on each node to ensure properties required by the application.

4.1   The Extended ADL

The ADL syntax is extended to allow the application developer to specify non-functional properties required by components and connectors. Using Olan, these latters are described as XML elements [11]. Non-functional properties are expressed as sub-elements of these elements:

```
<component name="...">
   <property_name attr_1="value" ... attr_n="value"/>
</component>
```

To illustrate this syntax, we consider below an example where the application developer wants to specify that message exchanges between the client interface "send" of component C1 and the server interface "receive" of component C2 have to be causally ordered:

```
<connector clientItf="C1.send" serverItf="C2.receive">
   <causality/>
</connector>
```

The specification of application component locations has also been extended. According to the Olan syntax, each application component location has to be specified by the application designer at configuration time. We allow the application designer to specify, for each application component, a (possibly empty) set of nodes that may host the application component. Note that specifying an empty set of nodes means that the application component may be located on any node.

4.2   The Configuration Algorithm

The customization algorithm determines the set of middleware modules — and their associated attributes — required by each server to meet the application non-functional requirements. As we want the customized middleware to be as efficient as possible, the customization algorithm also determines (when required) the location of application components that optimizes the middleware performances. For that purpose, assessments for the management cost of each non-functional property are required. By management cost, we mean the execution time overhead caused by non-functional property enforcement. Each middleware component responsible for a non-functional property implements a function whose goal is to determine the corresponding property management cost. This function has the following signature:

```
int managementCost ( deviceHWCaract, applicationConfig );
```

The first parameter characterizes the device hosting the server. Therefore the management costs differ from an embedded device to a workstation or a server. The second parameter is the configuration of the application (i.e. its ADL description). The function returns an integer which evaluates the non-functional property management cost.

Given all the non-functional properties management costs, the customization algorithm is able to determine the location of all application components that minimizes the overall cost. Note that the application designer can specify coefficients in order to change the weight of a property in the overall cost computation.

5   The Causal Ordering Example

We illustrate the middleware configuration tool with the causal ordering property. We have chosen this property for two reasons: (1) it is difficult to configure since this is a distributed property that involves several application components; (2) usual causal ordering mechanisms raise scalability problems, since increasing the number of nodes degrades their performances. Indeed, causal ordering protocols cause both network overload — due to timestamp data exchange for clock updates —, and high disk I/O activity to maintain a persistent image of the logical clocks used by the protocol.

The ScalAgent MOM provides two causal ordering modules. The first module implements the traditional matrix-clock based protocol, proposed by Fischer and Michael in 1982 [17]. Matrix-clocks are used to represent time. For a n-components application, each component c_i owns a $n \times n$ matrix. Configuring this module is easy and does not require a configuration tool.

Nevertheless, this module induces a very high overhead, since it considers that each component potentially communicates with all other components. We now propose another module that implements a protocol based on the knowledge of the application communication pattern, thus allowing a restriction of the causal ordering restricted to the components that actually communicate with each other. After its presentation, we will describe how this module is configured by the configuration algorithm. Finally, we present experiments and results that show the gain brought by the use of this module.

5.1   The Topology-Based Causal Ordering Module

This module implements a protocol that uses the application topology. This topology can be seen as a directed graph in which vertices represent application components, and directed edges represent directed communication channels between them. This graph is built using the ADL description of the application. The operating principle of the topology-based protocol is to group components into (possibly) overlapping domains. Each domain encompasses a set of components whose communication topology induces causal ordering problems. These domains are built from the directed graph mapping the architecture of the application, according to the following definition:

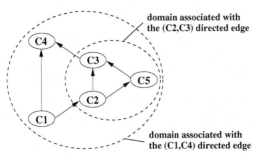

domain associated with
the (C2,C3) directed edge

domain associated with
the (C1,C4) directed edge

Definition: There exists a domain associated with a $(c1, c2)$ directed edge iff there exists an elementary (directed) path from $c1$ to $c2$ which is not $(c1, c2)$ itself. If so, the domain associated with the $(c1, c2)$ directed edge is defined as the $\mathcal{D}(c1, c2)$ components set containing $c1$, $c2$ and all others components c such that there exists an elementary (directed) path from $c1$ to $c2$ including c.

For each domain $\mathcal{D}(c1, c2)$ it belongs to, a component c owns a clock, noted $\mathcal{C}(c1, c2)$, which is an integer that represents c's knowledge about messages sent on the directed edge $(c1, c2)$. The (possibly empty) set of clocks owned by a component c is noted $\mathbb{C}_c$. Each message m carries a $\mathbb{S}_m$ (possibly empty) set of stamps defined as a subset of the sender's clocks set. The stamp associated to the $\mathcal{C}(c1, c2)$ clock is noted $\mathcal{S}(c1, c2)$. Figure 2 depicts the protocol that a component c must follow while sending or receiving messages in order to ensure causal delivery.

5.2   The Causal Ordering Configuration Algorithm

A causal ordering module only has to know the domains containing the components it manages. Except for applications involving very few components, this task cannot be performed by the application developer. The configuration algorithm implements a very simple Prolog program ($\approx$100 lines of code) that automatically computes these domains from the ADL description of the application. This is done in two steps: 1. construction of the directed graph using the ADL description of the application, then 2. computation of causality domains from the directed graph.

The current implementation of the module provides a very basic managementCost function. It does not take into account the

Initialization
```
// Set all clocks to 0
```
- $\forall \mathcal{C}(c1, c2) \in \mathbb{C}_c\; \mathcal{C}(c1, c2) = 0$

Sending message m to component c'
```
// Add the relevant stamps for component c'
```
- $\mathbb{S}_m = \{\mathcal{C}(c1, c2) \in \mathbb{C}_c \mid c' \in \mathcal{D}(c1, c2)\}$
```
// Send the message
```
- Send m
```
// Increment C(c,c') clock if it exists
```
- $\mathcal{C}(c, c') \in \mathbb{C}_c \Rightarrow \mathcal{C}(c, c') = \mathcal{C}(c, c') + 1$

$\left.\right\}$ *atomically*

Reception of message m from component c'
```
// Extract the TSm subset of m's stamps to
// be tested by c before delivering m
```
- $\mathbb{TS}_m = \{\mathcal{S}(c1, c2) \in \mathbb{S}_m \mid c2 = c\}$
```
// Wait for messages m causally depends on to arrive
```
- Delay delivery until $\forall \mathcal{S}(c1, c2) \in \mathbb{TS}_m\; \mathcal{S}(c1, c2) \le \mathcal{C}(c1, c2)$
```
// Deliver the message
```
- Deliver m
```
// Increment C(c',c) clock if it exists
```
- $\mathcal{C}(c', c) \in \mathbb{C}_c \Rightarrow \mathcal{C}(c', c) = \mathcal{C}(c', c) + 1$
```
// Update c's clocks according to m's stamps
```
- $\forall \mathcal{S}(c1, c2) \in \mathbb{S}_m\; \mathcal{S}(c1, c2) > \mathcal{C}(c1, c2) \Rightarrow \mathcal{C}(c1, c2) = \mathcal{S}(c1, c2)$

Fig. 2. The topology-based causal ordering protocol

deviceHWCharacteristics parameter. The cost returned by the function is equal to the number of clocks that the module owns (recall that for each component it manages, a module owns as much clocks as the number of domains the component belongs to). Let M be a module, its **managementCost** function returns:

$$\text{managementCost} = \sum_{c \in M} Card(\mathbb{C}_c)$$

Component locations are chosen so as to balance the number of clocks owned by each module. Consider the very simple example depicted on picture 3.

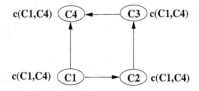

Fig. 3. An example of application with one domain.

According to the definition of domains, each component only belongs to the domain associated with the directed edge $(c1, c4)$. As a consequence, each component only requires one clock. Consider that there are two nodes (i.e. two modules) and component locations have to be determined. Regarding the causal ordering property, the best choice is to deploy two components per node.

5.3   Experiments and Results

Measurements have been performed on applications involving various numbers of components. The execution time has been compared for the same application running on the ScalAgent middleware in two scenarios: in the first case, messages are causally ordered using the first module (the matrix clock based algorithm); in the second case, messages are causally ordered using the second module (the topology-based protocol).

For the experiments, we have deployed a component on each server, which sends back received messages (ping-pong). Messages are sent by a main component on server 1, which computes the round-trip average time for 100 sends. We did three series of tests: application with sparsely, strongly and totally connected components. We setup a network of 30 hosts in order to increase the number of servers. We used a set of PC Pentium III 700MHz with 256 MB, connected by a 100Mb/s Ethernet adapter, running Linux kernel 2.4.6.

Measurements have been performed on different kinds of applications differing by the coupling degree of components. For each kind of application, a pattern has been designed. By reproducing this pattern, as depicted on figure 4, the number of application components may be increased.

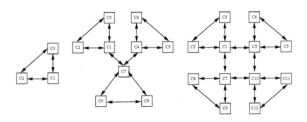

Fig. 4. Application construction by reproduction of a pattern.

Figure 5 presents performance results obtained for applications with sparsely-connected components. The pattern that has been reproduced is the one depicted in figure 4. We have done 4 tests that differ in the number of involved components: 15 (5× pattern), 30 (10×), 45 (15×) and 60 (20×). Figure 5 clearly shows the performance gain brought by the use of the protocol. The measurements made with a matrix-based causal ordering show the quadratic increase of the message ordering cost with the number of servers. This quadratic increase is the direct consequence of the quadratic increase of the matrix size. Our protocol allows the reduction of the message ordering costs since all components do not have to store and send/receive a matrix clock. In application with sparsely-connected components, servers do not have as much data to send/receive and store, which explains the observed gain.

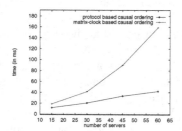

Fig. 5. Comparison of the cost with matrix based and protocol based causal ordering for applications with sparsely-coupled components.

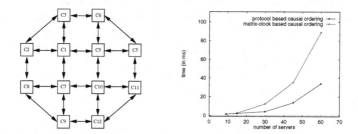

Fig. 6. Comparison of the cost with matrix based and protocol based causal ordering for applications with strongly-coupled components.

Figure 6 shows that there is still a gain for applications with strongly-connected components. However, this gain is lower since the average number of domains each component belongs to is higher than for applications with sparsely-connected components. A last result we observed that for an application with totally-connected components, the gain is almost null (but still positive) since each component exactly belongs to $n * (n - 1)$ domains (from itself to all other component and vice versa), n being the number of component involved in the application. This number is close to the matrix-clock size (n^2) but each server has still less data to handle, which explains the gain.

6   Conclusion

Today application designers are facing the problem of building complex distributed applications involving a large number of computing equipments ranging from traditional servers to mobile devices. The ScalAgent infrastructure aims at providing a coherent set of solutions based on an asynchronous messaging middleware and on a component-based approach of distributed software development. The ADL approach adopted in the ScalAgent infrastructure provides a first level of customization at the application level. Nevertheless, it does not provide support for middleware configuration, which is very important to face the lack of resources on some devices and to meet various application requirements.

This paper has shown how the ScalAgent infrastructure has been extended with a tool that allows middleware configuration according to hardware limitations and application needs. The approach we have taken can be viewed as a joint development of the distributed application and its operational run-time support based on a common ADL philosophy. The ADL used to describe the application has been extended to allow the specification of non-functional requirements. From this overall description, a customized runtime execution platform is automatically built. The configuration tool is controlled by an algorithm that tries to minimize the non-functional property management costs.

In our future work, we plan to study the conjunction of different types of non-functional properties that may interfere. At this time, all the available middleware modules provide compatible non-functional properties. Nevertheless two non-functional properties can be incompatible. We plan to examine detailed consequences of such interferences upon our approach. Our premise is that the interdependency among non-functional properties can be made explicit through the definition of a relation over properties.

References

1. M. Astley, D. Sturman, and G. Agha. Customizable Middleware for Modular Distributed Software. *Communications of the ACM*, 44(5), May 2001.
2. F. Kon, F. Costa, G. Blair, and R. H. Campbell. The Case for Reflective Middleware. *Communications of the ACM*, 45(6):33–38, June 2002.
3. M. Clarke, G. Blair, G. Coulson, and N. Parlavantzas. An Efficient Component Model for the Construction of Adaptive Middleware. In *Proceedings of the IFIP/ACM International Conference on Distributed Systems Platforms (Middleware' 01)*, pages 160–178, Heidelberg, Germany, November 2001.
4. P. Narasimhan, L. Moser, and P. Melliar-Smith. Eternal – A Component-based Framework for Transparent Fault-Tolerant CORBA. *Software Practice and Experience, Theme Issue on Enterprise Frameworks*, 32(8):771–788, July 2002.
5. E. Truyen, B. Vanhaute, W. Joosen, P. Verbaeten, and B. N. Jørgensen. Dynamic and Selective Combination of Extensions in Component-Based Applications. In *Proceedings of the 23rd International Conference on Software Engineering (ICSE'01)*, Toronto, Canada, May 2001.
6. F. Hauck, U. Becker, M. Geier, E. Meier, U. Rastofer, and M. Steckermeier. AspectIX: a quality-aware, object-based middleware architecture. In *3th IFIP International Working Conference on Distributed Applications and Interoperable Systems (DAIS'01)*, Krakow, Poland, 2001.
7. V. Issarny, C. Kloukinas, and A. Zarras. Systematic Aid for Developing Middleware Architectures. In *Communications of the ACM, Issue on Adaptive Middleware, Volume 45, Issue 6*, pages 53–58, June 2002.

8. G. Kiczales, J. Lamping, A. Mendhekar, C. Maeda, C. V. Lopes, J.-M. Loingtier, and J. Irwin. Aspect-Oriented Programming. In *Proceedings of the European Conference on Object-Oriented Programming (ECOOP'97)*, June 1997.

9. P. Pal, J. Loyall, R. Schantz, J. Zinky, R. Shapiro, and J. Megquier. Using QDL to Specify QoS Aware Distributed (QuO) Application Con.guration. In *Proceedings of the 3rd IEEE International Symposium on Object-Oriented Real-time distributed Computing (ISORC'00)*, Newport Beach, CA, March 2000.

10. M. Shaw, R. DeLine, D. V. Klein, T. L. Ross, D. M. Young, and G. Zelesnik. Abstractions for Software Architecture and Tools to Support Them. *Software Engineering*, 21(4):314–335, 1995.

11. L. Bellissard, N. de Palma, and D. Féliot. *The Olan Architecture Definition Language*. C3DS Technical Report, volume 24, 2000.

12. N. Medvidovic, D. S. Rosenblum, and R. N. Taylor. A Language and Environment for Architecture-Based Software Development and Evolution. In *Proceedings of the 21st International Conference on Software Engineering (ICSE'99)*, pages 44–53, 1999.

13. D. C. Luckham, J. J. Kenney, L. M. Augustin, J. Vera, D. Bryan, and W. Mann. Specification and Analysis of System Architecture Using Rapide. In *IEEE Transactions on Software Engineering, Special Issue on Software Architecture, Vol. 21, No. 4*, pages 336–355, April 1995.

14. R. Allen, D. Garlan, and R. Douence. Specifying Dynamism in Software Architectures. In *Proceedings of the Workshop on Foundations of Component-Based Software Engineering*, Zurich, Switzerland, September 1997.

15. G. A. Agha. Actors: A Model of Concurrent Computation in Distributed Systems. In *The MIT Press, ISBN 0-262-01092-5*, Cambridge, MA, 1986.

16. L. Bellissard, N. de Palma, A. Freyssinet, M. Herrmann, and S. Lacourte. An Agent Plateform for Reliable Asynchronous Distributed Programming. In *Symposium on Reliable Distributed Systems (SRDS'99)*, Lausanne, Switzerland, October 1999.

17. M. J. Fischer and A. Michael. Sacrifying Serializability to Attain High Availability of Data in an Unreliable Network. In *ACM Symposium on Principles of Database Systems*, pages 70–75, Los Angeles, March 1982.

dSL: An Environment with Automatic Code Distribution for Industrial Control Systems

Bram De Wachter*, Thierry Massart, and Cédric Meuter*

University of Brussels (ULB)
Département d'Informatique, Bld du Triomphe, B-1050 Bruxelles
{bdewacht,tmassart,cmeuter}@ulb.ac.be

Abstract. We present and motivate the definition and use of the language and environment dSL, an imperative and event driven language designed to program distributed industrial control systems. dSL provides transparent code distribution using simple mechanisms. Its use allows the industrial control system's designer to concentrate on the sequences of control required; the dSL compiler-distributer taking into account the distribution aspects. We show the advantages of our approach compared to others proposed using e.g. shared memory or synchronous languages like Esterel, Lustre or Signal.

Keywords: Industrial process control, transparent code distribution, execution migration

1 Introduction

An industrial control system is generally safety critical, event-driven, physically distributed and controls heterogeneous equipments whose response time can range from milliseconds to minutes. To be of any use in a real industrial environment, a control system must be reliable, efficient, robust and simple. Efficiency is needed to ensure that the controller is not overtaken by the system it controls. Robustness allows a maximal control even in case of hardware failure (sensor, actuator or processor). Simplicity is of main importance to allow a strong monitoring of the system and in case of maintenance or upgrade, to be able to easily update it without stopping the industrial system controlled.

The burden of combining the physical complexity of the process, the communication schemes of the distributed parts, the need to provide simple and fast control and the extreme reliability and robustness requirements make the development of such systems hard.

To simplify the work of the distributed systems designer, it is beneficial to design a development environment which handles the communication aspects and allows the programmer to concentrate on the functional aspects of the system. Classical solutions based on this idea exist (CORBA, DCOM, EJB). Unfortunately, due to the genericness of these solutions, they are quite heavy and

* Work supported by the *Region de Bruxelles Capitale*, grant no. RBC-BR 227/3298.

M. Papatriantafilou and P. Hunel (Eds.): OPODIS 2003, LNCS 3144, pp. 132–145, 2004.

completely hide all of the communication process, making the monitoring of such systems difficult.

More dedicated solutions to the problem of distributed execution of a system with transparent distribution mechanism, have been proposed. Examples of such solutions are distributed shared memory [19], or more specifically in the domain of control systems, synchronous languages like Esterel, Lustre or Signal (e.g. [1] and [11]).

Unfortunately, even if shared memory solutions are generally lighter than the distributed objects one, due to the cache coherence protocol, the time to access the memory can vary greatly and is not predictable. We also motivate why in our opinion, the latter solutions have, in practice, some drawbacks.

This leads us to the definition of $_d$SL[1], a new environment and language designed to program distributed industrial control systems, providing transparent code distribution using low level mechanisms adapted for the industrial environments. $_d$SL has been developed by the verification group of ULB[2] in collaboration with the company Macq Electronique[3].

$_d$SL offers both advantages to allow, most of the time, $_d$SL programmers to ignore all the communication aspects between controllers of the distributed systems and, by the simplicity of the distribution mechanisms, to easily monitor the behavior of the synthesized distributed system. $_d$SL can also be formally modeled and therefore allows links with the world of formal model-checking to verify the correctness of the systems. Another advantage of this approach is the ability to debug and verify the centralized program before its distribution.

In the remaining part of this paper, we first, in section 2, detail related proposals and justify the advantages of our solutions. In section 3 we present the $_d$SL syntax and in section 4, outline its semantics. In section 5, we describe the distribution procedure and $_d$SL environment. Finally in section 6, we discuss our future work.

2   Other Approaches and Motivations

The problem of distributing applications that control reactive systems has been studied for many years now and several interesting observations on these works shaped the design of $_d$SL. In particular, this problem has been studied conceptually in the world of process algebra and defined as a correctness preserving transformation of a centralized specification into a semantically equivalent distributed one. (e.g. for bisimulation equivalence [17], see [16]). It has also been studied on various types of labelled transition systems ([6] [20]).

These works solved part of the problem. However, contrary to other programming languages, the notion of variable does not exist in process algebra and these solutions had therefore to be extended. Work has also been done in the domain

---

[1] $_d$SL is the successor of the language SL (Supervision Language, based on ST, an industrial standard defined in IEC1131-3) developed at Macq Electronique company

[2] http://www.ulb.ac.be/di/ssd/groupverif.html

[3] a leading company in industrial process control, http://www.macqel.be

of synchronous languages such as Esterel [4], Lustre [5] and Signal [15], which answered questions on how to specify controllers in a natural and semantically well defined way. Unfortunately, in our opinion, the distribution of synchronous languages while preserving the semantics, suffer from a performance problem which, in practice, may not be acceptable.

Indeed, the synchronous programming scheme found in the synchronous languages supposes that time is defined as a sequence of instants To preserve determinism, these languages use the concept of synchronous broadcast [3] when several processes are composed in parallel. This implies that parallel branches in the high level description can be transformed into sequential deterministic code. The distribution of such programs, for example in Esterel [11], may suffer from severe performance penalties 1. because the instants must be respected, requiring a strong resynchronization scheme, and 2. because the distribution is applied on the determinized sequential code. The distribution of Esterel described in [11] can be summarized in 4 steps : (1) the centralized program (after being compiled in a single threaded sequential code) is duplicated on all participating sites; (2) the instructions that are not relevant to a given site are removed; (3) for data that is accessed on one site, but calculated on another, communication messages are inserted, and (4) synchronization messages are inserted to preserve the global instants. Remark that since the initial code is sequential, this solution suffers from the lack of parallelism (there are some ways to achieve higher concurrency such as weak synchronization but that does not preserve safety properties [11]). For Signal, the situation is very similar [1].

This strong synchronization has several undesirable drawbacks in an industrial environment. First of all, to keep all processes in pace, numerous messages need to be exchanged at each global instant. Secondly, all participating processes have to advance at the speed of the slowest process. Finally, the failure of one of the processes makes the whole system deadlock. To the best of our knowledge, the synchronous approach has no answer to these shortcomings.

These observations make us believe that, although perfectly suitable for tightly coupled homogeneous systems and having the benefit of simplicity when it comes to specifying a controller, the simplicity of the synchronous approach is too costly in terms of performance when applied to loosely coupled heterogeneous systems. Moreover, from the experience of our industrial partner specialized in process control, the strong synchronization of all processes is only rarely needed and must therefore not be used by default, but made available when needed.

To avoid these drawbacks, $_d$SL rejects the synchronous product used in the above languages at the detriment of indeterminism, and adopts an asynchronous composition of instantaneous (atomic) code and asynchronous (sequential) code. Asynchronous composition is therefore the keyword in $_d$SL's design. The instantaneous code uses an event driven scheme and, for a given component, must be able to run without any synchronization that would make it wait on other components. This asynchronous composition has the advantage that the failure of one site does not introduce deadlocks in atomic code on other sites. Moreover, as we detail later on, $_d$SL offers a way to detect and handle network or hardware failures. The sequentialcode, on the other hand, can be executed in a totally distributed and cooperative manner. These assumptions, of course, imply some restrictions on code and have consequences on the way data values are transmitted between distributed processes, as explained in section 5.

For the distributed execution of the sequentialcode, several models are proposed in the literature. These models can be divided into two sets based on the way they achieve data locality : either move data, or move the execution. Many systems have been studied that use the first solution, such as Distributed Shared Memory systems [19]. These systems, although offering a transparent distributed environment, suffer from undesirable border effects that make them unusable in an industrial environment. The need to replicate data to make such systems work in a performance responsible way [12], may cause thrashing[4] or false sharing[5] and these systems therefore do not guarantee stable performance as observed in [19]. Secondly, since data moves around, the supervision of such systems and its error-recovery - both indispensable features in industrial applications - may become too complicated [18] on dSL's target hardware.

For these reasons, dSL uses the second solution, which consists of moving the execution to the data, a concept known as process or thread migration [10]. In this concept, a thread of execution is halted on one site, its context (local variables and program counter) is sent to another site, where its context is restored and execution continues. Thread migration is known to enable dynamic load distribution, fault tolerance, eased system administration, data access locality and mobile computing [14]. In our system, all instructions and global variables are statically assigned to the participating sites and thread migration, decided at compile time, is used to obtain data access locality. The benefits are twofold: (1) following the state of the system is very easy, and (2) all communication and synchronization messages can statically be calculated, resulting in a predictable execution. However, we lose the benefits of dynamic load balancing and fault tolerance since the migration policy used in dSL is static.

The design of dSL can thus be synthesized as a hybrid execution scheme composed of two types of code : local or atomicinstantaneous code, and distributed sequentialcode that executes using statically calculated thread migration.

3   The dSL Concept

dSL is an imperative language with static variables. Each variable can be either (1) internal to a program, (2) linked to an input (sensor), or (3) linked to an output (actuator). dSL is event driven. This allows to specify that when the value of a boolean expression switches from false to true, some code must be executed. For instance, `when x >= 0 then run_motor1(); end_when` will trigger

---

[4] The effect of two (or more) processes competing for exclusive access to a given variable, resulting in high communication traffic and almost no productiveness

[5] Caused when two (or more) variables, used by different processes, are in the same page causing unnecessary communication traffic

the method **run_motor1()** every time the variable x switches from a negative to a positive value. dSL also offers limited O bject O riented features.

Moreover, the domains of all dSL primitive types are extended with the special value **unknown**. A variable linked to an I/O may take this special value in case of hardware failure. The **unknown** value propagates in expression evaluation and can be tested for with the builtin **is_unknown** statement. As shown in figure 1, this allows to construct more robust programs. In this figure, a sensor is duplicated in order to ensure correct behavior in case of hardware failure. Note that the body of a **when** whose condition evaluates to **unknown** is not executed.

```
WHEN temp1 > 30 AND          WHEN temp2 > 30 AND          WHEN IS_UNKNOWN(temp1) AND
     NOT handled THEN             NOT handled THEN              IS_UNKNOWN(temp2) THEN
     handled := TRUE;            handled := TRUE;              alarm := TRUE;
     ...                          ...                           ...
END_WHEN                     END_WHEN                     END_WHEN
```

Fig. 1. Fault tolerance in dSL with unknown.

A program in dSL is written in a centralized manner, as if every input or output can be accessed without the need for explicit communication or synchronization (we shall see that some restrictions are imposed to apply this principle). The designer must then fill in a localization table to specify the physical localization (execution sites) of each I/O. Other (internal) variables are either global in which case their localization will statically be fixed by the distributer, or local in which case they can move during execution. Since global variables do not move during execution, the distributer has to ensure that an instruction accessing a global variable is executed on the site of that variable. An execution site can be either a supervisor (typically a computer, possibly with a user interface) or a programmable controller (called automata from here on, which are connected to the industrial equipment through the sensors and actuators).

The dSL compiler/distributer automatically distributes the code among the execution sites, trying to minimize communications, and compiles the distributed code to an assembler-like language. This assembler-like code is interpreted by a dSL Virtual M achine A dSL virtual machine is available for both supervisors and automata. This is illustrated in figure 2.

This approach has many benefits such as (1) maintainability (only one language is used to program both the supervisors and automata) (2) flexibility (any change of an actuator or a sensor does not imply changes in the program),(3) simplicity (since communication / distribution is done implicitly, the programmer does not need to come up with synchronization schemes to handle particular tasks).

A dSL program contains several parts. (1) class declarations, (2) global variables declarations - including all I/O variables (3) method definitions (4) when definitions (5) sequence definitions and (6) a program initialization. Each Input (resp. Output) variable v_{in} (resp. v_{out}) is linked to a hardware sensor v_{in}^* (resp. actuator v_{out}^*) .

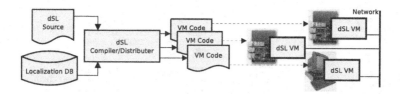

Fig. 2. dSL

Atomic and sequential code. The design of dSL has been dictated by the execution paradigm requiring an immediate reaction to events and their instantaneous treatment. In practice this forbids any implicit synchronization during the execution which implies inter-site communications (through a relatively slow network). A clear way must therefore exist to express that inter-site synchronization is allowed. Hence, in dSL, there is a distinction between:

- atomic code which must be executed in an atomic manner and therefore cannot be distributed,
- sequential code which can be distributed and use inter-site communications to synchronize or transfer values between sites.

Code inside a WHEN (the instruction inside its body and the condition) is forced atomic and must therefore be local to a given site. Sequential code is defined through the use of the SEQUENCE construct. The code inside a METHOD can be either atomic or sequential depending on the context in which it is called. If a METHOD can be reached from a WHEN, then the body of this METHOD is assumed to be atomic. It is assumed sequential otherwise. To relax the atomic constraints in a WHEN, two mechanisms have been defined (see figure 3) :

- The LAUNCH keyword allowing to call a SEQUENCE or a METHOD asynchronously (i.e without waiting for the control to return from the SEQUENCE or the METHOD), and possibly on a distant site. Note that a SEQUENCE can only be called asynchronously (using LAUNCH) and that it cannot have more than one instance executed simultaneously.
- The "~" operator allowing to reference the last locally known value of a variable possibly on a distant site. When the value of a variable is changed on the site governing it, its new value is sent to all necessary sites. One must be careful with tilded variables since it is never guaranteed that the value of the tilded variables corresponds to the real value of the variable. It can be interesting to use if the exact value is not imperative (e.g. temperature which evolves slowly), or if the program is built such that it is known that the tilded value is equal to the real one (e.g. using a procedure for explicit synchronization). A site that has a tilded copy of x, regularly checks if the site owning x is still alive. If not, the copy is set to unknown, indicating hardware or network failure.

```
CLASS Heater
    control, state : INT;
    maintenance    : BOOL;
END_CLASS

GLOBAL_VAR
    heater                   : Heater;
    temperature, fuel_cost : INT;
    alarm, led               : BOOL;
END_VAR

SEQUENCE set_heater(new_state : INT)
    heater.control := heater.control + 1;
    heater.state := new_state;
    IF (heater.state == 1) THEN
        led        := TRUE;
        fuel_cost := fuel_cost + 10;
    ELSE
        led := FALSE;
    END_IF
END_SEQUENCE

WHEN IN Heater (control==1000) THEN // W1
    control := 0;
    maintenance := TRUE;
END_WHEN
```

```
WHEN heater.maintenance THEN        // W2
    alarm := TRUE;
END_WHEN

WHEN ~temperature < 0 THEN          // W3
    IF (NOT heater.maintenance) THEN
        LAUNCH set_heater(1);
    END_IF
END_WHEN

WHEN ~temperature > 20 THEN         // W4
    IF (NOT heater.maintenance) THEN
        LAUNCH set_heater(0);
    END_IF
END_WHEN

PROGRAM
    heater.control := 0;
    heater.maintenance := FALSE;
    LAUNCH set_heater(temperature<0);
END_PROGRAM
```

Fig. 3. A temperature control system in dSL

dSL example. To illustrate the dSL concepts, let us examine a small example of a temperature control system. In this system, a temperature sensor is linked to an input variable `temperature`. A heater is turned on (off) if the temperature is below 0° (above 20°). The state of the heater (on/off) is controlled by the output variable `heater.state`. Moreover, there are two indicators on a control panel. The first indicator, (linked to the output variable `led`) is used to indicate the state of the heater, and the second (linked to the input variable `alarm`) is updated when the heater has been turned on a certain number of times. An additional variable `fuel_cost` estimates the amount of fuel consumed by the heater. The dSL program is presented in figure 3.

4   The dSL Semantics

In this section, we introduce the dSL semantics, concentrating on the distributed aspect of the language. We therefore skip a complete and formal review of well known program issues like method call, control flow, expression evaluation and the limited object oriented features.

The behavior of a dSL program depends on the localization of its variables. Our goal is to describe the semantics of a dSL program independently from any localization information. For that, we introduce the notion of maximal distribution, which expresses the most permissive way to distribute a dSL program. The semantics of a dSL program is then defined by the set of all behaviors of its maximal distribution

Maximal distribution. The maximal distribution is deduced from the locality constraints imposed on global variables by the atomic code, e.g (1) two global variables appearing in the same instruction and (2) two global variables accessed by the same WHEN must be governed by the same site. This defines a partition of the set of variables where each subset of the partition corresponds to an execution site. A formal description of how to find the maximal distribution can be found in [21].

Process behavior. The behavior of a dSL program P in its maximal distribution is given by

$$P_1 \parallel ... \parallel P_n$$

where each P_i is an independent process executing the part of code of P handling all the variables local to site i. These processes communicate through FIFO-channels between each pair of processes. We will note $F_{i,j}$ the FIFO-channels used from a process P_i to another process P_j.

Every process P_i is an infinite loop. Each cycle (i.e iteration) is composed of three phases: (1) the input phase, where each physical input is sampled and where the variables linked to those inputs are updated, (2) the process phase where the necessary WHENs are triggered and where the messages from other execution site are processed and (3) the output phase where the physical outputs are updated according to the variable they are linked to. The pseudo-code for this input-process-output cycle is given by :

> //input phase:
> **for each** $v_{in} \in P_i$ linked to an input **do** $v_{in} \leftarrow v_{in}^*$ **done**
> //process phase:
> **for each** $w \in W \cdot Var_W(w) \subseteq P_i$ **do** process w **done**
> **for each** $j \in \{1, 2..., i-1, i+1, ..., n\}$ **do** process messages from $F_{j,i}$ **done**
> //output phase:
> **for each** $v_{out} \in P_i$ linked to an output **do** $v_{out}^* \leftarrow v_{out}$ **done**

where v_{in}^* (v_{out}^*) denotes the hardware value of the variable v_{in} (v_{out}), W the set of WHENs, and $Var_W(w)$ the set of variables accessed by when w (for more details see [21]).

Processing WHENs. To each WHEN, we associate a hidden variable v_w keeping the previous value of the condition. This allows to trigger w of the form "**WHEN**" cond "**THEN**" instruction_list "**END_WHEN**" only when the condition switched from false to true. Note that the WHENs are processed in their order of appearance in the dSL program. The pseudo code for the execution of w is :

> **if** $cond \wedge \neg v_w$ **then** $v_w \leftarrow$ **true**; execute $instruction\_list$ **else** $v_w \leftarrow cond$ **fi**

Processing Messages. Conceptually, there are two types of messages: (1) messages concerning the update of tilded variables and (2) messages concerning the remote execution of sequential code. The first kind of message is of the form (v, new_value). Processing such a message simply consists in assigning this new_value to the local copy of v (see Assignment hereafter). The second kind of message, corresponding to the LAUNCH or continuation of sequential code, is simply a *label*. Indeed, when a process must execute remote code, it posts a message with the label corresponding to the first instruction of that code to the governing site. Processing such a message consists of the execution of the code associated with that *label*, until it reaches the end of that code or is migrated to another site.

Assignment. An assignment of the form v ":=" e ";" executed by the site S_i ($v \in S_i$) has the usual result (the variable v is set to value of the expression e), but ${}_d$SL adds two features to that. First of all, all WHENs w are processed, as explained previously. Secondly, if v has asynchronous distant copies (i.e. ~v), then these must be updated. Therefore, for all sites S_j governing a ~v, a message is posted in $F_{i,j}$ with v and its new value (i.e. the value of e). Note that the special behavior for assignment may cause infinite recursion in the processing of whens. A simple static check allows us to reject programs that may contain this unacceptable infinite recursion.

5   Static Distribution Process of ${}_d$SL

In this section, we discuss ${}_d$SL's distribution algorithms and the ${}_d$SL virtual machine. First, for atomic code, the distributer has to assign a unique localization to each instruction and each global variable such that the constraints on atomic code are met. Next, for the sequential code, the instructions that were not previously dealt with must be localized, taking into account the localization already imposed on the global variables at the level of the distribution of the atomic code. A second algorithm is introduced to solve this problem. Finally, we show how, from the computed information on localization, the distribution is actually achieved.

Satisfying the constraints on atomic code. In order to calculate independent components, and to satisfy the localization constraints on atomic code, a dependency graph is constructed whose purpose is to take into account the dependencies between all instructions and global variables involved in the WHEN-part of the ${}_d$SL program.

Before we can formalize the construction of this dependency graph, we need to introduce the following notation: (1) $GlobalVar(P)$ denotes the set of global variables of a program P; (2) $Instr(w)$ denotes the set of instructions appearing in or reachable through synchronous call from a WHEN w; (3) $Var(i)$ denotes the set of non-tilded variable appearing in an instruction i; (4) $Flow(i_1, i_2)$ is true if control may flow from instruction i_1 to instruction i_2.

The dependency graph of a ${}_d$SL program P, noted G_P, is an undirected graph (V_P, E_P) where $V_P = GlobalVar(P) \cup \{Instr(w)|w \in When(P)\}$ and $E_P = \{(i,v)|v \in Var(i)\} \cup \{(i_1,i_2)|Flow(i_1,i_2)\}$. Informally, an edge in this dependency graph G_P states that both vertices (either an instruction or a global variable) must be localized on the same site in order to keep the atomic code local to that site. Therefore, by computing the connected components of this graph, we can identify the different independent components of P. Each of these components can be localized on a different site.

Finally, the localization of each of the independent components is provided by the localization table. If a global variable must be localized on a certain site according to the localization table, then the whole independent component containing that variable must be localized on that site. If inside one of the components, two global variable are supposed to be localized on different sites according to the given localization table, the program cannot be distributed. In this case, the designer must relax the atomic constraints by introducing **LAUNCH**, "**~**" or **SEQUENCE**.

In our example, given the following localization table :

temperature	Site 2	heater.state	Site 2
alarm	Site 1	heater.control	Not imposed
led	Site 1	heater.maintenance	Not imposed
fuel_cost	Not imposed		

the dependency graph, obtained by applying the previous method on the example of figure 3 is represented in figure 4.a (the vertices W_i correspond to all instructions in W_i of figure 3).

Note that in this example, all variables but `fuel_cost` are localized once the atomic constraints are fulfilled and that imposing `heater.control` on a different site than `heater.maintenance` would make the program not distributable. Also remark that fields from a same class do not necessarily need to be localized on the same site. The ~ in W3 and W4 relaxes the atomic constraints, and allows `temperature` and `heater.maintenance` to be localized on different sites.

Localizing remaining sequential instructions. Now that the atomic instructions are localized, the sequential instructions remains. The localization of some of these instructions is already imposed. Indeed some global variables have been localized by the previous algorithm. The rest of them can be localized anywhere. However, it is important to find a good, and if possible, optimal localization. Indeed, as we show further on, if two consecutive instructions in a sequence are localized on different sites, the distributer inserts a migration point in order to stop the execution on the first site and to continue it on the second site. A bad localization may result in a program containing unnecessary migration points lowering the performance of the program at runtime.

To evaluate the performance of a particular localization, we introduced the notion of weighted colored control flow graph in [7] : a control flow graph with weights on the edges expressing the mean number of times control will flow following each edge during execution. In the case of an IF, these weights are based on the estimated probability of the test being satisfied. For a WHILE, they are based on an estimation of the mean number of times the body will be executed. The weights are then obtained by recursively combining these values for nested control structures (e.g. an IF branch with probability .3 nested in a loop executing 5 times results in a weight of 1.5). The colors on the vertices model the localization of each instruction (vertices with the same color are localized on the same site). We then define the communication load as the sum of the weights of the edges between vertices of different colors, which corresponds to the mean number of migrations during execution.

The problem of finding the localization minimizing the communication load can be defined as an instance of the NP-complete Colored Multiterminal Cut problem which finds the optimal coloring for the uncolored vertices[2]. For a formal definition of the problem and efficient heuristics, which are implemented in our system, see [7].

The figure 4.b illustrates this algorithm based on the example in figure 3 and the results of the previous algorithm. Remark that the algorithm should localize `fuel_cost` on site 1 in order to minimize the communication load.

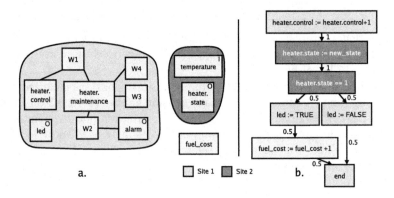

Fig. 4. a. Satisfying constraints on atomic code, b. Localizing sequential instructions.

Executable distributed code. Once every variable and instruction is uniquely assigned to a certain site, the distributer inserts migration points between instructions localized on different sites. The migration of the local context is based on extensive use of def-use chains(definition-use, a classical data-flow analysis technique). Since we have complete knowledge of live variables, the distributer can insert code that migrates only those local variables that are updated on the current site and read elsewhere. Technically, context migrating code builds messages to ask the remote update of either register or stack entries on distant sites. A valuable point of our migration method is that in contrast to many systems where the complete stack is migrated [9,13], dSL can use the information provided by the compiler to migrate only what is needed, saving valuable bandwidth. However, more instructions have to be interpreted to migrate the context than would be needed if the complete stack was migrated. Since in our target platform bandwidth is crucial because network speeds may be of very low quality, our solution yields higher performance.

Execution environment. dSL uses virtual machines. This is clearly indispensable since dSL's heterogeneous target platform consists of servers with a graphical user environment developed for Linux,UNIX,Windows on Intel or Power-PC processors and PLCs (16 bit Motorola 68340 @ 25Mhz with 4MB RAM of which 2MB is flash, no OS) interfaced to the environment. The dSL Virtual Machine, implemented for both server platforms and for the PLC hardware, can be classified as a CISC (i.e. Complex Instruction Set Computing) architecture, interpreting low level three-operand code, is single threaded and has a fixed amount of allocated memory. Simplicity and performance are essential in its design. The instruction set is very rich to optimize the interpretation/execution time ratio. In particular the instruction set contains specific instructions handling execution- and context-passing. Communications are guaranteed to respect message ordering and to be error free. In our implementation we use a simplified TCP/IP protocol stack.

The absence of a scheduler and preempted code is a design choice that aims at simplicity. Code is simply executed until it ends or migrates to another site. There is therefore no performance penalty for context switching and no need for a multi-threaded operating system.

An important feature of dSL's execution environment is that the memory size is bounded. Two reasons ensure this property : first, there is no dynamic memory allocation in dSL, so global memory can statically be allocated. Secondly, only a bounded number of processes with a local context coexist during execution. Indeed, each site has one process that handles uninterruptible synchronous code and remotely LAUNCHed methods. Finally, we can remark that since sequences have only one running instance at a time and that stacks are limited to a certain size, resulting in a statically known amount of memory.

In its current state, the dSL compiler/distributer and VM have been implemented in 20k+7k lines of C/C++ code as a proof of concept. The present implementation of the VM fits into 1MB of memory, including the dynamic program loader, debugger and interpreter. Further development, separate compilation, dynamic types, user interface, etc. is taken over by Macq Electronique. The introduction of pointers makes the static distribution process of dSL hard. We are working on a solution that uses extensive pointer analysis. Since dSL is integrated into Macq Electronique's OBviews, a commercial development environment and toolkit for the programming and supervision of PLCs, it benefits from a high number of existing utilities. The localization table as well as the description of types and global variables uses the graphical user interface of OB-Views' database subsystem. The dSL Virtual Machine is compatible with the OBViews' supervision subsystem that allows, amongst others, to create graphical representations of the controlled system, stimulated by the state of the controlling dSL program. In [8] we studied a controller, specified by a 200 lines dSL program, for the locks of a canal where various distributed constraints have to be respected (e.g. not to open both gates of the same lock). The resulting VM code was distributed on 3 PLCs. As a proof of concept, we actually built a small scale model of the locks using Lego M indstorm s^{Tm} and interfaced the PLCs to the engines and sensors[6].

6   Future Work

The main research we are conducting now and will pursue in the future is to enable the formal verification of $_d$SL. A first experiment has been conducted on the canal locks example of [8], where the $_d$SL source code is translated into Promela, and verified for the correctness of safety properties by the Spin model checker. We are working on the automatic translation of $_d$SL to Promela and more generally on an efficient way to verify $_d$SL programs avoiding the state space explosion problem. The indeterminism in $_d$SL is caused by the asynchronous composition and communications but not by the $_d$SL code itself. We hope to be able to use this fact to reduce the state space in addition to the classical methods like abstraction, symmetry and partial order reduction. We are also investigating how lightweight verification can offer a solution between testing and exhaustive verification. In order to achieve this validation, we developed a prototype debugger capable of generating traces. The model checker is used to explore the state space within a certain diameter of those traces.

In the case of exhaustive verification, we need to obtain a closed system. In order to do so, we must build a sufficiently detailed specification of the environment (i.e. the industrial process to control). This problem can be simplified by offering the user a verified library of pre-constructed and parameterizable common environments.

Further topics include efficiency (real-time behavior) and robustness issues.

References

1. P. Aubry. *Mises en oeuvre distribues de programmes synchrones (thèse).* Phd thesis, IFSIC, Rennes, France, October 1997.
2. E. Balas, G. Cornuéjols, and R. Kannan, eds. Algorithms and min-max theorems for certain multiway cuts. In *Proc. of the 2nd Integer Programming and Combinatorial Optimization Conference,* pages 334–345. Carnegie Mellon University, May 1992.
3. A. Benveniste and G. Berry. The synchronous approach to reactive and real-time systems. In *Proceedings of the IEEE,* volume 79, pages 1270–1282, 1991.
4. Gerard Berry and Georges Gonthier. The esterel synchronous programming language: Design, semantics, implementation. *Science of Computer Programming,* 19(2):87–152, 1992.
5. P. Caspi, D. Pilaud, N. Halbwachs, and J. Plaice. Lustre: A declarative language for programming synchronous systems. Conf Rec 14th Ann ACM Symp on Princ Prog Langs, 1987.
6. I. Castellani, M. Mukund, and P. S. Thiagarajan. Synthesizing Distributed Transition Systems from Global Specification. In *Foundations of Software Technology and Theoretical Computer Science,* pages 219–231, 1999.

---

[6] Pictures and videos available at http://www.ulb.ac.be/di/ssd/bdewacht/dsl

7. Bram DeWachter. Code Distribution in the dsl Environment for the Synthesis of Industrial Process Control. Technical report, U.L.B., 15 January 2003.

8. Bram DeWachter, Thierry Massart, and Cedric Meuter. An experiment on synthesis and verification of an industrial process control in the dsl environment. Proceedings of the 3rd Automated Verification of Critical Systems (AVoCS03), Technical Report DSSE-TR-2003-2, DSSE, Southampton (GB), April 2-3 2003.

9. B. Dimitrov and V. Rego. Arachne: A portable threads system supporting migrant threads on heterogeneous network farms. *IEEE Transactions on Parallel and Distributed Systems*, 9(5):459–, 1998.

10. M. Rasit Eskicioglu. Design issues of process migration facilities in distributed systems. In *IEEE Computer Society Technical Committe on Operating Systems and Application Environments Newsletter*, volume 4, pages 3–13, 1990.

11. A. Girault. *Sur la Répartition de Programmes Synchrones*. Phd thesis, INPG, Grenoble, France, January 1994.

12. J. Hennessy, M. Heinrich, and A. Gupta. Cache-coherent distributed shared memory: Perspectives on its development and future challenges. *Proc. of the IEEE, Special Issue on Distributed Shared Memory*, 87(3):418–429, 1999.

13. H. Jiang and V. Chaudhary. Compile/run-time support for thread migration. In *Proceedings of the 16th International Parallel and Distributed Processing Symposium*, Fort Lauderdale, Florida, April 2002.

14. H. Jiang and V. Chaudhary. On improving thread migration: Safety and performance. In *Proceedings: 9th International Conference on High Performance Computing 2002*, volume 2552 of *LNCS*, pages 474–484, Berlin, Germany, December 2002. Springer-Verlag.

15. P. LeGuernic, T. Gautier, M. LeBorgne, and C. LeMaire. Programming real time applications with signal. Proceedings of the IEEE, 79(9):1321-1336, September 1991.

16. T. Massart. A calculus to define correct transformations of LOTOS specifications. In *Proceedings of the FORTE'91 conference*, pages 281–296, 1992.

17. R. Milner. *Communication and Concurrency*. PHI Series in Computer Science. Prentice Hall, 1989.

18. C. Morin and I. Puaut. A survey of recoverable distributed shared memory systems. *IEEE Trans. on Parallel and Distributed Systems*, 8(9):959–969, 1997.

19. B. Nizeberg and V. Lo. Distributed shared memory: A survey of issues and algorithms. IEEE Computer, vol. 24, no.8, pp. 52-60, Aug. 1991.

20. Alin Stefănescu, Javier Esparza, and Anca Muscholl. Syntesis of Distributed Algorithm. In *To appear at 14th international conference on concurrency theory (CONCUR 2003)*, 2003.

21. Bram De Wachter, Thierry Massart, and Cédric Meuter. dsl : An environment with automatic code distribution for industrial control systems. Technical Report 512, ULB, 2004. Submitted to OPODIS 2003: 7th International Conference on Principles of Distributed Systems.

A Lower-Bound Algorithm for Load Balancing in Real-Time Systems

Cecilia Ekelin and Jan Jonsson

Department of Computer Engineering
Chalmers University of Technology
SE–412 96 Göteborg, Sweden
{cekelin,janjo}@ce.chalmers.se

Abstract. We study the problem of finding a safe and tight lower-bound on the load-balancing objective often found in real-time systems. Our approach involves the formulation of the *Multiple Bounded Change-Making Problem* which we efficiently solve by using a new symmetry-breaking algorithm. An experimental evaluation shows that the computed lower-bound is optimal in more than 70% of the cases and is able to find more than four times as many decidedly optimal solutions.

1 Introduction

The problem of load balancing is how to assign software tasks to processors in a distributed system such that the total execution time (i.e., load) on each processor is as similar as possible (i.e., balanced). In distributed computing, load balancing is an important objective since it increases the utilization of the system's resources and contributes to a higher throughput. In contrast, for real-time systems the primary concern is not throughput but rather predictability in meeting computational deadlines. However, load balancing is still desired to increase the likelihood of scheduling the tasks safely. Moreover, a balanced load increases the possibility of handling unexpected events such as aperiodic requests or task failure. Unfortunately, finding an optimal load-balance is an NP-hard problem. This means that (unless P=NP) the problem can only be solved either by using a suboptimal polynomial-time algorithm or an optimal exponential-time algorithm. In this work, we assume that the load balancing is to be performed as a part in the design of an embedded real-time system. Hence, algorithm runtime is not as crucial as in for example high-performance computing since the computation is performed off-line (at design time) rather than on-line (at run time). Furthermore, embedded real-time systems contain constraints on the execution of tasks (e.g., deadlines) that must be respected by the load-balancing algorithm. It is well known that the time spent by a search algorithm on verifying that a solution is optimal, typically is much longer than the time finding the solution. The reason is that for feasibility it is not always necessary to search all branches in the search tree. In contrast, to determine optimality (or infeasibility) all branches must be considered. However, given an objective function f (e.g.,

M. Papatriantafilou and P. Hunel (Eds.): OPODIS 2003, LNCS 3144, pp. 146–158, 2004.

for load balancing) it is possible to conservatively estimate the least (best) value
this function may assume, also known as the lower bound which can then be used
to prune the search space. In particular, if the objective value of a solution equals
the lower bound, the solution is decidedly optimal. Since the main purpose of the
lower bound is merely to boost the performance of the optimization algorithm,
it is not crucial that the lower bound is exact. Hence, it is possible to base the
lower-bound estimate on a simpler problem model, that is, a relaxation of the
original problem. The advantage of addressing the relaxed problem is that the
computational complexity can be significantly reduced. In this paper, we have
devised a lower-bound algorithm for the load-balancing objective which is based
on a relaxation to a certain kind of knapsack problem which we call the Multiple
Bounded Change-Making Problem. We present a new algorithm to address this
problem and also demonstrate the usefulness of our lower-bound algorithm by
evaluating its performance impact in a number of experiments.

2   Related Work

The load-balancing problem closely resembles the bin-packing problem although
they have been studied in different contexts. However, (in their abstract form)
the only difference is that in the load-balancing problem the number of bins
(processors) are fixed and the capacity is to be minimized whereas in the bin-
packing problem this relationship is reversed.

Optimal algorithms for these problems are usually based on the Branch-and-
Bound principle [14,11]. However, the fact that the problems are all NP-hard
has led to the development of heuristic algorithms that produce sub-optimal solutions [5,16,10]. In an optimization (minimization) context, solutions computed
by these algorithms can be said to be upper-bound estimates of the optimum.
That is, if f^* is the optimal value they compute that $f^* \leq f^{UB}$ (where f^{UB} is
the upper bound). In contrast, a lower-bound estimate computes that $f^* \geq f^{LB}$
(where f^{LB} is the lower bound). It is well known that dynamic lower-bounds
are essential for the performance of Branch-and-Bound algorithms (e.g., [4,1]).
This means that during search, the algorithm repeatedly estimate the potential
of partial solutions. However, the static counterpart, that we consider, is equally
important [3,15]. In this case the estimate is only computed once before the
search begins. The advantage of a static lower-bound is that the relaxed problem model can be more accurate since a higher computational complexity can be
tolerated. In our case, the relaxed problem is a kind of knapsack problem (Multiple Bounded Change-Making Problem) whose exact formulation has not been
previously presented. Previous work on the (single) change-making problem can
be found in [14,12].

3   Problem Description

We study the load-balancing problem within the context of real-time systems
which means that we want to assign n tasks (τ_i) to m processors (or nodes) and

also schedule the tasks on the nodes. It is assumed that a task can be assigned to any of the nodes (no locality constraints). Tasks are periodic meaning that they are invoked at regular time intervals. Invocation k of task τ_i is denoted τ_i^k. The schedule has to consider all task invocations in the time span dictated by the least common multiple of $\{\text{period}(i)\}$ also referred to as the least common period (lcp). It is assumed that all task invocations execute on the same node (no migration) and that the (worst-case) execution time (execution_time(i)) of a task is constant (identical processor speeds). The processor to which a task is assigned is denoted node(τ_i) and the actual start time of a task invocation is denoted start(τ_i^k). In addition, tasks may communicate through message passing over a bus (if they are located on different nodes) or through shared memory (if they are located on the same node). The communication delay (delay(τ_i, τ_j)) for a message between tasks τ_i and τ_j is the size of the message for inter-node communication and zero for intra-node communication. The actual transmit time of a message is denoted message_start(τ_i^k, τ_j^l). Note that, since tasks are periodic, a message may be sent several times during the lcp but the delay is the same every time due to that migration cannot occur. Tasks also have deadlines (deadline(i) $\leq$ period(i)) that restrict their finish time.

This model implies that the following constraints should hold in a feasible schedule:

- Periodicity: $\forall \tau_i^k$: start(τ_i^k) $\geq$ period(i) $\cdot$ ($k-1$) and start(τ_i^k) + execution_time(i) $\leq$ period(i) $\cdot$ ($k-1$) + deadline(i)
- Non-preemptiveness: $\forall \tau_i^k, \tau_j^l, i \neq j$: $\neg$(node(τ_i) = node(τ_j) $\wedge$ start(τ_i^k) $\leq$ start(τ_j^l) < start(τ_i^k) + execution_time(i))
- Communication[1]: start(τ_i^k) + execution_time(i) $\leq$ message_start(τ_i^k, τ_j^l) and message_start(τ_i^k, τ_j^l) + delay(i,j) $\leq$ start(τ_j^l)

The stated real-time assignment and scheduling problem will be modeled and solved using a constraint programming approach. In [6,7], we have shown how to devise such a scheduling algorithm that is also capable of performing optimization in a Branch-and-Bound fashion. The load-balancing objective is formally expressed as:

$$\text{minimize } f$$

subject to

$$
\begin{array}{ll}
f \geq \text{load}(j) & j = 1, ..., m \\
\text{load}(j) = \sum_{i=1}^{n} \frac{lcp}{period(i)} \cdot \text{execution\_time}(i) \cdot b_i & j = 1, ..., m \\
b_i \Leftrightarrow (\text{node}(\tau_i) = j) & j = 1, ..., m
\end{array}
$$

$$\text{integer node}(\tau_i) \in [1, m], b_i \in [0, 1]$$

---

[1] For communication we also require the non-preemptiveness constraint on the message transmission.

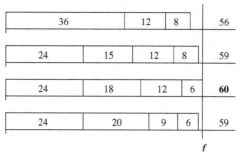

Fig. 1. Load-balancing example.

The problem we address is how to estimate a lower bound on f. From the definition it can be seen that only the task assignment ($\mathrm{node}(\tau_i)$ variables) directly contributes to the objective value. However, the constraints on the task and message scheduling ($\mathrm{start}(\tau_i^k)$/m essage_start(τ_i^k, τ_j^l) variables) affect which task assignment that will be allowed. This implies that we can speed up the search by only considering the scheduling constraints once we have found a promising task assignment. This property is in fact what we exploit to obtain a lower-bound estimate for f.

4 Algorithm Implementation

4.1 Motivational Example

Consider a system with four processors and a set of tasks with the following execution times: $\{36, 24, 24, 24, 20, 18, 15, 12, 12, 12, 9, 8, 8, 6, 6\}$. We can then view the processors as bins and the tasks as items to put in the bins where the execution time represent the size of an item. The objective function f can be viewed as a lid that is supposed to be pushed as far as possible down the bins. Fig. 1 shows one solution to this load-balancing problem where $f = 60$. The question now is whether it is possible to re-arrange the items such that $f < 60$. In theory, $f = 59$ could be possible since $\lceil \frac{56+59+60+59}{4} \rceil = \lceil \frac{234}{4} \rceil = 59$. In fact, this is the least possible value for f which is why we call it a lower bound (lb). We also know that the relationship $f \geq lb$ always holds. Hence, if we would know that there is no solution for $f = lb(= 59)$ we would also know that $lb = 60$ which would make the solution in Fig. 1 optimal. So how can we test whether $f = 59$ is feasible? The first thing we can do is to look at only one bin. Since 59 is the lower bound we know that at least one bin has to be filled exactly to the lid for all items to be accommodated. Hence, if it is not possible to fill even one bin exactly we know that the lid (lb) has to be increased. In this example, however, one bin can be filled exactly so we have to move on to the next step and consider all the bins again. We can now recognize that only filling one bin exactly may not imply that the problem is feasible since the remaining items must also fit into the remaining bins. In our example we would have to fill either two or three bins exactly since $234 = 2 \cdot 59 + 2 \cdot 58 = 3 \cdot 59 + 57$. (There are not enough items to fill all four bins exactly.) We proceed by finding the maximum number of bins that can be filled exactly when $f = 59$. In this example, it is in fact only possible to fill two bins which means that the three bin possibility is out of the question. So is it possible then to fill two bins exactly with $f = 58$? It turns out that there is only one such solution and therefore we know that the lid has to be increased to $lb = 60$ and thus the solution in Fig. 1 is decidedly optimal.

4.2   Basic Idea

From the example we see that a trivial lower-bound is obtained as $lb = \lceil \frac{\sum_{i=1}^{n} execution\_time(i)}{m} \rceil$. [2] We then want to test whether we can assign the tasks to the nodes such that $load(j) \leq lb$. This is done by relaxing the real-time assignment and scheduling problem into a (multiple) knapsack problem. That is, given a number of knapsacks (processors) with a certain capacity (the lower bound) how should we stuff a collection of items (tasks) into these such that all items fit. Unfortunately, this problem is also NP-complete even in the case of only one knapsack [14]. However, the knapsack problem may still be easier to solve than the original scheduling problem for a particular instance, mainly because fewer variables are involved. Furthermore, since we select the capacity to be the smallest possible it means that at least one node (the highest loaded) must have $load(j) = lb$. Hence, we can focus our attention to this single node case since if a fit for this node is not possible we know that $f^* > lb$ and can try to solve the problem with $lb + 1$ instead. However, when a fit is found we do not know whether there also exist any fits for the rest of the processors. In particular, we want to know the maximum number of processors, m_{lb}, that can be filled with tasks such that $load(j) = lb$ still holds. (In the following paragraphs we will show how m_{lb} is computed through the multiple knapsack problem.) Thus, the lower-bound iteration continues until the constraint $m_{lb} \cdot lb + \sum_{i=1}^{m-m_{lb}} m_{lb-\delta} \cdot (lb - \delta) \geq \sum_{i=1}^{n} execution\_time(i)$ is satisfied. That is, when all tasks have a chance of being fitted, either to one of the highest loaded processors (with load lb) or one of the remaining processors (with load $lb - \delta$). Our lower-bound algorithm operates in two similar stages where first the $lb - \delta$ and $m_{lb-\delta}$ values are determined and then the lb and m_{lb} values. Prior to presenting the lower-bound algorithm in detail we describe the different knapsack problems that are solved as part of the computation.

4.3   The Bounded Change-Making Problem

Following the previous reasoning, our lower-bound algorithm for the objective function for load balancing require us to solve a knapsack problem that is defined as:

---

[2] In the rest of this paper $execution\_time(i)$ will denote the total execution time of a task during the lcp.

$$\sum_{i=1}^{v} \text{size}(i) \cdot x_i = \text{lb}$$

$$\texttt{integer } x_i \in [0, \text{bounded}(i)]$$

Here, v denotes the number of distinct item sizes where $\text{size}(i)$ and $\text{bounded}(i)$ denotes the size and availability of item i respectively. It is assumed that $\text{size}(1) > \text{size}(2) > ... > \text{size}(v)$. In our case, the sizes are derived as the total execution times of the task during the lcp. Similarly, the availability is given by the number of tasks that have the same total execution time. Hence, $v \leq n$ and $1 \leq \text{bounded}(i) \leq n$.

This problem formulation is known as the Bounded Change-Making Problem (BCMP) [14,12]. Usually it is also assumed that the number of items ($\sum x_i$) is to be minimized but our primary concern is the feasibility problem. The problem is very straight-forward to implement in CLP(FD) [2,13] which our optimization framework is based on. Although the problem is known to be NP-complete [14], it is usually quite easy to solve in short time even for large instances ($v > 1000$) [12].

4.4 The Multiple Bounded Change-Making Problem

The method described in the previous paragraph finds one solution to the problem. However, since we actually deal with m problems (m processors), we need to know if there are any more ways to solve the problem. In particular, we want to know the maximum number of simultaneous solutions there are (without violating the availability constraints), since this number equals m_{lb}. Hence, we formulate the Multiple Bounded Change-Making Problem (MBCMP) as:

$$\sum_{i=1}^{v} \text{size}(i) \cdot x_{i,j} = \text{lb} \qquad j = 1, ..., m_{lb}$$
$$\sum_{j=1}^{m_{lb}} x_{i,j} \leq \text{bounded}(i) \qquad i = 1, ..., v$$

$$\texttt{integer } x_{i,j} \in [0, \text{bounded}(i)]$$

Compared to the BCMP this problem is significantly harder to solve in our context. Firstly, since we actually want to determine (the maximum) m_{lb} we would have to solve the problem for increasing m_{lb} until we have found an infeasible problem instance.[3] Secondly, (as mention earlier) determining infeasibility usually requires a large search effort which in many cases is caused by the presence of symmetries in the problem. For instance, the first constraint of the MBCMP formulation is a $v \times m_{lb}$-constraint matrix where each row corresponds to a solution to the BCMP. By reordering the rows it is possible to get several solutions to the MBCMP that in reality only count as one solution since we are not interested in the ordering of the individual BCMP solutions. These kind of symmetric solutions can be restricted by introducing lexicographic ordering constraints [9]. For the MBCMP, two vectors U and V are said to be lexicographically ordered, $U \geq_{lex} V$, when the following holds:

---

[3] In reality we start with the expected m_{lb} and decrease it if no feasible solution is found.

$\exists i \forall_{j<i} j : U(j) = V(j), U(i) \geq V(i)$. The reason for not using strict ordering is that we do not want to exclude those solutions where the availability constraint allows two (or more) equal BCMP solutions to exist together. Unfortunately, imposing this kind of ordering constraints does not break all the symmetries in the problem. Consider the following example:

$$size(i): \quad 40 \quad 20 \quad 10 \quad 5 \quad 2$$
$$bounded(i): 1 \quad 2 \quad 1 \quad 2 \quad 25$$
$$lb: \quad 50$$

s_1	1	0	1	0	0
s_2	1	0	0	2	0
s_3	0	2	1	0	0
s_4	0	2	0	2	0
s_5	0	0	0	0	25

These five solutions (to the BCMP) are lexicographically ordered such that $s_1 \geq_{lex} s_2 \geq_{lex}...\geq_{lex} s_5$. If we attempt to combine these BCMP solutions into a solution for the MBCMP (with $m_{lb} = 3$) and use lexicographic-ordering constraints on the row constraints, the only combinations that will be allowed are (s_1, s_4, s_5) and (s_2, s_3, s_5). Hence, the combinations (s_1, s_5, s_4), (s_4, s_1, s_5), (s_4, s_5, s_1), (s_5, s_4, s_1), (s_5, s_1, s_4), (s_2, s_5, s_3), (s_3, s_2, s_5), (s_3, s_5, s_2), (s_5, s_2, s_3), (s_5, s_3, s_2) are rejected because of symmetries which leads to a substantial complexity reduction. However, if solutions to the MBCMP are found by consecutively solving the BCMPs, the partial solutions (s_1, s_4) and (s_2, s_3) both result in the same subproblem to solve since the total amount of selected items are the same in both cases. Hence, the search for s_5 will be carried out twice. Clearly, for larger instances it is quite likely that several partial solutions to the MBCMP will result in the same subproblem. This property is particularly unfortunate when the subproblem is infeasible which, as mentioned, may very well be the case.

4.5 Symmetry Breaking by Enumeration

It can be argued that the unbroken symmetries in the MBCMP are a result of the solution method and could be avoided by solving the MBCMP as a single problem rather than through consecutive BCMPs. However, preliminary experiments indicate that the BCMP approach is indeed the faster method since a single BCMP is easy to solve. In fact, it is even easy to find all solutions to a single BCMP through backtracking which is why we can exploit this property to achieve a more efficient solution algorithm for the MBCMP. The pseudo-code for this general symmetry-breaking method which we call Symmetry Breaking by Enumeration is shown in Fig. 2.

The expression $(\mathcal{P}, s)$ denotes that the partial solution $\mathcal{P}$ is extended with the single solution s. If this extension fails, it is (sometimes) possible to identify exactly which subset s_Δ of the solution that caused the failure. This identification procedure is illustrated with the $\diamond$-symbol. A key part in reducing the

PROCEDURE: **symmetry-breaking-by-enumeration**
Input: A partial solution $\mathcal{P}_{i\square 1}$ (to the problem $\mathcal{P}$ consisting of symmetric subproblems p_i), $i \in [1, m_{lb}]$, the set $\mathcal{S}_i$ containing all possible solutions to $\mathcal{P}_i$
Output: A solution to $\mathcal{P}$ or $\emptyset$ if failure

```
(1)     IF i > m_lb THEN
(2)         RETURN P_i□1
(3)     ELSE
(4)         FOR each s_i ∈ S_i DO
(5)             P_i := (P_i□1, s_i)
(6)             S_i := S_i - s_i
(7)             S_{i+1} := S_i
(8)             FOR each s_{i+1} ∈ S_{i+1} DO
(9)                 IF not (P_i, s_{i+1}) THEN
(10)                    S_{i+1} := S_{i+1} - s_{i+1}
(11)                    s_Δ := P_i ◇ s_{i+1}
(12)                    FOR each s ∈ S_i DO
(13)                        IF s_Δ |= s THEN
(14)                            S_i := S_i - s
(15)                        END IF
(16)                    END FOR
(17)                END IF
(18)            END FOR
(19)            P :=symmetry-breaking-by-enumeration(P_i,i + 1,S_{i+1})
(20)            IF P ≠ ∅ THEN
(21)                RETURN P
(22)            END IF
(23)        END FOR
(24)        RETURN ∅
(25)    END IF
```

Fig. 2. Our symmetry-breaking algorithm.

computational complexity of this algorithm are lines (9)-(17). The test on line (9) implies that single solutions (s_{i+1}) that cannot extend the partial solution ($\mathcal{P}_i$) will not be considered on the next level of the search tree. Furthermore, since s_Δ expresses which part of $\mathcal{P}_i$ that prevented the extension, we also know that any single solution s_i that complies with s_Δ will result in the same failure. Hence, we can remove those single solutions as candidates for extending $\mathcal{P}_{i-1}$ (lines (12)-(16)).

In our case, the $\diamond$-operation means calculating which item sizes that become overused and by what amount. That is, for each item size we can compute its remaining availability in ($\mathcal{P}_i, s_{i+1}$). If this measure is less than zero, the usage of the item caused the constraint violation. We can then compute the minimum amount used of this item (s_Δ) that will result in a remaining availability of zero in $\mathcal{P}_i$. From this information we know that, if $\mathcal{P}_i$ contains a single solution s that use at least s_Δ of the considered item, a constraint violation will occur when extending $\mathcal{P}_i$. Hence, $\mathcal{P}_{i-1}$ may not be extended by solutions s containing s_Δ.

Example. The BCMP for our previous example (shown in Fig. 1) with $lb = 58$ has the following solutions: $\mathcal{S}_1 = \{(36, 8, 8, 6), (24, 20, 8, 6), (24, 18, 8, 8), (24, 12, 8, 8, 6), (20, 18, 12, 8), (20, 18, 8, 6, 6), (20, 15, 9, 8, 6), (20, 12, 12, 8, 6), (18, 15, 9, 8, 8), (18, 12, 12, 8, 8), (18, 12, 8, 8, 6, 6), (15, 12, 9, 8, 8, 6), (12, 12, 12, 8, 8, 6)\}$. If we then select $s_1 = (36, 8, 8, 6)$ we will discover that there is no s_2 that can exist together with our selected s_1. The reason is that either the number of 8:s or 6:s are over-used. That is, $s_\Delta = \{(2, 6), (2, 8)\}$ (where $(\#, i)$ is the maximum allowed usage of an item). This means that selecting any s_1 that contains either two 8:s or two 6:s will result in $\mathcal{S}_2 = \emptyset$. Hence, we can remove these solutions which gives us $\mathcal{S}_1 = \{(24, 20, 8, 6), (20, 18, 12, 8), (20, 15, 9, 8, 6), (20, 12, 12, 8, 6)\}$. We then select $s_1 = (24, 20, 8, 6)$ instead and again find that no extension is possible since $s_\Delta = \{(1, 20)\}$. This implies that $\mathcal{S}_1 = \emptyset$ and the algorithm terminates. (Note that the finial result will be the same regardless of which solution that is selected in each iteration.)

In summary, our algorithm **MBCMP-sym** for solving the MBCMP using symmetry breaking by enumeration consists of two steps: (i) the generation of $\mathcal{S}_1$ which contains all solutions to the BCMP and (ii) the call **symmetry-breaking-by-enumeration**$(\emptyset, 1, \mathcal{S}_1)$. Here it is assumed that **symmetry-breaking-by-enumeration** is extended to record the largest partial solution (with size m'_{lb}) in case the problem is infeasible. Note that when solving a single BCMP any duplicate solutions will only be found once. Hence, such solutions must be explicitly added to $\mathcal{S}_1$. (Thus, with strict mathematic notation $\mathcal{S}_i$ is not really a set.) The procedure runs in $O(|\mathcal{S}_1|^{m_{lb}})$ and breaks all symmetries in the problem. Furthermore, an item size selection that is identified to cause a failure will never be considered again as it would in a normal backtracking scheme. For comparison, we have also implemented **MBCMP-lex** which solves the MBCMP problem formulation using lexicographic-ordering constraints.

4.6   The Lower-Bound Algorithm

We have now presented the different parts of our lower-bound algorithm and are able to outline its pseudo-code in Fig. 3. Similar to the case of our previously developed lower bound [8] we can use the solution to the MBCMP as a suggestion for how to co-assign the tasks in order to find the optimal solution sooner.

Our algorithm has a certain similarity with dynamic programming in the sense that we divide the problem into smaller ones and then combine their solutions. However, in our approach we only solve one subproblem in isolation and we therefore do not know how to solve it such that the overall problem is guaranteed to be feasible. In general, the main arguments against dynamic-programming algorithms are that they require a lot of space and scale poorly. These properties also applies to our algorithm since the number of BCMP solutions may be extremly large. For instance, when most items have different size and the difference in size is only minor. However, since we address the MBCMP as derived from embedded real-time systems, the experienced run-time will in most cases be acceptable (as will be shown in the next section) when considering the overall performance gain. For example, since the item sizes correspond to task execution-times (over all invocations), the variation in size is likely to be rather large. Interesting enough, when the items have very similar (different) sizes it is in general easy (hard) to ■nd near-optimal solutions but hard (easy) to verify optimality.

PROCEDURE: **lower-bound**
Input: Number of processors m, $\mathcal{C} = \{execution\_time(i)\}$
Output: Lower-bound on f

$$
\begin{aligned}
&(1) \quad lb := \lceil \frac{c}{m} \rceil - 1 \\
&(2) \quad a_j := 0, (1 \le j \le m)^\dagger \\
&(3) \quad \text{WHILE } \exists a_j = 0 \text{ DO} \\
&(4) \quad\quad \mathcal{P} := \mathbf{MBCMP}(m, lb, sizes(i), bounded(i)) \\
&(5) \quad\quad \text{IF } |\mathcal{P}| > 0 \text{ THEN} \\
&(6) \quad\quad\quad <\text{replace } |\mathcal{P}| \text{ zero } a_j \text{ with } lb > \\
&(7) \quad\quad \text{END IF} \\
&(8) \quad\quad lb := lb - 1 \\
&(9) \quad \text{END WHILE} \\
\\
&(10) \quad lb := \lceil \frac{c}{\blacksquare} \rceil \quad \blacksquare \\
&(11) \quad \text{WHILE } \quad a_j < \quad \mathcal{C} \text{ DO} \\
&(12) \quad\quad \mathcal{P} := \mathbf{MBCMP}(m, lb, sizes(i), bounded(i)) \\
&(13) \quad\quad \text{IF } |\mathcal{P}| > 0 \text{ THEN} \\
&(14) \quad\quad\quad <\text{replace } |\mathcal{P}| \text{ least } a_j \text{ with } lb > \\
&(15) \quad\quad \text{END IF} \\
&(16) \quad\quad lb := lb + 1 \\
&(17) \quad \text{END WHILE} \\
&(18) \quad \text{RETURN } \mathtt{max}(a_j)
\end{aligned}
$$

† The vector a is used to store $m_{lb\blacksquare \ \delta}, lb - \delta$ and m_{lb}, lb.

Fig. 3. Our lower-bound algorithm.

5 Evaluation

The purpose of our evaluation is to investigate the quality of our lower-bound concerning reduction in run-time and deviation from optimum.

5.1 Experimental Setup

In our evaluation we have made five studies labeled A, B, C, D and E. Each study consists of 100 randomly generated task sets using the parameters in Table 1. Values indicated using ranges or sets were chosen randomly from a uniform distribution. The deadline of a task equals its period. Cyclic or mutual communication was avoided by only allowing a task τ_i to communicate with a task τ_j if $j < i$. The properties shown in italics are derived from the generated task sets and are thus not input parameters. Note that with this setup there is no guarantee that a task set is feasible.

We examined three different versions of the optimization algorithm: BB, which is plain B&B without a (static) lower-bound estimate, BB+sym which uses our lower-bound algorithm with **MBCMP-sym** (symmetry breaking by enumeration), and BB+lex which also uses our lower-bound algorithm but with **MBCMP-lex** (lexicographic-ordering constraints). To avoid too long runtimes, we had a time limit of one hour when the runs were terminated. In such cases, the best found solution so far was reported.

The purpose of the A and B studies is to investigate how the algorithms scale with the size of the problem. Similarly, studies C and D are made to illustrate how the algorithms are affected by the variation in the task execution-times. Study E is made to show the effect of communication constraints.

Table 1. Configuration parameters for the task sets.

Parameter	Study				
	A	B	C	D	E
Period	{20, 30, 40}	{20, 30, 40}	300	200	{40, 60}
Number of tasks	15	30	30	30	30
Average number of task invocations	65	128	30	30	74
Execution times	2–6	1–10	{11, 22, 33, 44, 55}	20–30	{3, 6, 9, 12, 15}
Average utilization	0.53	0.74	0.82	0.94	0.91
Communication probability	0	0	0	0	0.125
Average number of communication relations	0	0	0	0	15
Message sizes	0–0	0–0	0–0	0–0	1–5
Number of processors	4	8	4	4	6

5.2 Experimental Results

The results of running the different algorithm configurations, in terms of number of optimal solution, average load balance and average runtimes, are show in Table 2. Due to the potentially large variation in runtimes for the experiments we display both the arithmetic and geometric means for the runtimes.

As can be seen in the table, using the lower bound significantly increases the number of instances where optimality can be verified within the one hour time-limit, and at shorter runtimes. For instance, in study A the average runtime was decreased from 56 seconds to 2 seconds and in study C the number of optimal solutions increased over four times. We can also see that BB+lex/sym improve the quality of the solutions (study D and E), which is probably due to the suggested solution given by the lower-bound algorithm. In addition, we can see that BB+sym and BB+lex perform rather similarly for small problems whereas for larger problems (in terms of BCMP solutions) BB+sym outperforms BB+lex by at least an order of magnitude (studies B and D).

We also investigated how tight the computed lower-bounds are. This is done by simply adding the constraint $f = lb$. It turns out that more than 85% of the lower bounds were optimal when there were no communication constraints. In the presence of such constraints the figure drops to 72% due to that heavy communication tasks often have to be assigned to the same processor which is not recognized in the relaxed problem formulation. It could also be noted that it was only in study A that non-optimal lower-bounds was actually detected (within the one-hour time-limit).

6 Conclusions

We have presented a lower-bound algorithm for the load-balancing objective in the context of real-time systems. In experiments we found that over 70% of the computed lower-bounds were optimal and that they significantly reduced the search time. The lower-bound computation involves efficient solving of the Multiple Bounded Change-Making Problem which we achieve by introducing a new way of breaking symmetries in this problem. In our experimental evaluation, this Symmetry Breaking by Enumeration is shown to outperform the state-of-art approach of introducing lexicographic-ordering constraints.

Table 2. Algorithm performance. † For the remaining percentage, optimality was undecided.

Algorithm	Result	Study				
		A	B	C	D	E
BB	optimal solutions	100/100	31/100	22/98	26/100	9/67
	average f	65	90	251	191	113
	runtime (geo)	56 s	27 s	0.4 s	17 s	10 s
	runtime (arith)	5 min	4 min	0.4 s	4 min	55 s
BB+lex	optimal solutions	100/100	60/100	98/98	100/100	38/67
	average f	65	90	251	188	111
	runtime (geo)	2 s	8 min	0.6 s	1 min	20 s
	runtime (arith)	49 s	15 min	0.6 s	2 min	2 min
BB+sym	optimal solutions	100/100	77/100	98/98	100/100	38/67
	average f	65	90	251	188	111
	runtime (geo)	2 s	18 s	0.9 s	6 s	19 s
	runtime (arith)	48 s	2 min	0.9 s	7 s	53 s
sym/lex	optimal lower-bounds	93%	85%†	100%	100%	72%†

References

1. F. Bosi and M. Milano. Enhancing clp branch and bound techniques for scheduling problems. *Software-Practice and Experience*, 31(1):17–42, January 2001.
2. M. Carlsson, G. Ottosson, and B. Carlson. An open-ended finite domain constraint solver. In H. Glaser et al., editors, *Proc. of the Int'l Symposium on Programming Languages: Implementations, Logics, and Programs, volume 1292 of Lecture Notes in Computer Science*, pages 191–206, Southampton, UK, September 3–5, 1997. Springer Verlag.
3. H.-Y. Chao and M. P. Harper. A tighter lower bound for optimal bin packing. *Operations Research Letters*, 18:133–138, 1995.
4. G.-H. Chen and J.-S. Yur. A branch-and-bound-with-underestimates algorithm for the task assignment problem with precedence constraint. In *Proc. of the IEEE Int'l Conf. on Distributed Computing Systems*, pages 494–501, Paris, France, May 28–June 1, 1990.
5. W. W. Chu and L. M.-T. Lan. Task allocation and precedence relations for distributed real-time systems. *IEEE Trans. on Computers*, 36(6):667–679, June 1987.
6. C. Ekelin and J. Jonsson. A CLP framework for allocation and scheduling in embedded real-time systems. Tech. Rep. 01-12, Dept. of Computer Engineering, Chalmers University of Technology, S-412 96 Göteborg, Sweden, 2001.
7. C. Ekelin and J. Jonsson. Evaluation of search heuristics for embedded system scheduling problems. In *Proc. of the Int'l Conference on Principles and Practice of Constraint Programming*, pages 640–654, Paphos, Cyprus, November 26–December 1, 2001.
8. C. Ekelin and J. Jonsson. A lower-bound algorithm for minimizing network communication in real-time systems. In *Proc. of the Int'l Conference on Parallel Processing*, pages 343–351, Vancouver, Canada, August 18–21, 2002.
9. A. Frisch, B. Hnich, Z. Kiziltan, I. Miguel, and T. Walsh. Global constraints for lexicographic orderings. In *Proc. of the Int'l Conference on Principles and Practice of Constraint Programming*, pages 93–108, Ithaca, New York, September 2002.
10. D. S. Johnson. *Near-Optimal Bin-Packing Algorithms*. Ph.D. thesis, Massachusetts Institute of Technology, 1974.
11. Richard E. Korf. A new algorithm for optimal bin packing. In *Proc. of the National Conference on Artificial Intelligence*, pages 731–736, Edmonton, Canada, July 2002.

12. A. Kulanoot. *Algorithms for Some Hard Knapsack Problems*. Ph.D. Thesis, School of Mathematics and Statistics, Curtin University of Technology, Perth, Australia, January 2000.
13. Intelligent Systems Laboratory. *SICStus Prolog User's Manual*. Swedish Institute of Computer Science, 1995.
14. S. Martello and P. Toth. *Knapsack Problems: Algorithms and Computer Implementations*. Wiley, Chichester, 1990.
15. M. Milano and W. J. van Hoeve. Reduced cost-based ranking for generating promising subproblems. In *Proc. of the Int'l Conference on Principles and Practice of Constraint Programming*, pages 1–16, Ithaca, New York, September 2002.
16. S. S. Wu and D. Sweeting. Heuristic algorithms for task assignment and scheduling in a processor network. *Parallel Computing*, 20(1):1–14, January 1994.

A Simple Testing Technique for Embedded Systems

Hacène Fouchal and Antoine Rollet

LICA,Université de Reims Champagne-Ardenne
Moulin de la Housse, BP 1039, 51687 Reims Cedex 2, France
{Hacene.Fouchal, Antoine.Rollet}@univ-reims.fr

Abstract. Embedded systems are constrained and critical. They need to be validated before their development. They handle time constraints to model important aspects (delays, timeouts). This issue has to be taken into account in every step during its development life cycle, in particular in the testing step. This paper presents a methodology for the development of reliable embedded systems. A system is described as a timed automaton. It details an efficient derivation algorithm of test sequences able to identify controllable states on the system. Most of known errors of such systems are collected. They are automatically integrated on the derived sequences which are submitted to the implementation. If the system behaves correctly after this submission, the system is considered as robust.

1 Introduction

In software or hardware development, testing is highly needed in order to avoid catastrophic errors and to tackle industrial development of the product with confidence. Since few years, time is considered as a crucial feature of many sensitive systems as multimedia protocols, embedded systems, air traffic systems. Then it should be seriously considered by designers and developers.

This study deals with embedded systems described as Input Output Timed Automata [LV92,AD94](defined as automata where each transition can bear either an input action or output action with timing constraints in some cases). An embedded system (it is a reactive system too) is a system which reacts permanently with its environment, and which is subject to high time constraints. Here the whole system is seen as a graph where edges express actions or reactions of the system. On edges, we may have also some timing constraints which are related to the action execution.

In this paper, we suggest a methodology for robustness testing of embedded systems. First, we suggest a test derivation algorithm which extracts (from the specification) for each controllable state a sequence of actions starting with an input action and ends with an output one. If this sequence is not recognized by any other state, then this state is considered as identified. We will operate with a similar way for all other states with sequences containing at maximum a limited number of input actions. Then, test sequences are submitted to the

M. Papatriantafilou and P. Hunel (Eds.): OPODIS 2003, LNCS 3144, pp. 159–170, 2004.

IUT (assumed to be modelled also as a timed automaton). Its responses analysis allows us to check if every controllable state is correctly implemented.

Then, we intend to test, in addition to the conformance testing, the robustness of the system in a controlled way. We define formally the possible set of different faults that any system can perform. We show how to integrate these errors in test sequences in such a way to check reactions of the system when it performs faulty actions.

This paper is structured as follows: Section 2 contains related works to the timed testing field. In section 3, we present the robustness testing issues and some solutions to this aspect. In section 4, we discuss the observability and the controllability of such models, we detail also the assumptions we require for systems we study and then, we present an algorithm which produces, for controllable states, sequences of actions able to distinguish them from all others. Section 5 explains our technique on robustness testing. We first collect all possible errors and we show how to integrate them in test sequences. Section 6, illustrates our technique with a simple example. Section 7 gives the conclusion and some ideas about future works.

2   Related Work

There are many works and tools dedicated to timed automata verification. There are also other studies which proposed various testing techniques for timed systems. We will give an overview of them in the following section. But we will detail only one study about formal embedded system testing since the literature about this issue is quite unusual.

In [CL97], the authors derive test cases from specifications described in the form of a constraint graph. They only consider the minimum and the maximum allowable delays between input/output events. [COG98] presents a specific testing technique which suggests a practical algorithm for test generation. They have used a timed transition system model. The test selection is performed without considering time constraints. [RNHW98] gives a particular method for the derivation of the more relevant inputs of the systems. [PF99] suggests a technique for translating a region graph into a graph where timing constraints are expressed by specific labels using clock zones. [NS01] suggests a selection technique of timed tests from a restricted class of dense timed automata specifications. It is based on the well known testing theory proposed by Hennessy in [DNH84]. [HNTC01] derives test cases from Timed Input Output Automata extended with data. Automata are transformed in a kind of Input Output Finite State Machine in order to apply classical test generation technique. [SVD01] gives a general outline and a theoretical framework for timed testing. The study [AENK02] differs from the previous one by using discretization step size depending only on the number of clocks which reduces the timing precision of the action execution. [Cas02], an unique study on formal embedded systems testing, suggests to consider all possible faults that a system can execute. The designer has to insert them into the specification and finally derives test sequences from this modified specification.

As we notice, there are different ways to tackle the problem of timed and embedded testing. All of these studies focus on the reduction of the specification formalism in order to be able to derive test cases feasible in practice. In contrast to these studies, we use the timed automata model without neither translation nor transformation of labels on transitions.

3   Robustness Testing Issues

To tackle robustness testing, we need to answer the following questions: what are the (possible) differences between conformance testing and robustness testing? How to tackle the input domain of the test? How to interpret the output domain? How to model the system? And finally what testing architecture will we use?

We define the robustness notion as: a system is considered as robust if it is able to operate correctly in the presence of invalid inputs or stressful environment (IEEE definition). We will measure the ability of the system to have a "correct" or "acceptable" behavior in the presence of hazards (random errors). That means the IUT may accept unexpected (in the specification) actions without being blocked.

So, we can make out an idea to test the robustness of a system: we will use sequences obtained for the conformance testing as the basis of our method. We will apply them to the system, and in case of error (internal hazard, not provoked), we measure the ability of the system to deal with this error. Indeed, it is possible to insert some well chosen hazards in the test sequences, and apply the previous step again (we should simulate the external hazards). In this case, we should consider again the oracle and modify the verdicts. Then, the verdicts considered in robustness testing should be much more detailed than the notions of success or failure. We can add for example a robustness measure, or we can model robustness properties in some logics. Formally, we say that we have to extend the test input domain with hazards. Then, the input domain extension implies sometimes an output domain extension (moreover, even if the input domain is not extended, it is possible to extend the output domain).

We will investigate the case where the hazards are considered in the model. This case will bring us closer to the conformance testing process. We seperate in this model the aspects of "nominal" functioning from the "degraded" functioning (Fig. 1). In this case, it is possible to develop an approach where inputs are: a specification S, a fault model M, and a robustness property P and output are test sequences.

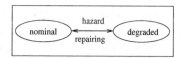

Fig. 1. Nominal, degraded modes

4   Test Sequence Generation

4.1   Input Output Timed Automata

In this section, we will recall the definitions of timed input output automaton TIOA. Timed input output automata have been proposed to model finite-state real-time systems. Each automaton has a finite set of states and a finite set of clocks which are real-valued variables. All clocks proceed at the same rate and measure the amount of time that has elapsed since they were started or reset. Each transition of the system might reset some of the clocks, and has an associated enabling condition which is a constraint on the values of the clocks. A transition can be taken only if the current clock values satisfy its enabling condition. The following definitions are mainly identical to those given in [AD94].

Definition 1 (Clock constraints and clock guard). A clock constraint over a set C of clocks is a boolean expression of the form x **oprel** z where $x \in C$, **oprel** is a classical relational operator ($<, \leq, =, \geq, >$), and z is an integer constant n. A clock guard over C is a conjunction of clock constraints over C.

Definition 2 (Timed Input Output Automata). A timed input output automaton [AD94] A is defined as a tuple $(\Sigma_A, L_A, l_A^0, C_A, E_A)$, where :

- Σ_A is a finite alphabet, split in two sets : $\mathcal{J}$ (input actions) beginning with a "?", and $\mathcal{O}$ (output actions) beginning with a "!".
- L_A is a finite set of states,
- $l_A^0 \in S$ is the initial state,
- C_A is a finite set of clocks,
- $E_A \subseteq L_A \times L_A \times \Sigma_A \times 2^{C_A} \times \Phi(C_A)$ is the set of transitions.

A transition (l, l', a, λ, G) goes from state l to state l' on input or output symbol a. The subset $\lambda \subseteq C_A$ allows the clocks to be reset within this transition, and G is a clock guard over C_A. $\Phi(C_A)$ is the set clock guards over C_A

4.2   Test Case Derivation Algorithm

We consider a TIOA $\mathcal{JA} = (\Sigma, \mathcal{S}, s_0, \mathcal{C}, \mathcal{J})$. $\mathcal{S}$ is the set of states. $\mathcal{C}$ is the set of clocks. $\mathcal{G}$ is the set of guards over $\mathcal{C}$. Σ is the set of actions, $\Sigma = \mathcal{J} \cup \mathcal{O}$ where $\mathcal{J}$ is the set of input actions and $\mathcal{O}$ is the set of output actions, $\mathcal{J}$ is the set of transitions, $\mathcal{J} = \{t_1, ..., t_M\}$ where $t_i = \langle a_i, g_i, Rset_i \rangle$ ($1 \leq i \leq N$) and $a_i \in \Sigma$, $g_i \in \mathcal{G}$ and $Rset_i \in \mathcal{C}$.

The basis of our test sequence generation algorithm is to identify specification states on the implementation. The specification timed automaton is denoted $\mathcal{JA}_\mathcal{S}$ and the implementation timed automaton is denoted $\mathcal{JA}_\mathcal{J}$. We are able to identify only states having outgoing transitions with input actions. These states are called *controllable* states where the system waits for input actions from the environment under the control of the tester. We denote $\mathcal{CS}$ this set, $\mathcal{CS} =$

$\{cs_1, ..., cs_{CSN}\}$ (CSN length set). The set denoted $\mathcal{NCS}$ contain non controllable states (they have outgoing transitions labelled by output actions).

For each state s, we need to define the set of outgoing transitions, denoted $Out(s)$. It will be used in many definitions.

Definition 3 (Output transitions). For a state s, Out(s) is the set of all transitions going from s.

The notion of controllability is expressed as: some states can be controlled by the user (they wait for an input action).

Definition 4 (Controllable state). cs is a controllable state if $cs \in \mathcal{S}$ and, if $Out(cs) = \{t_1, ..., t_n\}, \forall t_j \in Out(cs), t_j = \langle a_j, G_j, Rset_j \rangle$ and $a_j \in \mathcal{I}$

Our testing technique is based on the characterization of a controllable state by a specific sequence, if it exists. This sequence should start with an input action and should end with an output action. Between these actions, any action is possible.

Definition 5 (Possible identification sequence). seq_i is a Possible identification sequence for a state s if seq_i^s is defined as
$\{(s, t_{i_1}, s_{i_1}), (s_{i_1}, t_{i_2}, s_{i_2}), ..., (s_{i_{n-1}}, t_{i_n}, s_{i_n})\}$ where $\exists s' \in \mathcal{S}, (s, t, s') \in \mathcal{T}$ and $\forall j, 1 \leq j \leq n, t_{i_j} \in \mathcal{T}$ and $t_{i_1} = \langle a_{i_1}, G_{i_1}, Rset_{i_1} \rangle$ where $a_{i_1} \in \mathcal{I}$ and $t_{i_n} = \langle a_{i_n}, G_{i_n}, Rset_{i_n} \rangle$ where $a_{i_n} \in \mathcal{O}$.

A recognized sequence having a depth d is an identification sequence containing d input actions.

Definition 6 (Recognized sequence). rs_i^d is defined as a recognized sequence (with depth d) from a controllable state cs_i if rs_i^d is a possible identification sequence of cs_i and if rs_i^d contains d input actions.

We need to collect all the recognized sequences of a state having at maximum D input actions where D is fixed in advance.

Definition 7 (Recognised sequence set). Let cs_i a controllable state, let D the maximum number of input actions required in an identification sequence. RSS_i (Recognized Sequence Set) is the set of all recognized sequences of cs_i having at maximum D input actions. $RSS_i^D = RSS_{i_1} \cup ... \cup RSS_{i_D}$ where RSS_{i_j} is a recognized sequence of state cs_i with a depth of j.

We will be able to identify a controllable state if we are able to find a recognised sequence which is not recognized by any other state.

Definition 8 (Identification sequence). Id_i is the identification sequence for the controllable state cs_i if $Id_i \in RSS_i^D$ and $\forall cs_j \in \mathcal{CS}, Id_i \notin RSS_j^D$

A state is identified if it has an identification sequence.

Definition 9 (Identified state). cs_i is an identified state if $\exists seq_i \in RSS_i^D$ and seq_i is an identification sequence for cs_i.

Algorithm. This algorithm will produce a set $\mathcal{ID} = \{id_1, ..., id_K\}$ of identification sequences for some controllable states and having at maximum $MaxD$ input actions. But we may be able to identify all controllable states with sequences having less than $MaxD$ input actions. K is the number of identified states by this algorithm. id_i is an identification sequence for a state i. $\mathcal{CS}$ will contain the remaining states which have not been identified.

```
Data        : CS, CS1
Result      : ID, CS
d ← 1;
while CS ≠ ∅ and d ≤ MaxD do
    CurrentCS ← NextNonIdcs(CS);
    // CurrentCS contains the next non identified state of CS ;
    while CurrentCS ≠ NULL do
        // there are still unrecognized states ;
        RSS ← RecognizedSeqSet(CurrentCS, d);
        // RSS contains the set of sequences of depth d ;
        // that can potentially identify CurrentCS ;
        Identified ← FALSE;
        Count ← 1;
        while notIdentified and Count ≤ length(RSS) do
            OtherCS ← FirstCS(CS1);
            // OtherCS contains the first state of CS1 ;
            CurrentSeq ← RSS[Count];
            // CurrentSeq contains the count^th sequence of RSS ;
            Recognized ← FALSE;
            while notRecognized and OtherCS ≠ NULL do
                if CurrentCS ≠ OtherCS then
                    if RecognizedSeq(OtherCS, CurrentSeq) then
                        Recognized ← TRUE;
                    end
                end
                OtherCS ← NextCS(CS1);
                // OtherCS contains the next state of CS1 ;
            end
            if not Recognized then
                Identified ← TRUE;
                CS ← CS \ CurrentCS;
                ID[CurrentCS] ← CurrentSeq;
                // we add the sequence CurrentSeq into the set of UIO sequences;
            end
            Count ← Count + 1 ;
            // Computing with next sequence of RSS ;
        end
        CurrentCS ← NextNonIdCS(CS);
    end
    d ← d + 1;
end
```

Algorithm 1: Test sequence generation algorithm

Comments

1. We start with $\mathcal{CS}$ containing all controllable states. We will remove from $\mathcal{CS}$ all identified states. CS1 contains all controllable states during the whole algorithm. It will be needed to check each time if a sequence is not recognized by all other states.
2. We will first handle sequences having only one input action (d equal to 1).
3. For each state cs_i of $\mathcal{CS}$, we select one by one sequences starting from cs_i.
4. If the current sequence is recognized by any other state of $\mathcal{CS}$, then we deal with the next sequence going from cs_i.
5. If it is not recognized by any state, then cs_i is retrieved from $\mathcal{CS}$ and the selected sequence will be saved as the identification of cs_i.

6. If all sequences of cs_i do not discriminate it from others, we select the next state and apply the same process.

7. When all states have been handled, if $\mathcal{CS}$ is empty we stop the algorithm since all states are identified.

8. If $\mathcal{CS}$ is not empty, and If d is less than $Maxd$ then increment d by one and we repeat the algorithm from the 3.

9. If d has reached the value $MaxD$, then we stop the algorithm without total identification of all states.

10. Complexity of this algorithm: let e the number of states of the TIOA, $l_1 = max_i(card\,(RSS_i)), l_2 = card(CS1), t_{max}$ the maximum number of outgoing transitions for a state of the TIOA, then we have $C(RecognizedSeqSet) = O(e * (t_{max})^d)$ and the whole complexity is $O(e * (C(RecognizedSeqSet) + (l_1 * l_2)))$.

11. When the algorithm checks if a sequence seq_i is recognized by a state cs_j, it compares the labels of transitions going from cs_j. If it compares a transition $\langle a_i, G_i, Rset_i \rangle$ to a part of seq_i defined as $\langle a_i', G_i', Rset_i' \rangle$, this part will be recognized if and only if $a_i = a_i'$ and $Rset_i = Rset_i'$ and $G_i \cap G_i' = \emptyset$.

12. Notice that the real test sequences are longer than the UIO sequences, since every sequence is preceded by a preambule (in order to reach the state to identify) and followed by a postambule. The handled states in the algorithm will not appear in the test sequences, we only consider events in the test sequences.

5   Robustness Testing Method

In this technique, we will only handle external hazards, inserted in the test sequences. They are modelled as actions received by the system or incorrect timing constraints.

We consider that the system is described by two specifications written in the timed automata formalism (TIOA): a *nominal* specification $S = (\Sigma, \mathcal{S}, s_0, \mathcal{C}, \mathcal{T})$ which describes the behavior of the system, and a degraded specification $S_{degr} = (\Sigma_{degr}, \mathcal{S}_{degr}, s_{0degr}, \mathcal{C}_{degr}, \mathcal{T}_{degr})$ which describes the system in a degraded mode, i.e., it describes the vital functionalities and the minimum required behavior.

For example for a robot, we could require that it has to send its position at least every 10 seconds (in the degraded specification) whereas it sends its position every one second in the nominal specification.

We generate test sequences from the nominal specification. Then, we insert some hazards to these sequences. We can use a set of chosen events introduced randomly.

The tester has to send stimuli at the right moment respecting the timing constraints, and has to check the response validity. As soon as a fault is detected by the tester, we only record the system responses, and we continue to send the sequence inputs (of the nominal behavior). At the end of the sequence, if we have some unexpected responses, we check if the obtained execution trace (see the definitions below) is accepted by the degraded specification S_{degr}. If no fault has been detected by the tester, then the system is considered as robust enough regarding the considered hazards and the desired robustness level.

Furthermore, to measure the system robustness in case of internal hazards, we proceed as before without any insertion of hazards in sequences. In fact, each time we find an error during the execution step, we record the event and we continue testing. In fact, we observe the ability of the system to react to one of its own error. Notice that we do not use the degraded specification as a test sequence generation basis since we consider that the environment still sends the same inputs, and is not influenced by the system mode (normal or degraded).

In the following, we present some definitions needed to explain our test robustness algorithm.

We consider that we have at our disposal a set of test sequences produced by any derivation algorithm on Input Output timed automata.

Definition 10 (Set of test sequences). Let $S = (\Sigma, S, s_0, C, T)$ a timed automaton of the nominal specification, we denote TSS (Test Sequences Set)= $\{seq_1, ..., seq_n\}$, where $\forall i \in [1..n]$, $seq_i = < t_{i_1}, ..., t_{i_m} >$ and $t_{i_j} \in T, m = card(seq_i)$.

Definition 11 (Event). An event (a, t) is the execution of an action $a \in \Sigma$ at the time valuation t. In our case, each action is considered observable (not in our alphabet).

A timed trace is a sequence of actions (with their execution valuations) starting at the initial state.

Definition 12 (Timed trace). A timed trace is a sequence $\sigma = (a_1, t_1)(a_2, t_2)...(a_n, t_n)$ of observable events going from the initial state. From this initial state, σ allows us to know that the action a_1 is observed at the time valuation t_1, a_2 at t_2, etc ... $\forall j, t_j$ are time valuations.

Here, we define a relation between a sequence of actions and its possible clock valuations.

Definition 13 (Execute). Let σ a timed trace of the TIOA A, going from the initial state, and ending at a state considered as final. Let $L = \overset{i=0}{\underset{\infty}{\blacksquare}} \sigma_i$ the set of all timed traces. As each path p in the automaton can lead to a different observation, we define the relation $execute(p, A, \sigma)$ which unifies a path p of an automaton A and its timed trace σ ($\sigma \in L$). A path contains only action labels (without timing constraints).

Definition 14 (Observation set). Every possible observation of a path p for an automaton A is in: $ObservationSet(p, A) = \{\sigma \in L, execute(p, A, \sigma)\}$

$ObservationSet(p, A)$ is the union of all the timed traces obtained by going through the path p, and instead to handle an infinity of consecutive instants for a precise event, we gather them in an interval. This union allows us, in the following, to use an interval instead of a set of consecutive instants. For every path p in A, we denote $ObservationSet(p, A) = (a'_1, T'_1)...(a'_m, T'_m)$, with T_i a time interval, we have: $\forall j \in [1..(n-1)], \exists k$ so that $a'_j = a_k, t_k \in T'_j$ and $\exists k' > k$ so that $a'_{j+1} = a_{k\bullet}, t_{k\bullet} \in T'_{j+1}$. In other words, each action of a timed trace of $spec$ has to be in $exec$, respecting the timing constraints, and of course in the same order than the actions of $spec$.

We will present below our robustness testing algorithm (Algorithm 2). We consider $TSS = \{seq_0, ..., seq_n\}$ and $\forall i \in [1..n], seq_i = \{t_{i_1}, ..., t_{i_m}\}$ with $t_{i_j} \in \mathcal{T}$. $n = card(TSS)$ and $m = card(seq_i)$.

```
Data         : TSS , S_degr
Result       : trace , robusteEnough
robusteEnough ← true;
while there are hazards left to insert in TSS and robustEnough do
    i ← 1;
    while i ≤ n and robustEnough do
        j ← 1;
        trace ← NULL;
        errorFound ← faux;
        while j ≤ m do
            if t_{i_j} ∈ J then
                apply t_{i_j} to the system;
                if errorFound then
                    add t_{i_j} to trace;
                end
            else
                if t_{i_j} ∈ O then
                    if not(errorFound) then
                        verify that t_{i_j} is correct ;
                        if incorrect(t_{i_j}) then
                            errorFound ← true;
                            add t_{i_j} to trace;
                        end
                    else
                        add t_{i_j} to trace;
                    end
                end
            end
            j ← j + 1;
        end
        if errorFound then
            if inclusionTrace(S_degr, trace) then
                System robust enough in comparison to S_degr for seq_i;
            else
                System not robust enough in comparison to S_degr for seq_i;
                robustEnough ← false;
            end
        end
        System robust enough for seq_i;
        i ← i + 1;
    end
    if there are hazards left to insert to TSS then
        insert new hazards in TSS;
    end
end
```

Algorithm 2: Robustness testing algorithm

Then, we experiment all generated test sequences on the implementation and check their response validity. In case of error, we continue to experiment the rest of the test sequence (we assume that the system is not blocked after an incorrect action). Before staring any new test sequence, the tester checks if the obtained trace is conform to the degraded specification S_{degr}, by using the conformance relation defined below. At the end, if one sequence gives a non conform trace, then we consider that the system is not robust enough in comparison with the wanted robustnes

Notice that in order to check the validity of an output transition, the tester only checks the sent action is correct, and its time interval is also correct. Moreover, when an error is detected, we check that the execution trace is conform to S_{degr}. Complexity of this algorithm: let h the number of different scenari of insertion of hazards, $n = card(TSS)$ and $m = max_i(card(seq_i)))$, the complexity is $O(h * n * m)$.

6   Example

Suppose we have a robot in an hostile environment. The nominal specification of this robot describes that it sends its position after a position request (?position-Req), or the temperature after a temperature request (?temperatureReq). But the system must send its position and the temperature with regularity (the limit is 120s for temperature and 60s for position). The robot has a moving mode: it is able to turn or to go forward during a certain amount of time, interrupted by a stop signal (?stopTurn or ?stopForward). Fig. 2 (a) shows this specification, which is the specification in a "normal" mode.

An example of a degraded specification of this system could be the obligation for him to send its position at least every 300s, and to send the temperature at least every 600s. Then, the degraded specification is shown in Fig. 2(b).

An example of test sequences generated with our conformance testing method, using the nominal specification is :

- S1: (?temperatureReq,$x < 120$),(!temperature,$x := 0$);
- S2: Non Controllable;
- S3: Non Controllable;
- S4: (?endMove),(?positionReq,$y < 60$),(!position,$y := 0$);
- S5: (?stopTurn),(?endMove),(?positionReq,$y < 60$),(!position,$y := 0$);
- S6: (?stopForward),(?endMove),(?positionReq,$y < 60$),(!position,$y := 0$);

7   Conclusion

In this paper we introduced a simple approach for robustness testing. We have chosen the timed automata formalism as a specification model since it deals with time constraints with accuracy.

Then we have suggested a test case derivation algorithm for timed automata where on each transition we can have an input action or output action (it is different from the Input/Output FSM model). This algorithm derives test cases for controllable states only. Other states do not work under user control, we can not ensure a test sequence for them.

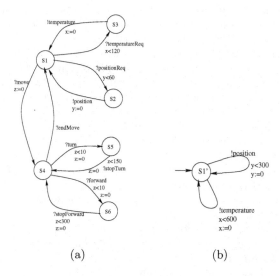

(a)   (b)

Fig. 2. (a) nominal specification (s1 initial location), (b) degraded specification

We have also suggested an approach to test robustness of critical systems. We first consider that we have two system specifications: one which contains all functionalities, denoted the nominal specification and a second one which contains the most important functionalities denoted as the degraded specification.

The robustness testing technique is based on the generation of test cases from the nominal specification. Then after the execution of these test cases on the implementation, we check if the implementation responses are valid on the degraded specification. In fact we test if the crucial behavior is ensured by the implementation.

The main limitation of this methodology is that we cannot guarantee an entire fault coverage since we are not able to generate test cases for all specification states. The fault coverage has to be improved. For the next future, we will iomprove our hazards insertion.

We have undertaken the implementation of our methodology in an integrated tool, then we will be able to experiment it on some real cases as a robot functioning or a multimedia protocol.

A long version of the paper is available on (www.univ-reims.fr/Labos/resycom).

References

[AD94]   R. Alur and D. Dill. A theory of timed automata. *Theoretical Computer Science*, 126:183–235, 1994.

[AENK02]   Rachida Dssouli Abdeslam En-Nouaary and Ferhat Khendek. Timed wp-method: Testing real-time systems. *IEEE Transactions on Software Engineering (TSE)*, 28(11):1023–1038, 2002.

[Cas02]   Richard Castanet. Les enjeux du test de robustesse. In *Journées du Réseau Thématique Prioritaire SECC*, November 2002.

[CL97]   Duncan Clarke and Insup Lee. Automatic generation of tests for timing constraints from requirements. In *Proceedings of the Third International Workshop on Object-Oriented Real-Time Dependable Systems*, Newport Beach, California, February 1997.

[COG98]   R. Cardel-Oliver and T. Glover. A practical and complete algorithm for testing real-time systems. In *Proc. of the 5th. Formal Techniques in Real-Time and Fault-Tolerant Systems*, volume 1486 of Lecture Notes in Computer Science, pages 251–261. Springer Verlag, 1998.

[DNH84]   R. De Nicola and M. Hennessy. Testing equivalences for processes. *Theoretical Computer Science*, 34:83–133, 1984.

[HNTC01]   Teruo Hogashino, Akio Nakata, Kenichi Taniguchi, and Ana R. Cavalli. Generating Test Cases for a Timed I/O Automaton Model. In *Proceedings of the 13th International Workshop on Test of Communicating Systems 2001 (Beinjin, China)*, October 2001.

[LV92]   N.A. Lynch and F.W. Vaandrager. Forward and backward simulations for timing-based systems. In J.W. de Bakker, C. Huizing, W.P. de Roever, and G. Rozenberg, editors, *Proceedings REX Workshop on Real-Time: Theory in Practice*, Mook, The Netherlands, June 1991, volume 600 of *Lecture Notes in Computer Science*, pages 397–446. Springer Verlag, 1992.

[NS01]   Brian Nielsen and Arne Skou. Automated Test Generation from Timed Automata. In T. Margaria and W. Yi, editors, *Proceedings of the Workshop on Tools and Algorithms for the Construction and Analysis of Systems*, Genova, Italy, volume 2031 of *Lecture Notes in Computer Science*, pages 343–357. Springer Verlag, April 2001.

[PF99]   E. Petitjean and H. Fouchal. From Timed Automata to Testable Untimeed Automata. In *24th IFAC/IFIP International Workshop on Real-Time Programming, Schloss Dagstuhl, Germany*, 1999.

[RNHW98]   P. Raymond, X. Nicollin, N. Halbwatchs, and D. Waber. Automatic testing of reactive systems, madrid, spain. In *Proceedings of the 1998 IEEE Real-Time Systems Symposium, RTSS'98*, pages 200–209. IEEE Computer Society Press, December 1998.

[SVD01]   J. Springintveld, F.W. Vaandrager, and P. R. D'Argenio. Timed Testing Automata. *Theoretical Computer Science*, 254(254):225–257, 2001.

Detecting Temporal Logic Predicates in Distributed Programs Using Computation Slicing*

Alper Sen and Vijay K. Garg

Dept. of Electrical and Computer Engineering
The University of Texas at Austin, Austin, TX, 78712, USA
{sen, garg}@ece.utexas.edu
http://www.ece.utexas.edu/~{sen,garg}

Abstract. Detecting whether a finite execution trace (or a computation) of a distributed program satisfies a given predicate, called *predicate detection*, is a fundamental problem in distributed systems. To solve this problem, we generalize an effective abstraction technique called *computation slicing*. We present polynomial-time algorithms to compute slices with respect to temporal logic predicates from a "regular" subset of CTL, that contains temporal operators EF, EG, and AG. Furthermore, we show that these slices contain precisely those global states of the original computation that satisfy the predicate. Using temporal predicate slices, we give an efficient (polynomial in the number of processes) predicate detection algorithm for a subset of CTL that we call regular CTL. Regular CTL contains nested temporal predicates for which, to the best of our knowledge, there did not previously exist efficient predicate detection algorithms. Then we show that we can enlarge the subset of CTL and still obtain effective results. Our algorithm has been implemented as part of a tool for analysis of distributed programs. We illustrate the effectiveness of our techniques on several protocols achieving speedups of over three orders of magnitude in one example, compared to partial order state-space search of SPIN. Furthermore, we were able to complete the verification for 250 processes for a partial order trace.

1 Introduction

A fundamental problem in distributed systems is that of *predicate detection* – detecting whether a finite execution trace of a distributed program satisfies a given predicate. There are applications of predicate detection in many domains such as testing, debugging, and monitoring of distributed programs. For example, when debugging a distributed mutual exclusion algorithm, it is useful to monitor the system to detect concurrent accesses to the shared resources. We can model a finite trace in two ways. The first model imposes a partial order between events, for example Lamport's *happened-before* relation [12]. The second model imposes a total order (interleaving) of events. We use the former approach in this paper, which is a more faithful representation of concurrency [12]. Furthermore we can obtain better coverage in terms of testing and debugging by capturing all interleavings in a partial order. This coverage may translate into finding bugs that are not found using a single interleaving.

---

* supported in part by the NSF Grants ECS-9907213, CCR-9988225, Texas Education Board Grant ARP-320, an Engineering Foundation Fellowship, and an IBM grant

M. Papatriantafilou and P. Hunel (Eds.): OPODIS 2003, LNCS 3144, pp. 171–183, 2004.

The main problem in predicate detection in the partial order model is the *state explosion problem*—the set of possible global states of a distributed program with n individual processes can be of size exponential in n. A variety of strategies for ameliorating the state explosion problem, including symbolic representation of states and partial order reduction have been explored [14,6,23].

In this paper, we present a provably efficient predicate detection algorithm using a technique called computation slicing. *Computation slicing* was introduced in [5,15] as an abstraction technique for analyzing *distributed computations* (finite execution traces). A *computation slice*, defined with respect to a global predicate, is the computation with the least number of global states that contains all global states of the original computation for which the predicate evaluates to true. This is in contrast to traditional slicing techniques which either work at the program level or do slicing with respect to variables. Computation slicing can be used to throw away the *extraneous* global states of the original computation in an efficient manner, and focus on only those that are currently *relevant* for our purpose.

The concept of slicing is useful for detecting temporal logic predicates since it enables us to reason only on the part of the global state space that could potentially affect the predicate. Many specifications of distributed programs are temporal in nature because we are interested in properties related to the sequence of states during an execution rather than just the initial and final states. For example, the liveness property in dining philosophers problem, "a philosopher, whenever gets hungry, eventually gets to eat", is a temporal property. We use the temporal logic CTL [1] to write specifications of distributed programs and interpret it on a finite distributive lattice of global states. Basic temporal operators of this logic include **EF**, **AF**, **EG**, **AG**, the rest may be found elsewhere [19]. We say that temporal predicate **EF**(p) (resp. **EG**(p)) holds at a global state G if and only if for some path starting from G and ending at the final state, the predicate p eventually (resp. always) holds on the path. We say that temporal predicate **AF**(p) (resp. **AG**(p)) holds at a global state G if and only if for all paths starting from G, the predicate p eventually (resp. always) holds on all the paths. For example a nested temporal predicate **AG**(**EF**$(reset)$) states that reset is possible from every state.

With the results of this paper, we can efficiently use computation slicing for predicate detection in the subset of CTL with the following three properties. First, temporal operators are **EF**, **EG**, and **AG**. Second, atomic propositions are regular predicates, which we will define later. Third, negation operator has been pushed onto atomic propositions. We call this logic *Regular* CTL *plus* (RCTL+), where plus denotes that the disjunction and negation operators are included in the logic. We also consider a disjunction and negation free subset of RCTL+ and denote this by *Regular* CTL (RCTL). In RCTL+, we use the class of predicates, called *regular predicates*, that was introduced in [5]. The slice with respect to a regular predicate contains *precisely* those global states for which the predicate evaluates to true. Regular predicates widely occur in practice during verification. Some examples of regular predicates are conjunction of local predicates [4,9] such as "all processes are in *red* state", certain channel predicates [4] such as "at most k messages are in transit from process P_i to P_j", and some relational predicates [4]. We show that temporal predicates **EF**(p), **EG**(p), and **AG**(p) are regular when p is regular and present polynomial-time algorithms to compute slices with respect to these temporal predicates.

We show that the complexity of predicate detection for a predicate p in RCTL is $O(|p| \cdot n^2|E|)$, where $|p|$ is the number of boolean and temporal operators in p, n is the number of processes and $|E|$ is the number of events in the trace. To the best of our knowledge, there did not previously exist efficient algorithms (polynomial in the number of processes) to detect predicates that contain nested temporal logic predicates such as $\mathbf{AG}(\mathbf{EF}(reset))$. Furthermore, we validate with experiments that even for RCTL+ predicates our computation slicing based technique is very effective.

We implemented our predicate detection algorithms for RCTL and RCTL+, which use computation slicing, in a prototype tool called Partial Order Trace Analyzer (POTA) [21]. We performed experiments using POTA on several protocols such as the Asynchronous Transfer Mode Ring (ATMR) [10]. In all cases, our technique completes fast and uses state space efficiently.

Due to space limitations, further experimental results and the formal proof of correctness of the algorithms are given in the extended version of the paper in [19].

2   Related Work

Predicate detection is a hard problem. Detecting even a 2-CNF predicate under $\mathbf{EF}$ modality has been shown to be NP-complete, in general [16]. Some examples of the predicates for which the predicate detection can be solved efficiently are: *conjunctive* [4,9], *disjunctive* [4], *linear* [4,18], and *non-temporal regular* [5,15] predicates. These predicate classes have been so far detected under some or all of the temporal operators $\mathbf{EF, EG, AG, AF}$ and under the *until* operator of CTL [18], but not under any nesting of these operators. For example, a predicate $\mathbf{EF}(p \wedge \mathbf{EG}(q))$, where p and q are conjunctive predicates, cannot be efficiently detected using only the efficient algorithms for conjunctive predicates. With the results of this paper, we can detect such nested temporal logic predicates efficiently. The idea of using temporal logic for analyzing execution traces (also referred to as runtime verification) has recently been attracting a lot of attention. We first presented a temporal logic framework for partially ordered execution traces in [18] and gave efficient algorithms for predicates of the form $\mathbf{EG}(p)$ and $\mathbf{AG}(p)$ when p is a linear predicate. The efficiency of those algorithms depended on the fact that p was a state predicate and therefore we could efficiently evaluate the satisfiability of p at a global state. However, in this paper we present implementation of efficient algorithms even when p is a temporal predicate.

Some other examples of using temporal logic for checking execution traces are the MaC tool [11], the JPaX tool [7], and the JMPaX tool [22]. The MaC and JPaX tools consider a totally ordered view of an execution trace and therefore can potentially miss bugs that can be deduced from the trace. JMPaX tool is closer to our tool POTA [21] because of the partial order trace model. JMPaX uses a subset of temporal logic with safety where atomic propositions can be arbitrary. Whereas we use a subset of temporal logic with both safety and liveness where atomic propositions are restricted. The complexity of the predicate detection algorithm in our approach is polynomial-time whereas the complexity is exponential-time in JMPaX.

3 Model

A *distributed program* consists of n sequential processes denoted by $P_1, P_2, \ldots, P_n$ communicating via asynchronous messages. In this paper, we are concerned with a single *computation* (*execution*) of a distributed program. Traditionally, a distributed computation is modeled as a partial order on a set of events, called happened-before relation [12]. In this paper we relax the restriction that the order on events must be a partial order. More precisely, we use directed graphs to model distributed computations as well as slices. Directed graphs allow us to handle both of them in a uniform and convenient manner.

Given a directed graph G, let $\mathsf{V}(G)$ and $\mathsf{E}(G)$ denote the set of vertices and edges, respectively. We define a *consistent cut* (global state) on directed graphs as a subset of vertices such that if the subset contains a vertex then it contains all its incoming neighbours. Formally, C is a consistent cut of G, if $\forall e, f \in \mathsf{V}(G) : (e, f) \in \mathsf{E}(G) \wedge (f \in C) \Rightarrow (e \in C)$. We say that a strongly connected component is *non-trivial* if it has more than one vertex. We denote the set of consistent cuts of a directed graph G by $\mathcal{C}(G)$. Observe that the empty set $\emptyset$ and the set of vertices $\mathsf{V}(G)$ trivially belong to $\mathcal{C}(G)$. We call them *trivial* consistent cuts.

We model a *distributed computation* (or simply a *computation*), denoted by $\langle E, \rightarrow \rangle$, as a directed graph with vertices as the set of events E and edges as $\rightarrow$. We use event and vertex interchangeably. A distributed computation in our model can contain cycles. This is because whereas a computation in the happened-before model captures the *observable* order of execution of events, a computation in our model captures the set of possible consistent cuts. Intuitively, each strongly connected component of a computation can be viewed as a *meta-event*; a meta-event consists of one or more primitive events, which are send, receive, or internal events.

We assume the presence of a fictitious *global initial* and a *global final event*, denoted by $\bot$ and $\top$, respectively. The global initial event occurs before any other event on the processes and initializes the state of the processes. The global final event occurs after all other events on the processes. Any non-trivial consistent cut will contain the global initial event and not the global final event. Therefore, every consistent cut of a computation in traditional model (happened-before model) is a non-trivial consistent cut of the computation in our model and vice versa. Note that the empty consistent cut, $\emptyset$, in the traditional model corresponds to $\{\bot\}$ in our model and the final consistent cut, E, in the traditional model corresponds to $E - \{\top\}$ in our model and we denote this by $\mathcal{E}$. We use uppercase letters C, D, H, V, and W to represent consistent cuts. Figure 1 shows a computation and its lattice of (non-trivial) consistent cuts. A consistent cut in the figure is represented by its frontier. A *frontier* of a consistent cut is the set of those events of the cut whose successors, if they exist, are not contained in the cut. For example, the consistent cut $C = \{e_3, e_2, e_1, f_2, f_1, \bot\}$ is represented by $\{e_3, f_2\}$.

Given a consistent cut, a predicate is evaluated with respect to the values of variables resulting after executing all events in the cut. If a predicate p evaluates to true for a consistent cut C, we say that C satisfies p. We leave the predicate undefined for the trivial consistent cuts. A global predicate is *local* if it depends on variables of a single process. We interpret predicates in our logic over the consistent cuts of a computation. We say that a consistent cut C satisfies $\mathbf{AG}(p)$ (resp. $\mathbf{EG}(p)$) if every cut on all sequences

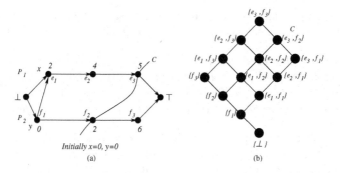

Fig. 1. (a) A computation $\langle E, \rightarrow \rangle$, (b) its lattice corresponding to $\mathcal{C}(G)$

of consistent cuts (resp. on some sequence of consistent cuts) from C to the final cut satisfies p. Similarly, we say that C satisfies $\mathbf{EF}(p)$ if there exists a consistent cut that satisfies p on some sequence from C to the final cut. The *predicate detection* problem is to decide whether the initial consistent cut of a distributed computation satisfies a predicate. In this paper we assume that atomic propositions are non-temporal regular predicates and their negations (which we will define in the next section). The formal syntax of RCTL+ is as follows. Every atomic proposition is an RCTL+ formula. If p and q are RCTL+ formulas, then so are $p \vee q$, $p \wedge q$, $\mathbf{EF}(p)$, $\mathbf{EG}(p)$, and $\mathbf{AG}(p)$. We define RCTL as the subset of RCTL+ where disjunction and negation operators are not allowed. Note that full CTL contains $\mathbf{X}$ and $\mathbf{U}$ operators, to denote *next-time* and *until* modalities.

4   Background on Slicing and Regular Predicates

The notion of computation slice is based on the Birkhoff's Representation Theorem for Finite Distributive Lattices [2]. The readers who are not familiar with earlier papers on slicing in [5,15] are urged to read [19]. Roughly speaking, a computation slice (or simply a slice) is a concise representation of all those consistent cuts of the computation that satisfy the predicate. More precisely,

Definition 1 (slice [15]). *A slice of a computation with respect to a predicate is a directed graph with the least number of consistent cuts that contains all consistent cuts of the given computation for which the predicate evaluates to true.*

We denote the slice of a computation $\langle E, \rightarrow \rangle$ with respect to a predicate p by $\mathsf{slice}(\langle E, \rightarrow \rangle, p)$. Note that $\langle E, \rightarrow \rangle = \mathsf{slice}(\langle E, \rightarrow \rangle, \mathsf{true})$. Every slice derived from the computation $\langle E, \rightarrow \rangle$ has the trivial consistent cuts ($\emptyset$ and E) among its set of consistent cuts. A slice is *empty* if it has no non-trivial consistent cuts [15]. In the rest of the paper, unless otherwise stated, a consistent cut refers to a non-trivial consistent cut. In general, a slice will contain consistent cuts that do not satisfy the predicate (besides trivial consistent cuts). In case a slice does not contain any such cut, it is called *lean*. We next give the regular class of predicates for which the slice is lean.

Given a computation, the set of consistent cuts satisfying a regular predicate forms a sublattice of the set of consistent cuts of the computation [5]. Equivalently,

Definition 2 (regular predicate [5]). *A predicate is regular if given two consistent cuts that satisfy the predicate, the consistent cuts obtained by their set union and set intersection also satisfy the predicate. Formally, given a regular predicate p,*
(C satisfies p) $\wedge$ (D satisfies p) $\Rightarrow$ (C $\cap$ D satisfies p) $\wedge$ (C $\cup$ D satisfies p)

We say that a regular predicate is *non-temporal* if it does not contain temporal operators such as **EF**, **AG**, and **EG**, otherwise it is a *temporal* regular predicate.

Some examples of non-temporal regular predicates are monotonic channel predicates such as "there are at least k messages in transit from P_i to P_j", conjunction of local predicates such as "P_i and P_j are in critical section", and relational predicates such as $x_1 - x_2 \leq 5$, where x_i is a monotonically non-decreasing integer variable on process i. From the definition of a regular predicate we deduce that a regular predicate has a least satisfying cut and a greatest satisfying cut. Furthermore, the class of regular predicates is closed under conjunction.

Also in [15] polynomial-time algorithms are given to compute slices with respect to boolean combination of regular predicates. Given the slices with respect to two regular predicates, the complexity of computing the slice for the conjunction and disjunction of these regular predicates is $O(n^2|E|)$. The complexity of computing the slice for the negation of a regular predicate is $O(n^2|E|^2)$. Note that regular predicates are not closed under disjunction and negation operators therefore slices obtained with respect to predicates that contain these operators may not be lean.

Temporal Regular Predicates
Now, we study regularity of a predicate p when temporal operators **EF**, **AG**, and **EG** are applied to it. Our results enable us to compute lean slices for these temporal predicates.

Lemma 1. *When p is regular,* **EF**(p), **AG**(p), *and* **EG**(p) *are regular.*

However, the regularity does not follow in the case of **AF**(p), **EX**(p), **AX**(p), **EU**(p, q) and **AU**(p, q). We now give an example in Figure 2 where consistent cuts D and H satisfy **AF**(p) but their intersection $(D \cap H)$ does not. This is because there exists a path starting from $(D \cap H)$ and ending at the final cut $\mathcal{E}$ where p never holds on the path. We present examples for the other temporal predicates in the extended version of the paper [19].

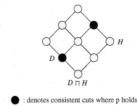

● : denotes consistent cuts where p holds

Fig. 2. AF(p) **may not be regular**

5   Computation Slices for Temporal Predicates

In this section, we describe computation slicing algorithms for *temporal* regular predicates to enable *efficient* predicate detection for RCTL+. Earlier, Mittal and Garg [5,15] presented computation slicing algorithms for *non-temporal* regular predicates, which they use to detect predicates such as $\mathbf{EF}(p)$, $\mathbf{EG}(p)$ and $\mathbf{AG}(p)$. We present algorithms for *temporal* regular predicates, which we use to detect *nested* temporal predicates such as $\mathbf{EG}(p \wedge \mathbf{EF}(q))$, and which is a much larger predicate class.

Since the consistent cuts of the slice of a computation is a subset of consistent cuts of the computation, the slice can be obtained by adding edges to the computation. In other words, the slice contains *additional edges* that do not exist in the computation. These additional edges may generate strongly connected components in the slice. For example, consider Figure 5(a) that displays the slice of the computation in Figure 1 with respect to $\neg((x = 5) \wedge (y = 2))$. The only consistent cut in the computation that does not satisfy the predicate is $\{e_3, f_1\}$. By adding the edge (f_2, e_3), we disallow this consistent cut from the slice. Similarly, since the consistent cuts of the slice for $\mathbf{AG}(p)$ is a subset of consistent cuts of the slice for p, the slice for $\mathbf{AG}(p)$ can be obtained by adding edges to the slice for p. Below, we will show which edges we should add to a computation (resp. to the slice for p) for computing slices for $\mathbf{EF}(p)$ (resp. for computing slices for $\mathbf{AG}(p)$).

Slicing Algorithms

Now we explain Algorithm A1 in Figure 4 for generating the slice of a computation with respect to $\mathbf{EF}(p)$. From the definition of $\mathbf{EF}(p)$, all consistent cuts of the computation that can reach the greatest consistent cut that satisfy p, say W, will also satisfy $\mathbf{EF}(p)$ and furthermore these are the only cuts that satisfy $\mathbf{EF}(p)$. We can find the cut W using slice($\langle E, \rightarrow \rangle, p$) when it is nonempty. We construct the slice for $\mathbf{EF}(p)$ from the computation so that the slice has the same consistent cuts as the computation upto the final cut of the slice W. To ensure that all cuts that cannot reach W do not belong to the slice, we add edges from $\top$ to the successors of events in the frontier of W in the computation. Adding an edge from $\top$ to an event makes any cut that contains the event trivial, therefore not of interest to us. Figure 3 shows the application of Algorithm A1. Given the slice of the computation in Figure 1(a) for some predicate p as shown in Figure 3(a), first we compute the final cut of the slice for p, that is, $\{e_2, f_3\}$. Then, on the computation, we add an edge from $\top$ to the successor of e_2, that is e_3. The successor of f_3 does not exist so we do not add any other edges. The resulting slice for $\mathbf{EF}(p)$ is displayed in Figure 3(c).

The complexity analysis is as follows. In Step 1 we can find the final cut of slice($\langle E, \rightarrow \rangle,$) p using the strongly connected components in $O(n|E|)$. Steps 2 to 4 take $O(n)$ time. The overall complexity is $O(n|E|)$.

Algorithm A2 in Figure 4 generates the slice for $\mathbf{AG}(p)$. We explained above that to obtain the slice for $\mathbf{AG}(p)$ we will add edges to the slice for p and therefore eliminate consistent cuts that do not belong to the slice for $\mathbf{AG}(p)$. We claim that consistent cuts of slice for p that do not include vertex e of each additional edge (e, f) in slice for p do not satisfy $\mathbf{AG}(p)$. For simplicity, let the slice($\langle E, \rightarrow \rangle, p$) have a single additional edge (e, f). Consider consistent cuts $\{\bot\}$, $\{f_1\}$, $\{e_1, f_1\}$, and $\{e_2, f_1\}$ of the slice in Figure 5(a) that do not include vertex f_2 of the additional edge (f_2, e_3). It is easy to see that

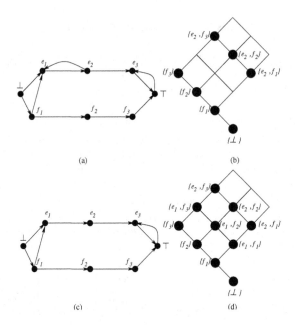

Fig. 3. (a) A slice of $\langle E, \rightarrow \rangle$ in Fig. 1 (b) the corresponding sublattice (c) The application of the temporal operator **EF** on the slice in (a) (d) the corresponding sublattice

these four consistent cuts do not satisfy **AG**(p). This is because there exists a consistent cut $\{e_3, f_1\}$ in the computation that does not satisfy p, yet which is reachable from these four consistent cuts.

For example, the slice in Figure 5(a) has an additional edge (f_2, e_3) so we add the edge $(f_2, \perp)$ and obtain the slice for **AG**(p) as in Figure 5(c).

In Step 2 we can add edges for each additional edge in slice$(\langle E, \rightarrow \rangle, p)$. From [15], there are $O(n|E|)$ such edges when the skeletal representation of a slice is used. Therefore, the overall complexity is $O(n|E|)$.

The algorithm for **EG**(p) slicing displayed in Figure 4 is similar to the **AG**(p) slicing algorithm. However in this case, for each additional edge (e, f) *that generates a non-trivial strongly connected component* in slice$(\langle E, \rightarrow \rangle, p)$, we add an edge from the vertex e to the vertex $\perp$. Intuitively, due to such a strongly connected component on all paths from the initial to the final state in the computation there exists a cut that does not satisfy p.

We give the formal proof of correctness of the algorithms in [19] .

Predicate Detection using Slicing

Given an execution trace and a predicate in RCTL+, we can compute the slice for the predicate recursively from inside-out by applying the appropriate temporal or boolean operator on the slices. The computation slice may contain more states than the ones that satisfy the predicate when slices are not lean. Therefore, we use the following strategy in POTA to decide whether the predicate is satisfied or not. Case 1, if the slice and the input trace have different initial states then the predicate is not satisfied. In this case a

---

Algorithm A1

Input: A computation $\langle E, \rightarrow \rangle$ and slice($\langle E, \rightarrow \rangle, p$)
Output: slice($\langle E, \rightarrow \rangle, \mathbf{EF}(p)$)
1.   Let G be $\langle E, \rightarrow \rangle$ and let W be the final cut of slice($\langle E, \rightarrow \rangle, p$)
2.   **If** W exists **then**
3. $\forall e \in frontier(W)$: add an edge from the vertex $\top$ to $succ(e)$ in G
4.   **return** G
5.   **else return** empty slice

Algorithm A2

Input: A computation $\langle E, \rightarrow \rangle$ and slice($\langle E, \rightarrow \rangle, p$)
Output: slice($\langle E, \rightarrow \rangle, \mathbf{AG}(p)$)
1.   Let G be slice($\langle E, \rightarrow \rangle, p$)
2.   For each pair of vertices (e, f) in slice($\langle E, \rightarrow \rangle, p$) such that,
            (i) $\neg(e \rightarrow f)$ in $\langle E, \rightarrow \rangle$, and (ii) $(e \rightarrow f)$ in slice($\langle E, \rightarrow \rangle, p$)
            add an edge from vertex e to the vertex $\bot$ in G
3.   **return** G

Algorithm A3

Input: A computation $\langle E, \rightarrow \rangle$ and slice($\langle E, \rightarrow \rangle, p$)
Output: slice($\langle E, \rightarrow \rangle, \mathbf{EG}(p)$)
1.   Let G be slice($\langle E, \rightarrow \rangle, p$)
2.   For each pair of vertices (e, f) in slice($\langle E, \rightarrow \rangle, p$) such that,
            (i) $\neg(e \rightarrow f)$ in $\langle E, \rightarrow \rangle$, and (ii) $(e \rightarrow f)$ and $(f \rightarrow e)$ in slice($\langle E, \rightarrow \rangle, p$)
            add an edge from vertex e to the vertex $\bot$ in G
3.   **return** G

Fig. 4. Algorithm for generating a slice with respect to $\mathbf{EF}(p)$, $\mathbf{AG}(p)$ and $\mathbf{EG}(p)$

counterexample is generated. Case 2, if the predicate is from RCTL and if the slice and the input trace have the same initial states then the predicate is satisfied.

The complexity of predicate detection for RCTL is dominated by the complexity of computing the slice with respect to a non-temporal regular predicates, which has $O(n^2|E|)$ complexity [5,15]. Therefore, the overall complexity of predicate detection for RCTL is $O(|p| \cdot n^2|E|)$, where $|p|$ is the number of boolean and temporal operators in p.

When the predicate does not belong to RCTL (that is, it contains disjunction or negation operators) the slice may not be lean. In this case, we may have to take an extra step. This is because the initial state of the slice may not satisfy the predicate. Therefore, we employ the translator module of POTA and translate the slice into Promela [8] . Then we use SPIN to check the trace assuming that there are equivalent specifications in LTL. Using SPIN may lead to exponential-time complexity for RCTL+. However, the slice is in general much smaller than the computation and therefore we still have efficient verification, which we validate with experiments in the next section.

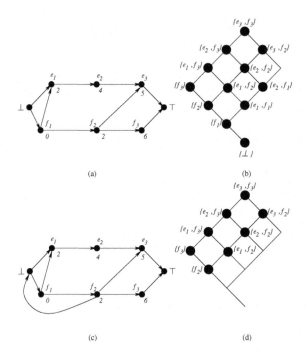

Fig. 5. (a) The slice of $\langle E, \rightarrow \rangle$ in Fig. 1 with respect to $\neg((x = 5) \wedge (y = 0))$ (b) the corresponding sublattice (c) The slice of $\langle E, \rightarrow \rangle$ in Fig. 1 with respect to **AG** $\neg((x = 5) \wedge (y = 0))$ (d) the corresponding sublattice

6   Experimental Results

We implemented our algorithms using Java in a prototype tool called Partial Order Temporal Analyzer (POTA) [21]. POTA consists of analyzer, translator and instrumentor modules. We have implemented slicing based predicate detection algorithms in the analyzer module. In order to evaluate the effectiveness of POTA, we performed experiments with scalable protocols, comparing our computation slicing based approach with partial order reduction based approach of SPIN [8]. Intuitively, when searching the state-space, at each consistent cut, partial order reduction approach allows only a small subset of enabled transitions to be explored. The translator module takes an execution trace and generates SPIN code. Currently, the instrumentation is being done manually. The instrumented program is such that when run every process outputs its local state where a local state contains the values of variables relevant to the predicate in question and a vector clock that is updated for each internal, send and receive event according to the Fidge/Mattern [3,13] algorithm. Vector clocks enable us to obtain a partial order representation of traces. All experiments were performed on a 1.4 Ghz Pentium 4 machine running Linux. We restricted the memory usage to 512MB, but did not set a time limit. The two performance metrics we measured are running time and memory usage. We run the programs for 20 seconds and our measurements are averaged over 20 traces for each program. Further experimental results can be obtained from POTA website [20] for protocols such as General Inter-ORB Protocol (GIOP), distributed dining philosophers and leader election.

We present experimental results for the Asynchronous Transfer Mode Ring (ATMR) protocol which was verified in [17] using SPIN. ATMR protocol [10] is an ISO standard based on a high-speed shared medium connecting a number of access nodes by channels in a ring topology. For controlling access to this type of shared medium, the ring is first initialized with a fixed number of ATM cells continuously circulating around the channel from one node to another. Within each access node there is an access unit which performs both the physical layer convergence function and the access control function. Access to the ring is requested by the client and controlled by a combination of a window mechanism and a reset procedure. The client can issue a sending request to the access unit and receive a data cell. The window mechanism limits the number of cells a node can transmit at a time, called the "credits" of this node. The reset procedure reinitializes the window in all access units to a predefined credit value.

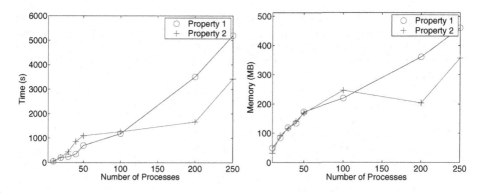

Fig. 6. ATMR verification results, SPIN runs out of memory for > 3 processes

We conducted experiments for several predicates used in [17]. Due to space limitations, we present two of them here.

1. Once an access unit exhausts its window size credit, the credit will eventually be renewed. $\mathbf{EF}((credit_i == 0) \wedge \mathbf{EG}(\neg(credit_i == 6)))$, for all access units i, where $credit$ stands for the number of credits which is being held by an access unit and 6 is the preset maximum value.
2. A client's request will be eventually acknowledged. $\mathbf{EF}(req_i \wedge \mathbf{EG}(\neg ack_i))$, for all clients i, where req is a cell sending request signal from a client to an access unit. If the requested cell has been sent out, the access unit will return an ack signal to the client.

The full state space verification of ATMR by Peng et al. [17] even for a configuration with 3 nodes was not completed due to state explosion. To enable verification for larger number of processes, they used an approximation technique in SPIN called *bit-state hashing* where two bits of memory are used to store a reachable state and they could verify upto 6 nodes on a 2GB memory machine with less than 98 percent coverage. In

Figure 6, we present experimental results for the two properties of ATMR. We generated execution traces for upto 250 nodes and completed full state space verification of these traces. Whereas, SPIN failed to complete full state space verification for more than 3 nodes even when the input were traces rather than the protocol.

7   Conclusion

We have presented an approach for detecting temporal logic predicates based on computation slicing. Application of our algorithms for detecting safety and liveness properties of distributed programs was presented. The experimental work proves that for large problem sizes, computation slicing is an effective technique. As a future work, we would like to apply our theory to multi-threaded Java programs.

References

[1] E. M. Clarke and E. A. Emerson. Design and Synthesis of Synchronization Skeletons using Branching Time Temporal Logic. In *Proc. of the Workshop on Logics of Programs*, volume 131 of *LNCS*, Yorktown Heights, New York, May 1981.

[2] B. A. Davey and H. A. Priestley. *Introduction to Lattices and Order*. Cambridge University Press, Cambridge, UK, 1990.

[3] C. Fidge. Logical Time in Distributed Computing Systems. *IEEE Computer*, 24(8):28–33, August 1991.

[4] V. K. Garg. *Elements of Distributed Computing*. John Wiley & Sons, 2002.

[5] V. K. Garg and N. Mittal. On Slicing a Distributed Computation. In *Proc. of the 15th Int'l. Conference on Distributed Computing Systems (ICDCS)*, 2001.

[6] P. Godefroid and P. Wolper. A partial approach to model checking. In *Proc. of the 6th IEEE Symposium on Logic in Computer Science*, pages 406–415, 1991.

[7] K. Havelund and G. Rosu. Monitoring Java Programs with Java PathExplorer. In *Runtime Verification 2001*, volume 55 of *ENTCS*, 2001.

[8] G. J. Holzmann. The Model Checker SPIN. *IEEE Transactions on Software Engineering*, 23(5), May 1997.

[9] M. Hurfin, M. Mizuno, M. Raynal, and M. Singhal. Efficient detection of conjunctions of local predicates. *IEEE Transactions on Software Engineering*, 24(8):664–677, 1998.

[10] ISO. Specification of the Asynchronous Transfer Mode Ring Protocol (ATMR). 1993.

[11] M. Kim, S. Kannan, I. Lee, O. Sokolsky, and M. Viswanathan. Java-MaC: A Run-time Assurance Tool for Java Programs. In *Runtime Verification 2001*, volume 55 of *ENTCS*, 2001.

[12] L. Lamport. Time, Clocks, and the Ordering of Events in a Distributed System. *Communications of the ACM*, 21(7):558–565, July 1978.

[13] F. Mattern. Virtual Time and Global States of Distributed Systems. In *Proc. of the Int'l Workshop on Parallel and Distributed Algorithms*, 1989.

[14] K. L. McMillan. *Symbolic Model Checking*. Kluwer Academic Publishers, 1993.

[15] N. Mittal and V. K. Garg. Computation Slicing: Techniques and Theory. In *In Proc. of the 15th Int'l. Symposium on Distributed Computing (DISC)*, 2001.

[16] N. Mittal and V. K. Garg. On Detecting Global Predicates in Distributed Computations. In *Proc. of the 15th Int'l. Conference on Distributed Computing Systems (ICDCS)*, 2001.

[17] H. Peng, S. Tahar, and F. Khendek. Comparison of SPIN and VIS for Protocol Verification. *Software Tools for Technology Transfer*, 4(2):234–245, 2003.

[18] A. Sen and V. K. Garg. Detecting Temporal Logic Predicates on the Happened-Before Model. In *Proc. of the Int'l Parallel and Distributed Processing Symposium (IPDPS)*, 2002.

[19] A. Sen and V. K. Garg. Automatic Generation of Slices for Temporal Logic Predicate Detection. Technical Report TR-PDS-2003-001, PDSL, ECE Dept. Univ. of Texas at Austin, 2003. Available at http://maple.ece.utexas.edu/.

[20] A. Sen and V. K. Garg. Partial Order Trace Analyzer (POTA). http://maple.ece.utexas.edu/˜sen/POTA.html, 2003.

[21] A. Sen and V. K. Garg. Partial Order Trace Analyzer (POTA) for Distributed Programs. In *Runtime Verification 2003*, volume 89 of *ENTCS*, 2003.

[22] K. Sen, G. Rosu, and G. Agha. Runtime Safety Analysis of Multithreaded Programs. In *Proc. of the 11th ACM Symposium on the Foundations of Software Engineering*, 2003.

[23] A. Valmari. A Stubborn Attack On State Explosion. In *2nd Int'l. Conference on Computer-Aided Verification (CAV)*, volume 531 of *LNCS*, pages 156–165, 1990.

Transformations for Write-All-with-Collision Model*

Sandeep S. Kulkarni and Mahesh (Umamaheswaran) Arumugam

Software Engineering and Network Systems Laboratory
Department of Computer Science and Engineering
Michigan State University
East Lansing MI 48824
{sandeep,arumugamcse.msu.edu
http://www.cse.msu.edu/~{sandeep,arumugam}

Abstract. In this paper, we consider a new atomicity model, *write all with collision* (WAC), and compare it with existing models considered in the literature. This model captures the computations in sensor networks. We show that it is possible to transform a program from WAC model into a program in read/write model, and vice versa. Further, we show that the transformation from WAC model to read/write model is stabilization preserving, and the transformation from read/write model to WAC model is stabilization preserving for timed systems. In the transformation from read/write model to WAC model, if the system is untimed (asynchronous) and processes are deterministic then under reasonable assumptions, we show that (1) the resulting program in WAC model can allow at most one process to execute, and (2) the resulting program in WAC model cannot be stabilizing. In other words, if a deterministic program cannot read then it is important that it can tell time.

Keywords: Model conversions, Preserving stabilization, Atomicity refinement, Write-all-with-collision model, Read/Write model

1 Introduction

The ability of modeling abstract distributed programs and transforming them into concrete programs that preserve the properties of interest is one of the important problems in distributed systems. Such transformation allows one to write a program in one (typically a simpler/restrictive) model and run it on another (typically a general/less restrictive) model. Hence, several algorithms (e.g., [1, 2, 3, 4, 5]) have been proposed for enabling such transformation.

In this paper, we are interested in a new model of computation that occurs in sensor networks. These sensors are resource constrained and can typically communicate with other (neighboring) sensors over a radio network. One of the important issues in these networks is message collision: Due to the shared medium,

---

* This work was partially sponsored by NSF CAREER CCR-0092724, DARPA Grant OSURS01-C-1901, ONR Grant N00014-01-1-0744, NSF Equipment Grant EIA-0130724, and a grant from Michigan State University

M. Papatriantafilou and P. Hunel (Eds.): OPODIS 2003, LNCS 3144, pp. 184–197, 2004.

if a sensor simultaneously receives two messages then they collide and, hence, both messages become incomprehensible. However, if a message communication does not suffer from a collision then the message is written in the memory of all neighbors of the sender.

Based on the above description, we can view the model of computation in sensor networks as a write all with collision (WAC) model. Intuitively, in this model, in one atomic action, a sensor (process) can update its own state and the state of all its neighbors. However, if two sensors (processes) simultaneously try to update the state of a sensor (process), say k, then the state of k is unchanged. (For precise definition, we refer the reader to Section 2.)

Moreover, in sensor networks, detecting such collisions is difficult due to several reasons. For example, it is possible that a sensor succeeds in updating the state of one of its neighbors even though its update causes collision at another neighbor. Hence, in this paper, we assume that collisions are not detectable. We would like to note that most of our results are also applicable for the case where collisions can be detected. We discuss this issue in Section 6.

While previous literature has focused on transformations among other models of computation (e.g., [1,2,3,4,5]), the issue of transformation from (respectively, to) WAC model to (respectively, from) other models has not been considered. To redress this deficiency, we focus on the problem of identifying the transformations that will allow us to transform programs in WAC model into read/write model (where a process can either read the state of one of its neighbors or write its own state, but not both), and vice versa.

Contributions of the paper. In this paper, we focus on transformation from WAC model under power-set semantics (where any subset of enabled actions can be executed concurrently) into read/write model, and vice versa. We show that concepts such as graph coloring (e.g., [6,7,8]), local mutual exclusion (e.g., [4]) and collision-free diffusion [9] can be effectively used for obtaining these transformations. The main contributions of the paper are as follows:

- For untimed (asynchronous) systems, we present an algorithm for the transformation of programs in read/write model into programs in WAC model. We also show the optimality of this transformation; specifically, we show that if the transformed program is deterministic, cannot use time and cannot perform redundant writes (see Section 3 for definition) then at most one process can execute at a time. Also, we argue that this transformation cannot be made stabilization preserving.
- For timed systems, we present an algorithm for the transformation of programs in read/write model into programs in WAC model. This transformation permits concurrent execution of multiple processes. We also show that if the given program in read/write model is stabilizing fault-tolerant [10,11], i.e., starting from an arbitrary state, it recovers to states from where its specification is satisfied, then, for a fixed topology, the transformed program in WAC model is also stabilizing fault-tolerant. In other words, for timed systems, we show that the transformation is stabilization preserving.

- We present an algorithm for the transformation of programs in WAC model into programs in read/write model. We show that this transformation is also stabilization preserving. This transformation does not assume that the topology is fixed or known in advance.
- We show how to transform programs in other models considered in the literature to WAC model, and vice versa.

Organization of the paper.   The rest of the paper is organized as follows. In Section 2, we introduce the read/write model and the WAC model. Then, in Section 3, we present an approach for the transformation of programs in read/write model into programs in WAC model under power-set semantics for untimed systems. Subsequently, in Section 4, we present the transformation for timed systems. Then, in Section 5, we present an approach for the transformation of programs in WAC model under power-set semantics into programs in read/write model. Finally, we make concluding remarks in Section 7.

2   Atomicity Models, Semantics, and System Assumptions

In this section, we first precisely specify the structure of the programs written in read/write model and in WAC model. Then, we present the assumptions made about the underlying system.

The programs are specified in terms of guarded commands; each guarded command (respectively, action) is of the form:

guard $\longrightarrow$ *statement*,

where *guard* is a predicate over program variables, and *statement* updates program variables. An action $g \longrightarrow st$ is enabled when g evaluates to true and to execute that action, st is executed. A computation of this program consists of a sequence $s_0, s_1, \ldots$, where s_{j+1} is obtained from s_j by executing actions (one or more, depending upon the semantics being used) in the program.

A computation model limits the variables that an action can read and write. Towards this end, we split the program actions into a set of processes. Each action is associated with one of the processes in the program. We now describe how we model the restrictions imposed by the read/write model and the WAC model.

Read/Write model.   In read/write model, a process consists of a set of public variables and a set of private variables. In the read action, a process reads (one or more) public variables of one of its neighbors. For simplicity, we assume that each process j has only one public variable $v.j$ that captures the values of all variables that any neighbor of j can read.

Furthermore, in a read action, a process could read the public variables of its neighbor and write a different value in its private variable. For example, consider a case where each process has a variable x and j wants to compute the sum of the x values of its neighbors. In this case, j could read the x values of its neighbors in sequence. Whenever j reads $x.k$, it can update a private variable $sum.j$ to be

$sum.j + x.k$. Once again, for simplicity, we assume that in the read action where process j reads the state of k, j simply copies the public variables of k. In other words, in the above case, we require j to copy the x values of all its neighbors and then use them to compute the sum.

Based on the above discussion, we assume that each process j has one public variable, $v.j$. It also maintains $copy.j.k$ for each neighbor k of j; $copy.j.k$ captures the value of $v.k$ when j read it last. Now, a read action by which process j reads the state of k is represented as follows:

$$\text{true} \quad \longrightarrow \quad copy.j.k = v.k$$

And, the write action at j uses $v.j$ and $copy.j$ (i.e., copy variables for each neighbor) and any other private variables that j maintains to update $v.j$. Thus, the write action at j is as follows:

$$predicate(v.j, copy.j, other\_private\_variables.j)$$
$$\longrightarrow \quad \text{update } v.j, other\_private\_variables.j;$$

WAC model. In the WAC model, each process consists of write actions (to be precise, write-all actions). Each write action at j writes the state of j and the state of its neighbors. Similar to the case in read/write model, we assume that each process j has a variable $v.j$ that captures all the variables that j can potentially write to any of its neighbors. Likewise, process j maintains $l.j.k$ for each neighbor k; $l.j.k$ denotes the value of $v.k$ when k wrote it last. Thus, an action in WAC model is as follows:

$$predicate(v.j, l.j, other\_private\_variables.j)$$
$$\longrightarrow \quad \text{update } v.j, other\_private\_variables.j;$$
$$\forall k : k \text{ is a neighbor of } j : l.k.j = v.j;$$

Remark. In the rest of the paper, we leave the additional private variables considered above implicit.

Semantics. For the WAC model considered in this paper, there are different types of semantics that can be used. Some of the commonly encountered semantics include, interleaving (also known as central daemon), maximum-parallelism and power-set semantics (also known as distributed daemon). In interleaving semantics, given a set of enabled actions, i.e., actions whose execution will change the state of some process, one of those actions is non-deterministically chosen for execution. In maximum-parallelism, all enabled actions (one from each process) are executed concurrently. And, in power-set semantics, any non-empty subset of enabled actions (at most one from each process) is executed concurrently. In this paper, unless stated otherwise, we assume that the program in WAC model is executed under power-set semantics.

System assumptions. We assume that the set of processes in the system are connected. If the set of processes are partitioned then the algorithms in this paper can be executed for each partition. Further, we assume that in the given program in read/write model, for any pair of neighbors j and k, j can never conclude that k does not need to read the state of k. In other words, we require that the transformation should be correct even if each process executes infinitely often. Further, in our transformation from read/write model to WAC model, we assume that the topology remains fixed during the program execution, i.e., failure or repair of processes does not occur. Thus, while proving stabilization, we disallow corruption of topology related information. This assumption is similar to assumptions in previous stabilizing algorithms where the process IDs are considered to be incorruptible. We note that our transformation from WAC model to read/write model does not assume that the topology is known up front and the topology can change at run time.

We consider two types of systems, timed and untimed. In a timed system, each process has a clock variable. We assume that the rate of increase of clock is same for all the processes. In an untimed (asynchronous) system, processes do not have the notion of time or the speed of processes. In both these systems, we assume that the execution of an action is instantaneous. The time is consumed between successive actions. Additionally, in an untimed system, we assume that the delay between successive actions is unpredictable.

3   Read/Write Model to WAC Model in Untimed Systems

In this section, we discuss the first of our transformations where we transform a program in read/write model into a program in WAC model. In the WAC model, there is no equivalent of a read action. Hence, an action by which process j reads the state of k in the read/write model needs to be modeled in the WAC model by requiring process k to write the appropriate value at process j. Of course, when k writes the state of j in this manner, it is necessary that no other neighbor of j is writing the state of j at the same time. Finally, a write action in read/write model can be executed in WAC model as is.

To obtain the transformed program that is correct in WAC model, we organize the processes in the given program (in read/write model) in a ring. Such a ring can be statically embedded in any arbitrary graph by first embedding a spanning tree in it and then using an appropriate traversal mechanism to ensure that each process appears at least once in the ring (cf. Figure 1).

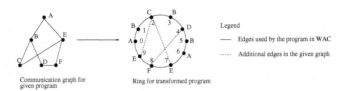

Fig. 1. In the transformed program, 'A' will execute actions of processes 0 and 6, 'B' will execute actions of processes 1, 3 and 5, and so on.

Let the processes in this ring be numbered $0 \ldots n-1$; note that if a process from the original graph is repeated in the ring then that process gets multiple numbers in this ring. Now, in the transformed program, process 0 executes first. When process 0 executes and writes the state of process 1 (and any other processes that are neighbors of process 0 in the original communication graph), process 1 is enabled and permitted to execute. When process 1 executes, it allows process 2 to execute, and so on. Figure 2 shows the actions of process j in the transformed program. If a process in the original graph has multiple numbers in the ring, it executes the actions corresponding to all those values.

```
process j
const   n;                      // number of processes in the ring
var     v.j, l.j, counter.j;
initially
        set v.j according to the initial value of v.j in read/write model;
        set l.j according to the initial value of copy.j in read/write model;
        counter.j = 0;
begin
        counter.j = j  ⟶  if(predicate(v.j, l.j)) update v.j;
                          counter.j = (j + 1) mod  n;
                          ∀k : k is a neighbor of j : l.k.j, counter.k = v.j, (j + 1) mod n;
                          // this write action will enable process numbered j + 1
end
```

Fig. 2. Read/write model to WAC model

Theorem 3.1 For every computation of the transformed program in WAC model under power-set semantics there is an equivalent computation of the given program in read/write model.

For reasons of space, we refer the reader to [12] for the proofs of all the theorems in this paper.   □

Optimality issues.   Now, we discuss the optimality of the transformation algorithm presented in Figure 2. Towards this end, we first identify the notion of redundant writes. Based on the definition of WAC model, the guard of any action, say of process j, in WAC model depends only on the local variables of j. Now, consider the case where process j executes its action (and writes its state as well as the state of its neighbors). If an action of j is still enabled after this execution, it follows that j can again execute and write the state of its neighbors. In this scenario, one of the writes of j is redundant if the system was untimed and no collision had occurred. To show the optimality of the above transformation, we assume that processes do not perform such redundant writes.

Redundant writes.   We say that process j does not perform redundant writes if after the execution of any action by j, all actions of j are disabled until a neighbor of j executes and writes the state of j.

Theorem 3.2 In an untimed system where processes cannot detect collisions, any algorithm that (1) transforms a given program in read/write model into an equivalent program in WAC model under power-set semantics, and (2) ensures that the processes in the generated program in WAC model are deterministic and do not perform redundant writes, must produce programs in WAC model in which at most one process executes at a time.   □

There are several ways to improve the performance of the transformation if we weaken some of the assumptions made above. Specifically, we can remove the assumption that processes cannot perform redundant writes in order to allow concurrency in the programs in WAC model. In [12], we present a solution that provides potential concurrency if processes are allowed to perform redundant writes. Another approach would be to remove the assumption about untimed systems. If the processes are allowed to use time, we can design transformation algorithms that allow more concurrency. In Section 4, we present such algorithms.

Stabilization issues.   Now, under the assumptions stated in the above theorem, we show that the transformation shown in Figure 2 cannot be stabilization preserving. Based on the assumption that processes do not perform redundant writes, for each process, say j, there exists a local state of that process where none of its actions are enabled. Also, since the guard of an action at process j depends only on local variables of j, we can perturb the given program to states where none of the actions are enabled. It follows that it will not be possible for the program to reach legitimate states from such a state.

In the context of the above result, a reader may wonder if a stabilizing token ring circulation algorithm (e.g., [11]) could be used to achieve stabilization in the transformation shown in Figure 2. To add stabilization to the program in Figure 2, we need a stabilizing token ring circulation algorithm that is correct under the WAC model. By contrast, existing stabilizing token ring circulation algorithms are correct under read/write model.

The above impossibility result depends on the assumption that the system is untimed and processes are deterministic, cannot detect collisions, and cannot perform redundant writes. If the assumption about untimed system is removed then it is possible to preserve stabilizing fault-tolerance. We present such stabilization preserving algorithms in Section 4.

4   Read/Write Model to WAC Model in Timed Systems

In this section, we present an algorithm for the transformation of a program in read/write model into a program in WAC model for timed systems. Specifically, we present a transformation for an arbitrary topology using graph coloring. Also, this transformation can be achieved using a collision-free time-slot based protocol like time-division multiple access (TDMA) [9, 13]. In these transformations, we initially assume that the clocks of the processes are initialized to 0 and the rate of increase of the clocks is same for all processes. Subsequently, we also present an approach to deal with uninitialized clocks; this approach enables us to ensure that if the given program in read/write model is stabilizing fault-tolerant then the transformed program in WAC model is also stabilizing fault-tolerant.

Transformation algorithm.   The main idea behind this algorithm is graph coloring. Let the communication graph in the given program in read/write model be $G = (V, E)$. We transform this graph into $G' = (V, E')$ such that $E' = \{(x, y) | (x \neq y) \wedge ((x, y) \in E \vee (\exists z :: (x, z) \in E \wedge (z, y) \in E))\}$ (cf. Figure 3). In other words, two distinct vertices x and y are connected in G' if distance between x and y in G is at most 2. Let $f : V \to [0 \ldots K-1]$ be the color assignments such that $(\forall j, k : k$ is a neighbor of j in $G' : f(j) \neq f(k))$, where K is any number that is sufficient for coloring G'.

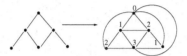

Fig. 3. Transformation using graph coloring. The number associated with each process denotes the color of the process.

Let $f.j$ denote the color of process j. Now, process j can execute at $clock.j = f.j$. Moreover, process j can execute at time slots $\forall c : c \geq 0 : f.j + c * K$. When j executes, it writes its own state and the state of its neighbors in G. Based on the color assignment, it follows that two write actions do not collide. Figure 4 shows the actions of process j.

process j
const $f.j, K$;
var $v.j, l.j, clock.j$;
initially
        set $v.j$ according to the initial value of $v.j$ in read/write model;
        set $l.j$ according to the initial value of $copy.j$ in read/write model;
        $clock.j = 0$;
begin
        $(\exists c : clock.j = f.j + c * K) \longrightarrow$ if($predicate(v.j, l.j)$) update $v.j$;
                              $\forall k : k$ is a neighbor of j in the original graph :
                                      $l.k.j = v.j$;
end

Fig. 4. Transformation for arbitrary topology

Theorem 4.1   For every computation of the transformed program in WAC model under power-set semantics there is an equivalent computation of the given program in read/write model.   □

Theorem 4.2 If the maximum degree of G is d, then the period between successive executions of a process is at most $d^2 + 1$.   □

Remark. The above theorem presents the upper bound on the performance of the transformation. For sensor networks (e.g., [14,15]), maximum degree d is usually small. Hence, the period between successive executions of a process is small. Moreover, $d^2 + 1$ is the upper bound for the period and the period can be smaller than $d^2 + 1$. For example, for a grid topology, maximum degree, $d = 4$, and $period = K = 5$.

Preserving stabilization during transformation. To show that stabilization is preserved during transformation, we first present how we deal with the case where the clocks are not initialized or clocks of processes are corrupted. Note that the rate of increase of the clocks is still the same for all processes. To recover from uninitialized clocks, we proceed as follows: Initially, we construct a spanning tree of processes. Let $p.j$ denote the parent of process j in this spanning tree. Process j is initialized with a constant $c.j$ which captures the difference between the initial slot assignment of j and $p.j$.

If clocks are not synchronized, the action by which $p.j$ writes the state of j may collide with other write actions in the system. Process j uses the absence of this write to stop and wait for synchronizing its clock. Process j waits for $K * n$ slots, where K is the period between successive slots and n is the number of processes in the system. This ensures that process j starts executing only when all its descendants have stopped in order to synchronize their clocks. When j later observes the write action performed by $p.j$, it can use $c.j$ to determine the next slot in which it should execute. Since the root process continues to execute in the slots assigned to it, eventually, its children will synchronize with the root. Subsequently, the grandchildren of the root will synchronize, and so on. Continuing thus, the clocks of all processes will be synchronized and hence, further computation will be collision-free.

In the absence of topology changes, the spanning tree constructed above and the values of $f.j$ and $c.j$ are constants. Hence, for a fixed topology, we assume that these values are not corrupted. Once the clocks are synchronized, from Theorem 4.1, for the subsequent computation of the transformed program, there is an equivalent computation of the given program in read/write model. Also, if the given program is stabilizing fault-tolerant then every computation of that program reaches legitimate states. Combining these two results, it follows that every computation of the transformed program eventually reaches legitimate states. Thus, we have

Theorem 4.3 If the given program in read/write model is stabilizing fault-tolerant then transformed program (with the modifications discussed above) in WAC model is also stabilizing fault-tolerant.   □

Remark. The above modification is meant to illustrate the feasibility of preserving stabilization while transforming a program in read/write model into a program in WAC model. The time for which a process waits, $K * n$ slots, after failing to observe the write action of its parent is an overestimate. The optimal time for which a process should wait is outside the scope of the paper.

5   WAC Model to Read/Write Model

In this section, we focus on the transformation of a program that is correct in the WAC model under power-set semantics into a program in read/write model. During this transformation, an action by which j writes its own state and the state of its neighbors in WAC model is split so that j writes its own state and then allows each of its neighbors to read its state.

However, if multiple fragmented WAC actions are executed simultaneously in the read/write model, their execution may not correspond to the sequential (respectively, parallel) execution of those actions in the WAC model. For example, consider the execution of two actions, $a.j$ and $a.k$, at neighboring processes j and k in the WAC model. In a fragmented execution of these two actions, the following execution scenario is feasible: j writes its own state as prescribed by action $a.j$, k writes its own state as prescribed by $a.k$, j reads the state of k, and k reads the state of j. However, such a scenario is not possible in WAC model. Specifically, if $a.j$ and $a.k$ are executed simultaneously then, due to collision, j (respectively, k) will not be able to write the state of k (respectively, j). And, in a sequential execution where $a.k$ is executed after $a.j$, k will be aware of the new state of j and use that in the execution of $a.k$. By contrast, in the above fragmented execution, this property was not true. Thus, the fragmented execution of two actions in the WAC model may not correspond to their sequential or parallel execution. Hence, to transform the given program in WAC model, we ensure that two neighboring processes do not simultaneously execute their fragmented WAC actions.

The problem of ensuring that neighboring processes do not execute simultaneously is a well-known problem in distributed computing. It has been studied in the context of local mutual exclusion (e.g., [4]), dining philosophers (e.g., [3,16]) and drinking philosophers (e.g., [3, 16]). Since either of these solutions suffices for our purpose, we simply describe the features of these solutions that are of importance here.

Each of the solutions in [4, 3, 16] has the following two actions: enterC S and exitC S. These solutions further guarantee that when a process is in its critical section (i.e., it has executed $enterCS$ but not $exitCS$) none of its neighbors are in its critical section. Using these two actions, in Figure 5, we demonstrate how one can transform a program in WAC model into a program in read/write model. Note that the last action in Figure 5 appears to allow j to read the state of all its neighbors; this action can be slow ly executed so that j reads the counters of its neighbors one at a time.

Rem ark.   For reasons of space, we refer the reader to [17], for an approach to bound $counter.j$ in the transformation shown in Figure 5.

Theorem 5.1 For every computation of the transformed program in read/write model there is an equivalent computation of the given program in WAC model under power-set semantics.   □

Preserving stabilization during transformation.   Now, we show that if we use a local mutual exclusion algorithm that is stabilizing (e.g., [3, 4]) then the transformation shown in Figure 5 is stabilization preserving. To show this,

process j
var $v.j$, $copy.j$, $counter.j$;
initially
       set $v.j$ according to the initial value of $v.j$ in WAC model;
       set $copy.j$ according to the initial value of $l.j$ in WAC model;
       $\forall k :: counter.j.k = 0$;
begin
       upon executing $enterCS$ $\longrightarrow$ $counter.j.j := counter.j.j + 1$;
                                       execute 'write part' of the program
                                       in WAC model to update $v.j$;
       $counter.j.k < counter.k.k$ $\longrightarrow$ $counter.j.k, copy.j.k := counter.k.k, v.k$;
       $(\forall k : counter.k.j \geq counter.j.j)$ $\longrightarrow$ execute $exitCS$;
                                         request for CS again;
end

Fig. 5. WAC model to read/write model

we first observe that any stabilizing solution for local mutual exclusion must ensure that eventually some process enters its critical section. Consider the case where process j is in critical section. If there exists a neighbor, say k, of j such that $counter.k.j < counter.j.j$ then k will copy $counter.j.j$. Thus, eventually, j will be able to exit critical section. Based on the above discussion, it follows that the stabilization property of local mutual exclusion is preserved. Hence, the program will recover to states from where no two neighboring processes are in their critical sections. Once every process enters C S sufficiently many times (equal to the maximum counter value in the initial state), the counter values will be restored, i.e., $\forall j, k : counter.k.j \leq counter.j.j$ will be true. Once counter values are restored, based on Theorem 5.1, for the subsequent computation of the transformed program in read/write model there is an equivalent computation of the given program in WAC model. Thus, we have

Theorem 5.2 If the given program in WAC model is stabilizing fault-tolerant then the transformed program in read/write model is also stabilizing fault-tolerant. □

6   Discussion

Our transformations from (respectively, to) WAC model to (respectively, from) read/write model raises several questions. We discuss some of these questions and their answers, next.

In this paper, we considered transformations of programs in read/write model to WAC model, and vice versa. Are similar transformations possible for other models considered in the literature?

Yes. It is possible to transform a program in shared memory model (where, in an atomic step, a process can read its local state as well as the state of its neighbors and write its own state) or message passing model (where, in an atomic step, a process can either send a message, receive a message, or perform an internal computation) to WAC model, and vice versa. Given a program in shared memory model, first, we can transform it to obtain a corresponding program in read/write model (e.g., [4, 3]). Then, we can use the algorithms in Sections 3 or 4 to transform it into a program that is correct under the WAC model. Moreover, given a program in WAC model, we can use the algorithm in Section 5 to transform it into an algorithm that is correct in read/write model. By definition, it is correct under shared memory model.

Regarding transformation from WAC model to message passing model, we can first use our algorithm from Section 5. Then, we can use the approach in [3] to transform it to a program in message passing model. Likewise, given a program in message passing model, we can first obtain a program in read/write model and then transform it into a program in WAC model.

How efficient are these transformations?

First, we compute the efficiency of the transformation from read/write model to WAC model. For untimed systems, according to Theorem 3.2, at most one process can execute at a time, if processes are deterministic, cannot detect collisions, and cannot perform redundant writes. Hence, the one enabled process may take up to $O(N)$ time before it can execute next, where N is the number of processes in the system. Thus, in untimed systems, the transformation from read/write model to WAC model can slow down the algorithm in WAC model. However, for this model this delay is inevitable (cf. Theorem 3.2). For timed systems, a process executes once in K slots where K is the number of colors used to color the extended communication graph. Thus, in timed systems, the transformation can slow down the given algorithm by a factor of K that is bounded by d^2, where d is the maximum degree of any node in the graph. This slow down is reasonable in sensor networks where topology is typically geometric and value of K is small (e.g., $K = 5$ for grid-based topology).

Likewise, in the transformation from WAC model to read/write model, the local mutual exclusion algorithm prevents two neighboring processes from executing concurrently. The slow down caused by this is $O(d)$ where d is the maximum degree in the given communication graph.

Are the transformations discussed in this paper possible if the processes can detect collisions?

Yes. The transformations proposed in Sections 3 and 4 are correct even if the processes can detect collisions. However, the optimality of the transformation for untimed systems may not hold. Specifically, in Theorem 3.2, we assume that a process can go from being disabled to being enabled only if its neighbor writes its state. In an algorithm where collision detection is possible, a process can also go from being disabled to being enabled when it detects a collision.

7   Conclusion and Future Work

In this paper, we considered a novel model of computation, write all with collision (WAC), and compared it with existing models of computation. The WAC model captures the computation in sensor networks where in an atomic step, a sensor can write its state and the state of its neighbors. However, if two sensors try to write the state of a sensor then none of the writes occur due to collision. Although, our transformation algorithms are designed for the case where collisions are undetectable, as discussed in Section 6, they can be easily used in contexts where collisions are detectable.

We compared the WAC model of computation with other models considered in the literature. We showed that it is possible to transform a program in read/write model into a program in WAC model, and vice versa. However, while transforming a program in read/write model into a program in WAC model, if the transformed program is deterministic and cannot use time then the transformed program is considerably slow; at most one process can execute at a time. We showed that this is optimal for an untimed, deterministic system where processes cannot detect collisions and cannot perform redundant writes (cf. Theorem 3.2). Also, we showed that, in a timed model, it is possible to allow processes to execute concurrently (cf. Section 4). Thus, we find that if the processes do not have the ability to read then the ability to determine time consistently is important.

For timed model, if the topology is fixed, our transformation preserves the stabilization property of the given program in read/write model. Further, the transformation of programs in WAC model to read/write model is also stabilization preserving. This transformation does not assume a fixed topology.

There are several open problems raised by our work. One of these problems is to develop fault-tolerance preserving transformations for WAC model. Since our algorithms require some offline setup (e.g., graph coloring), they cannot deal with topology changes. Based on the results in Section 3, we expect that such transformations would not be possible in untimed, deterministic systems. However, we expect that such transformations could be obtained for timed systems. One of the interesting extension to this work is to design primitives that would allow us to identify transformations where concurrent executions are possible. In this paper, we identified two such primitives, time and redundant writes. Another interesting extension of this work is to develop programs in WAC model that permit concurrent execution for untimed systems using the knowledge about the speed of processes. Another extension of this work is to design transformations for timed systems that allow clock drifts among processes.

Acknowledgments.   We thank Ted Herman for introducing the WAC model to us at the Seminar on Self-Stabilization, Luminy, France in October 2002.

References

1. M. Gouda and F. Haddix. The linear alternator. *In Proceedings of the Third Workshop on Self-stabilizing Systems*, pages 31–47, 1997.
2. M. Gouda and F. Haddix. The alternator. *In Proceedings of the Fourth Workshop on Self-stabilizing Systems*, pages 48–53, 1999.
3. M. Nesterenko and A. Arora. Stabilization-preserving atomicity refinement. *Journal of Parallel and Distributed Computing*, 62(5):766–791, 2002.
4. G. Antonoiu and P. K. Srimani. Mutual exclusion between neighboring nodes in an arbitrary system graph tree that stabilizes using read/write atomicity. *In Euro-par'99 Parallel Processing, Springer-Verlag*, LNCS:1685:824–830, 1999.
5. K. Ioannidou. Transformations of self-stabilizing algorithms. *In Proceedings of the 16th International Conference on Distributed Computing (DISC), Springer-Verlag*, LNCS:2508:103–117, October 2002.
6. T. H. Cormen, C. E. Leiserson, R. L. Rivest, and C. Stein. *Introduction to Algorithms*. The MIT Press, 2nd edition, September 2001.
7. G. Chartrand and O. R. Oellermann. *Applied and Algorithmic Graph Theory*. McGraw-Hill Inc., 1993.
8. S. Ghosh and M. H. Karaata. A self-stabilizing algorithm for coloring planar graphs. *Distributed Computing*, 7(1):55–59, 1993.
9. S. S. Kulkarni and U. Arumugam. Collision-free communication in sensor networks. *In Proceedings of the Sixth Symposium on Self-Stabilizing Systems (SSS), Springer-Verlag*, LNCS:2704:17–31, June 2003.
10. E. W. Dijkstra. Self-stabilizing systems in spite of distributed control. *Communications of the ACM*, 17(11), 1974.
11. S. Dolev. *Self-Stabilization*. The MIT Press, 2000.
12. S. S. Kulkarni and M. Arumugam. Transformations for write-all-with-collision model. Technical Report MSU-CSE-03-27, Department of Computer Science, Michigan State University, October 2003.
13. W. B. Heinzelman, A. P. Chandrakasan, and H. Balakrishnan. An application-specific protocol architecture for wireless microsensor networks. *IEEE Transactions on Wireless Communications*, 1(4):660–670, October 2002.
14. J. Hill, R. Szewczyk, A.Woo, S. Hollar, D. E. Culler, and K. Pister. System architecture directions for network sensors. *In Proceedings of the International Conference on Architectural Support for Programming Languages and Operating Systems (ASPLOS)*, November 2000.
15. D. Culler, J. Hill, P. Buonadonna, R. Szewczyk, and A. Woo. A network-centric approach to embedded software for tiny devices. In *Emsoft*, volume 2211 of *Lecture Notes in Computer Science*, pages 97–113, 2001.
16. K. M. Chandy and J. Misra. The drinking philosophers problem. *ACM Transactions on Programming Languages and Systems*, 6(4):632–646, 1984.
17. J. Couvreur, N. Francez, and M. Gouda. Asynchronous unison. *In Proceedings of the International Conference on Distributed Computing Systems*, pages 486–493, 1992.

Transient Model for Jackson Networks and Its Approximation

Ahmed M. Mohamed, Lester Lipsky, and Reda Ammar

Dept. of Computer Science and Engineering
University of Connecticut, Storrs, CT 06269, USA
{ahmed, lester, reda}@engr.uconn.edu

Abstract. Jackson networks have been very successful in so many areas in modeling parallel and distributed systems. However, the ability of Jackson networks to predict performance with system changes remains an open question, since they do not apply to systems where there are population size constraints. Also, the product-form solution of Jackson networks assumes steady state systems with exponential service centers and FCFS queueing discipline. In this paper, we present a *transient* model for Jackson networks. The model is applicable under any population size. This model can be used to study the transient behavior of Jackson networks and if the number of tasks to be executed is large enough, the model accurately approaches the product-form solution (steady state solution). Finally, an approximation to the transient model using the steady state solution is presented.

1 Introduction

Since the early 1970s, networks of queues have been studied and applied to numerous areas in computer science and engineering with a high degree of success. General exponential queueing network models were first solved by Jackson [10] and by Gordon and Newell [9] who showed that certain classes of steady state queueing networks with any number of service centers could be solved using a product-form solution. A substantial contribution to the theory was made by Buzen [5,6] who showed that the ominous-looking formulas the previous researchers had derived were actually computationally manageable. Basket et al [13] summarized under what generalizations the product form solution could be used (e.g., processor sharing, multiple classes, ...). Thereafter the performance analysis of queueing networks began to be considered as a research field of its own. Chandy et. al [14] and others developed many of the basic notions concerning several job streams, as well as some notions concerning non-exponential holding times.

Jackson networks have been so successful in so many areas that it is hard to see where they do not apply. However, the ability of Jackson networks to predict remains an open question. It is important to state that Jackson networks do not apply to systems where there are population size constraints. Also, the product-form solution of Jackson networks assumes steady state systems (number of customers is much greater than number of service centers). Finally, the model assumes exponential

M. Papatriantafilou and P. Hunel (Eds.): OPODIS 2003, LNCS 3144, pp. 198–209, 2004.

service centers with FCFS and other queueing discipline. If one of these assumptions is not satisfied, the steady state solution may not be valid.

In this paper we present a *transient* model to study the transient behavior of Jackson networks. The model is applicable to any population size. If the number of tasks to be executed is large enough, the model matches the product-form solution. However, there is a computational problem in attempting to use this model for large systems. An approximation to the transient model using the steady state solution is presented to overcome such problems when dealing with large systems.

In our analysis, we use the linear algebraic queueing theory approach. All the necessary background needed can be found in Lipsky [11]. The rest of the paper is organized as follows: In Section 2, we summarize the product-form solution of Jackson networks. A brief theoretical background is presented in Section 3. In Section 4, we introduce our transient model. In Section 5, we show how to use the model to analyze the performance of parallel and distributed systems. In Section 6, we show how the steady-state (product form) solution can be used to approximate the more accurate transient model.

2 Product-Form Solution

It has been shown by Jackson [9],Gordon and Newell [8] and Buzen [5] that for any network of K service centers with exponentially distributed service times , and serving a total of N customers the probability of being in the state $\overline{n} = \{n_1, n_2 \ldots\ldots n_k\}$ where $n_1 + n_2 + \ldots\ldots\ldots + n_k = N$ is

$$P(\overline{n}) = \frac{1}{G(N)} \prod_{i=1}^{K} [\frac{X_i^{n_i}}{\beta(n_i)}]$$

n_i is the number of customers at service center i, Xi is the fraction of time a customer spends at each visit service center i when there is no one else in the system and $\beta i(n)$ is the load function of service center i. The function $G(N)$ normalizes the probabilities so that their sum is 1, so

$$G(N) = \sum_{\substack{all \\ n^`}} \prod_{i=1}^{K} \frac{X_i}{\beta_i(n_i)}$$

One then can compute $G(N)$ using Buzen's algorithm to compute various performance parameters such as system throughput, which is given by,

$$Q_K(N) = G(N - 1) / G(N)$$

In the model, the average time to complete an application of N tasks running on a cluster of K Workstations is given by,

$$E(T_{app}(N)) = N / Q_K(N)$$

The above is what we call the steady state prediction model.

3   Theoretical Background

In the following section, we introduce some definitions that are important for our analysis. The reader is referred to [11] for more complete description.

3.1   Definitions

- Matrices used if only one customer in the system
S is a system consisting of a set of service centers. The service rate of each server is exponential.
Ξ is the set of all internal states of S.
p is the entrance row vector where p_i is the probability that upon entering S, a customer will go directly to server i.
q' is the exit vector where q_i is the probability of leaving the system when service completed at server i.
M is the completion rate matrix whose diagonal elements are the completion rates of the individual servers in S.
P is the transition matrix where P_{ij} is the probability that a customer will go from server i to server j when service is completed at i.
B is the service rate matrix, $\mathbf{B} = \mathbf{M}(\mathbf{I} - \mathbf{P})$.
τ' is a column vector where τ_i is the mean time until a customer leaves S, given that he started at server i.
V is the service time matrix where V_{ij} is the mean time a customer spends at j from the time it first visits i until it leaves the system. $\mathbf{V} = \mathbf{B}^{-1}$
ε' is a column vector all of whose components are ones.

- Matrices used if $K > 1$ task in the system
Ξ_k is the set of all internal states of S when there are k active customers there. There are D(k) such states.
$\mathbf{M}_k$ is the completion rate matrix where $[\mathbf{M}_k]_{ii}$ the service rate of leaving state i. The rest of the elements are zeros.
$\mathbf{P}_k$ is the transition matrix where $[\mathbf{P}_k]_{ij}$ $i,j \in \Xi_k$, is the probability that the system will go from state i to state j when service is completed at i.
$\mathbf{Q}_k$ is the exit matrix where $[\mathbf{Q}_k]ij$ is the probability of a customer leaving S when the system was in state $i \in \Xi_k$, leaves the system in state $j \in \Xi_{k-1}$.
$\mathbf{R}_k$ entrance matrix where $[\mathbf{R}_k]_{ij}$ is the probability that a customer upon entering S finding it in state $i \in \Xi_{k-1}$ will go to server that puts the system in state $j \in \Xi_k$.
$\mathbf{τ'}_k$ is a column vector of dimension D(k) where $[\tau k]i$ is the mean time until a customer leaves S, given that the system started in state $i \in \Xi_k$.

3.2   Matrix Representation of Distribution Functions

Every distribution function can be approximated closely as needed by some m-dimensional vector-matrix pair $< \mathbf{p}, \mathbf{B} >$ in the following way. The PDF is given by

$$F(t) =: \Pr(X \le t) = 1 - \mathbf{p} \exp(-t \, \mathbf{B}) \, \varepsilon'$$

Where $\mathbf{p} \, \varepsilon' = 1$. The matrix function $\exp(-t \, \mathbf{B})$ is defined by its Taylor expansion. Any $m \times m$ matrix $\mathbf{X}$ when multiplied from the left by a row m-vector and from the right by an m-column vector, yields a scalar. Since this function appears often in LAQT, it's been defined as [11],

$$\Psi[\mathbf{X}] := \mathbf{p} \, \mathbf{X} \, \varepsilon'$$

So, F(t) is a scalar function of t. It follows that the pdf is given by,

$$b(t) = \frac{dF(t)}{dt} = \mathbf{p} \exp(-t \, \mathbf{B}) \, \mathbf{B} \, \varepsilon' = \Psi[\exp(-t \, \mathbf{B}) \, \mathbf{B}]$$

and the reliability function is given by

$$R(t) := \Pr(X > t) = 1 - F(t) = \mathbf{p} \exp(-t \, \mathbf{B}) \, \varepsilon' = \Psi[\exp(-t \, \mathbf{B})]$$

It can also be shown that,

$$E(T^n) = n! \, \Psi[\mathbf{V}^n]$$

For more detailed description please see [11].

4 The Transient Model

Suppose we have a computer system made up of K workstations and we wish to compute a job made of N tasks where $N > K$. The first K tasks are assigned to the system and the rest are queued up waiting for service. Once a task finishes it is immediately replaced by another task from the execution queue. Assume that the system initially opens up and K tasks flow in. The first task enters and put the system in state $\mathbf{p} \in \Xi_1$. The second task enters and takes the system from that state to state $\mathbf{pR}_2 \in \Xi_2$ and so on. The state of the system after the Kth task enters is:

$$\mathbf{p}_K = \mathbf{pR}_2 \, \mathbf{R}_3 \ldots \ldots \ldots \mathbf{R}_K$$

It can be shown that the mean time until the first task finishes and leaves the system is [15],

$$\tau'_K = \mathbf{M}_k^{-1} \, \varepsilon'_k + \mathbf{P}_k \, \tau'_k = (\mathbf{I}_k - \mathbf{P}_k)^{-1} \, \mathbf{M}_k^{-1} \, \varepsilon'_k = \mathbf{V}_k \, \varepsilon'_k$$

The mean time until someone leaves is equal to the sum of two terms; the time until something happens, $[1/[\mathbf{M}_k]_{ii} = (\mathbf{M}_k^{-1} \, \varepsilon'_k)_i]$, and if the event is not a departure the system goes to another state, $[\mathbf{P}_k]$, and leaves from there. The mean time is given by,

$$t_k = \mathbf{p}_k \, \mathbf{V}_k \, \varepsilon'_k = \Psi[\mathbf{V}_k]$$

Next, we discuss how long does it take for the next task to finish?. There are two possibilities, either $N = K$ or $N > K$.

4.1 Case 1. ($N = K$)

The case when $N < K$ is ignored here because if $N < K$ we run the application in a smaller size cluster where $N = K$. First, define matrix $\mathbf{Y}_k$ where $[\mathbf{Y}_k]_{ij}$ is the probability the S will be in state $j \in \Xi_{k-1}$ immediately after a departure, given that the system was in state $i \in \Xi_k$ and no other customers have entered. An equation for $\mathbf{Y}_k$ can be obtained from the following argument. When an event occurs in S, either someone leaves, $[\mathbf{Q}_k]$, or the internal state of the system changes, $[\mathbf{P}_k]$, and eventually somebody leaves, $[\mathbf{Y}_k]$. Mathematically,

$$\mathbf{Y}_k = \mathbf{Q}_k + \mathbf{P}_k\,\mathbf{Y}_k$$

$$\mathbf{Y}_k = (\mathbf{I}_k - \mathbf{P}_k)^{-1}\,\mathbf{Q}_k = (\mathbf{I}_k - \mathbf{P}_k)^{-1}\,\mathbf{M_k}^{-1}\,\mathbf{M}_k\,\mathbf{Q}_k = \mathbf{V}_k\,\mathbf{M}_k\,\mathbf{Q}_k \qquad 1 \le k \le K$$

Then we can consider how long it takes for the second task to finish after the first one.

$$\mathbf{p}_k\,\mathbf{Y}_k\,(\mathbf{V}_{k-1}\mathbf{\epsilon'}_{k-1}) = \mathbf{p}_k\,\mathbf{Y}_k\,(\tau'_{k-1})$$

Where $[\mathbf{p}_k]_i$ is the probability that the system was in state i when the epoch (epoch is the time between two successive departure)began.

This means, after the first task leaves, the system is in state $\mathbf{p}_k\,\mathbf{Y}_k$ with $k-1$, tasks. The second task takes (τ'_{k-1}) to leave next. The time between the second and third departure is,

$$\mathbf{p}_k\,\mathbf{Y}_k\,\mathbf{Y}_{k-1}(\mathbf{V}_{k-2}\,\mathbf{\epsilon'}_{k-2}) = \mathbf{p}_k\,\mathbf{Y}_k\,\mathbf{Y}_{k-1}(\tau'_{k-2})$$

and so on. In general the mean time to finish executing all tasks is given by,

$$E(T) = \mathbf{p}_k\,[\tau'_K + \mathbf{Y}_k\,\tau'_{K-1} + \mathbf{Y}_k\,\mathbf{Y}_{K-1}\tau'_{K-2} + \ldots + \mathbf{Y}_k\,\mathbf{Y}_{K-1}\ldots\,\mathbf{Y}_1\tau'_1]$$

4.2 Case 2. ($N > K$)

The first K tasks are assigned to the system and the rest are queued up waiting for service. When a task leaves the system, another one immediately takes its place, putting the system in state

$$\mathbf{Y}_k\,\mathbf{R}_K = \mathbf{V}_K\,\mathbf{M}_K\,\mathbf{Q}_K\,\mathbf{R}_K$$

The mean time until the second task finishes is given by,

$$\mathbf{p}_k\,\mathbf{Y}_k\,\mathbf{R}_K\,(\mathbf{V}_K\,\mathbf{\epsilon'}_K) = \mathbf{p}_k\,\mathbf{Y}_k\,\mathbf{R}_K\,(\tau'_K)$$

Now, another tasks enters the system, putting the system in state,

$$\mathbf{Y}_k\,\mathbf{R}_K\,\mathbf{Y}_K\,\mathbf{R}_K = (\mathbf{V}_K\,\mathbf{M}_K\,\mathbf{Q}_K\,\mathbf{R}_K)^2$$

The mean time until the third task finishes is given by,

$$\mathbf{p}_k\,(\mathbf{Y}_k\,\mathbf{R}_K)^2\,(\mathbf{V}_K\,\mathbf{\epsilon'}_K) = \mathbf{p}_k\,(\mathbf{Y}_k\,\mathbf{R}_K)^2\,(\tau'_K)$$

Eventually we will reach case 1 again, where there will be only K tasks remaining but with here with initial state $\mathbf{p}_k\,(\mathbf{Y}_k\,\mathbf{R}_K)^{N-K}$. In general the mean time to finish executing all tasks is,

$$E(T) = \mathbf{p}_k \left[\sum_{i=0}^{N-K} (\mathbf{Y}_k \, \mathbf{R}_K)^i \right] (\tau'_K)$$

$$+ \mathbf{p}_k \, (\mathbf{Y}_k \, \mathbf{R}_K)^{N-K} \, \mathbf{Y}_k \, [\tau'_K + \mathbf{Y}_k \, \tau_{K-1} + \mathbf{Y}_k \, \mathbf{Y}_{K-1} \tau'_{K-2} + \ldots + \mathbf{Y}_k \, \mathbf{Y}_{K-1} \ldots \mathbf{Y}_I \tau'_I]$$

Each term of the above equation helps describe the transient behavior. When i is small the term $(\mathbf{Y}_k \, \mathbf{R}_K)^i$ gives different values for different values of i which gives different departure times for different epochs(transient region). Once i becomes large the term becomes constant which gives the steady state solution for Jackson networks. Once the number of tasks remaining becomes less than the number of processors, we have different values of k ($k < K$) for different system sizes, which leads to the other transient region (draining region).

5 Modeling Parallel and Distributed Systems

It is often assumed that tasks in parallel systems are independent and run independently using separate hardware (e.g. Fork/Join type applications). In this case the problem reduces to *order statistics* [16,17,18,19]. However, in many applications tasks must interact through shared resources (e.g. shared disks, communication channels). In this case order statistics analysis is not adequate and one must apply more general models. In our work, we focus on modeling clusters of workstations type systems [4,8]. We used the product-form solution for Jackson networks before to model clusters of workstations [1,3]. This model is satisfactory if the steady state region is much larger than the transient and draining region i.e. if $N \gg K$. However, if this is not the case, the transient model should be employed. For more details on how to use the transient model to analyze the performance of such systems, please see [2].

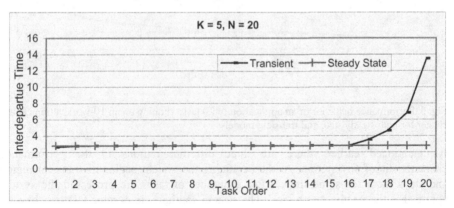

Fig. 1. Performance behavior of an application of 20 tasks running on a 5 workstation distributed cluster for both steady state and transient models

In Figure 1, 2 and 3, we use the transient and steady state models to calculate the performance behavior of an application running on distributed system of 5, and central system of 8 and 10 workstations. The application we use consists of 20 tasks.

Each tasks spends in average 11.33 at its local workstation, 1 units of time at the remote disk and 1 units of time at the communication channel. We use N = 20 to be able to show clearly the three performance regions.

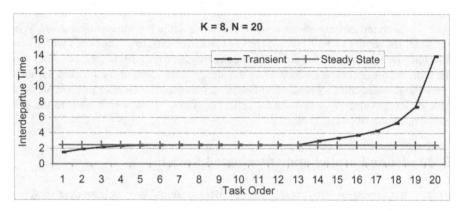

Fig. 2. Performance behavior of an application of 20 tasks running on an 8-workstation central cluster for both steady state and transient models

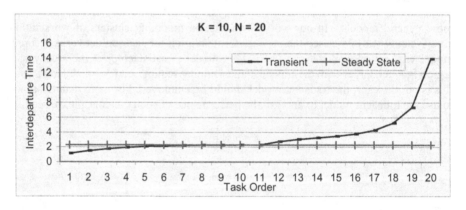

Fig. 3. Performance behavior of an application of 20 tasks running on an 10-workstation central cluster for both steady state and transient models

As mentioned earlier, there are three different regions in the performance characteristic of any system. At the beginning the system begins its transient region and stays there for some time. After a number of tasks are processed the system approaches the steady state region. The system continues to execute tasks as they are available in the execution queue. Once the number of tasks remaining in the execution queue becomes comparable to the number of nodes in the systems, the draining region starts. In all the cases shown here, the region where the inter-departure time appears to be constant is the steady state region.

6 An Approximation to the Transient Model

The transient model described earlier captures the performance behavior of the system more accurately than the steady state model. Also, it can be used where the steady state model can't be used. The problem with this model is that it can't be used for large system since the state space gets bigger as the system size increases. As shown in Table 1, for a distributed cluster of size 8 we need our matrices to be of size 24310 X 24310, which can't be achieved. In this section, we describe an approximation to the transient model using steady state values.

We have to approximate two performance regions, the transient and the draining. The transient region starts at the beginning of the execution where small tasks tend to finish first. The time needed for those tasks to finish depends on the service distribution. For the exponential distribution, the time for the first few to finish is less than the steady state time but close. So, the transient region can be approximated by the steady state value. On the other hand, where large tasks tend to finish at the end, the time needed per task is much more than steady state value due to large task and reduced parallelism. Assume we have the last K tasks from a given application that needed to be executed on K workstations. After the first one finishes, we only have $K - 1$ tasks left running on $K - 1$ workstations. According to the memoryless property of the exponential distribution, to calculate when the next task will finish, it is assumed like the $K - 1$ tasks just start execution. Thus it is reasonable to assume that the steady state time for a $K - 1$ workstation cluster would approximate the draining time for the second task to leave and so on. We continued doing that for each task until the last task in the execution queue. Based on the above argument, the transient approximation is given by,

Model approximation

$$E(T_{app}(N)) = \sum_{i=1}^{K} t_i + (N - K) * t_K$$

where, N is the number of tasks to be executed.

K is the number on workstations in the cluster.

t_i is the steady state service time per task in a cluster of i workstations.

To evaluate the accuracy of our approximation, we applied the approximation for many other system configurations and different system sizes and the percentage error between the approximation and the transient model did not exceed 3 %. We show some of our results in Figures 4, 5, 6, and 7.

The percentage error for the steady state model calculated as follows,

$$E = \frac{E_K(T_{app}(N))_{tr} - E_K(T_{app}(N))_{ss}}{E_K(T_{app}(N))_{tr}}$$

where,

$E_K(T_{app}(N))_{tr}$ is the mean service time for an application of N tasks on K workstation calculated using the transient model.

$E_K(T_{app}(N))_{ss}$ is mean service time for an application of N tasks on K workstation calculated using the steady state model.

The percentage error for the approximation model calculated the same way.

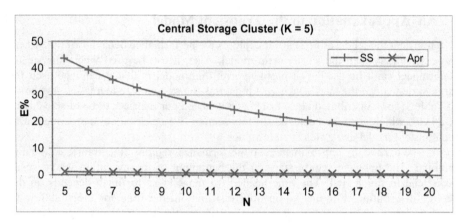

Fig. 4. The percentage error of the steady state and the approximation

In Fig. 4, we have a central cluster of 5 nodes. The application sizes is between 5 and 20. Each task spends 70% of its time with a high speed communication channel. The steady state error ranges from 44% to 18% while it is 2 % for the approximation model.

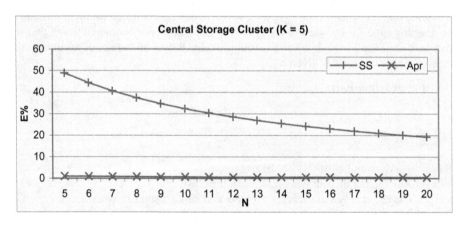

Fig. 5. The percentage error of the steady state and the approximation model

In fig. 5, we have a central cluster of five nodes. The application size is between 5 and 20. The steady state error ranges from 49% to 20% while it does not exceed 2 % for the approximation model. Same parameters have been used in Figures 6 and 7 but with a distributed cluster.

In the distributed clusters, the percentage error never reaches 1% while it ranges between 54% and 22% for the steady state. As the number of tasks to be executed gets bigger, the percentage error for both cases will get smaller. In figures 8,9 and 10, we show the same figures 1,2 and 3 but with the approximation model added.

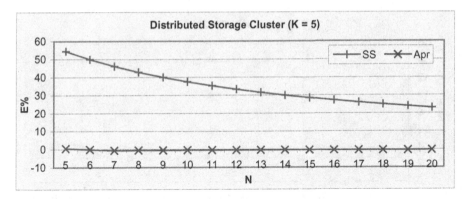

Fig. 6. The percentage error of the steady state and the approximation model

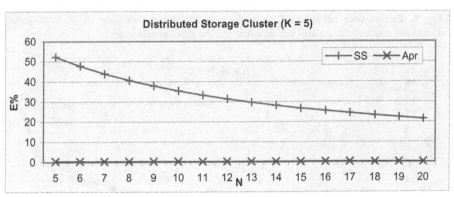

Fig. 7. The percentage error of the steady state and the approximation model

7 Conclusion

Since the early 1970s, networks of queues have been studied and applied to numerous areas in computer science and engineering with a high degree of success. Jackson networks do not apply to systems where there are population size constraints. Also, the product form solution of Jackson networks assumes steady state systems and exponential service centers with FCFS queueing discipline. In this paper, we presented a *transient* model for Jackson networks. This model can be used to study the transient behavior of Jackson networks. The model is applicable under any population size. We also compared steady state model with the more accurate but more complex transient model introduced in [2]. Finally, an approximation to the transient model using the steady state solution is presented. We also showed to what extent the steady state model can be used as an approximation to the transient model. In our future work we will investigate other probability distributions. Our preliminary results show that if the CPU time is not exponential, the transient results deviate greatly from the steady state.

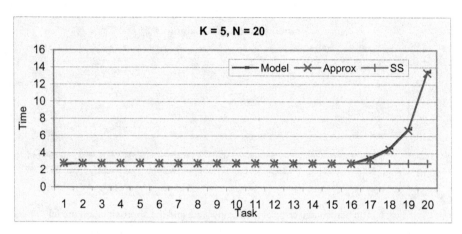

Fig. 8. Performance behavior of an application of 20 tasks running on an 5-workstation distributed cluster both steady state transient and the approximate models

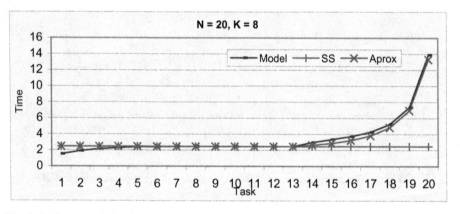

Fig. 9. Performance behavior of an application of 20 tasks running on an 8-workstation central cluster for steady state transient and the approximate models

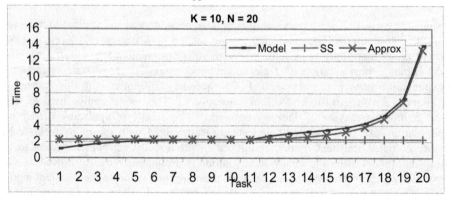

Fig. 10. Performance behavior of an application of 20 tasks running on a 8 workstation central cluster for steady state, transient and the approximate models

Table 1. The maximum dimension of matrices needed for different distributed cluster sizes

K	1	2	3	4	5	6	7	8
D(K)	3	10	35	126	462	1716	6435	24310

References

[1]   Ahmed Mohamed, Lester Lipsky and Reda Ammar,"Performance Modeling of a Cluster of Workstations." The 4th International Conference on Communications in Computing (CIC 2003), Las Vegas, NV.

[2]   Ahmed Mohamed, Lester Lipsky and Reda Ammar," *Transient Model for Jackson Networks and its Application in Cluster Computing.*" Sub. to J. of Cluster Computing, Nov. 03.

[3]   Ahmed Mohamed, Reda Ammar and Lester Lipsky, "Efficient Data Allocation for a Cluster of Workstations.",16th International Conference on Parallel and Distributed Computing Systems (PDCS2003), Reno, NV.

[4]   R. Buyya, "*High Performance Cluster Computing: Architecture and Systems,*" vol. 1, Prentice Hall PTR, NJ, 1999.

[5]   J. P. Buzen, "*Queueing Network Models of Multiprogramming*", Ph.D. Thesis, Div. Of Engr. and Physics, Harvard University, 1971.

[6]   J. Buzen, "*Computational Algorithms for Closed Queueing*", Comm. ACM, Vol 16, No. 9, Sep 1973

[7]   R. J. Chen, " *A Hybrid Solution of Fork/Join Synchronization in Parallel Queues*", IEEE Trans. Parallel and Distributed Systems, vol. 12, no. 8, pp. 829-845, Aug. 2001.

[8]   I. Foster and C. Kesselman, ""*The Grid: Blueprint for a New Computing Infrastructure,*" Morgan-Kaufman, 1998

[9]   W. J. Gordon, G. Newell,"*Closed Queueing Systems with Exponential Servers*", JORSA, Vol. 15, pp. 254-265, 1967.

[10] J. Jackson, "*Jopshop-Like Queueing Systems*", J. TIMS, Vol. 10, pp. 131-142, 1963.

[11] L. Lipsky, "QUEUEING THEORY: A Linear Algebraic Approach", McMillan and Company, New York, 1992.

[12] L. Lipsky, James D. Church, "*Applications of a Queueing Network Model for a Computer System,*" Computing Surveys, 9, pp. 205-221, Sep. 1977.

[13] F. Moore, "Computational Model of a Closed Queueing Network with Exponential Servers", IBM J. of Res. and Develop., pp. 567-572, Nov. 1962.

[14] R. Muntz, F. Baskett, K. Chandy," *Open, closed and Mixed Networks of Queues with Different Classes of Customers*", JACM, Vol. 22, pp. 248-260, Apr 1975.

[15] A. Tehranipour, L. Lipsky, "*The Generalized M/G/C//N-Queue as a Model for Time-Sharing Systems,*" ACM-IEEE Joint Symposium on Applied Computing, Fayetteville, AR, April, 1990.

[16] K. S. Trivedi, "Probability & Statistics with Reliability, Queueing and Computer Science Applications", Prentice-Hall, Inc., New Jersey, 1982.

[17] A. Qin, H. Sholl, R. Ammar, "*Micro Time Cost Analysis of Parallel Computations,*" IEEE Trans. Computers, vol. 40, no. 5, pp. 613-628, May 1991.

[18] Y. Yan, X. Zhang, Y. Song, "*An Effective and Practical Performance Prediction Model for Parallel Computing on Nondedicated Heterogeneous Networks of Workstations,*" J. Parallel Distributed Computing, vol.38, No.1, pp. 63-80, 1996.

[19] T. Zhang, S. Kang, L. Lipsky, " *On The Performance of Parallel Computers: Order Statistics and Amdahl's Law*", International Journal Of Computers And Their Applications, Vol 3, No. 2, August 1996.

Emulating Shared-Memory Do-All Algorithms in Asynchronous Message-Passing Systems[*]

Dariusz R. Kowalski[2,3], Mariam Momenzadeh[4], and Alexander A. Shvartsman[1,5]

[1] Department of Computer Science and Engineering, University of Connecticut,
371 Fairfield Rd., Unit 1155, Storrs, CT 06269, USA.
[2] Max-Planck-Institut für Informatik, Stuhlsatzenhausweg 85, Saarbrücken, 66123 Germany.
[3] Instytut Informatyki, Uniwersytet Warszawski, ul. Banacha 2, 02-097, Warszawa, Poland.
[4] Department of Electrical and Computer Engineering, Northeastern University, 409 Dana Research Center, 360 Huntington Ave., Boston, MA 02115, USA.
[5] Computer Science and Artificial Intelligence Laboratory, MIT, 200 Tech Square, Cambridge, MA 02139, USA.

Abstract. A fundamental problem in distributed computing is performing a set of tasks despite failures and delays. Stated abstractly, the problem is to perform N tasks using P failure-prone processors. This paper studies the efficiency of emulating shared-memory task-performing algorithms on asynchronous message-passing processors with quantifiable message latency. Efficiency is measured in terms of work and communication, and the challenge is to obtain subquadratic work and message complexity. While prior solutions assumed synchrony and constant delays, the solutions given here yields subquadratic efficiency with asynchronous processors when the delays and failures is suitably constrained. The solutions replicate shared objects using a quorum system, provided it is not disabled. One algorithm has subquadratic work and communication when the delays and the number of processors, K, owning object replicas, are $O(P^{0.41})$. It tolerates $\lceil \frac{K-1}{2} \rceil$ crashes. It is also shown that there exists an algorithm that has subquadratic work and communication and that tolerates $o(P)$ failures, provided message delays are sublinear.

Keywords: Distributed algorithm, fault-tolerance, work, communication, quorums.

1 Introduction

A fundamental problem in distributed computing is performing N tasks in a distributed system consisting of P processors, and despite the presence of failures. The abstract problem is called Do-All when processors communicate by exchanging messages and

---

[*] The work of the first author was performed at the University of Connecticut and supported in part by the NSF-NATO Award 0209588 and by the KBN Grant 4T11C04425; Email: darek@mimuw.edu.pl. This work is based on the second author's Masters thesis [15] at the University of Connecticut; Email: mmomenza@ece.neu.edu. The work of the third author is supported in part by the NSF CAREER Award 9984778 and the NSF Grants 9988304, 0121277, and 0311368; Email: alex@theory.lcs.mit.edu.

the tasks are similar in size and independent. Examples of such tasks include searching a collection of data, applying a function to the elements of a matrix, copying a large array, or solving a partial differential equation by applying shifting method. This problem has been studied in different settings, such as the message-passing model [5,6,8], and in the shared-memory model [1,11,12], where the problem is called Write-All. Depending on the model of computation, algorithmic efficiency is evaluated in terms of time, work, and message complexity. Work is defined as either the total number of steps taken by the available processors [11], or the total number of tasks performed [6]. Message complexity is expressed as the total number of point-to-point messages.

It has been observed that maintaining synchrony in real systems is expensive and models incorporating some form of asynchrony are considered to be more realistic. The Do-All problem has been substantially studied for synchronous failure-prone processors [4,6,5,8], however there is a dearth of asynchronous algorithms. This is not that surprising as it was shown by Kowalski and Shvartsman [13]. With the standard assumption that initially all tasks are known to all processors, the problem can be solved by a communication-oblivious algorithm where each processor performs all tasks. Such a solution has work $S = \Theta(N \cdot P)$, and requires no communication. For an algorithm to be interesting, it must be better than the oblivious algorithm, in particular, it must have subquadratic work complexity. However, if messages can be delayed for a "long time" (e.g., $\Theta(N)$ time), then the processors cannot coordinate their activities, leading to an immediate lower bound on work of $\Omega(P \cdot N)$. With this in mind, a delay-sensitive study of Do-All in [13] yields asynchronous algorithms achieving *subquadratic*[1] work as long as the message delay d is $o(N)$. The message complexity is somewhat higher than quadratic in some executions. The question was posed whether it is possible to construct asynchronous algorithms that simultaneously achieve subquadratic work and communication. It appears that in order to do so, one must strengthen the model assumptions, e.g., impose upper bounds on delays and constrain the failure patterns that may occur during the execution.

Contributions. We study emulation of shared-memory task-performing algorithms in asynchronous message-passing systems. Our goal is to obtain subquadratic bounds on work and communication for the Do-All problem:

Given N similar tasks, perform the tasks using P message-passing processors.

We consider an adversary that interferes with the progress of the computation by introducing delays and causing processors to crash. In order to obtain subquadratic work and message complexity, we restrict the power of the adversary. The best previous algorithm that achieves subquadratic work and message complexity [4,9] assumed synchronous processors and constant message latency. In this paper we present the first algorithms for Do-All that meet our efficiency criteria while allowing non-trivial processor asynchrony and message latency.

Let d be the worst case message latency, and e be the worst case time required for a processor to respond to a message (d and e are unknown to the processors). The summary of our results, for $P \leq N$ and a parameter K, is as follows.

---

[1] That is, the work complexity is $o(P^2 + PN)$, with the usual assumption that $P \leq N$.

1. We show that Do-All can be solved with work $S = O(\max\{K, d, e\}NP^{\log \frac{3}{2}})$ and message complexity $M = O(KNP^{\log \frac{3}{2}})$. The algorithm can be parameterized to have subquadratic work and message complexity of $O(NP^\delta)$ with $\log \frac{3}{2} < \delta < 1$, when the parameter K is $O(P^{\delta - \log \frac{3}{2}})$ (this is about $O(P^{0.41})$) and when $d, e = O(K)$. The algorithm tolerates $\lceil \frac{K-1}{2} \rceil$ crashes.

2. We show the existence of an algorithm that solves the Do-All problem with work $S = O(\max\{K, d, e\}NP^\varepsilon)$, and with message complexity $S = O(KNP^\varepsilon)$, for any $\varepsilon > 0$. The algorithm can be parameterized to have subquadratic work and message complexity of $O(NP^\delta)$ with $0 < \varepsilon < \delta < 1$, when the parameter K is $O(P^{\delta-\varepsilon})$, and when $d, e = O(K)$. The algorithm tolerates $\lceil \frac{K-1}{2} \rceil$ crashes.

3. We show a lower bound on work of $S = N + \Omega(P \log P)$ for the asynchronous Do-All problem that involves delays, but no processor crashes. (This matches the lower bound [12] for synchronous crash-prone processors, and the lower bound [11] for fail-stop/restartable processors.)

The results (1) and (2) are obtained by analyzing the emulations of shared-memory algorithms X [3] and AWT [1], respectively, in message-passing systems. We use the atomic memory service based on [14]. We replicate certain memory locations needed by the algorithms at K processors for fault-tolerance, with the atomic memory service maintaining replica consistency. The analysis of the algorithms is parameterized in terms of d, e, and K. The adversary is constrained not to disable the quorum configurations used by the atomic memory service, and to respect the bounds d and e.

Related work. The Do-All problem for the message-passing systems was introduced by Dwork, Halpern and Waarts [6]. There is a number of algorithms for the problem in the synchronous message-passing settings [6,5,8,9]. The algorithmic techniques in these papers rely on processor synchrony. Anderson and Woll gave an asynchronous shared-memory algorithm [1] that generalizes the algorithm of Buss et al. [3]. We convert these algorithms to run in message-passing systems with the help of atomic memory emulation. Attiya, Bar-Noy, and Dolev [2] showed how to emulate atomic shared-memory robustly in message-passing systems using processor majorities. Recently Lynch and Shvartsman [14] developed atomic multi-reader/multi-writer memory service for dynamic networks, allowing arbitrary new quorum configuration installations. We use a simplified version of the algorithm [14]. A quorum system is a collection of sets (quorums), where every pair of sets intersect. Quorums can be seen as generalized majorities [10,16], whose intersection property can be used to provide data consistency.

Structure of the document. Section 2 presents the model of computation and a lower bound. In Section 3 we review the shared-memory Write-All algorithms and a shared-memory emulation algorithm. In Sections 4 and 5 we present our message-passing algorithm and its analysis. Conclusions are in Section 6.

2   Model, Definitions, and a Lower Bound

We now define the model of computation, formalize the Do-All problem, define the complexity measures, and present a Do-All lower bound.

Processors. Our distributed system consists of P (asynchronous) processors with unique processor identifiers (PID) from the set $\mathcal{P} = \{0, \dots, P - 1\}$. P is fixed and is known to all processors. Processors communicate by passing messages (discussed later in this section) and have no access to shared memory.

Quorums. We are going to provide a shared-memory abstraction in message-passing systems using *quorum configurations*.

Definition 1 Let $\mathcal{R} = \{R_i\}$ and $\mathcal{W} = \{W_i\}$ be collections of subsets of processor identifiers, such that for all $R_i \in \mathcal{R}$ and for all $W_i, W_j \in \mathcal{W}$, we have $R_i \cap W_j \neq \emptyset$, and $W_j \cap W_i \neq \emptyset$. Then $\mathcal{C} = \langle \mathcal{R}, \mathcal{W} \rangle$ is a *quorum configuration*, where $\mathcal{R}$ is read quorums and $\mathcal{W}$ is write quorums. We use $mem(\mathcal{C})$ to denote the set of processors identifiers appearing in read and write quorums, and $size(\mathcal{C})$ to denote the total number of identifiers, that is, $size(\mathcal{C}) = |mem(\mathcal{C})|$.

Tasks. We consider N tasks, known to all processors. The tasks are similar, i.e., we assume that any task can be performed in one local time step. Task executions do not depend on each other and the tasks are idempotent, i.e., executing a task many times or concurrently has the same effect as executing the task once.

Communication. We assume a message-passing system. The network is fully connected and the processors communicate via *point-to-point* (asynchronous) channels. The delivery is unreliable and unordered, but messages are not corrupted. If a system delivers multiple messages to a processor, it can process these messages in one local time step. Similarly if a processor has several messages to send, the messages can be sent during a single local time step.

Given the motivation in [13] as discussed in the introduction, we are interested in settings where processors are asynchronous, but where there is an upper bound d on message delay (cf. [7]). We also assume that when a processor receives a message requiring a reply, it can send the reply in at most e time units. The bounds d and e need not be constant, and are unknown to the processors — the algorithms must be correct for any d and e.

Adversary Model. A processor's activity is governed by its local clock. We model asynchrony as an adversary that introduces delays between local time steps. The adversary may also cause message loss or delay, and processor crash failures. We use the term *adversary pattern* F to denote the set of events caused by the adversary in a specific execution and the term *adversary model* **F** to indicate the set of all adversary patterns for a given adversary.

The adversary is constrained in two ways: (1) the adversary must respect the bounds d and e (defined above), we call it (d, e)-adversary, and (2) when an algorithm uses a quorum configuration $\mathcal{C} = \langle \mathcal{R}, \mathcal{W} \rangle$, the adversary can cause any processor crashes as long as the processors of at least one read quorum and at least one write quorum remain operational and are able to communicate.

Let $\mathcal{Q} = \{\mathcal{C}_i\}$ be the set of all quorum configurations $\mathcal{C}_i$ used by an algorithm. We denote by $\mathbf{F}_\mathcal{Q}$ the adversary that respects the above constraints with respect to each $\mathcal{C}_i$.

Remark. Our definition of the adversary is somewhat involved for several reasons. If the adversary is allowed to cause arbitrary message delays, then communication is impossible and work complexity of any algorithm becomes quadratic. Hence we posit an upper bound on message delays. If the adversary is allowed to prevent processors from sending replies expediently, then a similar situation results. Hence we posit an upper bound on the time it takes a processor to send a reply. Lastly, our approach relies on the use of quorum systems. If the adversary is allowed to cause failures that disable the quorum systems used by the algorithms, then shared memory cannot be emulated, again leading to processors acting in isolation and performing quadratic work. Hence we assume that quorum systems are not disabled.   *Kramer.*

The Problem. Now we define the Do-All problem.

Definition 2 Do-All: Given P processors and N tasks, perform all tasks for any adversary pattern F in a specific adversary model.

While processors have no access to a global clock, we assume that the time of the local events can be measured on a discrete global clock.

Definition 3 Given a Do-All algorithm for P processors and N tasks, and an adversary model $\mathbf{F}_Q$, the algorithm solves the problem at step τ when all tasks are complete and at least one non-faulty processor has this completion knowledge.

Note that for correctness we do not require that every processor is aware of completion, since the bounds on delays are unknown to the processors.

Complexity Measures. In order to characterize the efficiency of our algorithms, we define two complexity measurements: work and message complexity. We assume that it takes a unit of time for a processor to perform a unit of work according to its local clock, and that a single task corresponds to a unit of work. By this definition the processors are charged for idling or waiting for messages.

Definition 4 Given a problem of size N and a P-processor algorithm that solves the problem at step $\tau(F)$ in the presence of the adversary pattern F in the model $\mathbf{F}_Q$, let $P_t(F)$ denote the number of processors completing a unit of work at global time t, then the work complexity S of the algorithm is: $S_{N,P} = \max_{F \in \mathbf{F}_Q} \{\sum_{t \leq \tau(F)} P_t(F)\}$.

For message-passing settings, message complexity is defined as follows.

Definition 5 Given a problem of size N and a P-processor algorithm that solves the problem at step $\tau(F)$ in the presence of the adversary pattern F in the model $\mathbf{F}_Q$, let $M_t(F)$ be the number of messages sent at global time t, then the message complexity M of the algorithm is: $M_{N,P} = \max_{F \in \mathbf{F}_Q} \{\sum_{t \leq \tau(F)} M_t(F)\}$.

A Lower Bound. A lower bound $\Omega(N + P \log P)$ on work for PRAM Write-All algorithms with crashes was shown by Kedem, Palem, Ragunathan, and Spirakis [12]. The same lower bound was later shown to apply to algorithms in the presence of processor crashes and restarts [3]. These results require the possibility of crashes. Here we show that the same bound holds for the asynchronous setting where no processor fails.

Theorem 1 *Any asynchronous P-processor Do-All algorithm on input of size N has* $S_{N,P} = N + \Omega(P \log P)$.

Proof: We present a strategy for the adversary that results in the worst case behavior. Let A be the best possible algorithm that solves the Do-All problem. The adversary imposes delays as described bellow:

Stage 1: Let $U > 1$ be the number of remaining tasks. Initially $U = N$. The adversary induces no delays as long as the number of remaining tasks, U, is more than P. The work needed to perform $N - P$ tasks when there are no delays is at least $N - P$.

Stage 2: As soon as a processor is about to perform some task $N - P + 1$ making $U \leq P$, the adversary uses the following strategy. For the upcoming iteration, the adversary examines the algorithm to determine how the processors are assigned to the remaining tasks. The adversary then lists the remaining tasks with respect to the number of processors assigned to them. The adversary delays the processors assigned to the first half remaining tasks ($\lfloor \frac{U}{2} \rfloor$) with the least number of processors assigned to them. By an averaging argument, there are no more than $\lceil \frac{P}{2} \rceil$ processors assigned to these $\lfloor \frac{U}{2} \rfloor$ tasks. Hence at least $\lfloor \frac{P}{2} \rfloor$ processors will complete this iteration having performed no more than half of the remaining tasks.

The adversary continues this strategy which results in performing at most half of the remaining tasks at each iteration. Since initially $U = P$ in this stage, the adversary can continue this strategy for at least $\log P$ iterations. Considering these two stages the work performed by the algorithm is: $S_{N,P} \geq \underbrace{N - P}_{\text{Stage 1}} + \underbrace{\lfloor P/2 \rfloor \log P}_{\text{Stage 2}} = N + \Omega(P \log P)$. $\square$

In the above strategy the adversary causes at most $\lceil \frac{P}{2} \rceil \log P$ delays, where the processor assigned to the last remaining task is delayed for $\log P$ iterations.

3   Algorithms X, AWT, and Shared Memory Emulation

We now overview two shared-memory algorithms for Write-All, called algorithm X [3] and algorithm AWT [1], and conclude with the shared memory emulation algorithm [14].

Algorithm X. This algorithm has subquadratic work of $S = O(NP^{\log \frac{3}{2}})$ using $P \leq N$ processors. It uses a full binary "progress" tree with P leaves. We assume that the N fixed-size tasks are associated with the leaves, where a "chunk" of $\lceil N/P \rceil$ tasks is positioned at each leaf. The boolean values at the vertices of the progress tree indicate whether or not all work below the current note is complete.

The algorithms proceeds as follows. Acting independently, each processor searches for work in the smallest immediate subtree that has work that needs to be done. The processor performs the work and when all work within the subtree is completed, it marks the root of the subtree as done and moves out of the subtree. The algorithm is presented in detail in [3,11]; its work for any pattern of asynchrony is as follows.

Theorem 2 *[3] Algorithm X solves Write-All of size N with P processors with work* $S_{N,P} = O(NP^{\log \frac{3}{2}})$, *for $P \leq N$.*

Algorithm AWT. In the algorithm [3], each processor traverses the unvisited subtrees of a vertex within the progress tree according to the permutation $(1, 2)$, i.e., first left, then right, if the bit of its PID at that tree level is 0, and according to the permutation $(2, 1)$, i.e., first right, then left, if the bit of its PID at that tree level is 1. This approach can be generalized to q-ary progress tree algorithms. Here the processors are equipped with q permutations of $\{1, \ldots, q\}$, and each processor traverses the q subtrees at a vertex according to the permutation that corresponds to the q-ary digit of its PID. It is possible to construct a set of q permutations so that the following result holds.

Theorem 3 *[1] Algorithm AWT solves Write-All of size N with P processors with work $S_{N,P} = O(NP^\varepsilon)$, for any $\varepsilon > 0$ when $P \leq N$.*

Algorithm AWT requires the set of q permutations of $\{1, \ldots, q\}$. The algorithm is correct for any q permutations, however the complexity result holds for a set of q permutations with certain combinatorial properties. These permutations can be found by searching the space of all sets of q permutations, and this space is very large even for moderately small ε. Since we do not show how to construct such permutations, in the rest of the paper we state results depending on algorithm AWT as existential results.

Shared Memory Emulation. We now present the algorithm implementing an atomic memory service based on [14] (the simplified version described here uses a single quorum configuration to access a data object and does not use reconfiguration). We call this atomic memory service *AM*. The algorithm implements read/write shared memory in asynchronous message-passing systems that are prone to message loss and processor crashes. In order to achieve fault-tolerance and availability, *AM* replicates objects at several network locations. In order to maintain memory consistency in the presence of failures, the algorithm uses a *quorum configuration*, consisting of a set of *members* (i.e., the set of processors "owning" a replica) plus sets of *read quorums* and *write quorums*. The quorum intersection property requires that every read-quorum intersect every write-quorum.

Every active node in the system maintains a *tag* and a *value* for each data object. Each new write assigns a unique tag, with ties broken by processor ids. These tags are used to determine an ordering of the write operations, and therefore determine the values that subsequent read operations return.

Read and write operations require two phases, a query phase and a propagation phase, each of which accesses certain quorums of replicas. Assume the operation is initiated at node i. First, in the query phase, node i contacts read quorums to determine the most recent available tag and its associated value. Then, in the propagation phase, node i contacts write quorums. The second phase of a read operation propagates the latest tag discovered in the query phase and its associated value. If the operation is a write operation, node i chooses a new tag, strictly larger than every tag discovered in the query phase. Node i then propagates the new tag, along with the new value, to the write quorums. Note that every operation accesses both read and write quorums. The protocol of each phase is formulated in terms of point-to-point messages. First the messages are sent to the members of the quorum configuration, then the replies are collected until a complete quorum responds.

Each of the two phases of the read or write operations, accesses quorums of processors, incurring a round-trip message delay. Assuming that there is an upper bound d on message delays and that local processing is negligible, this means that each phase can take at most $2d$ time. Given that all operations consist of two phases, each operation takes at most $4d$ time. (The full algorithm that includes a reconfiguration service, and its analysis, is given in [14].)

4   The Message-Passing Algorithm

We now present the emulation of the shared-memory algorithm X in the message-passing model. We call this algorithm *Xmp*. The shared data used in the algorithm is replicated among the processors. Each processor has a local progress tree containing the replicas of the vertices used by the shared-memory algorithm. Specific vertices are *owned* by certain designated processors as described below (each processor has a replica of each vertex, but not all processors are owners).

Memory Management. The progress tree is stored in the array $d[1, \ldots, 2P - 1]$. This array is replicated at each processor. We use the index x to denote the vertex $d[x]$ of the progress tree. For each x, let $\mu(x)$ be some non-empty subset of processor identifiers. We call the processors in each $\mu(x)$ the *owners* of the vertex $d[x]$. These processors are responsible for maintaining consistent (atomic) replicas of the vertex. We assume that all *owner* sets in the system have the same size (this is done for simplicity only—both the algorithms and the analysis readily extend to quorum configurations with owner sets of different sizes). For a set Y containing some indices of the progress tree, we let $\mu(Y) = \cup_{x \in Y} \mu(x)$.

When a processor needs to read or write a vertex x in its local progress tree, it uses the atomic memory service *AM*, which accesses the *owners* of the vertex, i.e, processors in $\mu(x)$, until it obtains responses from the necessary quorums (as described in the previous section).

Algorithm Description. Algorithm *Xmp* for each processor has the structure identical to algorithm X, except that each processor has a local copy of the progress tree and may use *AM* to access the vertices of the tree. The processors access the progress tree vertices as follows:

- If a processor needs to read vertex x, and its local value is 0, it uses *AM* to obtain a fresh copy of x.
- If a processor needs to read vertex x, and its local value is 1, the processor uses this value — this is safe because once a progress tree vertex is marked done, it is never unmarked.
- If a processor needs to write (always value 1 according to the algorithm) to vertex x, and its local value is 0, it uses *AM* to write to x and it updates the local value accordingly.
- If a processor needs to write vertex x, and its local value is already 1, the processor does not need to write — once a progress tree vertex is marked done, it is never unmarked.

The tasks are known to all processors and are associated with the leaves of the tree (as in algorithm X). Initially the values stored in each local tree are all zeros. Each processor starts at the leaf of its local tree according to its PID and it continues executing the algorithm until the root of its local tree is set to 1.

Algorithm AWT [1] can also be emulated in the message-passing system considered here using the memory service AM. Recall that the main distinction is that algorithm X uses a binary tree, while algorithm AWT uses a q-ary tree.

Correctness. We claim that algorithm Xmp (as well as the q-ary tree algorithm based on algorithm AWT) correctly solves the Do-All problem. This follows from the following observations: (1) The correctness of the memory service AM (shown in [14]) implies that if a vertex of the progress tree is ever read to be 1, it must be previously set to 1. (2) A processor sets a vertex of the progress tree to 1 if and if only it verifies that its children (if any) are set to 1, or the processor performed the task(s) associated with the vertex when it is a leaf. (3) A processor leaves a subtree if and only if the subtree contains no unfinished work and its root is marked accordingly.

Quorum Configuration Parameterization. We use the size of the *owner* sets, $|\mu(\cdot)|$, to parameterize algorithm Xmp. This will allow us later to study the trade-off of algorithm efficiency and fault-tolerance.

Definition 6 For each data object x we define a *quorum configuration* $\mathcal{C}_x = \langle \mathcal{R}_x, \mathcal{W}_x \rangle$, where $mem(\mathcal{C}_x) = \mu(x)$, and $\mathcal{R}_x, \mathcal{W}_x \subseteq 2^{\mu(x)}$. We define K to be the size of the largest quorum configuration, that is, $K = \max_x \{|\mu(x)|\}$. We define $\mathcal{Q}$ to be the set of all quorum configurations, that is $\mathcal{Q} = \{\mathcal{C}_x\}$.

We now discuss the assignment of vertices to owners. Each vertex of the progress tree is owned by K processors. This results in $\binom{P}{K}^{2N-1}$ combinations of "owned" replica placements. Examples 1 and 2 illustrate two possible placements, when $N = P$.

Example 1 Let N and K be powers of 2. The processors are divided into N/K segments with contiguous PIDs. Each segment owns the leaves of the progress tree corresponding to its processors' PIDs along with the vertices in the subtree of the owned leaves. Moreover, each vertex at the height greater than $\log K$ is owned by the owner of its left child. It is not hard to show that the processors with PID $= 0, \ldots, K - 1$ (the first segment) own $2K - 1 + \log(N/K)$ vertices but processors with PID $= N - K, \ldots, N - 1$ (the last segment) own $2K - 1$ vertices. Therefore the first segment processors are more likely to be busier than other processors responding to messages as *owners*. Figure 4 illustrates this example where $N=16$ and $K=4$: Here, $\mu(\{1,2,4,8,9,16,17,18,19\})= \{P_0, P_1, P_2, P_3\}$, $\mu(\{5, 10, 11, 20, 21, 22, 23\}) = \{P_4, P_5, P_6, P_7\}$, etc. (to avoid confusion between tree indices and PIDs we use P_i to denote the processor with PID i).

Example 2 The processors are divided into N/K segments and each segment has K processors with contiguous PIDs. Vertex i of the progress tree is owned by the $j + 1^{th}$ segment, where $i \stackrel{K}{\equiv} j$. Since there are $2N - 1$ vertices in the progress tree, each processor owns either $\lfloor K(2N - 1)/N \rfloor$ or $\lceil K(2N - 1)/N \rceil$ vertices. Hence there is an almost uniform distribution of vertices among the owners.

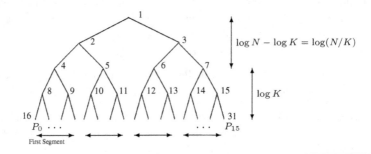

Fig. 1. Owners for $N = 16$ and $K = 4$ (Example 1).

5   Algorithm Analysis

We assess the efficiency of our algorithm against the (d, e)-adversary $\mathbf{F}_Q$ (that respects the delays d and e, and that does not disable the quorum system Q). We start with the following lemma about the cost of reads and writes.

Lemma 4 *Using the atomic memory service AM, each read or write operation contributes at most $4(K + d) + 2e$ to the work complexity and at most $4K$ to the total number of messages.*

Proof: The processor performing a read or a write operation uses the service *AM* with quorum configurations of size at most K. Thus each quorum consists of no more than K processors. In a single phase (see the overview of the service *AM* in Section 3), it takes no more than K units of work to send messages to K processors. After sending the last message, the processor may have to wait additional $2d + e$ time steps to receive the responses. If some K' responses are received, then it it takes at most K units of work to process them (since $K' \leq K$). Thus it takes time $2K + 2d + e$ to process a single phase. The second phase similarly takes time $2K + 2d + e$. Thus the two phases of an operation take time $4(K + d) + 2e$.

Each stage involves sending K messages and receiving no more than K responses. The total number of messages is no more than $4K$. □

Now we present the work and communication analysis.

Theorem 5 *Algorithm Xmp solves Do-All of size N with $P \leq N$ processors, for (d, e)-adversary $\mathbf{F}_Q$, with work $S_{N,P} = O(\max\{K, d, e\}NP^{\log \frac{3}{2}})$ and message complexity $M_{N,P} = O(KNP^{\log \frac{3}{2}})$.*

Proof: Using Theorem 2, the work of algorithm X is $S_x = O(NP^{\log \frac{3}{2}})$, counting local operations, and shared-memory read/write operations. In algorithm *Xmp*, each local operation takes one local time step, and each read or write operation takes time $4(K + d) + 2e$ by Lemma 4. Thus the total work is $S_{N,P} = (4(K + d) + 2e) \cdot S_x = (4(K + d) + 2e) \cdot O(NP^{\log \frac{3}{2}}) = O(\max\{K, d, e\}PN^{\log \frac{3}{2}})$.

Using Theorem 2 again, we note that the vertices of the progress tree will be updated by the processors a total of $O(NP^{\log \frac{3}{2}})$ times. In algorithm *Xmp*, by Lemma 4, each update contributes $4K$ messages to the message complexity. Thus the total number of messages is $M_{N,P} = 4K \cdot S_x = O(KNP^{\log \frac{3}{2}})$. $\square$

By using algorithm AWT [1] as the basis, and following the identical emulation approach, we obtain the following result with the help of Theorem 3.

Theorem 6 *There exists an algorithm that solves Do-All of size N with $P \leq N$ processors, for (d, e)-adversary $\mathbf{F_Q}$, with work $S_{N,P} = O(\max\{K, d, e\} \cdot NP^\varepsilon)$, and with message complexity $M_{N,P} = O(KNP^\varepsilon)$, for any $\varepsilon > 0$.*

Given K, we use quorum systems with all majorities of size $\lceil (K + 1)/2 \rceil$, so that we can tolerate the crash of any minority of processors in a configuration.

Theorem 7 *Algorithm Xmp tolerates any pattern of f failures, for $f \leq \lfloor (K - 1)/2 \rfloor$.*

The algorithm is most efficient when $K = 1$, that is when the shared memory has a single owner; unfortunately this is not fault-tolerant at all. Thus we are interested in parameterizations that achieve subquadratic work and communication, while maximizing the fault-tolerance of the algorithm.

Theorem 8 *Algorithm Xmp solves Do-All of size N, with $P \leq N$ processors, and for any adversary pattern in $\mathbf{F_Q}$, with (subquadratic in N and P) work and message complexity of $O(NP^\delta)$ with $\log \frac{3}{2} < \delta < 1$, when the parameter K is $O(P^{\delta - \log \frac{3}{2}})$ and when $d, e = O(K)$.*

Note that if δ is chosen to be close to $\log 3/2$ (≈ 0.59), the algorithm tolerates only a constant number of failures, but it is as work-efficient as its shared-memory counterpart. As δ approaches 1, the complexity remains subquadratic, while the fault-tolerance of the algorithm improves. In particular, when δ is close to 1, the algorithm is able to tolerate about $O(P^{0.41})$ crashes.

Theorem 9 *There exists an algorithm that solves Do-All of size N, with $P \leq N$ processors, and for any adversary pattern in $\mathbf{F_Q}$, with (subquadratic in N and P) work and message complexity of $O(NP^\delta)$ with $0 < \varepsilon < \delta < 1$, when the parameter K is $O(P^{\delta - \varepsilon})$, and when $d, e = O(K)$.*

Remark. One may be interested in measuring the impact of using our emulation on the performance (work) of the original shared-memory algorithms. It is difficult to do this directly, given that in message-passing systems there exists a natural interdependence between the efficiency and fault-tolerance in the emulation. In order to lower the cost of the emulation one needs to assume fewer failures. On the other hand, tolerating a linear number of processor failures causes the emulation to impose a linear overhead, resulting in worse-than-quadratic work. This is in contrast with the shared-memory solutions where a large number of failures may not necessarily degrade performance: consider a situation where after the initial failures only a constant number of processors remains—in this case work can be optimally linear in the size of the input.   *Kramer.*

6   Conclusion and Future Work

We presented and analyzed emulation of asynchronous shared-memory Do-All algorithms in the message-passing model. We focused on the trade-offs between efficiency and fault-tolerance in our algorithms as we examined how the replication of resources affects efficiency. We also presented a lower bound for the asynchronous Do-All problem that involves delays, but no failures. Several aspects of our work are open for future exploration, not the least of which is the narrowing if the existing gap between the upper and lower bounds. Another direction is to characterize the impact of the emulation efficiency, and the reconfiguration of memory replication, on the upper bounds.

Acknowledgements. The authors thank Lester Lipsky, Alex Russell, and the anonymous referees for suggestions that helped improve the presentation in this paper.

References

1. R.J. Anderson and H. Woll, "Algorithms for the Certified Write-All Problem", *SIAM Journal of Computing*, vol. 26, no. 5, pp. 1277-1283, 1997.
2. H. Attiya, A. Bar-Noy, and D. Dolev, "Sharing Memory Robustly in Message Passing Systems", *Journal of the ACM*, vol. 42, no. 1, pp. 124-142, 1996.
3. J. Buss, P. Kanellakis, P. Ragde, and A. Shvartsman, "Parallel Algorithms with Processor Failures and Delays", *Jour. of Algorithms*, vol. 20, no. 1, pp. 45-86, 1996.
4. B.S. Chlebus, L. Gąsieniec, D. Kowalski, and A.A. Shvartsman, "Bounding work *and* communication in robust cooperative computation", *Proceeding of the 16th Int-l Symp. on Distributed Computing*, Springer LNCS 2508, pp. 295-310, 2002.
5. R. De Prisco, A. Mayer, and M. Yung, "Time-Optimal Message-Efficient Work Performance in the Presents of Faults", *Proceedings of the 13th Symposium on Distributed Computing*, pp. 161-172, 1994.
6. C. Dwork, J. Halpern, and O. Waarts, "Performing Work Efficiency in Presence of Faults", *SIAM Journal on Computing*, vol. 27, no. 5, pp. 1457-1491, 1998.
7. C. Dwork, N. Lynch, and L. Stockmeyer, "Consensus in the presence of partial synchrony", *Journal of the ACM*, vol. 35, no. 2, pp. 288-323,1988.
8. Z. Galil, A. Mayer, and M.Yung, "Resolving Message Complexity of Byzantine Agreement and Beyond", *Proceedings of the 36th IEEE Symposium on Foundation of Computer Science*, pp. 724-733, 1995.
9. C. Georgiou, D. Kowalski, and A.A. Shvartsman, "Efficient Gossip and Robust Distributed Computation", *Proc. of the 17th International Symposium on Distributed Computing*, pp. 224-238, 2003.
10. D.K. Gifford, "Weighted Voting for Replicated Data", *Proceedings of the 7th Symposium on Operating Systems Principles* , pp. 150-159, 1979.
11. P.C. Kanellakis and A.A. Shvartsman, "Fault-Tolerant Parallel Computation", ISBN 0-7923-9922-6, *Kluwer Academic Publishers*, 1997.
12. Z.M. Kedem, K.V. Palem, A. Raghunathan, and P. Spirakis, "Combing Tentative and Definite Executions for Dependable Parallel Computing", *Proceedings of the 23rd Symposium on Theory of Computing*, pp. 381-390, 1991.
13. D. Kowalski and A.A. Shvartsman, "Performing Work with Asynchronous Processors: Message-Delay-Sensitive Bounds", *Proceedings 22nd ACM Symposium on Distributed Computing*, pp. 211-222, 2003.

14. N. Lynch and A.A. Shvartsman. "RAMBO: A Reconfigurable Atomic Memory Service for Dynamic Networks", *Proceedings of the 16th International Symposium on Distributed Computing (DISC)*, pp. 173-190, 2002.
15. M. Momenzadeh, *Emulating Shared-Memory Do-All in Asynchronous Message Passing Systems*, Masters thesis, University of Connecticut, 2003.
16. R. Thomas, "A Majority Consensus Approach to Concurrency Control for Multiple Copy Databases", *ACM Trans. on Database Sys.*, vol. 4, no. 2, pp. 180-209, 1979.

Acknowledged Broadcasting and Gossiping in Ad Hoc Radio Networks

Jiro Uchida[1], Wei Chen[2], and Koichi Wada[3]

[1] Nagoya Institute of Technology Gokiso-cho, Syowa-ku, Nagoya, 466-8555, Japan,
jiro@phaser.elcom.nitech.ac.jp, wada@nitech.ac.jp
[2] Tennessee State University 3500 John A MerritBlvd, Nashville, TN 37205, USA,
wchen@tnstate.edu

Abstract. A radio network is a collection of transmitter-receiver devices (referred to as nodes). ARB (Acknowledged Radio Broadcasting) means transmitting a message from one special node called source to all the nodes and informing the source about its completion. In our model each node takes a synchronization per round and performs transmission or reception at one round. Each node does not have a collision detection capability and knows only own ID. In [1], it is proved that no ARB algorithm exists in the model without collision detection. In this paper, we show that if $n \geq 2$, where n is the number of nodes in the network, we can construct algorithms which solve ARB in $O(n)$ rounds for bidirectional graphs and in $O(n^{3/2})$ rounds for strongly connected graphs and solve ARG (Acknowledged Radio Gossiping) in $O(n \log^3 n)$ rounds for bidirectional graphs and in $O(n^{3/2})$ rounds for strongly connected graphs without collision detection.

Keywords: broadcasting, gossiping, distributed, deterministic, radio network

1 Introduction

A radio network is a collection of transmitter-receiver devices (denoted as nodes). Each node can transmit data to the nodes that exist within its transmitting capability region. A radio network can be modeled by a directed graph (we simply call it graph) $G = (V, E)$ called reachability graph where V denotes a set of nodes and when a node u can transmit to a node v, there exists an edge $(u, v) \in E$. If $(u, v) \in E$, u is called an in-neighbor of v, and v is called an out-neighbor of u. If the power of every transmitter is the same, then the reachability graph is bidirectional[4], that is, if there is an edge from node u to node v, then there exists the edge from v to u, and vice versa. We assume that all nodes in a radio network have access to a global clock (like GPS) and work synchronously in discrete time steps called rounds. At every round, each node transmits data or receives data. A node acting as a receiver in a given round gets

---

[4] bidirectional is called symmetric in [1].

M. Papatriantafilou and P. Hunel (Eds.): OPODIS 2003, LNCS 3144, pp. 223–234, 2004.
© Springer-Verlag Berlin Heidelberg 2004

a message iff exactly one of its in-neighbors transmits in this round. If at least two in-neighbors v and v' of u transmit simultaneously in a given round, none of the messages is received by u in this round. In this case we say that a conflict or a collision occurred at u. When collision occurs, two cases are considered: u notices the occurrence of a collision (i.e. it has collision detection), and u cannot distinguish between the background noise and the interference noise. It depends on the capability whether a node can detect a collision or not.

One of the fundamental tasks in network communication is radio broadcasting (RB). Its goal is to transmit a message from one node of the network, called the source, to all other nodes. The message which is disseminated is called source message. Remote nodes get the source message via intermediate nodes, along directed paths in the network. In an acknowledged radio broadcasting (ARB) the goal is not only to achieve RB but also to inform the source about the completion of RB. This may be essential, e.g., when the source has several messages to disseminate, none of the nodes should receive the next message until all nodes get the previous one [1]. Another task is radio gossiping (RG) which broadcasts the message of each node to all other nodes. We also consider the task acknowledged radio gossiping (ARG) which achieves RG and inform every node about the completion of RG.

In this paper, we consider the standard model of unknown radio networks, called the ad-hoc radio network model. We assume that each node does not know any information of the network (e.g. its neighbor, the number of nodes and the topology). The network is assumed to have a fix topology during the execution of algorithms. However, since no information of the network is used in our algorithms, they can be applied to networks with any topology. We evaluate algorithms with the number of rounds used to complete the tasks.

1.1 Previous Results

The standard collision-free communication procedure for ad hoc radio networks is called Round Robin [2]. Round Robin contains n rounds. In the i-th round the node with identifier i transmits its whole knowledge to all its out-neighbors. In every round at most one node acts as a transmitter, hence collisions are avoided. Round Robin is used as a subroutine in many RB and RG algorithms. An RG completes in $O(n^2)$ rounds, where n is the number of nodes.

There are two situations for communication procedures in radio networks: one is that nodes have full knowledge of the network (such as the topology of the network, the number of the nodes in the network, IDs of the neighbors etc.), the other is that nodes are ignorant of the network information. Various algorithms are studied in radio networks, e.g. the centralized algorithms with the mechanism in which all nodes are concentrated and managed, and the distributed algorithms without such a mechanism; the deterministic algorithms whose process become settled uniquely, and randomized algorithms which are not so [3,4,5,6,1,7,8,9, 2,10].

Under the assumption that the nodes have full knowledge of the network, in [3] the authors proved the existence of a family of n-node networks of radius

2, for which any broadcast requires $\Omega(\log^2 n)$ time, while in [4] it was proved that broadcasting can be done in $O(D + \log^5 n)$ time, for any n-node network of diameter D.

Hereafter, we assume that the nodes have neither the knowledge of the network nor the knowledge of their neighborhood.

For randomized algorithms, the lower bound of $\Omega(D \log(n/D))$ for bidirectional graphs is shown by Kushilevitz and Mansour [6], and the lower bound of $\Omega(\log^2 n)$ for constant diameter networks is obtained by Alon et al.[3].

For deterministic distributed algorithms, on the model without collision detection, Chlebus et al have presented an optimal linear-time broadcasting protocol for bidirectional ad hoc radio networks [1]. Also, on the model with collision detection, they presented an $O(n \cdot ecc)$-time RB algorithm for strongly connected graphs, an $O(r \cdot ecc)$-time RB algorithm for arbitrary graphs, an $O(n)$-time ARB algorithm for bidirectional graphs, and an $O(n \cdot ecc)$-time ARB algorithm for strongly connected graphs, where ecc is the maximum distance from the source. Note that on the model without collision detection there does not exist any algorithm for ARB, even for bidirectional graphs [1]. The best $O(n^{1.5})$ time gossiping algorithm for strongly connected graphs is shown in [10].

· About the lower bounds of deterministic RB, the lower bound of $\Omega(n)$ for bidirectional graphs [5] and the lower bound of $\Omega(n \log n)$ for arbitrary graphs [9] are shown.

Table 1 shows the results of these deterministic algorithms.

Table 1. Previous results(Deterministic and Distributed)

Problem	Collision detection	Graphs	Computation time
RB	without	bidirectional	$O(n)$ [1]
			$\Omega(n)$ [5]
		arbitrary	$O(n \log^2 n)$ [8]
			$\Omega(n \log n)$ [9]
	with	bidirectional	$O(r + ecc)$ [7]
		strongly connected	$O(n \cdot ecc)$ [1]
		arbitrary	$O(r \cdot ecc)$ [1]
RG	without	strongly connected	$O(n^{3/2})$ [10]
ARB	without	bidirectional	algorithm does not exist [1]
	with	bidirectional	$O(n)$ [1]
			$O(r + ecc)$ [7]
		strongly connected	$O(n \cdot ecc)$ [1]

(n:number of nodes, ecc:largest distance from the source, r:length of the source message)

1.2   Our Results

In this paper, we consider the ARB and the ARG algorithms on the model of ad hoc radio networks without collision detection. As we mentioned on the model without collision detection, there does not exist any ARB algorithm even for bidirectional graphs [1], which is proved by using a special case: when the source does not receive any message about the completion of the RB, the source can not distinguish between the situations that the network has only the source node (thus the source does not receive any message) and that at least two in-neighbors of the source transmit some messages (thus collision occurs).

If we assume that the network contains at least one node other than the source node and each node knows the number of nodes or its in-neighbors, RB algorithms can be easily modified to ARB ones. It is interesting to know the weakest conditions needed for performing an ARB. In this paper, we show that if the network contains at least two nodes, we can construct algorithms which solve ARB for bidirectional graphs and strongly connected graphs under the assumption that the network has no collision detection and each node knows only its ID.

The computation time of our ARB algorithm for bidirectional graphs is the same as the existing best RB algorithm which uses $O(n)$ rounds. The computation time of our ARB algorithm for strongly connected graphs is $O(6n + \sum_{i=1}^{\lceil \log n \rceil} \{2 \cdot RB(2^i) + RG(2^i)\})$, where $RB(n)$ and $RG(n)$ is the number of rounds which an RB and an RG requires for n-node strongly connected graphs, respectively. It becomes $O(n^{3/2})$ when using the $O(n^{3/2})$-time gossiping algorithm from [10].

In addition, we consider acknowledged radio gossiping (ARG) algorithms. We show that our ARB algorithms can be extended to ARG algorithms for both of bidirectional graphs and strongly connected graphs. Our ARB algorithm for bidirectional graphs needs a leader, and we use the source node to be the leader in the algorithm. In ARG, since no source node is given, we need to elect a leader for ARG when we extend the ARB algorithm to an ARG algorithm. For strongly connected graphs our ARB algorithm does not need a leader, therefore , in this case, the ARB algorithm can be extended to an ARG algorithm directly. The computation time of the extended ARG algorithms is $O(n + \sum_{i=1}^{\lceil \log n \rceil} \{LE(2^i)\})$ for bidirectional graphs and $O(6n + \sum_{i=1}^{\lceil \log n \rceil} \{RB(2^i) + 2 \cdot RG(2^i)\})$ for strongly connected graphs, respectively, where $LE(n)$ denotes the number of the rounds needed to elect a leader for n-node bidirectional graphs. The computation times of ARG algorithms become $O(n \log^3 n)$ and $O(n^{3/2})$, respectively, by using the $O(n \log^3 n)$-time leader election algorithm from [8] and the $O(n^{3/2})$-time gossiping algorithm from [10].

2   Model and Definitions

In this paper, we consider the radio networks without a collision detection. We describe the model of radio networks we consider :

- The knowledge of every node is limited to its own ID.
- Each node knows whether itself is a source or not in broadcasting.
- Nodes in a radio network work per round synchronized by a global clock.
- In every round, each node acts either as a transmitter or as a receiver.
- A node acting as a receiver in a given round gets a message iff exactly one of its in-neighbors transmits in this round.
- If more than one in-neighbor transmits simultaneously in a given round, collision occurs and none of the messages is received in this round.
- A node cannot notice the occurrence of a collision (i.e. without collision detection).

For simplicity we assume that each node is labeled with distinct integers between 1 and n in an n-node network. But all the arguments hold if the labels are distinct integers between 1 and $Z = O(n)$, and we do not use the property that the labels are in $\{1, 2, \ldots, n\}$.

3   ARB and ARG in Bidirectional Graphs

In this section, we describe ARB and ARG algorithms for bidirectional graphs where the number of nodes in the network is at least 2. First, we describe the overview of our algorithms, secondly we show an ARB algorithm and then modify it to an ARG algorithm.

3.1   Overview of Our Algorithm

The main idea of our algorithm is that each node confirms all of its in-neighbors in every phase, where in the k-th phase nodes with ID at most 2^k works. In the k-th phase, first the in-neighbors of any node v whose IDs are no more than 2^k send their own IDs, thus the node v can recognize its in-neighbors' IDs that are no more than 2^k. Then in the same phase the node whose ID is the minimum one among the in-neighbors with IDs no more than 2^k, and nodes whose IDs are more than 2^k send their IDs simultaneously. If the node v receives the minimum ID (i.e. collision does not occur), it recognizes that it knows all of the in-neighbor in this phase. It is easy to perform the ARB if every node knows all of its in-neighbors. If the node v does not receive the minimum ID (i.e. collision occurs), v recognizes that it does not know all of the in-neighbors and the algorithm performs the next phase.

3.2   Algorithm bi-ARB

We show an ARB algorithm named bi-ARB for bidirectional graphs in an n node radio network, where $n \geq 2$.

Algorithm bi-ARB works phase by phase, numbered by consecutive positive integers. Phase k lasts $9 \cdot 2^{k-1}$ rounds divided into four stages. Stage A consists of 2^{k-1} rounds, Stage B consists of 2^k rounds, Stage C consists of 2^k rounds, and Stage D consists of 2^{k+1} rounds. We denote the ID of node v as $\mathrm{ID}(v)$. We define the following notations.

- L_k : the set of nodes with IDs $1, \ldots,$ and 2^k.
- G_k : the connected component containing the source of the network induced by L_k. $G_k = \phi$ if the ID of the source node is larger than 2^k.
- N_v^k : the set of IDs smaller than or equal to 2^k from the in-neighbors of node v.
- $\min(N_v^k)$: the minimum ID in N_v^k. If $N_v^k = \phi$, $\min(N_v^k) = \perp$.

Note that in bidirectional graphs the in-neighbors of each node v are the same as the out-neighbors of v.

Informally we show the algorithm of phase k. Stage A is a Round Robin which intends to let each node v know its in-neighbors (and out-neighbors) whose IDs are at most 2^k (N_v^k). In Stage B each node v in L_k sends $min(N_v^k)$, which will be the only node in in-neighbors of v can transmit to v in the next stage C. Stage C is used to judge whether the node v of G_k knows all of its in-neighbors or not. In Stage C the node whose ID is $\min(N_v^k)$ and nodes not in L_k send their IDs, then according to whether receiving $\min(N_v^k)$ or not every node v in G_k recognizes whether it knows all its in-neighbors or not. In Stage D the source node in G_k broadcasts the source message to every node of G_k. The stage also collects the information that whether each node in G_k knows all its in-neighbors. Thereby the source node can confirm the completion of RB. We use the broadcast algorithm shown in [1] in this stage.

bi-ARB. Phase 0 consists of one round, the node with ID 1 acts as transmitter and sends its ID in this phase. The other nodes act as receivers.

Hereafter, we explain phase $k > 0$, of bi-ARB. We assume that every node is either a transmitter or a receiver in each round.

Stage A. The rounds in Stage A of phase k are numbered by integers $2^{k-1} + 1, \ldots, 2^{k-1} + 2^{k-1}$. In round number i of Stage A only the node v with ID i acts as a transmitter and sends a message ID(v).

Stage B. The rounds of this stage are numbered by integers $1, \ldots, 2^k$. In round i of Stage B only the node v with ID i acts as a transmitter and sends a message $\min(N_v^k)$. If $\min(N_v^k) = \perp$, the node v sends no message. The node w that receives $\min(N_v^k)$ stores it if ID(w)=$\min(N_v^k)$.

Stage C. The rounds in Stage C of phase k are numbered by integers $1, \ldots, 2^k$. In round i of Stage C, the node v with ID i acts as a receiver. The node with ID=$\min(N_v^k)$ acts as transmitter and sends its ID (if $\min(N_v^k)$ $\min()$), and all the nodes whose IDs are larger than 2^k (not only in-neighbors of v) also send their own IDs in the round.

Every node v not receiving $\min(N_v^k)$ in the round ID(v), is set to the state **warned** which means that v does not know all its in-neighbors, or in other words, v has the in-neighbors whose IDs are larger than 2^k.

Stage D. The rounds in Stage D of phase k are numbered by integers $1, \ldots, 2^{k+1}$. The source initiates Stage D if its ID is less than or equal to 2^k. Otherwise all nodes do nothing in these 2^{k+1} rounds. We use a message called token. At the beginning of this stage every node $v \in G_k$ knows its out-neighbor N_v^k in G_k and maintains a list Q_v containing the set of its out-neighbors in G_k which were not yet visited by the token. Q_v is initialized to N_v^k.

When a **warned** node sends the token to an out-neighbor, it appends a **warning** message to the token, and the out-neighbor getting the token becomes **warned**.

When node v gets the token, it acts as follows:

step 1. Node v sends the message <ID(v), visited>. If a node u receives the message, it removes v from the list Q_u.

step 2. Node v sends the token <source message, ID(w), (warning)> to the following node w:

- (i) If $Q_v = \phi$, w is the node from which v got the message in step 1 for the first time.
- (ii) If $Q_v \neq \phi$, w is the node with the smallest ID in the list Q_v.

the messages are concatenated and are sent in a single round. Node w which gets the token repeats the procedure of step 1 and step 2.

If, at the end of phase k, the source is **warned**, it knows that the RB has not been completed, and shifts to the next phase. Otherwise the algorithm terminates.

Correctness of Algorithm bi-ARB

Lemma 1. The following invariants are maintained after phase k of bi-ARB, for any positive integer k.

- Every node v knows the N_v^k, the set of IDs at most 2^k from the in-neighbors (and out-neighbors) of v.
- Every node in G_k knows the source message, if G_k contains the source node.

Proof. See [11].

Theorem 1. Algorithm bi-ARB performs an ARB in time $O(n)$, for any n-node bidirectional graph with $n \geq 2$.

Proof. See [11].

Message size. Let S be the maximum length of the message transmitted each time and let r be the length of the source message. In Stage A,B and C each node transmits at most one ID respectively, thus $S = O(\log n)$. In Stage D each node transmits message <ID(v), visited> and the token <source message, ID(w), (warning)>, thus $S = O(r + \log n)$. Hence the maximum message size is at most $O(r + \log n)$ for algorithm bi-ARB.

3.3   Algorithm bi-ARG

The ARG algorithm bi-ARG for bidirectional graphs is obtained by changing a part of bi-ARB.

Algorithm bi-ARG works in phases, numbered by consecutive positive integers similar to bi-ARB. Each phase consists of four stages A,B,C and D. Stage A,B,C are the same as these of algorithm bi-ARB but Stage D is different. It needs a leader election procedure and an extra token patrolling. Recall that in bi-ARB, the source node is used to be the starting point of the token patrolling. Furthermore, each node knows whether itself is a source or not. But the source node does not exist for ARG. We have to elect one leader for each connected component induced by L_k so that the token patrolling can be performed in each component. We use a leader election procedure. The leader of each connected component acts as initiator and makes the token patrol twice in its connected component in Stage D. In the first patrol the leader of each connected component collects the messages which each node has and **warning** messages from the nodes to the leader (the same as that in bi-ARB), then in the second patrol it disseminates the messages which were collected in the first patrol to all the nodes in the component. Thereby any node knows whether RG have completed or not.

In order to use an leader election algorithm, each node must know the completion time of the algorithm, since the leader election procedure must finish in each phase of bi-ARG.

Theorem 2. Algorithm bi-ARG performs an ARG in time $O(n + \sum_{i=1}^{\lceil \log n \rceil} \{LE(2^i)\})$, for any bidirectional graph with $n \geq 2$, where $LE(k)$ denotes the number of the rounds of any leader election algorithm for k-node bidirectional graphs in which each node knows the completion time.

We use the algorithm FIND MAX shown in [8] as a leader election procedure. The algorithm FIND MAX elects a leader by calculating the maximum ID on a strongly connected graph under the assumption that each node knows the upper bound of IDs of nodes in the network. Moreover, if each node knows (the upper bound of) the number of nodes n in the network, it can compute the completion time of FIND MAX, which is $cn \log^3 n$ for some known constant c. Algorithm FIND MAX finds the leader based on binary search. At each step, all nodes know that the minimum ID (the node having this ID is elected as a leader) among all nodes is between a and b by broadcasting a message, where $a \leq b$. Initially $a = 0$ and $b = n$. If $a = b$, then the minimum ID is equal to a, and the computation of minimum ID is complete. In each phase we use this algorithm to elect a leader for each connected component. In phase k, the upper bound of IDs and that of the number of nodes in the connected components induced by L_k is known to be 2^k. We obtain the following corollary from Theorem 2 using the $O(n \log^3 n)$-time leader election algorithm FIND MAX.

Corollary 1. Algorithm bi-ARG performs ARG in time $O(n \log^3 n)$, for any bidirectional graph with $n \geq 2$.

$$\left(\because \sum_{i=1}^{\lceil \log n \rceil} 2^i \log^3 2^i \leq 2(2^{\lceil \log n \rceil} - 1) \cdot (\log n + 1)^3 \leq 2(2n - 2) \cdot (\log n + 1)^3 \right)$$

Our algorithm bi-ARG is improvable if more efficient leader election algorithms can be designed for bidirectional graphs under the condition that each node knows the maximum of IDs and n.

Message size. Let S be the maximum length of the message transmitted each time and let r be the length of the message each node has. In Stage A,B and C, $S=O(\log n)$ which are the same as that of bi-ARB. In Stage D first $S=O(\log n)$ for the leader election procedure FIND MAX [8]. Next each node adds its own message to the token, $S=O(rn + \log n)$. Hence the maximum message size is at most $O(rn + \log n)$ for algorithm bi-ARG.

4 ARB and ARG in Strongly Connected Graphs

4.1 Algorithm st-ARB

The ARB algorithm st-ARB for strongly connected graphs is obtained by changing a part of bi-ARB. Algorithm st-ARB works in phases, numbered by consecutive positive integers. Every phase starts in the round following the end of the previous phase. Phase $k(> 0)$ lasts $3 \cdot 2^{k-1} + 2 \cdot RB(2^k) + RG(2^k)$ rounds divided into four stages. Stage A consists of 2^{k-1} rounds, Stage B consists of $RG(2^k)$ rounds, Stage C consists of 2^k rounds, and Stage D consists of $2 \cdot RB(2^k)$ rounds.

Here we show the outline of this algorithm in phase k. Stage A and C of st-ARB are the same as those of bi-ARB, and the purpose of Stage B and D also does not change. Although in bidirectional graphs a node v can transmit $\min(N_v^k)$ to its in-neighbor w whose ID$=\min(N_v^k)$ because the in-neighbors of v is also its out-neighbors, node v cannot do that in strongly connected graphs since w may not be an out-neighbor of v. To do this, v must gossip on the subgraph induced by L_k in Stage B. In Stage D each node other than the source node in L_k transmits the **warning** message and the source node broadcasts the source message. Thereby the source node can confirm the completion of RB.

In st-ARB we use the RB and RG in the subgraph induced by L_k (not necessarily strongly connected). In order to apply the RB algorithm for strongly connected graphs to our algorithm, it is sufficient to perform the task for all reachable nodes. About RG algorithm, it is not necessary to perform the task for all reachable nodes. Any algorithm of RB and RG can be applied to our algorithm if each node knows the completion time. We consider an extension of the RB that broadcasts from several source nodes with the same messages to all reachable nodes, and use the algorithm that performs such an extended RB in Stage D. Since the algorithm does not depend on the information of the source node, it can perform an RB in the situation such that several source nodes exist.

st-ARB Phase 0 consists of one round, the node with ID 1 acts as transmitter and sends its ID in this phase. The other nodes act as receivers.

Hereafter, we explain phase $k(> 0)$ of st-ARB. Stage A and C is the same as that of bi-ARB. Every node that is not transmitter is receiver in the explanation.

Stage A . Rounds in Stage A of phase k are numbered by integers $2^{k-1} + 1, \ldots, 2^{k-1} + 2^{k-1}$. In round number i of Stage A the only node v with ID i acts as a transmitter and sends a message ID(v).

Stage B . Stage B consists of $RG(2^k)$ rounds. In Stage B each node v in L_k acts as a transmitter, gossiping the message `<ID(v), min(N`$_{v}^{k}$`)>`. If $\min(N_v^k) = \lambda$, the node v sends no message.

Stage C . Rounds in Stage C of phase k are numbered by integers $1, \ldots, 2^k$. In round number i of Stage C the node v with ID i acts as a receiver. The node with ID $\min(N_v^k)$ and the nodes whose IDs are larger than 2^k act as transmitter, sending their own IDs.

Every node v not receiving $\min(N_v^k)$ in the round ID(v), is set to the state **warned**.

Stage D . Stage D consists of $2 \cdot RB(2^k)$ rounds. First, each node sends a **warning** message if it is **warned**. Next, if the source does not receive the **warning** message, it knows that there is no node in L_k whose in-neighbors with ID$> 2^k$ and then broadcasts the source message, otherwise it knows that there still exist nodes in L_k whose in-neighbors with ID$> 2^k$ and then it becomes **warned**, and shifts to the next phase.

Correctness of Algorithm st-ARB

Lemma 2. If there are **warned** nodes in the strongly connected graph after phase k of st-ARG then there is a path from at least one **warned** node to the source node that contains only nodes whose IDs are not larger than 2^k.

Proof. Let v be some **warned** node. In the original graph there is a path from v to the source. If there are nodes with ID$> 2^k$ in this path, let the out-neighbor of the last of them in the path be v'. The path from v' to the source proves the lemma.   □

Theorem 3. Algorithm st-ARB performs ARB in time $O(6n + \sum_{i=1}^{\lceil \log n \rceil} \{2 \cdot RB(2^i) + RG(2^i)\})$, in any strongly connected graphs with n nodes, where $n \geq 2$ and $RB(k)$ and $RG(k)$ denotes the number of the rounds of any extended RB and RG algorithm for k-node strongly connected graphs in which each node knows the completion time, respectively.

Proof. See [11].

We obtain the following corollary from Theorem 3 using the $O(n \log^2 n)$-time broadcasting algorithm from [8] and the $O(n^{3/2})$-time gossiping algorithm from [10]. The broadcasting Algorithm from [8] can perform the extended RB. The algorithm consists of stages, with each stage having $\log n + 1 = O(\log n)$ steps. For each $j = 0, \ldots, \log n$ let $\overline{S}_j = (S_{j,0}, S_{j,1}, \ldots, S_{j,m_j-1})$ be a 2^j-selector with $m_j = O(2^j \log n)$ sets, and the transmission set at the jth step of stage s

is $S_{j,\ s \bmod m_j}$, where w-*selector* is defined as follow; Given a positive integer w, a family $\overline{S}$ of sets is called a w-*selector* if it satisfies the following property: For any two disjoint sets $X, Y \in \{1, \ldots, n\}$ with $w/2 \leq |X| \leq w$ and $|Y| \leq w$ there exists a set in $\overline{S}$ such that $|S \cap X| = 1$ and $S \cap X = \phi$. Since each node does not use the information whether it is the source or not and does not depend on the message it received in the previous round, RB can be done on condition that several source nodes have the same message. Each node can compute the completion time of each algorithm under the assumption that it knows the upper bound of IDs of nodes in the network.

Corollary 2. Algorithm st-ARB performs ARB in time $O(n^{3/2})$, for any strongly connected graphs with $n \geq 2$.

Message size. Let S be the maximum length of the message transmitted each time and let r be the length of the source message. In Stage A and C each node transmits at most one ID, thus $S = O(\log n)$. In Stage B each node v gossips $ID(v)$ and $\min(N_v^k)$, thus $S = O(n \log n)$. In Stage D each node transmits a **warning** message, the source node transmits the source message, thus $S = O(r)$. Hence the maximum message size is at most $O(r + n \log n)$ for algorithm st-ARB.

4.2   Algorithm st-ARG

The ARG algorithm st-ARG for strongly connected graphs is obtained by changing a part of st-ARB.

Algorithm st-ARG works in phases, numbered by consecutive positive integers as well as st-ARB. Stage A,B and C is the same as that of st-ARB. We perform ARG by changing Stage D. Stage D consists of $RB(2^k) + RG(2^k)$ rounds. First step where each node confirms whether it receives the **warning** message or not is the same as that of Stage D of st-ARB. If a node does not receive **warning** message, it knows that there is no node with ID$> 2^k$ and gossip its own message, otherwise it knows that there still exist nodes with ID$> 2^k$ and becomes **warned**, then shifts to the next phase.

Theorem 4. Algorithm st-ARG performs ARG in time $O(6n + \sum_{i=1}^{\lceil \log n \rceil} \{RB(2^i) + 2 \cdot RG(2^i)\})$, for any strongly connected graph with n nodes, where $n \geq 2$ and $RB(k)$ and $RG(k)$ denotes the number of the rounds of any RB and RG algorithm for k-node strongly connected graphs in which each node knows the completion time, respectively.

We obtain the following corollary from Theorem 4 using the $O(n \log^2 n)$-time broadcasting algorithm from [8] and the $O(n^{3/2})$-time gossiping algorithm from [10] as well as Corollary 2.

Corollary 3. Algorithm st-ARG performs ARG in time $O(n^{3/2})$, for any strongly connected graph with n nodes, where $n \geq 2$.

Message size. Let S be the maximum length of the message transmitted each time and let r be the length of the message each node has. In Stage A,B and C $S = O(n \log n)$ is the same as that of st-ARB. In Stage D each node v broadcasts a **warning** message and gossips its own message, thus $S = O(rn)$. Hence the maximum message size is at most $O(rn + n \log n)$ for algorithm st-ARG.

5   Conclusion

In this paper, on the model without collision detection we show that we can construct deterministic and distributed ARB algorithms for symmetric digraphs in time $O(n)$, and for strongly connected digraphs in time $O(6n + \sum_{i=1}^{\lceil \log n \rceil} \{2 \cdot RB(2^i) + RG(2^i)\})$, where n is the number of the nodes in the graphs and $n \geq 2$. We also show that our each ARB algorithm can be extended to ARG algorithm. Our algorithms can be improved if we can find more efficient leader election algorithms for symmetric digraphs and if ARB can be achieved without using RG for strongly connected digraphs.

References

1. B.S. Chlebus, L. Gąsieniec, A.M. Gibbons, A. Pelc, and W. Rytter. Deterministic broadcasting in ad hoc radio networks. *Distributed Computing 15*, pages 27–38, 2002.
2. L.Gąsieniec, M.Christersson and A.Lingas. Gossiping with bounded size messages in ad hoc radio networks. *29th International Colloquium on Automata, Languages and Programming, (ICALP'02)*, pages 377–389, 2002.
3. N.Alon,, A.Bar-Noy, N.Linial, and D.Peleg. A lower bound for radio broadcast. *Journal of Computer and System Sciences 43*, pages 290–298, 1991.
4. I.Gaber and Y.Mansour. Broadcast in Radio Networks. *6th Ann. ACM-SIAM Symp. on Discrete Algorithms, SODA'95*, pages 577–585, 95.
5. R.Bar-Yehuda, O.Goldreich, and A.Itai. On the time-complexity of broadcast in radio networks: an exponential gap between determinism and randomization, *6th ACM Symposium on Principles of Distributed Computing*, pages 98–107, 1987.
6. E.Kushilevitz and Y.Mansour. An $\Omega \left(D \log \frac{n}{D} \right)$ lower bound for broadcast in radio networks. *12th Ann. ACM Symp. on Principles of Distributed Computing*, 65–73, 1993.
7. T.Okuwa, W.Chen and K.Wada. An optimal algorithm of acknowledged broadcasting in ad hoc networks, Proc. of 2nd Int'l Symp. Parallel and Distributed Computing(2003)(to appear).
8. M.Chrobak, L.Gąsieniec, and W.Rytter. Fast broadcasting and gossiping in radio networks. *st IEEE Symp. on Found. of Computer Science (FOCS'2000)*, pages 575–581, 2000.
9. D.Brusci and M.Del Pinto. Lower bounds for the broadcast problem in mobile radio networks. *Distributed Computing 10*, pages 129–135, 1997.
10. Y.Xu. An $O(n^{1.5})$ deterministic gossiping algorithm for radio networks. *Algorithmica, May 2003*, pages 93–96, 2003.
11. Jiro Uchida, Wei Chen, and Koichi Wada. Acknowledged Broadcasting and Gossiping in ad hoc radio networks. *Nagoya Institute of Technology, Wada Lab, TR2004-01*, 2004.

Decoupled Interconnection of Distributed Memory Models[*]

Ernesto Jiménez[1], Antonio Fernández[2], and Vicente Cholvi[3]

[1] Universidad Politécnica de Madrid, 28031 Madrid, Spain
ernes@eui.upm.es
[2] Universidad Rey Juan Carlos, 28933 Móstoles, Spain
afernandez@acm.org
[3] Universitat Jaume I, 12071 Castellón, Spain
vcholvi@inf.uji.es

Abstract. In this paper we present a framework to formally describe and study the interconnection of distributed shared memory systems. In our models we minimize the dependencies between the original systems and the interconnection system (that is, they are decoupled) and consider systems implemented with invalidation and propagation.

We first show that only fast memory models can be interconnected. We then show that causal and pRAM systems can be interconnected if they fulfill some restrictions, and for these cases, we present protocols to interconnect them. Finally, we present a protocol to interconnect cache systems.

1 Introduction

Distributed shared memory is an abstraction used for process communication. In this abstraction, processes read and write variables of a shared memory, which is usually implemented with distributed memory and message passing. Depending on the semantics of the shared memory a number of consistency models have been proposed in the literature [1,9]. Some of the most popular models are the sequential [16], causal [3], pRAM [18], and cache [12]. Informally, the sequential model requires that the read and write (memory) operations obtained in an execution of a distributed system could have been obtained if they had been executed in a single processor. Therefore, in this model there must be a total order (a view) of the operations such that they seem to have been executed in that sequential order. This sequential view must be the same for every process. The causal model relaxes the memory semantics because it allows several views (one for each process), where only causally related memory operations must be ordered. Therefore, two processes could have different causal views if there are operations that are not causally related. Similarly, the pRAM model is a

[*] This work has been partially supported by the Spanish MCyT under grants TIC2001-1586-C03-01 and TIC2001-1586-C03-02, the Comunidad de Madrid under grant 07T/0022/2003, and the Universidad Rey Juan Carlos under grant PPR-2003-37.

M. Papatriantafilou and P. Hunel (Eds.): OPODIS 2003, LNCS 3144, pp. 235–246, 2004.

relaxation of the causal model, because it only requires that in each process all write operations of another process seem to have been executed in the same order as they were issued. Finally, the cache model is like the sequential model but applied on each variable independently. That is to say, there is a sequential view formed by all operations on variable x (for every variable x of the shared memory). Many protocols have been proposed in distributed shared memory systems that implement these consistency models.

In this work we study the interconnection of distributed shared memory systems. By this we mean the adding of an interconnection system to several existing distributed shared memory systems that implement a given consistency model to obtain a single distributed shared memory system that implements the same consistency model. This line of work was started in [10], where the interconnection of causal propagation-based systems was studied. In this work we use much weaker assumptions on the systems to be interconnected, consider also invalidation-based systems, and explore other models as well.

Our Contributions. In this work we first define a framework for the interconnection of systems. We formalize several classes of interactions, both for propagation and invalidation-based protocols, between the existing systems and the interconnection system. All these classes decouple the systems from the interconnection system, unlike the previous model [10].

Then, we show that systems that implement non-fast consistency models cannot be interconnected in these classes. A fast consistency model is one that allows implementations of read and write operations that return control after only local computations. After that, we study the interconnection of pRAM and causal systems. We show that they can not be interconnected in general, but can under certain restrictions. We give sufficient conditions and the corresponding protocols to do so. Finally, we also show that systems that implement cache consistency can always be interconnected.

Note that this is the first work that studies the interconnection of pRAM and cache systems, that considers both propagation and invalidation, and that shows that certain interconnections are in fact impossible. Our protocols need not be very useful nor efficient in practice, since all we try to do with this work is to define the bounds of the possibilities of interconnection.

The rest of the paper is organized as follows. In Section 2 we introduce our framework for the interconnection of systems. In Section 3 we show the impossibility result for non-fast consistency models. In Section 4 we study the interconnection of pRAM systems, in Section 5 the interconnection of causal systems, and in Section 5 we show how to interconnect cache systems. Finally, in Section 7 we present concluding remarks.

2   Definitions and Notation

We consider distributed shared memory systems (or systems for short) formed by a collection of application processes that interact via a shared memory formed by a set of variables All the interactions between the application processes and the memory are done through read and write operations (m em ory operations) on variables of the memory.

Each memory operation is applied on a named variable and has an associated value. A write operation of the value v in the variable x, denoted $w(x)v$, stores v in the variable x. A read operation of the value v from the variable x, denoted $r(x)v$, reports to the issuing application process that the variable x holds the value v. To simplify the analysis, we assume that a given value is written at most once in any given variable and that the initial values of the variables are set by using fictitious write operations.

Consistency Model of a System. An execution α of a system S is the set of read and write operations observed in some run R of system S.

Definition 1 (Process Order). Let p be a process of S and $op, op' \in \alpha$. Then op precedes op' in p's process order, denoted $op \prec_p op'$, if op and op' are operations issued by p, and op is issued before op'.

Definition 2 (Execution Order). Let $op, op' \in \alpha$. Then op precedes op' in the execution order, denoted $op \prec op'$, if:
1. op and op' are operations from the same process p and $op \prec_p op'$, or
2. $op = w(x)v$ and $op' = r(x)v$, or
3. $\exists op'' \in \alpha : op \prec op'' \prec op'$

We denote by α_p the subset of operations obtained by removing from α all read operations issued by processes other than p. We also denote by $\alpha(x)$ the subset of operations obtained by removing from α all the operations on variables other than x.

Definition 3 (View). Let $\prec^o$ be an order on execution α, and let $\alpha' \subseteq \alpha$. A view β of α' preserving $\prec^o$ is a sequence formed by all operations of α' such that this sequence preserves the order $\prec^o$.

Note that if $\prec^o$ applied on α' is not a total order, there can be several views of α'. We use $op \overset{\beta}{\to} op'$ to denote that op precedes op' in a sequence of operations β. We will omit the name of the sequence when it is clear from the context. We will also use $\beta_1 \to \beta_2$, where β_1 and β_2 are sequences of operations, to denote that all the operations in β_1 precede all the operations in β_2.

Definition 4 (Legal View). Let $\prec^o$ be an order on execution α, and let $\alpha' \subseteq \alpha$. A view β of α' preserving $\prec^o$ is legal if $\forall r(x)v \in \alpha'$:
a) $\exists\, w(x)v \in \alpha' : w(x)v \overset{\beta}{\to} r(x)v$, and
b) $\nexists\, w(x)u \in \alpha' : w(x)v \overset{\beta}{\to} w(x)u \overset{\beta}{\to} r(x)v$.

By using this definition of legal view, we can define systems satisfying the causal, pRAM, and cache consistency models.

Definition 5 (Causal, pRAM, or Cache System). A system S is causal if for every execution α and every process p there is a legal view β_p of α_p preserving $\prec$ on α. A system S is pRAM if for every execution α and every process p there is a legal view β_p of α_p, preserving $\prec_q$ on α_p, for all q. A system S is cache if for every execution α and every variable x there is a legal view β_x of $\alpha(x)$ preserving $\prec$ on $\alpha(x)$.

System Architecture. From a physical point of view, we consider distributed systems formed by a set of nodes and a network that provides communication among them. The essence of this model has been taken from [6]. The application processes of the system are actually executed in the nodes of the distributed system. We assume that the shared memory abstraction is implemented by a memory consistency system (MCS). The MCS is composed of MCS-processes that use the local memory at the various nodes and cooperate following a distributed algorithm, or MCS-protocol, to provide the application processes with the impression of having a shared memory. The MCS-processes are executed at the nodes of the distributed system and exchange information as specified by the MCS-protocol. They use the communication network to interact if they are in different nodes. Each MCS-process can serve several application processes, but an application process is assigned to only one local MCS-process. For each application process p we use $mcs(p)$ to denote its MCS-process.

An application process sequentially issues read or write operations on the shared variables by sending (read or write) calls to its MCS-process. After sending a call, the application process blocks until it receives the corresponding response from its MCS-process, which ends the operation.

We consider MCSs implemented with propagation and invalidation. For simplicity, in both cases we consider that each MCS-process has a copy (replica) of the whole shared memory. In an MCS with invalidation, some of the copies of a variable x can be "invalid" or outdated. If an MCS-process' copy of a variable x is invalid and one of its application processes tries to read x, the MCS-process has to obtain the current value of x from some other MCS-process (following the MCS-protocol). When an application process issues a write operation $w(x)v$, the local copy of x in its MCS-process is updated with the current value v, and the valid copies of x in the rest of MCS-processes are marked as invalid. In an MCS with propagation no copy is ever invalid and holds the current value (as seen by the MCS-process). This value is returned to an application process that issues a read operation. New written values are propagated among MCS-processes to maintain the copies up to date.

The Interconnection System. This paper deals with the interconnection of systems. This means that, after the interconnection, the set of original systems will behave as one single system. Using the terminology defined above, interconnecting systems is, in fact, interconnecting MCSs. In our model, the load of such an interconnection will fall on an interconnection system (IS). An IS is a set of processes (IS-processes) that execute some distributed algorithm or protocol

(IS-protocol). For simplicity in the IS design, we consider one IS-process for each MCS to be interconnected. The IS-process of each system is at the same level as an application process and has its own MCS-process. The IS-process uses the MCS-process to read and write on the shared memory of the local system. In particular, the only way a value written by an application process in some system can be read by an application process in another system is if the IS-process of the latter system writes it. IS-processes exchange information among them (as specified by the IS-protocol) by using a communication network. Note that, after the interconnection, the overall system has a global MCS formed by the MCSs of the original systems plus the IS that interconnects them.

For system interconnections we extend the interface between the MCS and the IS beyond read and write operations issued by IS-processes. We assume that MCS-processes are connected with its corresponding IS-process through a reliable FIFO channel and send messages to it with the changes on the local memory replicas by using these FIFO channels. We consider the following classes of interfaces between the MCS and the IS.

(a) **Weak decoupled class with propagation (WDP).** The MCS-process of the IS-process sends a message to the IS-process every time a variable copy is updated. Each of these messages, denoted by $msg(p, x, u)$, carries the process p that issued the corresponding write operation, the variable x, and the new value u.

(b) **Strong decoupled class with propagation (SDP).** Every MCS-process in the system sends a message to its corresponding IS-process every time a variable copy is updated. Each of these messages, denoted by $msg(p, m, x, u)$, carries the application process p that issued the corresponding write operation, the MCS-process m that updated, the variable x, and the new value u. Trivially, in the SDP class, the IS-process receives at least as much information as in the WDP class. Thus, in this sense, SDP is stronger than WDP.

(c) **Strong decoupled class with invalidation (SDI).** Every MCS-process in the system sends a message to its corresponding IS-process every time a variable copy is invalidated or updated (by a write operation issued by one of its application processes). Each of these messages, denoted by $msg(p, q, x, u)$, carries the process p that issued the corresponding write operation, the MCS-process q that updated or invalidated this replica, the variable x, and the new value u (if it is an update). For each write operation $w(x)u$ issued by some process p, the IS-process will receive an update message $msg(p, mcs(p), x, u)$ from p's MCS-process, and an invalidation message $msg(p, m, x)$ from each MCS-process m that had a valid copy of x, and has invalidated it.

Model and Notation. In this paper we assume an asynchronous model. This means that there is no bound on the time instructions and message transmissions take. We do not assume synchronized clocks among processes. We also assume that no system component (processes, nodes, and networks) fails.

In the rest of the paper we will use N to denote the number of systems to be interconnected. The systems to be interconnected will be denoted by

$S^0, \cdots, S^{N-1}$, and the resulting interconnected system by S^T. The IS-process for each system S^k (where $k \in \{0, \cdots, N-1\}$) is denoted by isp^k. It is worth to remark that isp^k is part of the system S^k. For that reason, the MCS-process $mcs(isp^k)$ has a local replica of each variable of the shared memory, and those replicas are updated or invalidated (depending on the method used to maintain the coherence of these replicas) following the MCS-protocol implemented in the MCS of S^k. We also assume that the IS-processes are interconnected among them through reliable FIFO communication channels which will be used to propagate write operations from one system to the other. We consider that the set of processes of S^T includes all the processes in $S^0, \cdots, S^{N-1}$ except for $isp^0, \cdots, isp^{N-1}$ (they are only used to interconnect the systems $S^0, \cdots, S^{N-1}$).

Regarding executions, we will use the next notation. α^T will denote an execution of S^T. Similarly, α^k (where $k \in \{0, \cdots, N-1\}$) will denote the execution of S^k obtained in the same run. Note that α^k and α^T have in common all the operations issued by processes in S^k. We also extend the notation used with read and write operations. We denote by $w_p^k(x)v$ the write operation $w(x)v$ issued by process p of system S^k. Similarly, we denote by $r_p^k(x)v$ the read operation $r(x)v$ issued by process p of system S^k. A write operation $w_q^l(x)v$ in α^T issued by some processes q in S^l appears in α^k, $k \neq l$, as the write operation $w_{isp^k}^k(x)v$ issued by the process isp^k in S^k. This is so because every write operation issued by isp^k in α^k is, from the IS-protocol, just the propagation of a write operation issued by a process of another system S^m, $m \neq k$. We denote by $orig(op)$ the original write operation propagated as operation op in α_p^k by process isp^k. Similarly, given a write operation op issued in S^l, $l \neq k$, we denote by $prop(op)$ the write operation issued by isp^k as a result of propagating op to S^k as defined by the IS-protocol.

We will say that a consistency model can be interconnected if there is an IS-protocol that interconnects systems implementing this consistency model. The IS-protocol can specify the number of systems it interconnects. (However, it cannot restrict how applications processes are mapped to nodes.)

3   Non-fast Consistency Models

In this section we show that systems implementing "non-fast" consistency models can not be interconnected in any of the classes defined in the previous section. We say that a consistency model is fast if there is an MCS–protocol that implements it, such that memory operations only require local computations before returning control, even in systems with several nodes. There is a number of consistency models (e.g., causal or pipelined RAM) that are fast, while there are stronger memory models (e.g., the sequential or atomic) that are not. This implies that the property of being fast classifies the set of memory models in a non trivial way.

The proof of the following theorem is omitted due to space limitations.

Theorem 1. There is no IS that guarantees the interconnection of systems implementing some non-fast memory model.

As a consequence of this theorem, we can derive that a number of popular memory models can not be interconnected. In [6] it is shown that the sequential consistency model is not fast. Hence it cannot be interconnected and neither can the atomic consistency model, nor its derivations, safe and regular [17]. Similarly, Attiya and Friedman [4] have shown that the processor consistency models PCG and PCD [12,2] are not fast and hence cannot be interconnected. Finally, in [4] Attiya and Friedman also proved that any algorithm for the mutual exclusion problem using fast operations must be cooperative. This implies that any synchronization operation that guarantees mutual exclusion must be non–fast. Therefore, any synchronized memory model that provides exclusive access cannot be interconnected. As a result, we have that memory models such as the eager release [11], the lazy release [15], the entry [7] or the scope [13] can not be interconnected.

4   pRAM Consistency Model

In this section we study the interconnection of pRAM systems. We first show that in general the interconnection is not possible. Then present IS-protocols for the different classes defined under different restrictions.

Impossibility for Interconnecting pRAM Systems. In this subsection we show that we can not guarantee the interconnection, through some IS in any class, of every pair of pRAM systems. The proof of the following theorem is based on the fact that, when some process p in S^k, $k \in \{0,1\}$, issues several write operations, it may update the corresponding variables in its local memory in a different order from $p's$ process order.

The proof of the following theorem is omitted due to space limitations.

Theorem 2. There is no IS in SDP that guarantees pRAM interconnection for every pair of pRAM systems.

We know, by definition, that SDP is stronger than WDP. Hence, we can also apply this impossibility result to ISs interconnecting pairs of pRAM systems in WDP. Note also that the above proof can be easily adapted to the SDI class. Hence, we have that there is no IS in SDI that guarantees pRAM interconnection for every pair of pRAM systems.

IS-protocols for pRAM Systems. In this section we show how to interconnect systems implementing the pRAM [18] consistency model in SDP, WDP, and SDI, as long as these systems satisfy certain restrictions. First, we present an IS-protocol in SDP, for MCSs that satisfy the following property, which is fulfilled by all pRAM MCSs we have found.

Property 1. In any computation α^k of system S^k ($k \in \{0, \cdots, N-1\}$), for each process p in S^k, there is an MCS-process $s(p)$, known by isp^k, such that if p issues two write operations $w_p^k(x)v \prec_p w_p^k(y)u$, then $s(p)$ updates its local replica of x with the value v before updating the variable y with the value u.

Property 1 guarantees that each process isp^k knows MCS-processes in system S^k that locally apply the write operations in the same order as they were issued in S^k by the application processes. Furthermore, isp^k knows at least one such MCS-process for each application process p. With this knowledge, isp^k will be able to propagate the write operations to other systems preserving the process order $\prec_p$ (see Definition 1). Then, in our algorithm, each IS-process isp^k, $k \in \{0, \cdots, N-1\}$, contains two concurrent tasks, $Propagate_{out}^k$ and $Propagate_{in}^k$. $Propagate_{out}^k$ deals with transferring write operations issued in S^k to every S^l, $l \neq k$, while $Propagate_{in}^k$ deals with applying within S^k the write operations transfered from the systems S^l, $l \neq k$. The two tasks that form the pRAM IS-protocol in SDP operate as follows (see Fig. 1):

– Task $Propagate_{out}^k$ is activated after a message $msg(p, s(p), x, v)$, for some process p, is received by isp^k. Then, $Propagate_{out}^k$ sends the pair $\langle x, v \rangle$ to every isp^l, $l \neq k$. From the above Property 1, the sending of the pairs generated from the write operations issued by p follows p's process order. We avoid to re-propagate write operations received from other systems, by checking that the write operation was not issued in S^k by isp^k.

– Task $Propagate_{in}^k$ is activated whenever a pair $\langle x, v \rangle$ is received from some process isp^l, $l \neq k$. As a result, it performs a write operation $w_{isp^k}^k(x)v$, thus propagating the value v to all the replicas of variable x within S^k.

1	Task $Propagate_{out}^k$ :: upon reception of $msg(p, s(p), x, v)$	1	Task $Propagate_{in}^k$ :: upon reception of $\langle x, v \rangle$ from isp^l, $l \neq k$
2	begin	2	begin
3	if $p \neq isp^k$ then	3	$w_{isp^k}^k(x)v$
4	send $\langle x, v \rangle$ to every isp^l, $l \neq k$	4	end
5	end		

Fig. 1. The pRAM IS-protocol in isp^k in SDP.

The correctness of the IS-protocol of Fig. 1 is omitted due to space limitations. There, we show that the system S^T, obtained by connecting N systems $S^0, \cdots, S^{N-1}$ using this pRAM IS-protocol in SDP, is pRAM.

We now consider an IS-protocol in WDP such that this IS only interconnects MCSs that fulfill the following Property 2.

Property 2. In any computation α^k of system S^k ($k \in \{0, \cdots, N-1\}$), for each process p in S^k, if p issues two write operations $w_p^k(x)v \prec_p w_p^k(y)u$, then $mcs(isp^k)$ updates its local replica of x with the value v before updating its local replica of y with the value u.

Property 2 guarantees that the MCS-process of isp^k applies the write operations in the same order as they are issued in S^k. We can observe that this

Property 2 is a particular case of Property 1 where process $s(p)$ is now $mcs(isp^k)$, for all p. Hence, we can use the same IS-protocol of Figure 1.

Finally, to end this section, we consider an IS-protocol in SDI such that this IS only interconnects MCSs that fulfill the following Property 3.

Property 3. In any computation α^k of system S^k ($k \in \{0, \cdots, N-1\}$), for each process p in S^k, if p issues two write operations $w_p^k(x)v \prec_p w_p^k(y)u$, then $mcs(p)$ updates its local replica of x with the value v before updating its local replica of y with the value u.

Now Property 3 guarantees that every MCS-process of system S^k applies the write operations in the same order as they are issued in S^k. Again, this property is a particular case of Property 1 where process $s(p)$ is now $mcs(p)$. Hence, we can use the same IS-protocol of Figure 1 to interconnect pRAM systems in SDI.

5 Causal Consistency Model

In this section we study the interconnection of causal systems. Note that the pRAM model is strictly weaker than causal model [3,8]. Therefore, the results of impossibility of Section 4 are also applicable to causal systems.

In Section 4 we present an IS–protocol in SDP for interconnecting pRAM systems satisfying Property 1. We can show that there is no IS in SDP that interconnects every pair of causal systems satisfying Property 1. The proof is omitted due to space limitations. This result can be easily extended to WDP with Property 2 and SDI with Property 3.

We now propose an IS–protocol in SDP for causal systems. We also show in this subsection that the resulting system of this interconnection is causal. For our IS, we will only consider MCSs that fulfill the following Property 4 (which is in fact satisfied by all the causal protocols we have found).

Property 4. Consider any execution α^k of the causal system S^k (where $k \in \{0, \cdots, N-1\}$). For each two write operations $w_p^k(x)v \prec w_q^k(y)u$ on α^k, each MCS–process of system S^k updates its local replica of x with the value v before updating its local replica of y with the value u.

Property 4 guarantees that every MCS-process of system S^k applies the write operations preserving the execution order $\prec$ (see Definition 2). In Figure 2 we present the causal IS-protocol we propose. This protocol requires that the communication among IS-processes is totally ordered. There are well-known message-passing protocols (e.g., [5, pp. 177-179]) to provide total ordering of messages.

It can be observed that the IS-protocol is composed by two task, like the IS-protocol of Fig. 1. In fact, the $Propagate_{in}^k$ task is the same. However, the key difference is found in task $Propagate_{out}$. In this task a pair $\langle x, v \rangle$ is not sent to the other systems until all the MCS replicas of x have been updated. Note that, from Property 4, write operations are propagated to the rest of systems following

1	Task $Propagate_{out}^k$ :: upon reception of $msg(p, q, x, v)$, from every MCS-process q	1	Task $Propagate_{in}^k$ :: upon reception of $\langle x, v \rangle$ from isp^l, $l \neq k$
2	begin	2	begin
3	if $p \neq isp^k$ then	3	$w_{isp^k}^k(x)v$
4	send $\langle x, v \rangle$ to every isp^l, $l \neq k$	4	end
5	end		

Fig. 2. The causal IS-protocol in isp^k in SDP.

the causal order in system S^k. We need the communication among IS-processes to be totally ordered to enforce that two write operations from different systems and casually ordered, are applied in the rest of systems in the causal order.

Let us now show that the system S^T, obtained by connecting N systems $S^0, \cdots, S^{N-1}$ using the causal IS–protocol of Fig. 2 in SDP, is causal.

Let p be some process in system S^k, $k \in \{0, \cdots, N-1\}$, and let $mcs(p)$ be its MCS-process. Recall that α_p^k (resp. α_p^T) is the set obtained by removing from α^k (resp. α^T) all read operations except those from process p. We define β_p^k as a sequence with the same operations as α_p^k that preserves the order in which all operations of α_p^k are issued by process p, and the order in which every write operation is applied in $mcs(p)$. Formally,

Definition 6. Let β_p^k a sequence of the operations in α_p^k. Let op and op' in α_p^k. Then $op \rightarrow op'$ in β_p^k, if any of the following happens:

1. op and op' are operations from the same process p of S^k and $op \prec_p op'$.
2. $op = w_q^k(x)u$, $op' = w_s^k(y)v$, and in $mcs(p)$ the local copy of x is updated with u before updating y with v.
3. $op = w_q^k(x)u$, $op' = r_p^k(y)v$, and in $mcs(p)$ the local copy of x is updated with u before p issues op'.

Note that, like in α_p^k, every write operation of process isp^k in β_p^k is the propagation of a write operation issued by a process of S^l, $l \neq k$. We define β_p^T as the sequence obtained by replacing in β_p^k every write operation op from isp^k by the write operation $orig(op)$. The proof of the following results is omitted due to space limitations.

Lemma 1. β_p^T is formed by all operations of α_p^T, preserves the execution order $\prec$ on α^T, and is legal.

Theorem 3. The system S^T is causal.

6   Cache Consistency Model

In this section we study the interconnection of cache systems. We show that, unlike the previous models, the interconnection of cache systems is always possible, independently of how they are implemented. The interconnection only uses read and write operations, without any other consideration about the interface between the MCS and the IS. Hence, we can use the same IS-protocol for SDP, SDI and WDP classes.

The IS-protocol we propose only works for the interconnection of two systems. However, it can be repeatedly used to interconnect as many systems as desired. Each isp^k (in this case $k \in \{0,1\}$) has one task for each variable of the shared memory, presented in Figure 3. Note that each IS-process maintains a copy of

1	Task $Propagate^k(x)$ :: upon reception of $\langle x, v \rangle$ from isp^{1-k}
2	begin
3	if $v \neq$ "$NoData$" then
4	$w_{isp^k}^k(x)v$
5	$last(x) = v$
6	$r_{isp^k}^k(x)u$
7	if $u = last(x)$ then
8	$u =$ "$NoData$"
9	send $\langle x, u \rangle$ to isp^{1-k}
10	end

Fig. 3. The cache IS-protocol in isp^k for variable x.

the latest value propagated from the other system in $last(x)$ for each variable x. That copy must be initialized with a special value (e.g., "$NoData$"). Note also that initially one of the IS-processes (for instance isp^0) must send to the other a message with $\langle x, NoData \rangle$ for each variable x to start the interconnection. The proof that this cache IS-protocol interconnects two cache systems is omitted due to space limitations.

7 Conclusions

In this paper we have formalized and studied the interconnection of distributed shared memory systems. We have shown that non-fast, pRAM, and causal systems cannot be interconnected in general, while cache systems can. Then, we have given sufficient conditions to interconnect pRAM and causal systems. Then, with the results presented in this paper we can determine, for example, whether several systems, that implement certain memory models, can be interconnected by merely looking at the properties that these systems satisfy, and independently of what specific protocols they use.

Limitations of space have made impossible to include all the proofs. A complete version of this paper can be found in [14].

References

1. S.V. Adve. *Designing Memory Consistency Models for Shared-Memory Multiprocessors*. PhD thesis, University of Wisconsin-Madison, 1993.

2. M. Ahamad, R. Bazzi, R. John, P. Kohli, and G. Neiger. The power of processor consistency. In *Proceedings of the 5th ACM Symposium on Parallel Algorithms and Architectures*, pages 251–260, 1993.
3. M. Ahamad, G. Neiger, J.E. Burns, P. Kohli, and P.W. Hutto. Causal memory: Definitions, implementation and programming. *Distributed Computing*, 9(1):37–49, August 1995.
4. H. Attiya and R. Friedman. Limitations of fast consistency conditions for distributed shared memories. *Information Processing Letters*, 57:243–248, 1996.
5. H. Attiya and J. Welch. *Distributed Computing: Fundamentals, Simulations, and Advanced Topics*. McGraw-Hill, 1998.
6. H. Attiya and J.L. Welch. Sequential consistency versus linearizability. *ACM Transactions on Computer Systems*, 12(2):91–122, 1994.
7. B.N. Bershad, M.J. Zekauskas, and W.A. Sawdon. The Midway distributed shared memory system. In *COMPCON*, 1993.
8. V. Cholvi. *Formalizing Memory Models*. PhD thesis, Department of Computer Science, Polytechnic University of Valencia, December 1994.
9. V. Cholvi. Specification of the behavior of memory operations in distributed systems. *Parallel Processing Letters*, 8(4):589–598, December 1998.
10. A. Fernández, E. Jiménez, and V. Cholvi. On the interconnection of causal memory systems. In *Proceedings of the 19th Annual ACM Symposium on Principles of Distributed Computing*. ACM, July 2000.
11. K. Gharachorloo, D. Lenoski, J. Laudon, P. Gibbons, A. Gupta, and J. Hennessy. Memory consistency and event ordering in scalable shared-memory multiprocessors. In *Proceedings of the 17th Annual International Symposium on Computer Architecture*, pages 15–26. ACM, May 1990.
12. J.R. Goodman. Cache consistency and sequential consistency. Technical Report 61, IEEE Scalable Coherence Interface Working Group, March 1989.
13. L. Iftode, J. Singh, and K. Li. Scope consistency: A bridge between release consistency and entry consistency. In *Proc. of the 8th Annual ACM Symposium on Parallel Algorithms and Architectures*, 1996.
14. Ernesto Jiménez, Antonio Fernández, and Vicente Cholvi. Decoupled Interconnection of Distributed Memory Models. Technical Report TR-GSYC-2003-2, Universidad Rey Juan Carlos, October 2003, http://gsyc.escet.urjc.es/publicaciones/tr.
15. P. Keleher. *Distributed Shared Memory Using Lazy Consistency*. PhD thesis, Rice University, 1994.
16. L. Lamport. How to make a multiprocessor computer that correctly executes multiprocess programs. *IEEE Transactions on Computers*, 28(9):690–691, September 1979.
17. L. Lamport. On interprocess communication: Parts I and II. *Distributed Computing*, 1(2):77–101, 1986.
18. R.J. Lipton and J.S. Sandberg. PRAM: A scalable shared memory. Technical Report CS-TR-180-88, Princeton University, Department of Computer Science, September 1988.

Author Index